$16.54

B$15.75

J. Bomgardner

W9-CKI-840

ANTHROPOLOGICAL
PERSPECTIVES
ON
EDUCATION

ANTHROPOLOGICAL PERSPECTIVES ON EDUCATION

EDITED BY

MURRAY L. WAX

STANLEY DIAMOND

FRED O. GEARING

Basic Books, Inc., Publishers

NEW YORK   LONDON

© 1971 by Basic Books, Inc.
Library of Congress Catalog Card Number: 71–147020
SBN 465–00341–9
Manufactured in the United States of America
DESIGNED BY THE INKWELL STUDIO

76 77 78 79 80   10 9 8 7 6 5 4 3 2

Acknowledgments

Our thanks are due to the following for permission to reprint from their works:

To the editor for excerpts from "Instruction and Affect in Hopi Cultural Continuity" by Dorothy Eggan, *Southwestern Journal of Anthropology*, 12 (1956): 347–370.

To the editor and the author for excerpts from "Critical Periods in Behavioral Development" by J. P. Scott, *Science*, 138 (November 1962): 949–958; copyright © 1962 by the American Association for the Advancement of Science.

To the publisher for excerpts from "Contrasts between Prepubertal and Postpubertal Education" by C. W. M. Hart in *Education and Anthropology*, edited by George D. Spindler (Stanford: Stanford University Press, 1955).

To Charles Mac Spellman for use of figure 18–1 from his *The Shift from Color to Form Preference in Young Children of Different Ethnic Backgrounds* (Austin: University of Texas Child Development and Research Center, 1968), p. 69.

To Karol Fishler for use of table 18–1.

To the International African Institute (London, England) and Monica Wilson for excerpts from her *Good Company: A Study of Nyakusa Age-Villages* (published in the United States by the Beacon Press, Boston, 1963).

For preparation of the manuscript, our thanks to Mary Wolken, Barbara Johnson, and Debbie Huff, members of Professor Murray Wax's staff.

Contributors to This Volume

WORLD BIBLIOGRAPHY OF ANTHROPOLOGY
AND EDUCATION
assembled, annotated, and introduced by
HARRY M. LINDQUIST
University of Kansas, Lawrence

EDITORS, AND AUTHORS OF CHAPTERS

COURTNEY B. CAZDEN
Graduate School of Education, Harvard University

YEHUDI A. COHEN
Livingston College, Rutgers University

STANLEY DIAMOND
New School for Social Research

FRED O. GEARING
State University of New York—Buffalo

THOMAS F. GREEN
Educational Policy Research Center, Syracuse University

VERA P. JOHN
Yeshiva University, New York

JULES HENRY (Deceased)
Washington University, St. Louis

DONALD HORTON
Bank St. College of Education, New York

DELL HYMES
University of Pennsylvania, Philadelphia

BUD B. KHLEIF
University of New Hampshire, Durham

ELEANOR B. LEACOCK

   Polytechnic Institute of Brooklyn

CHARLES MC REYNOLDS

   Adelphi College

MARGARET MEAD

   American Museum of Natural History

HELEN I. SAFA

   Livingston College, Rutgers University

ROBERT K. THOMAS

   Montieth College, Wayne State University

ARTHUR J. VIDICH

   New School for Social Research

ALBERT L. WAHRHAFTIG

   Montieth College, Wayne State University

HARRY F. WOLCOTT

   Center for Advanced Study of Educational Administration, University of Oregon, Eugene

MURRAY L. WAX

   University of Kansas, Lawrence

ROSALIE H. WAX

   University of Kansas, Lawrence

TOPICAL Commentary and Brief Statements by

PAUL GOODMAN, FRANCIS A. J. IANNI, JULES HENRY, JOHN R. SEELEY, SHERWOOD L. WASHBURN

Preface

The essays of this volume have been written during a time when schools all over the world are being afflicted with grave problems and are becoming the focus of major political battles, including riots and sit-ins, injuries to persons and destruction of property. To study schools is thus to examine the body politic, and the analysis of school systems affords a critical perspective, not only on American society, but on societies everywhere.

Penetrating into rural villages and urban enclaves, the school is frequently an arm of an exteriorly based agency (the mission church, the nation state, a foreign empire) uncontrolled by the local folk. The schoolmaster and the schoolteachers are strangers accorded an ambivalent welcome, as their presence can easily be intrusive and troublesome. Moreover, the school itself is a novel social form creating a peer society among its pupils and thus providing the matrix for the emergence of what is often known as "adolescent" or "youth" subculture. Where the school is bureaucratic and authoritarian, the subculture of the pupils may in turn be rebellious and cynical; where the school is posited on the superiority of an alien language and culture, the subculture of the pupils may crystallize about an ethnic nationalism. And, to the extent that the school is "successful," it introduces ideas that are alien and disquieting.

It follows naturally that the school system becomes the focus for major social and political conflicts generated by critical questions: Should the schools train an elite for political, economic, and scientific leadership, or should they provide rudimentary training for the mass of the population? Should the schools introduce children to an international language (such as English, French, Russian or Chinese), or should they concentrate on local dialects, or the language of the state? Should the schools be oriented toward vocational training for the many, or toward a broader cultural apprenticeship that will permit the option of higher education in Western universities? Should the system be strictly meritocratic, with crucial decisions being made impartially on the basis of standardized examinations (and state support for the "talented" elite), or should the schools accommodate themselves to status, family, and personal relationships? Demanding resolution, such conflicts are manifest everywhere—in New York City, India, China, Ghana, the Soviet Union, and on American Indian reservations.

Questions of the above order have provided the stimulus for the papers in this volume. Most of these essays emerged out of a series of conferences on anthropology and education that were organized by Stanley Diamond as an aspect of the Culture of Schools Program (see bibliography), with the assistance of funds from the U.S. Office of Education. After a year and a half, Diamond as principle investigator, suggested that the program be transferred to the sponsorship of the American Anthropological Association, while maintaining Office of Education support, and this was achieved by the end of 1965. The result was the Program in Anthropology and Education (PAE), directed by Fred O. Gearing. Together with Murray L. Wax, Gearing subsequently organized a further series of conferences, and Wax then assumed major responsibility for a projected book, jointly edited. The Wenner-Gren Foundation for Anthropological Research assisted PAE's efforts, graciously providing funds in an unrestricted fashion that served to make the organizing of the conferences easier and more efficient.

Conventionally, a book of this scope begins with an editorial definition "of the field." In the present instance, such an effort by the editors would be redundant, as several of the essays (notably those by Cohen, Hymes, Mead, Washburn, Wax-and-Wax) were originally prepared as introductions to an aspect of the area of anthropology and education, or to the field at large. On the other hand, we wish to call the attention of the reader to the inner unity of the volume, various and extensive as its content is. Although holding different assumptions, the authors, nevertheless confront the same set of phenomena.

For example, Helen I. Safa approaches "nation-building" from the perspective of those who wish to create a state from disparate ethnic and regional groupings. However, it would be equally legitimate to adopt the view of people who once constituted a nation and who are now losing the last vestiges of their autonomy to a larger political society. Thus, Thomas-and-Wahrhaftig eloquently reflect the attitudes of the Tribal Cherokee of northeastern Oklahoma, who are, as the authors put it, "out-of-it" because they have lost the power to conduct their own affairs (or to operate their own schools).

The issue of "nation-building" is approached by Thomas F. Green in yet a different fashion: following Jefferson, he considers the contribution of the schools to the creation of a democratic citizenry. Green contends that, as schools have increasingly assumed functions in the sorting and preparing of persons for jobs, they have neglected the task regarded by Jefferson as crucial. While Green continues to hope for an enlightened citizenry, Jules Henry in "Is Education Possible?" argues that schools are designed to cultivate stupidity, inasmuch as a society (or nation) can tolerate only a limited amount of rational inquiry: On this issue, Sherwood Washburn offers a ray of hope, since he assumes that the survival of the species depends on adaptive—*i.e.,* intelligent—decisions. Another case pertinent to the issue of national integration and rural autonomy is the suburban residential community, described by Donald Horton as divided by conflicts over the nature of education and the proper level of community support, while in fact it is losing its autonomy to the larger bureaucracies of the state and the professional associations as these assume increasing control over the organization of schools.

Just as Horton discusses the linkages between small town and large bureaucracy, so Wax-and-Wax differentiate between "The Great Tradition which reaches the village from a central urban elite and "The Little Tradition" which is transmitted internally from one generation of villagers to another. Although the larger tradition is more rationalized. it is also less relevant to the needs and interests of the local people, so that its use as a basis for education is always more problematic. Yehudi Cohen elaborates such distinctions abstractly, distinguishing "socialization" from "education" and associating particularistic values and customs with the former, and formal law and universalistic values with the latter.

More briefly, we should note that many of the papers center on the problem of the differential performances in learning by school children of diverse ethnic and racial backgrounds. Cazden-and-John summarize the various research findings on the comparative performances of Black, American Indian, and Anglo (White) children. Dell Hymes discusses "sociolinguistic interference" and criticizes as restrictively narrow several of the conventional approaches to the study of language difficulties of children. Margaret Mead analyzes the critical role of early childhood experiences with particular reference to the acquisition and uses of literacy. Eleanor B. Leacock reports upon a study of multi-racial, multi-class classrooms in urban schools. Henry relates classroom to familiar problems of Negro children and presents a case with a surprising outcome. Wax-and-Wax expose the effect of imposing the ethos of competitive individualism on traditional Indian children.

Several of the papers concern themselves with method. Bud Khleif reviews a series of models for the study of schools. Harry Wolcott offers a cautionary analysis of the role of the anthropologist studying schools. Wax outlines a set of research possibilities. Harry M. Lindquist provides a global bibliography of anthropology and education which certainly will become a major research tool in the field.

We have also included a few short and pointed essays. Their authors will be familiar to those who have been reading the critical literature on education during the past several years—Paul Goodman, Jules Henry, John Seeley, and Francis Ianni. Together with the more programmatic and expository papers, they help define the range, and the responsibilities, of anthropology in the educational turmoil of our time.

MURRAY L. WAX

STANLEY DIAMOND

FRED O. GEARING

Contents

PART I
Theoretical and Methodological

PART II
Schools in Modern Urban Society

PART III
Tools for Further Research in Anthropology and Education

PART I

Theoretical and Methodological

CULTURAL AND LINGUISTIC

1: *Great Tradition, Little Tradition,*
and Formal Education

MURRAY AND ROSALIE WAX

From a comparative and historical perspective, the vast body of research literature on schools and education appears both pseudoempirical and pseudotheoretical. Researchers have been administering hundreds of tests to thousands of pupils and intellectual critics have devoted countless pages to the criticism of textbooks and other curricular materials. Yet, the bulk of their efforts contrasts markedly with its quality and its impact, because their vision has been constricted by an interlocking chain of assumptions: that schools are primarily and exclusively agencies of formal education (rather than being social institutions); that pupils are isolated individuals (rather than social beings who participate in the life of peer societies, ethnic groups, and the like); that formal education is synonymous with education; and that the principal task of the teacher is to educate. Thus, instead of inquiring what sort of social processes are occurring in— and in relation to—the schools, researchers and critics have defined their problem as being one of discovering how to make the schools teach their individual pupils more, better, and faster. Only a few of the many researchers and critics have had the patience, fortified by the faith in ethnographic empiricism, to observe the social processes actually occurring in relation to the schools: among the pupils, among the teachers, within the classrooms, between the pupils and their parental elders, and so on.

Teachers and pupils being docile and available, it has been far easier and far more pretentiously scientific (while less threatening to the local power structure) to administer reams of tests that are then scored mechanically. As a result, the research literature lacks a solid body of data on the ethnography of schools.

Seemingly, the theoretical literature on education would be far superior.

The intellectual critics number some of the most formidably trained scholars in the country, as well as some of the most irate journalists and pontifical classicists. Unfortunately, most seem to lack that sense of history and feeling for comparison that the Classical Curriculum (or its modern "Liberal Arts" variant) is presumed to produce. As but a small instance, consider that most of the classically trained critics laud the Hellenic system of education, and, from that vantage point, denounce as trivial and unworthy of our schools such courses as driver training. Yet, it is surely arguable that being able to drive an automobile courteously, deftly, and responsibly, restraining aggressive impulses, and focusing attention upon the task, is a sign of good citizenship and moral excellence. Really good training in driving an automobile would merit as much approbation as the Hellenic cult of body culture. If the invidious slur on driver training courses is typical of the logic of the critics (and we take it to be so) then they are sadly deficient in the perspective and knowledge required for an evaluation of modern schools.

Asking the right questions is the path to acquiring wisdom, but to ask good questions, rather than trivial ones, the investigator has to break out of conventional frameworks. In the early part of this essay we proceed autobiographically, outlining how this happened to us so that we came to perceive freshly some of what is going on in relation to the schools. Later in the essay, we build on these experiences and elaborate a more theoretical argument which, in turn, leads us to a series of research questions for the study of the culture of schools.

THE SCHOOL AND THE LITTLE COMMUNITY

We begin in traditional anthropological fashion by describing some of what we learned about the educational problems of the Oglala Sioux on Pine Ridge Reservation. The patient reader will find that this is not simply an ethnographic excursion but leads to a consideration of the nature of education in a modern industrial society.

Our interest in Indian education developed during the several years in which we directed the Workshops for American Indian college students held during the summer on the campus of the University of Colorado. These workshops had been designed to provide young Indians with a broad perspective about Indian affairs, so that they could later serve their communities as advisors and leaders. As we worked with these young people, we were appalled. Supposedly the cream of the Indian population, they were so provincial in their knowledge of the United States and so ignorant of Indian history and current affairs as to make us doubt their rank as college students. Yet, at the same time, most of them could be excited, and to an intense glow, by lectures on Indian history, or on Indian religious cults or social organization, in which we treated these phenomena as worthy of serious intellectual attention. Judging by their response, none of these students had ever participated in a discussion that treated Indian religious cults as vital and meaningful subjects (rather than as superstitious, primitive, or archaic). Accordingly, we developed a critical curiosity about the nature of the educational system in which these students had been schooled, and we deliberately decided to study an Indian population (the Pine Ridge Sioux) that had for some years been subjected to federal programs for education and assimilation.

At the time we designed the study, we envisioned the school as a battleground: on the one hand, the educators—flanked by the Bureau of Indian Affairs, the mission churches, and kindred agencies—would be fighting to pull the children out of Indian society, while, on the other hand, the Indian elders would be clinging desperately to their young, trying to hold them within their traditional society. Indeed, this was exactly the picture drawn for us by a high Bureau of Indian Affairs (BIA) official on our first day on the reservation, except that, instead of the Indian elders, he blamed "grandma," who craftily lured her grandchildren "back to the blanket."

Our hypothesis about battlegrounds was to prove as inaccurate as his was about grandmas and blankets. Nevertheless, it turned out to be extremely advantageous, for it predisposed us to approach the Sioux pupils, their teachers, and the administration, as living members of social groups rather than as isolated respondents to questionnaires administered from a distance. Thus, we were obliged to sit for weeks and months in classrooms, watching what was going on and, in like manner, to talk not only to administrators and educational experts but also to Indian parents and to the children themselves. In due time we realized that the educators and Indian elders were not locked in battle for the soul of the Indian child, because the Sioux elders, faced with the power of the educational establishment, simply withdrew. In this tactic they were encouraged by the educational administrators who exhorted them: just send your children to school every day and we will educate them. The educators found the absence of the parents convenient and proper, since the parents would have had no background for understanding the operations of the school and could only have interfered. Yet, here, the educators were overconfident, for within the schoolrooms they were confronting children who were alien and who could elude their ministrations. Issuing from small local communities of kith and kin, and sharing a common set of values and understandings, as well as a language (Lakota) that was unknown to most teachers, the Sioux children could and did create within the formal structure of the educational institution, a highly cohesive society of their own. As the children matured, their society of peers became ever more solidary, and the teacher confronting them was reduced to operating at the level they would permit. Whereas an occasional teacher might gain the approval of this peer society, most teachers found themselves talking to a wall of apparent indifference and assumed incompetence. Interestingly, many teachers remarked that after the sixth or seventh grade their pupils became more "withdrawn" or "apathetic" every year, but not one realized that the wall was the outward manifestation of a subtle and highly organized rejection. The withdrawal remained a mystery to the educators.

In another respect, the design of our study differed from the more conventional ethnographic or social anthropological investigations, for we committed ourselves to a study of the Indian children *in the schools.* This meant that we were obliged to consider and try to understand not only Sioux society or culture but the reservation system (teachers and administrators), and how the Indians related generally to the agencies of the greater society as well. This commitment helped us to perceive very early that the administrators and most of the teachers looked upon the Sioux children not as members of a different or exotic culture but as members of an ethnic and inferior caste. Their task, as they saw it, was to help their pupils become members of the superior caste.

The status of the Sioux as being lower caste was so conspicuously visible among the educators that we singled out one of its manifestations for analysis under the label of "The Vacuum Ideology." The reference is to the experiential background of the Sioux child, for the educators, especially the administrators, did not regard this child as participating in a distinctive culture and society but, instead, as lacking in those preschool experiences that distinguish the desirable kind of pupil. Judging by the experiences that were listed, the ideal pupil would have been of urban middle-class, Protestant (and White) background, and, insofar as the Sioux pupil lacked those particular experiences, it was not that he had had others but that he was deficient. Since his parents had not read *Peter Rabbit* to him, he lacked familiarity with stories; and since they did not sing Anglo-Saxon lullabies to him, he lacked familiarity with music. The same ideology is also prevalent among educators confronting children of urban lower-class and ethnic backgrounds. (Compare the further discussions of these issues in the essays of Hymes and of Cazden-and-John in this volume.)

Subsequent experience has convinced us that many educators are passionately attached to the notion that their disprivileged or poor pupils come to them with empty minds that must be filled before they can compete with youngsters from "the usual middle-class home." Nevertheless, they withdraw in horror from the suggestion that a denial of experience constitutes a denial of socialization or human development. That a little child might not respond warmly to a teacher who sees him and his family as empty vessels does not occur to them.

Almost in spite of ourselves, we have been led to the conclusion that some of our most important general educational goals constitute ruthless attacks on the solidarity and self-respect of the ethnic and lower-class communities, and, indeed, on their very existence (on this point, see the essays by Cohen, Safa, and Thomas-and-Wahrhaftig). The Vacuum Ideology is only one of the more recent tactical offenses. Another is the goal of individualistic achievement.

The modern school system is premised on the notion that its population is an aggregate of social atoms, among whom there are no significant or permanent linkages. In the ideology of the educators, these social atoms begin at the same starting line and then move onward in haphazard clumps, each atom achieving independently of the others and according to its own inner strength and motives. What an individual does in school, and later, in his vocation, is an achievement—his individual achievement—deriving from his own initiative and effort, and of benefit only to himself and his immediate family. Contrary to this ideology is the normative system of a folk community that confronts an alien society. For in this system the individual may excel only when his excellence enhances the position of his brethren. If this achievement were to derogate them before others, then it would be incumbent on him to conceal his talents. Thus, in the schools on Pine Ridge, our staff observed classrooms where, when the teacher called upon a pupil to recite, he would become the target of jibes and jokes whispered in Lakota and unperceived by the teacher, with the result that he would stand or sit paralyzed and unable to respond; meanwhile, the teacher, being oblivious to the secret life of the classroom, would be perplexed and distressed at her inability to secure responses indicating that she had covered the day's lesson. Similar observations were made by Harry Wolcott, who, for his doctoral dissertation, taught in a one-room school among Indians on an island off the West coast of Canada. Wolcott reports that, although he taught for a full year, living among the community, he was never able to learn just how much or how little most of his pupils knew, because, no matter what the nature of the classwork—whether test or seatwork or other areas—no student could be induced to work solely for himself.

The fact that the educators themselves seem unaware that individualistic achievement as they define it is considered grossly immoral behavior by the children they are trying to instruct is an obvious case of selective inattention. But the fact that social researchers are so often indifferent to this type of conflict and to its implications is more surprising and puzzling. This brings us to the second part of this paper: a consideration of the inadequacy of past and current research on schools and education.

PSEUDOEMPIRICAL RESEARCH ON EDUCATION

Because of the fundamental orientation of their research, most investigators have managed to avoid looking at what actually occurs within schools. Since they collect much data, their research appears to be empirical, but in actuality they have been selectively inattentive to important classes of phenomena. Educational psychologists, for example, convert the society of pupils into an aggregate of individual animals, each of whom must be trained to perform certain tasks established by the curriculum. Discovering what the pupils are actually engaged in doing and experiencing is irrelevant to the job that the psychologist has defined for himself, namely structuring the school situation so that each of the human animals is made to learn more and faster. The educational psychologist thus comes to function like the industrial psychologist whose role is to help increase production. For both, the fundamental tasks are established by the bureaucratically given structure, and the researcher accepts as his goal the devising of ways to accomplish those tasks most expeditiously. Whatever else may be going on within the school, or however else the child may be being educated, becomes relevant for the researcher only insofar as it clearly affects the performance of the curricularly given tasks.

In a like manner, structural-functionalists among sociologists have tended to orient themselves by defining their discipline as "the sociology of education" and by assuming that the school is that institution having education as its primary function. In effect, these plausible assumptions serve to transform the scientific problem of *the nature of the school* (and its relationship to other social activities) into the problem of evaluating the school in terms of the extent to which it performs a particular *educational function* (cf. Brotz, 1961). If further, the sociologist relies principally upon survey procedures, with rigid schedules administered to large numbers of pupils, then he has thoroughly inhibited himself from the observation of the school as a species of social organization. The pupils are perceived as social atoms, differing from each other only in terms of their ethnic-religious and social-class backgrounds, but the school is rarely studied as a society or social system that is more than an arena for the movement of these atoms.

Lest we be misunderstood, we should like to emphasize that the issue is not the learning theory of some psychologists nor the structural-functionalism of some sociologists. Either theory and discipline could be utilized in the empirical study of schools, but in fact they seldom have been, and the research that is done has a flavor that is tragicomic. For example, some investigators known to us are now engaged in elaborate investigations involving, on the one hand, the administration of large batteries of tests to hundreds of Indian and White pupils, and, on the other hand, the observation in detail of the relationships between Indian mothers and their children. The hypothesis informing the research is that the progressive "withdrawal" characteristic of Indian pupils in schools is the outcome of a psychic inadequacy related to their upbringing. Were these investigators to perform some elementary ethnography, inquiring as to how the Indians perceive their community situation and the role of the schools, and if they were then to observe classroom interactions, their comprehension of what they presume to be a psychic inadequacy might be thoroughly transformed. But for this to occur, they would have to be prepared to examine the school as a real institution affecting a real interethnic community of Indians and Whites, instead of reducing the school to an educational function and dissolving the Sioux child out of his community and his lower-caste situation.

On the other hand, research conducted along Community Study lines has often contributed a great deal to the understanding of the schools (whether or not the research has utilized a structural-functionalist or learning theory conceptualization). The major endeavors (Hollingshead, Havighurst, and Wylie), which have had the school as the focus of the community study, are well recognized, but it is important to note that almost any thorough study of a geographic community can contribute to our knowledge of the schools. In Whyte's study of Cornerville, it is necessary to read between the lines to learn about the schools, but in Gans's later study of an ethnically similar community, much can be gained from the brief pages on the topic (1965:129–136). Similar value can be found in the pages relating to the schools in the studies by Withers (1945), Vidich and Bensman (1960), the Lynds, Hughes (1963), Warner and associates (1949), and others of the better investigators of small American communities. Indeed, the fact that these studies are not focused on the schools has a certain advantage, for the educationally focused studies allow their research to be excessively oriented by the ideology of the schools, and so they spend too many pages in demonstrating that the schools do not provide equal opportunity for achievement and too few pages in describing what the schools actually are doing.

In contrast to these contemporaneous varieties of social research on education is a study so old as to be dated, having been published forty years ago. Yet this study, which, to our knowledge, has had no successor, is the only one that comes close to describing the school as an institution. We have in mind Waller's *The Sociology of Teaching*. Waller's research procedures appear to have been informal, and he seems to have relied mainly upon his own experiences and the reports and diaries of teachers who were students of his, yet, nonetheless, he systematically reviewed the major sorts of interactions associated with being a teacher. As compared with the several, methodologically sophisticated readers in the sociology of education on the market, Waller's has been the only book to discuss such significant topics as the elementary forms of collective behavior within the classroom or the role of ceremonies in the life of the school (the anthropologist, Burnett, revived the study of these ceremonies in 1966). In a sense, Waller viewed the school as a community, and its educators and pupils as social beings participating in the life of the community, and so he produced a monograph that can serve to suggest directions for research on contemporary schools. Stimulated by his book, we would like to advance several questions for research on the schools: What kinds of social roles emerge within the schools, among the teachers, the pupils, and the lay public associated with the schools? What social forms emerge within the context of the schools? Are there typical cycles of reform associated with the school system, similar, perhaps, to the reforming movements within the Catholic Church, of which some culminated in the founding of religious orders and others in the rise of new sects? What happens to children within the schools; how are children transformed into *pupils?*

A knowledgeable and shrewd anthropologist can advance a number of hypotheses in response to the questions we have just raised. He could, for instance, point to the differences between the kind of age-grading that occurs among the children of hunting peoples who roam in small bands and that which occurs within our public schools, where children are associated with a narrow stratum of other children of almost exactly the same chronological age. From there he could argue about the differences that would develop because the first kind of children would have the opportunity to associate with others much older than themselves and would have also the association with and responsibility for other children much younger than themselves; and, continuing the train of logic, he could argue as to the kinds of differences in personality that might ensue. Yet, much as we welcome such broad speculation, we do wish to insist that there is much about our schools that we don't know for certain because investigators have not been looking—they have administered tens of thousands of tests and conducted hundreds of interviews, but only a handful have looked systematically, diligently, and sympathetically at all phases of the school in relationship to pupils, educators, and parents.[1]

Just as we need to know more about how children are transformed into

---

[1] After reading this essay in manuscript, Howard S. Becker commented that

> We may have understated a little the difficulty of observing contemporary classrooms. It is not just the survey method of educational testing or any of those things that keeps people from seeing what is going on. I think, instead, that it is first and foremost a matter of it all being so familiar that it becomes almost impossible to single out events that occur in the classroom as things that have occurred, even when they happen right in front of you. I have not had the experience of observing in elementary and high school classrooms myself, but I have in college classrooms and it takes a tremendous effort of will and imagination to stop seeing only the things that are conventionally "there" to be seen. I have talked to a couple of teams of research people who have sat around in classrooms trying to observe and it is like pulling teeth to get them to see or write anything beyond what "everyone" knows.

pupils, so must we know more about how young persons (usually college students) are transformed into *teachers.* The research in this area has been limited and is mostly represented by tests or other fixed schedules of questions that are administered to samples of teacher trainees and veteran teachers (cf. Guba, Jackson, and Bidwell in Charters and Gage 1963:271–286). In accounting for the attitudes and conduct of veteran teachers, most critics have stressed the relationship between the teacher and the school administration, the latter usually being bureaucratic, conservative, and timorous. However, we would also be inclined to suggest a Goff-manical posture of inquiry that would inquire as to the effects upon a person of having to be on public display before—and in constant disciplinary control of—a large audience of alien children for many hours per day. It is not, we would guess, the school administration per se that develops the teacher type, but the administrative requirement of facing and controlling so large a body of youngsters. We are impressed by the fact that the problem of maintaining discipline in the classroom is foremost among the anxieties of the novice teacher, and also foremost among the demands made upon the teacher by his supervisors, and yet the literature of social research on the issue is so weak and so focused on individual children as "disciplinary problems." We are also impressed by the fact that most novices do manage to maintain discipline in their classes, and that critical attention is usually directed only to the conspicuous failures of discipline, but that few scholars ask how the stunt is performed. Yet the question of how discipline is maintained throughout a school is, we suggest, a paradigm for the question of how order is maintained in civil society.

THE SCHOOL AND THE GREAT TRADITION

To propose the foregoing questions—how do children become pupils? how do young people become teachers? how is discipline maintained within the schoolroom?—is to declare that the cross-cultural comparisons that anthropologists have conventionally attempted are limited in their relevance to formal education. By comparing the experiences of the contemporary schoolchild in the Bronx with that of a juvenile in New Guinea thirty years ago, we can say something significant about the personality development of the child, but we are in limbo so far as concerns much that is significant about formal education, as is evident in terms of the content of the readers and textbooks on anthropology and education produced but a generation ago. The authors of these works are well qualified, their essays are frequently of intrinsic interest, but their pertinence to the contemporary educational drama is negligible. For these anthropologists, trying to be culturally relativistic, defined "educational practices" in broad terms. Viewing cultures as separate and distinct entities that could be compared as independent individuals, they conceived of each as having its own system of child-rearing and, therefore, of education. Such a procedure did have and still has some uses, but it cannot hope to characterize the contemporary situation where *education* is of the order of an international mission activity, being exported from the U.S. and other Western societies. *Education* in this sense is avowedly intended to decrease the isolation of other ("backward") societies and to alter drastically their cultural configurations. In its aggressive impact, this education is similar to the spread of Christianity, Islam, Communism, or capitalistic business practices.

Indeed, the traditional anthropological procedure was not even accurate for the history of Western society or of other civilized societies. For the Western system of formal education is rooted in its Great Tradition (Redfield, 1956 chap. 3; Singer, 1960) and can only be understood on that basis. Great Traditions, it will be recalled, are borne by a literate corps of disciples, and are in tension with the little traditions transmitted informally within the little community. Or, in the pithy language of Bharati (1963):

what the missionary in a particular religion wants the less knowledgeable votaries to do, defines the "big tradition," and what he wants them to give up and to desist from in the future, defines the "little tradition" in any religious area.

Christianity has epitomized that tension, for, on the one hand, there have been its dedicated disciples, oriented toward the millennial creed of its scriptures, while, on the other hand, there have been the folk, who have required a religion, which, through its values and symbols, expressed the unity and morality of the little community. This tension has been clearly visible in the American churches, especially of the contemporary South: for, as its dedicated ministers affirm, the Christian message would require thorough desegregation, since all men are brothers in Christ; yet, to the members of the local White community, the local church embodies their moral unity and necessarily excludes the Negroes as alien and profane. The school stands in a similar situation, for, on the one hand, it, too, is a kind of local church, embodying the sacred values of the little community. Yet, on the other hand, the school is connected, organizationally and ideationally, with the greater society and with the Great Traditions of the West.

In their relationship to the contemporary and actual school systems, intellectual critics—such as ourselves—play somewhat the role of the fervent religious orders within the medieval church. The critics are painfully conscious of the true message; they are prepared to be tolerant of some of the little traditional beliefs, provided they can be incorporated within the body of dogma; but they are appalled at the heresy and corruption within the institutional church. They debate theories of education with their fellows, as if these were theological creeds, and they are perturbed that the school as a reality bears so little a resemblance to the school as the gateway to salvation.

If we may be permitted to continue this metaphor, we would suggest that what social scientists, especially anthropologists, could now accomplish in their research upon education is a purification of the dogma. The world of today is in the midst of a vast expansion and elaboration of the system of formal education: more peoples are sending their children to school, and more children are spending longer periods of their lives as students. This transformation is of such magnitude and abruptness as to deserve the label of *revolution*, and it appears quite comparable in scope to movements, such as the spread of Christianity in the ancient world, or to the Industrial Revolution. While both of these did become worldwide movements, in order to do so each has had to purify itself of much ideological dross. Christianity did not become really effective in Northern Europe until its populace had eliminated many of the peculiarities distinctive to the Mediterranean world from the dogma and had reformulated this dogma in terms of their own ethnic traditions. The Industrial Revolution did not begin to permeate many areas of the world, until its dogma of Manchester Liberalism was dismembered and replaced by local or nativistic creeds disguising themselves behind the flexible vocabularies of nationalism and socialism. Now, we should like to suggest that our United States educational system is similarly loaded with ideological irrelevancies that make it unsuited to other countries (cf. Thomas, 1966:72–74) and have made it clearly unsuited to our own ethnic and lower-class populations. We would hazard that the unsuitability of our system in other countries is, at present, disguised by the outpourings of financial and moral assistance from the West coupled with the native willingness of other nations to accept our institutional complexes in the dizzy hope of becoming as prosperous and powerful as the United States. In about a decade, the twin impetus should have disappeared, and anthropologists may then be in a position to observe some interesting attempts to reshape the educational structure. More than this, it should be possible for anthropologists to be of marked assistance in the reshaping and purification of education, provided that they are astute and critical and that they begin their work in the near future, and discard the restrictive blinders of irrelevant or system-biased research as we noted earlier.

Let us give an example of an ideological tenet that, as we have indicated, hampers the adjustment of some peoples to the Western system of formal education. United States and other Western schools have, generally, been organized about the notion of individual achievement with rewards of personal advancement and benefit. Looking historically and comparatively, we believe it can be argued that this tenet may not be essential and may even be somewhat of a hindrance, unless suitably modified. Great traditions, generally, and Western scholarship, specifically, have as we have noted been borne by associations of disciples, who have shared common goals and been subject to a common discipline. Anthropologists (or other social-scientists) would not accomplish what they do, wrestling with the hardships they must face, unless sustained by their association of compeers. There is individualistic competition, which does stimulate to achievement, but it is a competition that is regulated by formal norms against deceit and plagiarism and by informal norms of courtesy, fellowship, and camaraderie. Whenever the attempt has previously been made to widely disseminate great traditional knowledge throughout a population, it has been associated with a social movement having superpersonal goals. The Jews, who were among the first to do so, accomplished widespread literacy, and it was in a strictly religious context, in order to bring about the salvation of Israel and the participation of the individual in that joyous event. With Protestantism a similar movement for literacy developed, more individualistic perhaps, but nonetheless set in the context of a social movement and communal aspirations. Today, in the United States, we seem to be pushing the notion of individualistic competition within the framework of the school to an almost superhuman pitch. Yet, it is striking that real progress toward spreading literacy among lower-class or ethnic groups has so often occurred in the context of social movements: civil rights, the Black Muslims and Black Panthers, and, as always, the evangelistic churches.

Another example of an ideological tenet that has hampered the adjustment of some peoples to the system of formal education is, we believe, the notion that each child must be identified with a unique nuclear family and that the community encompassing the school is a community of nuclear families. As anthropologists, we are bound to ask whether as efficient an educational establishment could be fitted into a society with extended families and elaborate systems of kinship? Speaking from our observations among the Sioux (and our readings about other peoples, or even about the Hutterites and Amish), this is no idle question. So much of the procedures of the systems of schooling and welfare and public health are geared to the assumption that each child must be part of an intact family or else he is a neglected child, and the power of the state and the wealth of its agencies is thereby used to disrupt the extended family and cement the nuclear one. In the case of the American Indian, it is not yet too late to ask whether we should be doing this, and we may also bear in mind that many more peoples of the world are and will be increasingly involved with this issue.

THE SCHOOL AND THE LITTLE TRADITION

Because researchers have focused on curricularly given tasks, and critics have focused on great traditional knowledge, no one has been looking systematically at the impact of formal educational institutions on little traditional processes of child rearing. Instead, there has been recourse to the concept of "cultural deprivation," which (like the vacuum ideology of Sioux educators) has enabled the theorists and administrators to ignore the culture of the impoverished and ethnic peoples, on the ground that it either scarcely exists or exists in such distorted form as best to be suppressed. Some social scientists have been arguing as if these peoples are lacking—linguistically, psychically, and culturally (Roach, 1965 and the retort by Hughes). Surely, here it is necessary to be concrete and ethnographic, and to ask in specific detail about the experiences of the child in various contexts. Continuing our usage of the great/little traditional dichotomy and tension, we would suggest that the process of formal schooling is, to a large degree, the struggle to substitute one kind of tradition (or knowledge) for another within the mind of the child. Where, in a folk society, the child would have to master a great variety of particular bits of knowledge, concerning particular persons, topographic features, rites, skills, and so on, the archetypical urban school is oriented toward instilling a knowledge that is abstract, general, and in some sense, "rational," and, thereby, deracinated. In like manner, where in folk society there is a great stress on the function of language to promote consensus and maintain the integrity of the community (Wright), in the urban middle-class world and its schools the stress is on language as a vehicle for imparting "rational" knowledge to strangers. Within the hierarchy of schools, it is the elite university with its graduate education that has epitomized this type of knowledge and language dialect, but the demand now is being made that the elementary school system participate even more intimately in this effort.

But knowledge, or tradition, does not exist in a vacuum. It is borne by individual human beings. And the demand that is being made on the schools to rationalize their curricula even further is also a demand to produce a certain type of human being—abstract, theoretical, rational, and, hence, deracinated—the academic man writ large. But we are sufficiently disenchanted with our colleagues, and with the middle class of the United States, to ask that researchers and critics examine the issue. In making the school more efficient in its transmission of formal knowledge, to what extent will the reformers be helping to create human beings who are more thoroughly deracinated and dehumanized? Conversely, to what extent are the current, so-called "inefficiencies" and stupidities of the school system really a blessing or a source of hope, because it is in these interstices (and irrationalities) that the child still has some chance of developing as a human being? We can even ask about the little traditions of the school, the lore and experience that is transmitted informally among pupils, between teacher and pupils (and vice versa), within the school system. How much of what it means to be a man does a boy learn from his schoolmates (rather than from the curricular content of the school)? As reforms eat away the irrationalities and inefficiencies of the school, will they likewise reduce even further the opportunity to observe and experience the meaning of manliness? The skeptical reader may counter that we are here indulging in ethnographic nostalgia, and to be frank we are recalling the youthful Sioux, and their fine personal sensibility, the brilliance of their singing, the virility of their dancing, and their exuberant vitality. During one summer when we were examining Head Start programs operated for Indian children, there was one occasion in which we stepped from a powwow—distinguished by the most exciting singing and dancing—into a classroom where some well-meaning teacher was leading children through the familiar, dreary, off-key rendition of a nursery song. Later, members of this staff were to talk with us about what they were doing for these "culturally deprived" children.

As we look at the youth of the contemporary United States, we are not impressed by the success of our system of education and training. So many of our young men can perform well on the national test of achievement and yet they lack the pride and self-confidence in their manliness. We recognize full well that to an audience of anthropologists and intellectuals, these criticisms may seem overly familiar. Yet, we think someone has to raise these questions, as *research* questions, and we think that this is part of our task as intellectuals and anthropologists, because otherwise all of us tend to concentrate so exclusively on the issue of educational tasks— how the schools can teach better, faster, and more: how can kids be taught Russian at three, calculus at four, and nuclear physics at five—and neglect to ask a far more important question: what is happening to our children as human beings?

Let us summarize by using an economic model. Theoretically, it would be possible to isolate children in an environment free of all stimulation. Such environments, we would surmise, are fairly rare and would exist only in the most misguided and understaffed institutions. Given an actual environment, whether it be Harlem, Pine Ridge, or Summerfield, children will be experiencing and learning. If they are part of a folk society, they will be learning a folk culture. If they are part of the general middle-class of the United States, they will be learning its culture, and becoming better fitted for early achievement in school. For example, the child reared among the middle class may acquire a larger vocabulary than the child reared in the slum or the reservation. Yet, while the size of vocabulary is predictive of early scholastic achievement, it is not a statement of linguistic or social maturity; for, as but one illustration, consider that some people of a modest vocabulary can be far more eloquent than scholars whose vocabulary is huge. What the child experiences in home and school is but a selection from a vast possible range, so that, in economic terms, if the child is having one kind of experience, then he cannot be having another. If he is learning calculus, then he is not simultaneously learning to dance, powwow style. We are suggesting that most intellectuals, including anthropologists, are so sold on the value of children learning calculus that they have forgotten about the value of dancing, and that they are made so irate by the diction of incompetent educators who prate about the value of learning to play *with* others, that they have forgotten the intimate relationship between play and freedom.

REFERENCES

Bell, Robert R.
  1962 The sociology of education: a sourcebook. Homewood, Ill.: Dorsey Press.
Bharati, A.
  1963 Eclectic patterns in Indian pilgrimage. Paper delivered at the annual meeting of the American Anthropological Association, San Francisco. Dittoed.
Brotz, Howard
  1961 Functionalism and dynamic analysis. European Journal of Sociology. (Archives Européenes de Sociologie) 2:170–179.
Burnett, Jacquetta Hill
  1966 Ceremony, rites, and economy in the student system of a rural high school. Paper delivered at the annual meetings, American Anthropological Association, Pittsburgh.
Charters, W. W., Jr., and N. L. Gage
  1963 Readings in the social psychology of education. Boston: Allyn & Bacon.
Friedenberg, Edgar Z.
  1965 Coming of age in America: growth and acquiescence. New York: Random House, Inc.
Gans, Herbert J.
  1965 The urban villagers: group and class in the life of Italian-Americans. New York: The Free Press.
Goffman, Erving
  1959 The presentation of self in everyday life. Garden City: Doubleday & Co.
Guba, Egon G., Philip W. Jackson, and Charles E. Bidwell
  1963 Occupational choice and the teaching career. *In* Readings in the social psychology of education, edited by W. W. Charters and N. L. Gage, pp. 271–286. Reprinted *from* Educational Research Bulletin 38 (1959):1–12, 27.
Halsey, A. H., Jean Floud, and C. Arnold Anderson
  1961 Education, economy, and society. New York: The Free Press.
Havighurst, Robert J. et al.
  1962 Growing up in River City. New York: John Wiley & Sons, Inc.
Henry, Jules
  1963 Culture against man. New York: Random House, Inc.
Hollingshead, A. B.
  1949 Elmtown's youth. New York: John Wiley & Sons, Inc.
Hughes, Everett Cherrington
  1963 French Canada in transition. Chicago: University of Chicago Press, Phoenix Books, p. 139.
  1965 Comment *on* Sociological analysis and poverty by J. L. Roach. American Journal of Sociology 71:75–76.

Redfield, Robert
  1956 Peasant society and culture. Chicago: University of Chicago Press, Phoenix
       Books, p. 53.
Roach, Jack L.
  1965 Sociological analysis and poverty. American Journal of Sociology 71:68–75,
       76–77.
Singer, Milton
  1960 The great tradition of Hinduism in the city of Madras. *In* Anthropology of
       folk religions, edited by Charles Leslie, New York: Random House, Vintage
       Books (V 105). (Reprinted *from* Journal of American Folklore 71:347–388.)
Spindler, George D.
  1963 Education and culture: anthropological approaches. New York: Holt, Rinehart,
       and Winston, Inc.
Thomas, Elizabeth Marshall
  1966 Warrior herdsmen. London: Secker & Warburg.
Vidich, Arthur J. and Joseph Bensman
  1960 Small town in mass society. New York: Doubleday & Co., Inc.
  ———, and Maurice R. Stein
  1964 Reflections on community studies. New York: John Wiley & Sons, Inc.
Waller, Willard
  1932 The sociology of teaching. New York: John Wiley & Sons, Inc., Science
       Editions, 1965.
Warner, William Lloyd
  1949 Democracy in Jonesville: a study of quality and inequality. New York: Harper
       & Row, Publishers, Inc.
Withers, Carl
  1945 Plainville by James West (pseud.). New York: Columbia University Press.
Wolcott, Harry F.
  1965 A Kwakiutl village and its school: cultural barriers to classroom performance.
       Unpublished doctoral dissertation, Department of Anthropology, Stanford
       University.
Wright, Rolland
  1964 The urban man. Detroit: Montieth College Readings.
Wylie, Laurence
  1964 Village in the Vauclose. New York: Harper & Row, Publishers, Inc., Colophon
       Books CN 24.

2: *The Shaping of Men's Minds: Adaptations to Imperatives of Culture*[1]

YEHUDI A. COHEN

INTRODUCTION

One of the earliest and most significant of anthropology's discoveries was that culture is a particular way of shaping the mind. More than being a series of habits and patches of exotic customs, of ways of earning a livelihood, or of being clothed and adorned, anthropologists learned that the essence of a culture is to be sought in the material and intellectual symbols to which people respond in their social relations and in meeting their basic necessities. Indeed, many anthropologists are agreed that in their daily lives people in all societies respond to cultural symbols rather than to objective reality. Close on the heels of this insight was the awareness that the symbolizations of cultural life do not have their roots in race or any other aspect of biology but are learned as the result of systematic and consistent experiences to which the individual is exposed in the course of growing up.

With this also came another significant realization that has served as one of the cornerstones of modern anthropology, namely, that one way of conceptualizing a culture is as a self-perpetuating system. Thus, an important group of anthropologists asserted that one of the most important tasks in the study of culture is to seek an understanding of the means by which social systems shape the minds of their members in order to assure the perpetuation of their cultures. These principles underlay much of the work of Sapir (1949) and Mead (1939), among others, especially during the 1930s.

During the 1940s, these concepts were given an added dimension as a result of Hallowell's investigations (1955) of the psychological components of acculturation among the Ojibwa, in which he found that the adoption of formal features of Euro-American culture, especially of material items, did not necessarily involve the reshaping of modes of mind;

[1] I want to thank James L. Gibbs, Jr., for his very helpful comments about this paper and for sharing with me some of his unpublished observations on the Kpelle of Liberia. I alone am responsible for errors and misinterpretations in this paper.

instead, he found that traditional patterns of cognition, motivation, and emotional functioning can often covary with the radios, guns, clothing, and money of their conquerors. More than suggesting that appearances can be deceiving, and in addition to the idea that culture is manifest in more than directly observable phenomena, these findings—sharpened further by the Spindlers' (1955, 1962, 1963) studies of the Menomini, among others—contributed immeasurably to our understanding of some of the processes in sociocultural and psychological adaptation. Most recently, these hypotheses and insights have been systematically and comparatively explored by Goldschmidt (1965) and his coworkers (especially Edgerton 1965) in East Africa.

With growing attention by anthropologists generally to the concepts emerging from the study of biological evolution (see the essay by Washburn in this volume), and the timely resurgence of interest in the processes underlying the evolution of social organization, the conviction has been strengthened among anthropologists that it is the population, rather than the individual, that is the adaptive unit. Whether the problem under investigation is a group's modes of marriage, political organization, or manner of controlling impulses, the cultural patterning of behavior must be seen, at least in part, as a complex set of adaptive mechanisms that are designed to assure the group's self-perpetuation under highly specific conditions. Similarly, it is commonly accepted by many anthropologists today that although there is variability in every society—for example, with regard to marriage, law, economic arrangements, political organization, the psychological makeups of individuals, and the like—it is the adaptive mechanisms in the population that must be focused on.

Adaptation refers to the relationship maintained by a group to its environment. The adaptive mechanisms that develop in a population to facilitate its survival are not only to be found in its technology and in its economic, political, and legal organizations but also in patterns of cognition, motivation, and impulse control. Whether we are dealing with technology, formal institutions, or psychological processes, patterns of institutional organization must be seen as aspects of adaptation by a population to highly specific environmental pressures. The environment in regard to which a group develops its sociopsychological adaptations is highly complex and, as a matter of fact, includes most of the universe in which the individual is expected to live and make his way.

I am going to deal in this paper with a limited aspect of the ways in which society shapes the individual's mind. Specifically, I am going to distinguish between *socialization* and *education*, and examine their relationships to each other. My contention is that the proportion assumed by one vis-à-vis the other is an adaptation to certain imperatives in the sociocultural environment, especially its structure of social relations. In terms of the principal focus of this paper, the modes of upbringing in a society—the means by which the mind is shaped—are to be regarded as mechanisms that are designed to create the kind of person who is going to be able to meet the imperatives of the culture in which he is going to participate as a mature adult, especially in respect to the maintenance of effective social relations. The notion that modes of shaping the mind must be understood within the total sociocultural context in which they develop is expressed in the following programmatic statement. If we substitute the phrase "any social system" for "the kibbutz" in this statement, it has universal or cross-cultural applicability:

> Education of the children cannot be for educational purposes as such. . . . Rather it must be intrinsically tied to the major objectives of the kibbutz and to prepare the children for the kibbutz way of life. . . . The kibbutz is a complicated economic, social and political organism and all educational efforts must be directed to prepare the children to accept the institution and to serve its aims. [Golan, quoted in Stern 1965, p. 118]

I am going to concentrate on the imperatives of social relations because I want to stress that the individual in society confronts a complex set of realities that are foreordained, over which he has little (if any) control, and that are the products of his society's history. I emphasize this because of the proclivity among many behavioral scientists to disregard the principle that men must adapt to the realities in which they find themselves. I also emphasize this in order to make explicit the idea that programs that advocate changes in modes of socialization and education must be congruent with the cultural realities for which individuals are being prepared.

By definition, the concept of culture includes change. Social systems not only prepare their succeeding generations to maintain their ways of life but they also seek to prepare their members for new conditions of life, for new modes of acquiring a livelihood, and for new political realities when these undergo change (compare the essay by Safa in this volume). In the discussion that follows, I am going to speak of cultures as if they were stable systems, but this will be done only for heuristic purposes and for the sake of parsimony; one of my basic premises is that when a culture changes, there must be congruent changes in the manners of shaping the minds.

SOCIALIZATION AND EDUCATION

My point of departure is that *socialization* and *education* are two fundamentally different processes in the shaping of mind. They are found in all societies, albeit in different proportions. Although socialization and education are aspects of growing up in all social systems, their quantitative roles in preparing individuals for participation in adult cultural life vary from one society to another. This variation is an adaptive response to—or a function of—different cultural imperatives.

By the socialization of children I mean the activities that are devoted to the inculcation and elicitation of basic motivational and cognitive patterns through ongoing and spontaneous interaction with parents, siblings, kinsmen, and other members of the community. These activities are geared toward the creation of attitudes, values, control of impulses, cognitive orientations, and the like, in the course of daily and routine activities, both within and outside the household. Education is the inculcation of standardized and stereotyped knowledge, skills, values, and attitudes by means of standardized and stereotyped procedures. Such procedures and content exist in all cultures, ranging from the repetitive recitation of lore, myth, and etiquette by grandparents to grandchildren around open fires in crude shelters to the stereotyped instruction of large groups of children and adolescents (and sometimes adults) by non-kinsmen, using electronic media of communication, in elaborate and permanent buildings (compare Wax and Wax in this volume on Great/Little Tradition).

Socialization consists of such daily events in the life of a child as a parent expostulating "No!" when the child does something undesirable, or receiving a reward after having done something well. The interaction between the parent and child might be predictable—as when a child tortures a cat or a younger sibling—but it is not stereotyped and standardized in the sense that the interaction occurs at regular times, in predictable ways, and at set places.

I hypothesize that the quantitative role played by socialization in the development of the individual is in direct proportion to the extent to which the network of kin relations coincides with the network of personal relations. Correlatively, education tends to increase proportionately with the degree to which the network of kin relations fails to coincide with the network of personal relations.

Education does not take place only in schools, although, as will be seen, such institutions play an important role in the shaping of mind. Education—in the sense of formal, stereotypic, predictable learning experiences—takes place in even the most primitive societies. One example of this is Hart's description (1963, p. 410) of puberty rites among the Tiwi; the implications of this passage for other societies in which there are initiation ceremonies are readily apparent.

Among the Tiwi of North Australia, one can see the traumatic nature of the initiation period in very clear form, and part of the trauma lies in the sudden switch of personnel with whom the youth has to associate. A boy reaches thirteen or fourteen or so, and the physiological signs of puberty begin to appear. Nothing happens, possibly for many months. Then suddenly one day, toward evening when the people are gathering around their campfires for the main meal of the day after coming in from their day's hunting and food-gathering, a group of three or four heavily armed and taciturn strangers suddenly appear in camp. In full war regalia they walk in silence to the camp of the boy and say curtly to the household: "We have come for So-and-So!" Immediately pandemonium breaks loose. The mother and the rest of the older women begin to howl and wail. The father rushes for his spears. The boy, himself panic-stricken, tries to hide, the younger children begin to cry, and the household dogs begin to bark. It is all terribly similar to the reaction which is provoked by the arrival of the police at an American home to pick up a juvenile delinquent. This similarity extends to the behavior of the neighbors. These carefully abstain from identifying with either the strangers or the stricken household. They watch curiously the goings-on but make no move that can be identified as supporting either side. This is particularly notable in view of the fact that the strangers are strangers to all of them too, that is, they are from outside the encampment, or outside the band, who, under any other circumstances, would be greeted by a shower of spears. But not under these circumstances.

In terms of the hypotheses to be explored in this paper, I would like to take exception to one statement in the foregoing paragraph and, at the same time, add another dimension to the difference between education and socialization. I do not think that the comparison between the Tiwi experience just described and the American family's reaction to a visit by the police is apt—even though the overt behavior might be similar— because of its implications for the individual. In American society, having one's child picked up by the police as a delinquent is—at least in some circles—considered to be an unusual, if not an idiosyncratic, experience. It sets one off as being different from most other people. But the staged performance among the Tiwi has quite different consequences: it establishes a bond of common experience with others.

One of the pitfalls in many applications of psychological theories to the phenomena of culture is the prevailing implicit assumption that the formative experiences of early life have their effects—in the manner of information inputs—only at the times at which they occur. Without gainsaying the determinative effects of early life experiences for the shaping of personailty, what is often overlooked is that adults frequently think back to their experiences in growing up, and that remembrances of things past themselves have their effects. All adults look back from time to time on their childhood and adolescent experiences in the privacies of their minds and—whether they are aware of it or not—they distinguish between those experiences that were shared with all peers and those that were unique or idiosyncratic. The latter are important in contributing to a sense of personal identity—the sense of being unique— while the shared experiences contribute immeasurably to identification with other members of the group. When an adult thinks back to the experiences of his childhood and later stages of development, each formative event also contains, explicitly or implicitly, a recollection of whether he alone had a particular experience or whether it was one that all people like him had gone through. In addition to its other consequences, an experience that is recalled as unique is an important contributor to the sense of exclusiveness that each person must maintain. An experience that is recalled as one that had been undergone by others—a vision quest, group circumcision, marriage, learning how to hunt or cultivate, a doctoral oral examination, and the like—is an important psychological contributor to the feeling of "I am like all the others." This, too, is necessary for social life, and can be generated by socializational or educational experiences.

I suggest that the experience described by Hart for the Tiwi makes its mark three times, each with its own effects on the mind. The first occurs when a prepubertal child observes this happening to an older sibling or neighbor. His terror must be profound. The second occurs when it happens to him. Painful as the event must be when he is called for, he must somehow recall having seen this happen to others, and it certainly contributes to his sense of being a Tiwi, in addition to its other repercussions for him. The third time that the incident leaves its mark is when he is an adult, when he observes its occurrence in the lives of future adult Tiwi. This observation must strengthen his bond with the others in the group, knowing that he had undergone the experience and that it is now part of the lives of others: it is part of becoming and being a Tiwi. As will be discussed more fully, the preponderance of such shared institutionally stereotypic experiences in the course of growing up, vis-à-vis more idiosyncratic experiences, contributes to the sense of sameness with others, and is an adaptive response to the pressures of certain of social systems.

Another example of stereotypicality and standardization of instruction that can be designated as education is provided by George Spindler (1963, p. 389) from the Menomini:

> Grandparents still tell children "bedtime stories," and the adults in the group remember when their grandparents told them stories. "Grandmaw told us kids a story every night before we went to sleep. First thing next morning she would ask us what the story was about. If we couldn't tell her, she would tell the same story again the next night. She would do that until we could tell her what the story was about." What Grandmaw was looking for was the moral point of the story, "that we shouldn't offend anybody's feelings," or "not to envy what someone else has got."

I am not trying to establish a taxonomy on the basis of which one particular behavior or another with respect to children can be designated as an example of socialization or education. Instead, my concern is with the proportion of the two to each other—and their institutional contexts—in the total experience of growing up and in being prepared for participation in the culture. The balance struck between the two in the shaping of mind, and their placement in different institutional settings, is in itself a formative experience; the proportions that are maintained in this regard are preparations for different styles of life

Socialization

Socialization—the inculcation of basic psychological patterns through spontaneous interaction with parents, siblings, and others—is the predominant mode of the shaping of mind in social systems in which kinship is the primary principle in the organization of economic, political, and other social relations. One of the salient features of kinship as a standard for the organization of social relations is its emphasis on *particularistic* criteria in recruitment and in the evaluation of behavior. This is best expressed in the fundamental paradigmatic dictum that your brother is your brother, and you must get along and cooperate with him, regardless of how you feel about him. Such a value is often given religious and ritual validation in many societies in which kinship is the principal articulator in the organization of social relations, as in the rule that brothers may not sacrifice together when they are in a state of enmity. Expectations for performance, bases of reciprocity, access to the desiderata of the culture, and the like, are phrased in terms of who a person is instead of *what* he has accomplished. The particularistic values of kinship prescribe that solidarity and anchorage—what I have referred to elsewhere as "sociological interdependence" (Cohen 1964)—are to be sought within narrowly defined sociological limits often within the boundaries of the corporate kin group or the community. An excellent example of particularism in social life is provided by Wilson for the Nyakyusa (1959, p. 201): "In [traditional Nyakyusa] thought moral obligations are limited to kinsmen and neighbors: they do not extend beyond the chiefdom except to those relatives who may live beyond its bounds."

The predominance of socialization—vis-à-vis education—in the shaping of mind is thoroughly congruent with an emphasis in the social structure on particularism. This must be seen in two different frames. On the one hand, it is a mode of upbringing that prepares the individual for responsiveness to particularistic criteria. On the other hand, it represents a consistency between the over-all institutional structure of the society and its methods of culturalizing its future members. The latter is an especially important consideration because a society's modes of bringing up its children are not something apart from the total institutional structure of the society. If it is correct to characterize a culture as, *inter alia*, a self-perpetuating system, it is necessary to acknowledge explicitly that the enculturation of the future members of the society is one of the most important institutional activities of the group. Since one of the features of a social system is the achievement and maintenance of consistency in the values and criteria of its principal institutions, there is usually also an attempt to achieve and maintain consistency between the group's methods in shaping the mind and its other institutional activities.

The family is almost always the primary locus of socialization, and relationships within it are governed by particularistic considerations. Thus, as Parsons has described the articulation of socialization and family organization (1964, pp. 48–49),

> In the case of the family . . . the paramount value is particularism-quality; it is the maintenance by the family as a collective unit of an appropriate "style" or pattern of life, including of course the treatment of children as part of this. But in this subsystem the father-husband role is differentiated in terms of the primacy *for* this role, *i.e.*, the second place for the family, of the particularistic performance pattern, *i.e.*, of responsibility for the interests of the collectivity in its *relations to the situation*, while the mother-wife role is differentiated in terms of particularism-quality (from her husband's); it is, that is to say, the more direct embodiment of the familial values.

In family-socialization, the child learns behaviors and feelings that are appropriate to *his* family, *his* parents, *his* siblings, and the like, in addition to expressive patterns that are appropriate to general social life. Of course, children become aware at very early ages that there are other families and that there are variations among these families with respect to customary and permissible conduct. But when family-socialization predominates as the context in which the mind is shaped, children also learn very early that it is to the norms of their own and closely related families to which they must respond. Where the family is the principal institutional vehicle for the transmission of culture, the embodiment of familial values serves as a prototype for an adult style of life in which the individual is expected to respond in terms of particularistic criteria—behavior that is appropriate to *his* kin group, *his* age set, *his* cult, *his* sex, and the like.

In no society, however, is the shaping of children's minds confined exclusively to the family. Another important locus of socialization is the network of kinsmen outside the household, and kinsmen are often assigned responsibility for the imposition of particular disciplines and the transmission of particular skills and knowledge to each other's children. The socialization of children by extrahousehold kinsmen is also intimately tied to a particularistic orientation in the culture as a whole, and kinsmen are responsible for a significant portion of the upbringing of each other's children in societies in which the network of kin relations coincides with the network of personal relations. Furthermore, as I showed in *The Transition from Childhood to Adolescence* (1964), the members of a child's descent group (e.g., clan, lineage) are obligated to participate in his upbringing in societies in which the rule of joint legal liability is found, that is, the rule of law that if the perpetrator of certain unlawful acts cannot be apprehended or meet his liability, then that liability falls on members of his descent group, usually in predetermined order. One of the aims that I attributed to being brought up by members of the descent group in addition to parents and others is that it helps to establish an identification and solidarity with the descent group. Thus, this practice can be viewed, among its other connotations, as a means of inculcating an orientation to the particularistic values of certain kin groups. Correlatively, the rule of joint liability embodies particularistic criteria within the legal system; it does not assert that all men are equal under the law but, instead, connotes that different rules of law obtain when men are kinsmen than when they are not.

Peer groups and socialization: Another important locus of socialization —which, although it is found in all societies, has not received the systematic attention it warrants—is the peer group (note the discussion on peer society in the essay by Wax and Wax in this volume). Although the peer group is an important feature of the individual's growth in all societies, there seem to be very important—if not fundamental—differences in the relationship of the peer group to adult institutions, depending on the general orientation of social relations in the culture. Peer groups are particularistically oriented but, at the same time, are almost always prototypes of adult structuralizations of social relations, at least in part, and are important vehicles for the transmission of adult patterns of authority and cooperation. It appears that in societies in which the network of kin relations greatly coincides with social relations, parents play an important role in overseeing and controlling the content or nature of peer-group activities. On the other hand, it appears that in societies in which the network of kin relations does not coincide with social relations, parents are not directly involved in the behavior and activities of their children in relation to peers; instead, they seem to focus their control on the children's choice of friends.

This can be illustrated by reference to three different cultures. Among the Nyakyusa and Gusii, where kinship plays an important role in economic, political, and other spheres of activity, parents are directly involved in the behavior of their children within the peer group. In contemporary American society, where kinship is not supposed to be a factor affecting either the recruitment of children into systems of training for adult positions or in the evaluation of performance, parents do not seem to control the activities of the peer group directly; instead, their influence appears to be confined to choice of friends.

In societies such as Nyakyusa and Gusii, each of which is ethnically homogeneous, children learn the idiom and values of kinship—and its significance in the organization of social relations—from their earliest days. The choice of friends in the formulation of peer groups does not present much of a problem in societies such as these because group memberships and affiliations are largely predetermined. On the other hand, in a heterogeneous society, contemporary United States for example, group memberships and affiliations are not foreordained, at least ideally. Hence, one of the principal concerns of parents is to teach their children the criteria by which their peers are to be selected. This is not to say that parents in American society do not influence the nature of social relations within their children's peer groups; they do, but by indirection. I suggest that it makes a great deal of difference whether parents explicitly control social relations within the peer group—as among the Nyakyusa and Gusii —or whether they do so indirectly, as in contemporary American society. This is a matter for further research, but it must be viewed within the context of the organization of social relations within the culture at large.

Among the Nyakyusa, children—especially boys—are incessantly pressured into peer-group participation, and the latter association is one of the major vehicles in the shaping of the individual to become a good Nyakyusa.

One of the values most constantly stressed by the Nyakyusa is that of *ukwangala* which, in its primary sense, means "the enjoyment of good company" and, by extension, the mutual aid and sympathy which spring from personal friendship. It implies urbane manners and a friendliness which expresses itself in eating and drinking together; not only merry conversation, but also discussion between equals, which the Nyakyusa regard as the principal form of education. "It is by conversing with our friends," said one of our witnesses, "that we gain wisdom (*amahala*); it is bad to sit quite still in men's company. A man who does this is a fool; he learns no wisdom, he has only his own thoughts. Moreover, a man who does not spend time with other people is always dirty, he does not compare himself with any friends. For we learn cleanliness of body in company, those who are dirty learning from their more cleanly friends. . . . It is better to live with other people. [Wilson 1963, p. 66]

To make certain, in part, that the individual does not develop "only his own thoughts" (my interpretation),

the value of good fellowship with equals is constantly talked about by the Nyakyusa, and it is dinned into boys from childhood that enjoyment and morality alike consist in eating and drinking, in talking and learning, in the company of contemporaries. The solitary and aloof, those who enjoy the company of women (as opposed to direct sexual satisfaction) and those who seek intimacy with members of another generation, are derided. [Wilson 1963, p. 163]
Men and boys are expected to eat regularly with age-mates. . . . From the time a small boy begins to herd he is encouraged to bring home two or three friends to eat with him, and in turn he visits each of them. Since boys have no fields of their own until they marry, but co-operate in cultivation with their parents, it is to their own mothers they go for food, and parents are proud of a son bringing many friends. "Perhaps," said Angombwike, "a son will come with his friends and cut a huge bunch of bananas, and take thick milk and eat with them. When the father comes back his wives will tell him: 'Your son has eaten all the thick milk and cut a banana bunch!' Then he will ask: 'How many men were with my son?' 'Six!' 'Ah, he's a chief!' the old man will say, smiling proudly." "And formerly if a young man came home often alone to eat, his father would beat him, or even take a spear and wound him, and when people asked why he would say: 'This great fool comes alone to my place, again and again.' It is good to eat with friends, for boys to go round in groups of four or five." [Wilson 1963, p. 67]

Another illuminating description of the relationships of childhood peer groups to the adult generation is provided by LeVine and LeVine for the

Gusii of Kenya. Noting that the structure of peer groups is often determined by economic considerations, such as whether families have cattle
that have to be herded (1963, p. 170), they observe that

at home and in the pastures, older children dominate younger ones. To
some extent this is promulgated by parents, many of whom said they felt
it important for one child to be in charge of the others and tell them what
to do, and who select the oldest in the group of children for the position
of leadership. . . . Since the parents may hold the appointed leader accountable
for misdemeanors by and harm befalling the younger children, he is highly
motivated to keep them in line and boss them around, though he is not
permitted to punish them. In herding groups consisting of children from
several homesteads, the oldest dominates the others, ordering them about,
occasionally beating them, taking whatever articles they own. . . . Parents
consider such behavior natural and even proper, but they do not accept the
idea of the group or its leader dominating a boy so as to make him ignore
or violate his parents' wishes. In fact, parents do not entirely recognize the
existence of children's groups beyond those of siblings, and they try to maintain direct control over their children regardless of the amount of peer
activity. [LeVine and LeVine 1963, p. 171]

Now to compare the foregoing accounts from the Nyakyusa and Gusii
with material from a village in contemporary New England. From the
descriptions of Nyakyusa and Gusii peer-group relationships, it can be
gathered that parents are very concerned with the structure of relations
within the group. In the New England community, called Orchard Town
by Fischer and Fischer (1963), one gathers that parents are primarily
concerned with the choices of friends made by their children, and little
with the structure of relationships within the group.

Although the parents try to give the play groups considerable autonomy,
they do continue to exercise some influence, mostly indirect, on their elementary school child's choice of playmates. Mothers sometimes make critical
remarks to their child about undesired playmates and also show differential
hospitality to neighbors' children according to their suitability as playmates
from the point of view of morals and manners. [Fischer and Fischer 1963,
p. 994]

The role played by the peer group in the shaping of the individual's
mind for participation in the culture represents one of the major gaps
in our knowledge of how culture is transmitted and perpetuated. Nor,
aside from a few brief ethnographic descriptions, do we have systematic
comparative information about the role played by the peer group in
cultural change. More important, however, peer groups are not only the
province of children; they are also the concerns of adults who, it can be
hypothesized, make certain that these networks are maintained in a culturally approved manner in the interest of the transmission and perpetuation of the culture. But we know very little, at least in any systematic
fashion, about the activities of adults in attuning the peer group with the
rest of the social structure. While it is clear enough from the data that
adults play an active role in Nyakyusa and Gusii peer groups in limited

spheres, we need to know whether they do so in others, and from which aspects of peer-group activities their influences are systematically excluded. We also need to know how adult values with respect to seniority are conveyed from household to peer group. And, importantly, in terms of the hypotheses being explored in this paper, we need to know whether there are any significant differences in the socializing roles of peer groups between societies in which the network of kin relations coincides with the network of personal relations and those in which the two are disparate (cf. Parsons 1964, pp. 221–229).

Techniques of socialization: Just as the social nexuses devoted to the upbringing of children differ in the roles that they play according to the emphasis in the social structure on particularistic values, so are there also important variations in the techniques by which children are taught to respond to expectations in their performances. It is not necessary to belabor the point that children in all societies are disciplined and rewarded, and that children are subjected to pressures for conformity in all societies.

In societies where socialization plays a greater role in the shaping of the child's mind than does education, the techniques of the former are generally designed to elicit conformity to *small-group* pressures. Many students of patterns of child upbringing (see, for example, Pettit 1946) have stressed the important role of guilt and ridicule in the systems of socialization—and the general eschewal of corporal punishment—in many primitive societies. Many anthropologists and others have quoted parents' assertions that corporal punishment is "cruel" and that they "love" their children too much to punish them physically. Unfortunately, however, these statements fail to relate the techniques of socialization to the total social systems in which they are used, that is, to the goals of such modes of upbringing.

We have several excellent studies of social systems in which the elicitation of guilt is an important technique in gaining conformity in children. (Although many authors have sought to distinguish guilt and shame, I assume that there is little difference between them, or that they are at least correlative.) Among the best of these are DeVos' analysis of Japanese patterns (1960) and Dorothy Eggan's of the Hopi (1956). What emerges consistently from these studies is that a heavy reliance on the elicitation of guilt is a systematic means of training people to respond to the pressures for conformity from a small and solidary group. Eggan made this clear for the Hopi (1956, pp. 361–362):

For through the great strength of the emotional orientations conveyed within the kinship framework and the interwoven religious beliefs, young Hopi learned their world from dedicated teachers whose emotions were involved in teaching what they believed intensely, and this in turn engaged the children's emotions in learning. These experiences early and increasingly made explicit in a very personal way the values implicit in the distinction between a good heart and a bad heart. For public opinion, if intensely felt and openly expressed in a closely knit and mutually dependent group . . . can be more effective potential punishment than the electric chair. It is perhaps easier to die quickly than to live in loneliness in a small community in the face of contempt from one's fellows, and particularly from one's clan from whence . . . comes most of one's physical and emotional security. Small wonder that the children who experience this constant pressure to conform to clan dictates and needs, and at the same time this constant reinforcement of clan solidarity against outsiders, are reluctant as adults to stray too far from the clan's protective familiarity or to defy its wishes.

A Hopi wondering whether he is of "bad heart" is experiencing the guilt that is attuned to the imperatives of life in a Hopi clan. It is an effective orientation of mind to the social realities of the clan world.

There was, therefore, a constant probing of one's own heart, well illustrated by the anguished cry of a Hopi friend, "Dorothy, *did* my son die as the old folks said because my heart was not right? Do *you* believe this way, that if parents do not keep good hearts children will die?" And there was a constant examination of one's neighbors' hearts: "Movensie, it is those _____ clan people who ruined this ceremony! They have bad hearts and they quarrel too much. That bad wind came up and now we will get no rain." Conversation among the Hopi is rarely censored, and the children heard both of these women's remarks, *feeling*, you may be sure, the *absolute belief* which these "teachers" had in the *danger* which a bad heart carries for everyone in the group. [Eggan 1956, p. 361]

Training for sensitivity to group pressures for conformity by means of eliciting guilt does not take place in a vacuum; instead, it always takes place in the concrete interactions between the child and highly specific individuals who are charged by the social system with the responsibility of producing the guilt, of manipulating it, and of teaching the instrumental responses by which it can be assuaged. Usually, it is the mother who is most often responsible for this training, and the reasons for this are understandable. The mother is generally the most highly affectively charged individual in a growing child's life, and he often spends more time with her than with any other person.

But what is important in this connection is not only that the mother is the central object of the child's guilt, but that she performs this role as the representative of the group. This is abundantly illustrated in DeVos' analysis of the deep undercurrent of guilt as the psychological fulcrum in traditional Japanese socialization. Guilt toward the mother in this situation is specifically related to the child's failure to meet expectations that are phrased in terms of the individual's duties and obligations in respect to the family and extended kin grouping. The overt phraseology of the consequences of transgressions, as taught in Japanese socialization—laziness and other nonproductive behavior—is that they "injure" the parents. But the thrust of the argument is not lost on the child, who also sees and hears his parents themselves responding consistently to the pressures of the kin group and community. Furthermore, the systematic use of guilt as a means for eliciting conformity during childhood and adulthood must also be seen as an integral aspect of the particularistic orientation of a social system. It is in terms of the consequences for a specific solidary grouping—family, lineage, community, and the like—that an individual in such societies must weigh his actions. Guilt can become an object of humor and a primary concern of psychotherapeutic systems when its elicitation is inappropriate to—and incongruent with—the imperatives of a social system in which the principal (or at least growing) emphasis is on *universalistic* values and criteria.

The systematic development of sensitivity to ridicule and the loss of esteem by the group is another technique of socialization that is intimately tied to an orientation to particularistic values and to life in relatively self-contained and solidary groups. It is not the ridicule of everyone to which an individual is taught to respond in many primitive and peasant societies but rather to the threats of loss of esteem of the specific group in which he is expected to find his social and emotional anchorage. Ridicule is only effective when an individual's self-value is equated with the worth placed on him by the group with which he is expected to identify, and within which he expects to function. It is an extremely potent means of assuring conformity when the solidary, limited, and circumscribed group constitutes the individual's universe wherein he seeks to secure a place. Ridicule is a rejection—or at least a threat of it—by the universe as it is subjectively experienced; the narrower the social stage on which the individual can maneuver during his life, the more effective is ridicule as a device of control.

The individual must learn the idiom and nuances of ridicule if it is to be an effective weapon in the hands of the group; hence, the sensitivity to ridicule and threats of loss of esteem must be established early in his life. It might be self-evident that pressures to conformity are ineffective if people have not been sensitized to them, but the point has to be made explicit if we are to untangle the skein of a culture and its mechanisms of self-perpetuation.

It is in contrast with guilt and ridicule that corporal punishment can be understood as a technique of socialization. Corporal punishment is rare as a standard means of socialization in primitive and peasant societies because of its personalized quality. It is an activity that takes place in a dyadic context; its goal is to elicit conformist response to the demands of a particular individual who is exercising—or who is capable of exercising—force. The impact of corporal punishment is not only physical; it is also social and emotional. Specifically, the emphasis in corporal punishment is on person-to-person relationships at the expense of an emphasis to group pressures to conformity. One of the socioemotional messages conveyed in the relatively regular reliance on corporal punishment—as, for example, in Alor (DuBois 1944, p. 137) or in a highland peasant Jamaican community (Cohen 1958)—is that if one can avoid detection by the punishing agent he can "get away with it." By contrast, one of the lessons taught in societies in which great reliance is placed on guilt and ridicule—and these are generally groups in which the individual is constantly exposed to group surveillance—is that the group is always present, even if it is only one other person who symbolizes the group, and that it is almost impossible to escape detection.

As an important technique of socialization, corporal punishment is eminently suited for preparation to participate in a social system of atomized relationships, but it is incompatible with preparation to participate in a solidary system with firmly bounded social relationships. But the close correspondence between corporal punishment in socialization and atomized relationships among adults does not rest exclusively on the fact that corporal punishment generally takes place in the context of a dyadic relationship. Corporal punishment in childhood arouses intense emotions in children, and evidence provided from animal experimentations suggests that this mode of socialization is effective in heightening and strengthening the emotional bond between child and parent; as I have tried to show elsewhere (1964), such intense relationships are established at the expense of wider extrafamiliar identifications.

While extrapolations from experimental work with animals should not be taken literally, they can be very suggestive for understanding human behavior. Scott has observed in his review of animal experimentation (1962, pp. 950–955) that

all [the] evidence indicates that any sort of strong emotion, whether hunger, fear, pain, or loneliness, will speed up the process of socialization. . . . We may also conclude that the speed of formation of a social bond is dependent upon the degree of emotional arousal, irrespective of the nature of that arousal. . . . In short, it seems likely that the formation of a social attachment through contact and emotional arousal is a process that may take place throughout life, and that although it may take place more slowly outside of certain critical periods, the capacity for such an attachment is never completely lost.

Evidence is accumulating . . . that given any kind of emotional arousal a young animal will become attached to any individual or object with which it is in contact for a sufficiently long time. . . . It should not be surprising that many kinds of emotional reactions contribute to a social relationship. The surprising thing is that emotions which we normally consider aversive should produce the same effect as those which appear to be rewarding. This apparent paradox is partially resolved by evidence that the positive effect of unpleasant emotions is normally limited to early infancy by the development of escape reactions. Nevertheless, this concept leads to the somewhat alarming conclusion that an animal (and perhaps a person) of any age, exposed to certain individuals or physical surroundings for any length of time, will inevitably become attached to them, the rapidity of the process being governed by the degree of emotional arousal associated with them.

I have suggested in my exploration of initiation ceremonies (Cohen 1964) that this might provide an explanation for the widespread use of physical—especially genital—mutilations in the course of these rites of passage. Specifically, I hypothesized that these painful experiences might help to strengthen the attachments to the kinsmen who are performing the operations in order to add to the individual's feelings of solidarity with the kin group of which they are all a part. But when corporal punishment is one of the principal means of socialization, it contributes to the emotional attachment between parent and child, and this is almost always at the expense of wider identifications.

Socialization and traditionalism: Finally, socialization—vis-à-vis education—is oriented to traditionalism. As is well known, there tends to be a direct relationship between levels of sociotechnological development and the rate of cultural change. Without going into the reasons that the rate of change of a society is locked into its culture—and must be seen as an aspect of the culture—the fact also remains that every society maintains a highly specific attitude toward change; this is part of its value system, and it must be inculcated as part of the process of the shaping of mind. I hypothesize that in those societies in which the rate of change is slow and in which change is disvalued, socialization will predominate in the upbringing of the members of the group. I am not suggesting that socialization is in any way a source of a slow rate of change or that it is responsible for negative values associated with change. If a causal relationship is in order, I would hypothesize the converse, that a slow rate of change is a sociocultural feature that can underlie the predominance of socialization in the transmission of culture.

One of the most outstanding characteristics of socialization—especially within the family—is the high affective charge that is associated with almost everything that is learned within that context. The reason for this is that the content of learning, especially in children, is often inseparable from the identity of their teachers. Furthermore, this is an important aspect of particularism in general—*who* states a proposition is directly relevant to its value. It is a general characteristic of highly traditional people that they are not only fundamentalist in outlook but that they are also generally guided by particularistic values in the organization of their social relationships and by particularistic criteria in the evaluation of performance.

Because agents of socialization (as distinct from agents of education) are so highly charged emotionally, the patterns of behavior that they inculcate—socially acceptable norms, the organization of social relationships, modes of belief and of thought, and the like—are equally charged. What is important with respect to the maintenance of traditionalism and resistance to change is that the relinquishment of such patterns can often arouse—unconsciously, to be sure—anticipations of loss of love and primary security, whereas the retention of traditional modes can elicit equally deep and subtle connotations of approval, reward, and a sense of belonging. This is not to imply that a predominance of socialization in the total experience of maturation will lead to a complete rejection of change; adults are usually oriented to reality and do adapt when the conditions in which they find themselves require change. But what is important is that the requirements for change do elicit different degrees of resistance and personal turmoil in different societies. The reliance on agents and techniques of socialization for the transmission of culture is an adaptive mechanism in many societies whose rate of change is slow and who, therefore, maintain negative values in connection with change.

This relationship between traditionalism and a predominant reliance on socialization—in which, to reiterate, the latter is the dependent variable —is illustrated by "the early learning hypothesis," explored by Bruner (1956) on the basis of material from the Mandan-Hidatsa. Bruner suggested that what is learned early in life is resistant to change while that which is learned later in life is most susceptible to change. In a discussion of Bruner's analysis, I added to his hypothesis the suggestion (Cohen 1961, p. 112) that what is learned inside the family is most resistant to change and that which is learned outside the family is most susceptible to change.

This discussion of the relationship between traditionalism and socialization would be incomplete, however, without pointing, at least, in passing, to another very important variable. In social systems in which change is disvalued, the individual more or less tends to grow up, live out his life, and die among the same people. In such environments, as noted, there tends to be little chance of escaping the scrutiny of affectively charged people for long. These relatively stable groupings of people are those with whom some of the most fundamental patterns of behavior were learned in childhood. The shame, guilt, need for approval, desire for belongingness, and the like, which are learned during the earliest years of psychological vulnerability are always the strongest; and the patterns of behavior that they underlie also tend to remain the strongest when the associations with those in whose midst such patterns were acquired are retained.

Also, in most of these societies, the family is a unit of both production and consumption and it involves the most inalienable ties. In addition to its symbolization of solidarity, such a family also carries with it the sociological imprints and emotional associations with one's parents, grandparents, and the traditions that they represent. In such social systems, people behave traditionally and tend not to follow their own inclinations because, in part, of the scrutiny of those with whom they have been in lifelong association and who are the symbolic reminders of the emotions associated with things their parents and other affectively charged persons had taught them (Cohen 1961, pp. 106–111). Thus, the experiences of childhood not only often underlie adult modes of behavior, but it is also important to recognize that the institutional structures in which adults participate underlie the means by which the culture is transmitted, as in the balance struck between socialization and education.

Education

Education—the inculcation of standardized knowledge and skills by standardized and stereotyped means—is the predominant mode of shaping the mind in social systems in which nonkinship and *universalistic* considerations are of primary significance in the organization of economic, political, and other social relations. Although, as noted, education is found in all societies, it begins to assume a predominant role in the course of history when it is institutionalized in schools. Considered as techniques of society for molding the individual to serve the aims of the social system, socialization and education are in competition. Coleman has noted this in his introduction to *Education and Political Development* (1965, p. 22) when he referred to "the wide gap between the modern and traditional sectors of the developing countries. "Yet," he observes, "it is the very existence of this gap which . . . elevates the formal educational system to a more determinative role in the political socialization process, and diminishes, if it does not extinguish, the role of the family, the prime socializer." While the latter assertion in this statement is somewhat overdrawn, it does point clearly to the proportionate relationship between socialization and education. The family is not faced with extinction; like all other social institutions, it is merely changing adaptively to meet new sociocultural pressures.

Every social system tends to insist that its members be quite blind, especially with respect to history (compare Henry's discussion of "stupidity" in his remarks, "Is Education Possible?"). Every culture requires that the people participating in it see the institutions of their society as unique, as outgrowths of present and immediate needs, and as expressions of its genius. Were this otherwise, most social systems would find it more difficult than they do to win loyalty and allegiance. Hence, most people in society tend to approach an understanding of the institutions by which they live in a manner akin to the proverbial blind man who is trying to describe an elephant. We thus observe many people—behavioral scientists among them—variously suggesting that our contemporary educational institutions are designed to cope with the demands of an industrially oriented technology; a mechanism for transmitting knowledge gained by our contemporaries and by other societies at different times in history; an institutional complex devoted to the life of the mind; a means of transmitting political values; an instrument for eliminating social inequality; a key to utopia, in which Everyman will be "creative" and self-expressive, and the like.

However, when we remove our historical blinders and look at educational institutions from their beginnings in human history, and at our own systems of education as outgrowths or products of history, we must conclude that they are all—and none—of these. Instead, we are compelled to look at these institutions as changing adaptations to changing sociocultural environments. As private citizens taking personal stands, we might not like what we see—there are, after all, some advantages to blindness—but a social system is more than, and different from, the sum of personal stands and likes or dislikes in the polity. Few institutions in history have been changed by conscious and deliberate means, except through violent revolution. Furthermore, no educational system in history—or at least any of which we know—has been consciously and deliberately transformed without first heaving over the entire social system to which it is an adaptation. Our task here is to understand the elephant rather than to write a manifesto for or about one of his hind legs. How and why did formal educational systems first develop, and what do today's institutions of learning have in common with the first schools?

One of the important lessons that can be learned from studies of cultural evolution is that a social system in complete equilibrium—one that manifests only the characteristics appropriate to the stage of development that it represents—is almost nonexistent. An important derivation of the axiom that every culture is, *inter alia*, a changing system is that it is generally possible to find in each the retention of some social patterns that are indicative of its earlier modes of adaptation and the emergence of patterns that anticipate a subsequent stage. While I recognize the teleological element in this proposition, this is not an appropriate place at which to tarry and argue its feasibility, and I will use it as an axiom and a point of departure for the following analysis.

If we examine the historical emergence of schools in the context of stages of cultural development, rather than chronologically, their first recorded appearance seems to have occurred during the stage represented by some West African societies, such as the Kpelle, in the form of the so-called "bush" schools (see Gibbs 1965; Watkins 1943). "The Kpelle have an incipient class system that distinguishes three classes" (Gibbs 1965, p. 214). While kinship does play an important role in the organization of social relations among them, it is secondary to tribal fraternities and other secret societies. These, too, are embodiments of particularistic orientations, although somewhat less so than kin-group organizations, like the lineage.

Kpelle culture has two conflicting dominant themes. The first is a stress on personal autonomy and the individual achievement of status. Eligibility for high rank such as chieftaincy is not ascribed primarily on the basis of birth as a member of a particular lineage or clan as it is in many middle-range African societies. Rather, it is achieved on the basis of individual effort. A Kpelle may climb ahead of his fellows through the possession of certain obtainable skills Most important is the ability to work hard, that is, to farm well, and to manage his economic resources skillfully. . . . The counterweight to the theme of individual achievement is the stress on conformity and regulation as exemplified in the tribal societies. Through the initiation ["bush"] schools they assure the continuity of basic Kpelle values and by the application of combined ritual and

secular sanctions, they ensure adherence to those values. This means that individual Kpelle are guided by the same expectations in the competition for power.
They play by the same rules and for the same stakes, which means that no one
goes too far in the means he uses to acquire position. If he does, the sanctions
are forceful and effective. Through its officials, the Poro [tribal fraternity, secret
society] regulates the speed with which a man with a following may acquire
formal political or Poro office. [Gibbs 1965, pp. 229–230]

In terms of the hypotheses being explored in this paper, the "bush"
schools of the Kpelle and other West African societies constitute an in-
triguing problem. On the one hand, these cultures exhibit many of the
characteristics of societies in which socialization predominates over education. Until adolescence, the household is the principal context in which the
individual matures (Gibbs 1965, pp. 207–210). On the other hand—and,
at first blush, somewhat anomalously—they have a system of schools for
initiates; this schooling, however, is not compulsory, and nowadays the
person who does not attend does not suffer any severe social disabilities
(Gibbs 1965, pp. 221–223). In some of these West African societies, attendance at these schools during early adolescence lasts several years.

How can we reconcile the presence of schools in a social system with
the fact that kinship and secret societies—matrixes that inevitably sub-
serve particularistic values and orientations—play such important roles in
the organization of its economic, political, and other spheres of social
relations? One of the keys to this paradox is the fact that after each group
has completed its period of instruction, the buildings of its school are
abandoned or destroyed; in either event, they may not be used again for
any other group or for any other purpose. Moreover, Gibbs informs me
(in a personal communication) that his recent investigations among the
Kpelle indicate that there is a minimum of formal and standardized
instruction in Kpelle "bush" schools.

There are strong parallels between the formalized training of Kpelle
youths during their initiation ceremonies and that which is found among
many Australian aboriginal societies. While none of the Australians can
be considered to have "schools" to an extent approaching those of the
Kpelle, it needs to be borne in mind that Kpelle "schools" are part of the
secret (Poro) society. As a result, and in view of the high degree of
particularism represented by the secret society, the formal and specialized
training received by youths in Kpelle initiation schools must also be regarded as important contributors to the maintenance of particularistic
values.

In the light of these considerations, it can be suggested that these
"bush" schools are not schools at all, if we mean by a school an institution
with specialized personnel, permanent physical structures, special apparatus (of which texts are an important part), formal and stereotyped
means of instruction, a curriculum, and rationally defined manifest objectives. The Kpelle and others like them have, as it were, tasted the

educational cake without ever really having it or being able to eat it. So-called West African "bush" schools represent a symbolic elaboration or maximization of the universal process of education within the limits permitted by the social structure.

The retention of the school structures after each age grade has "graduated" and the adoption of a curriculum and standardized instruction would be incompatible with the total institutional structures and value systems of these societies. If they were not repetitively demolished or abandoned and were allowed to be used again, the schools would soon come to be used more extensively, at earlier ages, and as a much more integral vehicle for the transmission of the culture. They would thus replace the household and other primary local groups as the principal mold for the shaping of the individual. If a standardized curriculum and formal and stereotyped instruction were introduced, the *particularistically* oriented sector of the culture's value system—household, kin group, secret society —would be subverted because, as will be illustrated, such means of instruction are designed to serve *universalistic* values. The recurrent demolition or abandonment of these "schools" and the eschewal of standardized instruction represent an avoidance of a pattern of upbringing that is incompatible with the rest of the social system.

Schools and states: The development of schools—the institutionalized predominance of education over socialization in the shaping of men's minds—is a characteristic feature of state societies. Not all state societies develop schools, but the important point is that schools do not emerge historically prior to the creation of states. By a state society is meant here a society in which "a single person, by whatsoever name he may be distinguished, is entrusted with the execution of the laws, the management of the revenue, and the command of the army" (Gibbon I, p. 52).

The essence of education—vis-à-vis socialization—is that one of its principal emphases is on universalistic values, criteria, and standards of performance. It is in these terms that, from the point of view of the total social system, education competes with socialization. The thrust of learning acquired in a context of socialization is the identity of the teacher— *who* states a proposition is the relevant consideration. The impact of learning in a context of education is that "*who* states a proposition is as such irrelevant to the question of its . . . value" (Parsons 1954, 42); instead, the relevant consideration in education is *what* is being taught and learned, regardless of who teaches it. One of the underlying premises of a system of education—whether it is conducted on an individual basis or in schools—is that teachers can be changed daily, or that the child can go from one teacher to another, without altering the content of what is being learned.

It is the universalistic orientation that is inherent in education that makes it eminently suitable as a predominant mode of shaping the mind to prepare people to serve the aims of a state society. Two outstanding characteristics of a state society that are relevant to our present consideration serve the growth of universalistic values in the society as a whole. First, one of the goals of a state is to subvert local—especially kin—sources of solidarity, loyalty, and authority. Engels was among the first to make this conflict clear (1942 edition, p. 99) when he spoke of "the irreconcilable opposition between gentile society and the state; the first attempt at forming a state consists in breaking up the gentes by dividing their members into those with privileges and those with none, and by further separating the latter into two productive classes and thus setting them one against the other." Spencer also observed this when he asserted (1891, p. 283) that "naturally, as a whole nation becomes more integrated, local integrations lose their separateness, and their divisions fade . . . though they long leave their traces. . . ." As Diamond stated in his reconstruction of the building of the Dahomean state (1951, pp. 3–4; 10; 14):

> The civil power must, in one way or another, subvert kin solidarity and deflect that esprit de corps towards itself, in order to extend its authority throughout the social structure.
> . . . It appears that the whole region of [Dahomey] from the northern boundary of Whydah to Yoruba country was, up to the beginning of the seventeenth century, divided into tiny local sovereignties. . . . These autonomous sovereignties were probably localized clans, or clusters of clans, each with a paramount chief. . . . [As] the scattered kin societies within the Whydah-Abomey axis were coagulating into civil society . . . the Aladaxonu became the civil authority, building and manipulating a power structure that was designed to wrest from the subordinated kin groups their customary political, social, economic and religious functions.

A second major task confronted by a state in the legitimation of its authority is that it must establish an ideology—if not a reality—of uniformity among its polity. While there are many ways by which states accomplish this, one is the attempt to inculcate a universalistic or uniform and standardized set of symbols to which all the members of the society can be trained to respond uniformly (compare Safa's discussion of nation building in this volume). Such symbol-systems must be implanted early if they are to be effective. The implantation of standardized responses to the symbol-system of the state can appear in many guises, but their goals are the same—to contribute to the establishment of conformity to the aims and imperatives of a state system. Whether the means to this end take the form of uniform dress for schoolchildren (or even for their teachers), standardized sacred books and paraphernalia or fetishes, flags, pictures of culture heroes or rulers that students face throughout the school day, and the like, the object is to present all future participants in the society with uniform ideological symbols. The goal is to make these symbols integral parts of shaped minds, so that responses to them in adulthood will be uniform when the state bureaucracy feels that it needs to use them to gain acquiescence or mass participation in an activity of the society.

Without going into a discussion of why some state societies develop school systems and others do not—although it can be noted in passing that writing is a necessary, but not the only, requisite—it is essential to bear in mind that schools are an important part of the political bureaucracies in those state societies in which there are schools. It goes without saying that each part of a state bureaucracy has its own relevant and specialized tasks: the collection of taxes, control of religious organization, management of economic activities, administration of law, leadership of the military, and the like. Similarly, the educational part of a state's bureaucracy has its relevant and specialized tasks, to implant politically meaningful and legitimating symbols and to elicit approved and appropriate responses to those symbols as one means among many for the maintenance of order and uniformity of response throughout the polity. If we are to understand educational institutions in terms of their provenance, we must remember that schools were not established originally to foster the life of the mind or the spirit of free inquiry. That they have in a few cases become devoted to such pursuits is another matter, and they are exceptional. But every organization and bureaucracy is self-serving; this is no less true of a state system than any other (compare Horton's discussion of educational bureaucracy in this volume). Every state organization constantly looks to the sectors of its bureaucracy to make certain that its interests are being served. To expect that a state will allow its schools to serve aims other than those of the national political structure is to expect that a state will not behave like a state.

To take some examples from contemporary societies, we can ask, of what relevance is a daily oath of allegiance to a flag—and the flag itself, which the child faces throughout the learning period—to the acquisition of knowledge and skills? Of what relevance is the ubiquitous portrait of Washington, Mao, or Lenin to the teaching of grammar and the use of a slide rule in an American, Chinese, or Soviet classroom? Of what relevance is a cross in a religiously sponsored school to the learning of geography, history, literature, and the like? The relevance is this: As part of the state bureaucracy, schools are generally maintained under the sponsorship of the state organization that controls and supports them in one way or other. Just as courts are part of the state bureaucracy and display the material symbols of the state organization of which they are a part, so do schools. The relevance is also this: Learning is a rewarding experience for most children. Hence—as every variety of behavioristic psychology has demonstrated repeatedly—it is hardly a startling insight to suggest that, whether anyone is consciously aware of it or not, the child comes to associate everything he learns with the state's symbols that face or en-

velop him while he is learning. These symbols become as much a part of
his mind as the alphabet and the concept of zero. School is not only the
place to learn arithmetic; it is also the place to learn zealotry.

One of the major institutional sources for the spread of universalistic
orientations in a state society, and thus a major underpinning to the
predominance of education over socialization—however indirect—is to
be found in its legal system; a fundamental distinction that can be made
between *customary* and *formal* law. Although traces of each can always
be found in the application and practice of the other, nevertheless basic
differences exist between them, especially in the roles that they play in
total legal systems. Generally speaking, *customary law* is made up of
established laws, but without formal or impersonal procedures. Customary
law is enforced in face-to-face relationships within the community, and
justice—however it is culturally conceptualized—emerges more or less
automatically in the community. When customary law prevails in a
society, the personalities of the individuals involved in a dispute, and the
backgrounds of their previous interactions, are of considerable importance.
Thus, a man with a reputation for belligerence is *a priori* at a great legal
disadvantage when accused of assault. The force of customary law is the
consensus of the community. Customary law is therefore often interlaced
with particularistic values—*who* has committed an act is sometimes more
important than the act itself and the evidence in the case—and generally
predominates in societies whose value systems are heavily particularistic.
Correlatively, the predominance of socialization over education is an important technique in preparing people to serve the aims of a legal system
in which particularism often obtains.

Formal law, by contrast, is made up of established laws that are
administered through formal—that is, stereotyped—legal procedures. Lawyers and judges are frequent accompaniments of a system of formal law;
they are specialized technologists who study the wordings of the law with
microscopic care, focusing on precedent and stereotyped procedures. The
criteria that they are expected to apply in the administration of law are
impersonal: rules of evidence, solemn ritual, the claim that the law is the
respecter of no person, and the like. Thus, one of the most fundamental
premises of a system of formal law is that it is grounded in universalistic
orientations.

What is important in this connection is that formal law tends to
become predominant over customary law in state societies or conditions of
urbanization. One of the reasons for this is that both sets of conditions
tend to favor the disparity between kinship networks and those of social
relations as well as universalistic orientations. The processes underlying
these trends are readily apparent and need not be spelled out here.

But legal systems do not operate in a vacuum; if they are to be effective
in the maintenance of order in long-range terms, they must be in harmony
with the general value orientations of the polity. The fostering of uni-

versalistic values and criteria is one of the goals of a state organization, as, for example, in the ideal that all citizens are subject to the same laws, regardless of origin and affiliation. Schools serve the same ends. Thus, for example, it is not mere coincidence that schools and courts are currently among the major battlegrounds between the universalistic orientations of the central American government and the regional or community particularism of many sectors of the American South. The histories of colonialized societies also repeat this pattern with recurrent regularity.

How does education contribute to the predominance of a universalistic orientation; that is, why do social systems in which the balance of values and the criteria for performance are weighted on the side of universalism favor a reliance on education, vis-à-vis socialization, in the shaping of the minds of polities? Whether a curriculum is devoted to catechetical instruction, skills (like learning the multiplication tables), executing "proper" penmanship, learning the dates of wars and treaties (in which one's own society somehow always manages to emerge as wronged or righteous, or both), the names of rivers, mountains, cities, or ports, such learning is wholly independent of family background, ethnic or religious affiliation, regional membership, or any other nexus that is a natural breeding ground for particularistic orientations. While I do not intend to suggest that there is no difference between learning a catechism and the other subjects mentioned, the essence of education is that there is only one correct answer to a problem or to a question. The essence of a universalistic orientation is that there is only one correct way of behaving within the society as a whole—no matter where one goes within its borders—and that there is only one standard of loyalty to the state. The bane of university professors who demand that the student-products of secondary schools think for themselves instead of performing by rote is the fruit of a successful state system rather than of the ideology of any particular system of schooling.

It is in these terms that an educational system without regular and recurrent examinations is difficult to imagine. (I am speaking here principally of what are called in our society elementary and secondary schools, in which the overwhelming majority of the population are educated. One consequence that can be anticipated from mass college education is an even heavier reliance on procedures such as examinations.) The manifest or rational purpose served by examinations is, of course, to determine the degree to which material has been learned. However a latent purpose is also served by examinations, namely, the application of universalistic criteria for the evaluation of performance: there is only one correct answer to a question, and everyone is evaluated by the same criteria. I suggest that this is the more important of the two in terms of the preparation of the individual for later participation in a social system in which universalism is the predominant orientation.

The techniques of education, especially in rote and standardized learn ing and in the use of examinations, explicitly deny and conflict with the conveyance of particularistic values and criteria. Individual differences in personality, or family, kin, and community backgrounds and traditions count for little, if anything, in the procedures of education. Instead, what is emphasized is uniformity.

The pressures of a society encouraging the training of students for a universalistic orientation are familiar to most of us. Let me give one concrete example from my own experience. In an introductory course to cultural anthropology in which there were several hundred students— hardly conducive to getting to know each student, and thus in itself encouraging the application of impersonal and universalistic standards— considerable emphasis is placed in the first part on the dynamics and mechanics of kinship organization. One of the students in the class is an extraordinarily bright person who shows promise of a very successful intellectual career. While she performs much better than most of the other students in answer to essay questions, she is unable to cope with a single problem in kinship analysis, and is in danger of failing the first half of the course. In talking with her, I learn that she comes from an ethnic group in which kinship obligations and reciprocities constitute the central moral focus of life. One result of her attempts to become "Americanized" is her total inability to cope with kinship on an intellectual level. For a professor to take this problem "into account" is to run counter to the institutional demands for the evaluation of students by universalistic criteria. To disregard such a problem, and to allow the evaluation of the student to be carried out on a calculating machine, poses its own ethical dilemma.

Techniques of education: There are several facets to the uniformity which is the inevitable by-product of education. Most readily apparent is the demand for standardization in performance. In this connection, one of the most important factors is the child's awareness that he is learning precisely the same things as all his peers throughout the realm, and that he must give the same responses. He does not know what the authority for this is and whence it derives, but that is one of the points of it all: he is expected to acquire the realization, which is not necessarily conscious, that such authority exists. He is not trained to conceptualize that authority as localized in a nexus of named lineal ancestors or collateral kinsmen.

Nor is he expected to associate that authority with a particular teacher of unique personality, whose attributes he might adopt for his own. Children tend to identify with those people who meet their needs, including those who teach them. Identification is an important source of particularistic values, and a society whose predominant orientation is to universalistic values must make certain that lasting emotional identifications do not become part of the mind that is being shaped for participation in that culture. Thus, an important aspect of the educational systems of societies that are primarily universalistic in their value orientations is that when these orientations become increasingly pervasive in the institutional structure there is a parallel tendency to thwart or interfere with the identifications of children with their teachers. One of the ways by which this is accomplished is by having children taught by a variety and succession of teachers. Whether a child's teachers change annually or several times a day, one of the consequences is to break into or seriously weaken any tendency to identify with a particular teacher. Such identifications during the formative years are dangerous to a social system whose principal reliance is on universalistic values and criteria. In the social system of the future, hints of which are already upon us, this danger will have been obviated even more by mechanical or electronic instruction on a mass scale.

Another very important facet of the uniformity that is instilled through education as a technique in the shaping of men's minds is the allocation of standardized rewards and punishments for standardized performance. There are no surprises for the student who excels above all others in his grade—unless he is fortunate enough to experience surprise in knowledge itself. He knows in advance—and such knowledge is as important to an educational system as the multiplication table and the chronology of wars and culture heroes—which mass-produced medals he will receive, and which accolades, monetary awards, conscription status, occupations, and the like, will be his due as a result of universalistically evaluated performances. What needs to be stressed in this connection is that this is not an expression of an "educational policy." It is, instead, the policy of a state system that seeks to maintain its authority and control through the establishment of homogeneity throughout its polity. One of the means to this end is the inculcation of reflexes of mind by which the individual is brought to expect automatic standard consequences for standard performance.

It is necessary to reiterate at this point that no society achieves these goals overnight. The dominance of universalistic values and criteria is a gradual process of accretion at the expense of particularism; the latter is displayed slowly and, in the experiences of many individuals in the society, painfully. Similarly, the development of techniques of education in the service of these goals is also a gradual process, and must be understood as an aspect of history, not unlike parallel developments in the legal sphere of social organization or in patterns of recruitment to the state bureaucracy. An excellent illustration of this is provided in Dore's *Education in Tokugawa Japan* (1965), which, unfortunately, stands alone as an analysis of the development of an educational system in tandem with a nascent state organization.

Education, stratification, and change: It would be misleading to convey the impression that educational systems, especially in state societies, are designed to prepare people only for universalistic values and criteria for performance. All educational systems are discriminatory to some extent, whether by sex, social class, caste, ethnic or religious membership, or the like. These differentials in education are not only unequal distributions of privilege with respect to education but they are also preparations for differences in access to participation in the political apparatus. Educational differentials not only perpetuate systems of social stratification but are also affirmations of the relative political statuses of the groups making up a social system (compare the discussion by Thomas and Wahrhaftig of the Cherokee and others who are "out-of-it"). Such institutionalized inequalities continue to serve as seedbeds of particularistic values, but they are also in conflict with a state's rational ideology that seeks to establish homogeneity. One of the consequences of the elimination of social enclaves or ghettos, and the like, is to remove the sociological bases of particularistic values in the society. Uniform mass education is an important means to this end.

Hence, it is necessary to understand that education *per se* is not a vehicle of mobility in a system of social stratification. Whether we speak of the emancipation of women in primitive and peasant societies, of the access to higher status by commoners in modern emergent states, or of the mobility of ethnic groups in the United States, and although education almost invariably plays a role in these events, access to the educational system is always one aspect of the lowering of barriers generally. In these terms, the opening of schools to groups who had previously been barred from them is a by-product—not a cause—of social mobility.

I have suggested that the predominance of socialization in the shaping of the mind is oriented to traditionalism. In similar vein, I hypothesize that as the rate of change in a society accelerates, and as positive valuation of social change increases, commensurately greater emphasis is placed on education in preparing people to serve the aims of society's institutions. Just as a correlate of socialization is the affective charge of learned patterns, one of the consequences—if not a goal—of education is the relative "neutrality" or "secularization" of acquired knowledge. One of the ways by which this is accomplished is by impeding the development of strong emotional identifications between student and teacher; another, and closely related, is the reliance on nonkinsmen as agents of education.

An increasing reliance on education is adaptive to a rapid rate of change and to a high valuation of change because it contributes to the development of a habit of mind by which the individual evaluates an item of information in terms of its utility instead of the particular individuals or settings in association with whom it was learned. It not only contributes to an amenability to new knowledge but also to new social responses to changing conditions. Education, especially when it predominates over socialization, contributes to the establishment of a particular attitude toward change.

CONCLUSION

The study of educational institutions has been one of the stepchildren of social science, and has often been left by default to the educationists. The consequences are analagous to child neglect, abandonment, and abuse. What I have tried to show in this paper is that educational institutions—and others involved in the self-perpetuation of culture through the shaping of man's mind—warrant, and are amenable to, the same modes of analysis that have been developed by anthropologists for the study of kinship and marriage, legal and political institutions, economic activities, and religion and social stratification.

I am not seeking to idealize education. There are many standards which, when applied to the fruits of educational systems, cast a pall on one's hopes for the future of man. But that is sentimentalism, which is inappropriate to standards of universalism. I have, however, tried to place some aspects of education in a historical perspective in order to try to understand whence we have come—so that we might perhaps better appreciate where we are and get some hints into where we might be headed. While I do not think of education as the panacea to the ills of mankind, I have tried to convey the idea that, no matter what its other by-products, it has contributed much to an amelioration of the human situation. It has not done this alone; it has, as a matter of fact, committed some of its own horrors, about which we are sometimes too silent in our classrooms. But with other sociocultural developments of which it is an integral part, the predominance of education over socialization has contributed somewhat to the ability of a few people to realize their personal potentials—people who, in previous stages of cultural development, were charged with heresy, sorcery, or unconscionable deviance, and sentenced either to the stake or to bland compliance. That most educated people have substituted the gray flannel suit for the gray flannel loincloth is not entirely the fault of the educational institutions of society.

In stressing what seem to be the principal goals of education, I have also tried to convey the hypothesis that educational institutions were never designed—and thus cannot really be criticized for failing—to convert people to the intellectual life. That a few individuals have managed to develop a commitment to the life of the mind despite the ends and means of educational institutions sheds light only on man's evolutionary capacity, and on little else. Thus, when I say that education contributes to the establishment of a particular attitude toward change, I do not wish to sound like a commencement orator and suggest that it establishes these attitudes in the minds of all, or even most, who pass through its portals. It contributes to the establishment of these attitudes in the culture, which is very different than the sum of its carriers. While twentieth-century educated man often sounds like a socialized medieval peasant when faced with the inevitability of adaptive social change, the important fact is that many of these adaptive changes do take place nevertheless. Although he may sound like a medieval peasant, the important thing is that he behaves like one less and less. With a few relatively insignificant exceptions, he watches witch hunts on his television screen but does not ordinarily seek to lead them. He might personally empathize with the residents of Watts, California, and Cicero, Illinois, but education has played a role, albeit a small one, in the fact that the world is no longer all Watts and Cicero.

Thus, what I have also tried to say in this paper is that any social development—such as the unfolding of the potentials of educational institutions—never occurs rapidly. Nor are the consequences of educational experiences, such as attitudes toward change, ever established in a vacuum and without the support of other social institutions. I am not suggesting the eschewal of a critical stance with respect to educational institutions; but to demand that they be changed immediately, or to insist on new educational philosophies as though they were coffee in a vending machine, is to espouse an extreme anti-intellectualism that is grounded in the same assumptions as are found in the thinking of the maunfacturer who has programmed his dies to produce little artifacts on demand or at monotonously regular intervals.

I have also tried to make a methodological point in this paper. This is that if we wish to measure the successes and failures of educational institutions—and it should be noted that most critics of school systems have been quite cavalier about making explicit the criteria by which they attribute success and failure in this regard—we do not focus on individuals but, rather, on generations (see the remarks by Seeley in this volume). The danger in surveying individuals is that one can almost invariably find what he is looking for if he is skilled in designing survey instruments; is it any wonder that so many survey-tested hypotheses seem to be borne out? In order to understand the consequences—as well as the content—of education, it is necessary to compare generations or historical periods in the cycles of a society's development. Did education have the same effects on people who completed their schooling in 1867 or 1937 as on those who finished theirs in 1967? Why were schools different 30 or 100 years ago? If they have retained anything from these earlier periods, why did they do so? Attitudes and institutions do change, often without the awareness of the members of the society. If we confine our time spans to a single day, or even to five years, we necessarily have to conclude that nothing has changed. If, however, we adopt a historical perspective, we might emerge with a much more balanced picture.

I have tried to illustrate the hypothesis that the means adopted by different societies to shape the minds of their growing members are mechanisms of adaptation to the sociocultural environment. Historical analysis is essential to the study of adaptation generally; it is also indispensable to an understanding of educational institutions in particular. Without such understanding it is impossible to take sensible action.

REFERENCES

Bruner, Edward M.
  1956 Cultural transmission and cultural change. Southwestern Journal of Anthropology 12:191–199.
Cohen, Yehudi A.
  1958 Character formation and social structure in a Jamaican community. Psychiatry 18:275–296.
  1961 Social structure and personality: a casebook. New York: Holt, Rinehart & Winston, Inc.
  1964 The transition from childhood to adolescence: cross-cultural studies of initiation ceremonies, legal systems, and incest taboos. Chicago: Aldine Publishing Company.
Coleman, James S.
  1965 Education and political development. Princeton, New Jersey: Princeton University Press.
DeVos, George
  1960 The relation of guilt toward parents to achievement and arranged marriage among the Japanese. Psychiatry 23:287–301.
Diamond, Stanley
  1951 Dahomey: a proto-state in West Africa. Doctoral dissertation, Columbia University, University Microfilms, No. 2808. Ann Arbor, Michigan.
Dore, R. P.
  1965 Education in Tokugawa Japan. Berkeley and Los Angeles: University of California Press.
DuBois, Cora
  1944 The people of Alor: a socio-psychological study of an East Indian island. Minneapolis: University of Minnesota Press.
Edgerton, Robert B.
  1965 "Cultural" vs. "ecological" factors in the expression of values, attitudes, and personality characteristics. American Anthropologist 67:442–447.
Eggan, Dorothy
  1956 Instruction and affect in Hopi cultural continuity. Southwestern Journal of Anthropology 12:347–370.
Engels, Frederick
  1942 The origin of the family, private property, and the state. New York: International Publishers.
Fischer, John L. and Ann Fischer
  1963 The New Englanders of Orchard Town, U.S.A. In Six cultures: studies of child rearing, edited by Beatrice B. Whiting. New York and London: John Wiley and Sons, Inc.
Gibbon, Edward
  n.d. The decline and fall of the Roman empire. Modern Library edition. New York: Random House, Inc.
Gibbs, James L., Jr.
  1965 The Kpelle of Liberia. In Peoples of Africa, edited by James L. Gibbs, Jr. New York: Holt, Rinehart and Winston, Inc.
Goldschmidt, Walter
  1965 Theory and strategy in the study of cultural adaptability. American Anthropologist 67:402–408.

Hallowell, A. I.
 1955 Culture and experience [selected papers]. Philadelphia: University of Pennsylvania Press.
Hart, C. W. M.
 1963 Contrasts between prepubertal and postpubertal education. *In* Education and culture, edited by George D. Spindler. New York: Holt, Rinehart and Winston, Inc.
LeVine, Robert A. and Barbara B. LeVine
 1963 Nyansongo: a Gusii community in Kenya. *In* Six cultures: studies of child rearing, edited by Beatrice B. Whiting. New York and London: John Wiley and Sons, Inc.
Mead, Margaret
 1939 From the South Seas. New York: William Morrow and Company, Inc.
Parsons, Talcott
 1954 Essays in sociological theory (revised edition). New York: The Free Press.
 1964 Social structure and personality. New York: The Free Press.
Pettit, George A.
 1946 Primitive education in North America, University of California Publications in American Archaeology and Ethnology 63:1–182.
Sapir, Edward
 1949 Selected writings of Edward Sapir, edited by David Mandelbaum. Berkeley and Los Angeles: University of California Press.
Scott, J. P.
 1962 Critical periods in behavioral development. Science 138:949–958.
Spencer, Herbert
 1891 The principles of sociology, II. New York: D. Appleton Company.
Spindler, George D.
 1955 Sociocultural and psychological processes in Menomini acculturation. University of California Publications in Culture and Society 5.
 1963 Personality, sociocultural system, and education among the Menomini. *In* Education and culture, edited by George D. Spindler. New York: Holt, Rinehart and Winston, Inc.
Spindler, Louise S.
 1962 Menomini women and culture change. Memoir 91, American Anthropological Association.
Stern, Boris
 1965 The kibbutz that was. Washington, D.C.: Public Affairs Press.
Watkins, Mark Hanna
 1943 The West African "bush" school. American Journal of Sociology 48:666–675.
Wilson, Monica
 1959 Communal rituals of the Nyakyusa. London: Oxford University Press.
 1963 Good company: a study of Nyakyusa age-villages. Boston: The Beacon Press.

3: *On Linguistic Theory, Communicative Competence, and the Education of Disadvantaged Children*

Good practical work must have an eye on the current state of theory; it can be guided or misguided, encouraged or discouraged, by one or another theoretical view. Moreover, the problems of language development in disadvantaged children have a particular pertinence for theory at this time. The burden of my discussion will be that the practical and theoretical problems in this area converge.

For it is not that there exists a body of linguistic theory that practical research can merely apply. It is rather that work motivated by practical needs may help elicit and help build the theory that we need. Let me review the present state of linguistic theory in order to show why this is so.

Consider the recent statement:

Linguistic theory is concerned primarily with an ideal speaker-listener, in a completely homogeneous speech-community, who knows its language perfectly and is unaffected by such grammatically irrelevant conditions as memory limitations, distractions, shifts of attention and interest, and errors (random or characteristic) in applying his knowledge of the language in actual performance.[1]

From the standpoint of the children who are disadvantaged, such a statement may seem to be almost a declaration of irrelevance. All the difficulties that confront the children and us seem to be swept from view.

One's response to such indications of the nature of linguistic theory might be what can be called "pick-and-choose." Useful models of language structure, after all, can be of benefit in ways not formally envisioned in the theoretical statements of their authors. Some linguists use transformational generative techniques to characterize ways in which some speaker-listeners in the same general speech community differ from one another; moreover, some of these differences clearly involve imperfect knowledge of the language. Perhaps one's attitude, then, ought to be simply to disregard what linguists say about theory, as being primarily concerned with something not of primary concern to us. One can point to various models of language structure available to us—Hallidayan, tagmemic, transformational-generative (in its MIT, Pennsylvania, and other variants), stratificational; one can note that there are distinguished scholars actively involved with the use of each of these models in the analysis of English; one can regret that linguists remain unable to agree on the analysis of English (let alone on attitudes toward schooling and children); and one can pick and choose, depending upon the problem and local situation, leaving grammarians otherwise to their own devices.[2]

Only to "pick and choose," however, would be a mistake for two reasons: the sort of linguistic theory quoted, despite its narrowness, *is* relevant in a special way that is always important to have in mind; and there is a body of linguistic problems and data that will be left without theoretical insight, if linguistic theory is left with such a narrow definition.

First, as to the special relevance of the view of linguistic theory cited, its representative anecdote (to use Kenneth Burke's term), the image it puts before our eyes, is that of a child, born with the ability to master any language with almost miraculous ease and speed. It is a child who is no mere passive object of conditioning and reinforcement, but who actively applies a truly cognitive skill to the unconscious theoretical interpretation of the speech that comes its way, so that in a few years and with a finite experience, it is master of an infinite ability, that of producing and understanding in principle any and all grammatical sentences of its language. When the image of the unfolding, mastering, fluent child is set beside the real children in many of our schools, the theoretical basis of the image is seen for what it is, not a doctrine of irrelevance, but a doctrine of poignancy. Such theory is based on the essential equality and potential of each child in his or her capacity simply as a human being. It is noble in that it can inspire one with the belief that even the most dispiriting conditions can be transformed; and it is an indispensable weapon against views that would explain the communicative difficulties of groups of children as inherent, and perhaps racial.

As to the narrowness for our needs of the theoretical standpoint just described, it is, if I may say so, rather an Adam and Eve, a Garden of Eden standpoint. I do not think that the restriction of theory to an ideal speaker-listener is merely a simplifying assumption of the type that all scientific theories must make. If that were the case, then some explicit place for social complexities might be left, and no such place is defined. In particular, the concepts of linguistic competence and linguistic performance, as discussed in the work from which the quotation is taken, do not provide the theoretical scope that is required. *Linguistic competence* is understood as being exactly concerned with an idealized knowledge of language structure—semantics, syntax, phonology. *Linguistic performance* is understood as being concerned with the modifications introduced by the processes that have often been termed encoding and decoding. Some aspects of performance have a constructive role to play, e.g., cycling rules that help to properly assign stress; but if the passage quoted previously is recalled, and if the examples of performance phenomena in the chapter quoted are reviewed, it will be noticed that the note struck is one of limitation. I do not think this note of limitation to be accidental. Rather, I take the motivational core of the theoretical stance to be one that views linguistic competence as an idealized Garden of Eden sort of power, and the exigencies of performance as rather like the eating of the apple of the Tree of Knowledge, thrusting the once perfect speaker-hearer out into a fallen world. But of this fallen world, where meanings must be won by the sweat of the brow, and recreated in labor, almost nothing at all is said. The image is of an abstract and isolated individual, not, except contingently, of a person in a social world.

I take such limitations to disclose an ideological aspect to the theoretical standpoint in question. The theoretical stance of any group should always be examined in terms of the interests and needs unconsciously served. Now a major characteristic of modern linguistic theory has been that it takes structure as a primary end in itself, and tends to depreciate use while not relinquishing any of its claims to the great significance that is attached to language. (Contrast classical antiquity, where structure was a means to use, and the grammarian subordinate to the rhetor.) The result can sometimes seem a very happy one. On the one hand, by narrowing concern to independently and readily structurable data, one can enjoy the prestige of an advanced science; on the other hand, despite ignoring the social dimensions of use, one retains the prestige of dealing with something fundamental to human life.

In this light Chomsky is quite correct when he writes that his conception of the concern of linguistic theory seems to have been also the position of the founders of modern general linguistics. Certainly if modern structural linguistics is meant, then a major thrust of it has been to define the subject matter of linguistic theory in terms of what it is not. In de Saussure's linguistics, as generally interpreted, *la langue* was the privileged ground of structure, and *la parole* the residual realm of variation (among other things).[3] Chomsky associates his conceptions of competence and performance with the Saussurean conceptions of langue and parole, but sees his own conceptions as superior, going beyond the conception of language as a systematic inventory of items to the renewal of the Humboldtian conception of underlying processes. Chomsky's conception is superior, not only in this respect, but also in the very terminology that it introduces to mark the difference. "Competence" and "performance" much more readily suggest concrete persons, situations, and actions. Indeed, from the standpoint of the classical tradition in structural linguistics, Chomsky's theoretical standpoint is at once its revitalization and its culmination. It carries to its perfection its desire to deal in practice only with what is internal to language, yet to find in that internality what in theory is of the widest, or deepest, human significance. No modern linguistic theory has spoken more profoundly of either the internal structure or the intrinsic human significance.

This revitalization flowers while around it emerge the sprouts of a conception that before the end of the century may succeed it. If such a succession occurs, it will be because, just as the transformational theory could absorb its predecessors and handle structural relationships beyond their grasp, so new relationships, relationships with an ineradicable social component, will become salient that will require a broader theory to absorb and handle them. I shall return to this historical conjecture at the end of the chapter. Let me now develop some of the particular sorts of data that motivate the development of a broader theory. And let me do this by first putting forward some alternative representative anecdotes.

As against the ideal speaker-listener, consider Bloomfield's account of one Menomini he knew:

> White-Thunder, a man around forty, speaks less English than Menomini, and that is a strong indictment, for his Menomini is atrocious. His vocabulary is small; his inflections are often barbarous; he constructs sentences of a few threadbare models. He may be said to speak no language tolerably. His case is not uncommon among younger men, even when they speak but little English.[4]

Bloomfield goes on to suggest that the commonness of the case "perhaps . . . is due, in some indirect way, to the impact of the conquering language." Social factors are suggested to have entered here not merely into outward performance but into inner competence itself. And the one thing that is clear in studies of subcultural differences in language development is stated by Courtney Cazden in her excellent review article as follows:

> The findings can be quickly summarized. On all the measures, in all the studies, children of the upper socio-economic status, however defined, are more advanced than those of the lower socio-economic status.[5]

The point of course is not that social factors enter only to interfere. The differences summarized involve positive social factors on the one side as much as negative ones on the other (compare Mead's discussion of the same problem in this volume). It may indeed be the case that some or many lower socioeconomic status children excel in aspects of verbal skill not observed or measured in the reported tests.

The generic role of social factors has been stressed by Labov, reporting on information as to the ability to perceive phonological contrasts:

> The contention that native speakers can hear phonemic distinctions much better than nonphonemic distinctions was not borne out by the evidence. Instead, one might say that the ability to perceive distinctions is determined largely by the social significance of the distinction to the listener.[6]

Here are recurrently found differences between one and the same speech-community, entering again into the inner competence itself. It seems clear that work with disadvantaged children needs a theory of competence that can take account of socially conditioned differences in a natural and revealing way.

What would such a theory be like? No one knows better than myself that very little of the content of such a theory can now be specified. Permit me, however, to take up the representative anecdote of the child in order to sketch briefly what a *broad* (as distinct from *narrow*), or perhaps a strong (as distinct from weak) theory of linguistic competence would entail. Recall that in terms of the narrow theory one is concerned to explain how a child can come to produce and understand (in principle) any and all grammatical sentences. Consider a child with just that ability; it would be disadvantaged in a severe sense. Someone who went about producing any and every sentence without concern for anything else might be quickly institutionalized. We have then to account for the fact that a normal child acquires a knowledge both of proper sentences and of their appropriate use. He or she develops abilities to judge when to speak, when not, and what to talk about with whom, in what way, and when and where.

It is especially important not to confuse an account of such abilities with an account of performance. The broad theory, like the narrow theory, has both competence and performance aspects. Indeed, one of the chief dangers of leaving the field of linguistic theory to the narrow view is that it may encourage one to relegate all questions of use to the category of performance. As has been noted, performance here amounts essentially to the exigencies of realization and interpretation in encoding and decoding. The abilities with which a broad theory of competence is concerned are in the first instance equally matters of underlying intuitive knowledge, of "mentalistic" competence, just as much as are the abilities with which grammar and semantics are concerned.[7] Moreover, although the notion of rules of use carries with it an indication of restraints, such rules are not to be taken just as limitations on an otherwise infinite capacity. First of all such rules are not a late grafting. Data from very early in life, the first years of the acquisition of grammar, show that children develop rules for the use of different forms in different situations (Susan Ervin-Tripp, personal communication). Competency for use is part of the same developmental matrix as competency for grammar.

Second, like competency for grammar, competency for use has a dimension of productivity. Within the development matrix in which children can acquire the knowledge in principle of the set of sentences of a language, they also acquire the knowledge in principle of a set of ways in which sentences are used; and they internalize attitudes toward a language and its uses, and indeed, toward language itself (including, e.g., attentiveness to it) or its place in a pattern of mental abilities.[8]

The words "in principle" in the last sentence should no doubt have been in quotes. No child has knowledge of all sentences, no more than he or she has knowledge of all application of the rules of use. The matrix formed in childhood continues to develop and change throughout life in both respects. Either or both may indeed be supplanted. Competency in either respect is not a matter of childhood alone, but of the succeeding stages of life as well.[9] Perhaps here one should contrast a long and a short range view of competency. The short-range view is concerned primarily in innate capacities as they unfold during the first years of life, and the long-range view, is necessarily concerned with the continuing socialization and shifting competence of lives through adulthood. In any case, here is one important respect in which a theory of competency must go beyond a narrow one, if it is to be of value to the work with disadvantaged children. For when one is dealing with recurrently found differences, social in part or whole, with an intent to change, one is presupposing the very possibility that competency that has "unfolded" in the natural way can be altered, perhaps drastically so, by environmental factors. One is assuming from the outset a confrontation of different systems for competency within the same community, and focusing on the way in which one affects or can be made to affect the other. In short, one's theoretical perspective can be limited neither to young children of preschool age nor to homogeneous communities. One encounters linguistic phenomena that pertain not only to the structures of languages, but also to what has come to be called *interference* between them: problems of perception, understanding, and acquisition of habits that result from perception of the manifestations of one system in terms of the structures of another.

Since the interference one confronts involves language features and features of use together, it would be well to adopt the phrase introduced by Alfred Hayes (at the Yeshiva University conference October 1965), and to speak of *sociolinguistic interference* (see also the review of that topic by Cazden-and-John in this volume).

When a child from one developmental matrix enters a situation in which the communicative expectations are defined in terms of another, misperception and misanalysis may occur at every level. As is well known, words may be misunderstood because of differences in phonological systems; sentences may be misunderstood because of differences in grammatical systems; intents, too, and innate abilities, may be misevaluated because of differences of systems for the use of language and for the import of its use (as against other modalities).

With regard to education, some years ago I stated the matter thus:

New speech habits and verbal training must be introduced, necessarily by particular sources to particular receivers, using a particular code with messages of particular forms via particular channels, about particular topics and in particular settings—and all this from and to people for whom there already exist definite patternings of linguistic routines, of personality expression via speech, of uses of speech in social situations, of attitudes and conceptions towards speech. It seems reasonable that success in such an educational venture will be enhanced by an understanding of this existing structure, because the innovators' efforts will be perceived and judged in terms of it, and innovations which mesh with it will have greater success than those which cross its grain.[10]

The notion of sociolinguistic interference is of the greatest importance for the relationship between theory and practice. First a theory of sociolinguistic interference must begin with heterogeneous situations, whose dimensions are social as well as linguistic, situations of a sort from which the narrow theory seems in principle to cut itself off. (The fruits of such theory in the understanding of language systems can of course be *utilized* in dealing with sociolinguistic interference.)

Second, the notion of sociolinguistic interference helps one see how to draw on a variety of researches for practical purposes, researches that might otherwise be overlooked or set aside (as the social dimensions of Black dialects were set aside when the educational problem was labeled as "second language learning"). One main virtue of the notion of sociolinguistic interference is that it fits into a conception of an *integrated theory of sociolinguistic description*. And such a theory of description does not begin with the notion of a language, or of counting numbers in languages but with notions that have to do with codes and number of codes. In particular, such a theory of description recognizes that the historically derived status of codes as separate languages, related dialects, alternative styles, or whatever, is entirely secondary from the standpoint of their use in actual human relationships. From the functional standpoint that a sociolinguistic description must take, quite different means can be employed in equivalent ways for equivalent ends. A striking example from another area, that of modes of address, is that of the function served by the shift of the second-person pronoun in French, *tu : vous*, may be served by the shift of the entire language in some situations in Paraguay (Guarani : Spanish). In short, we have to break with the entire *a* language: *a* cultural tradition of thought, a fixation that has dominated linguistic thought for generation and indeed centuries. In order to deal with the practical problems faced among disadvantaged children, theory must begin with the conception of the speech habits of a population. Within those speech habits, it may find one language; three languages; dialects widely divergent or divergent by a hair; styles almost mutually incomprehensible or barely detectable as different to the outsider; but these objective differences in terms of linguistic structure are secondary and do not tell the story. What must be known is the attitude toward the differences, the functional slot assigned them, the use made of the varieties so distinguished. Only on the basis of such a functional description can comparable cases be established and a valid theory developed.

Now with regard to the sociolinguistic interference among schoolchildren, much relevant information and theoretical insight can come from the type of cases variously labeled "bilingualism," "linguistic acculturation," "dialectology," or "creolization." The value of an integrated theory of sociolinguistic description to the practical work would be that (1) it would attempt to place studies, diversely labeled, within a common analytical framework; and (2), by placing such information within a common framework, where one can talk about the relation among codes, and types of code-switching, and types of intereference as between codes, one can make use of the theory while perhaps avoiding the connotations that attach to such labels as "second language learning." ("Perhaps" because of course it is very difficult to avoid unpleasant connotations for any terms used to designate situations that are themselves intrinsically sensitive and objectionable.)

William Stewart's suggestion that some code relationships in the United States might be better understood if viewed as part of a continuum of case ranging to the Caribbean and Africa, for example, seems to me from a theoretical standpoint very promising.[11] It is not that most code relationships in the United States are to be taken as involving different languages, but that they do involve relationships among different codes, and that the full series illuminates the part. Stewart has seen through the different labels of dialect, creole, pidgin, language, bilingualism, to a common sociolinguistic dimension (compare Mead's references in this volume to Metraux's research in the Caribbean). Getting through different labels to the underlying sociolinguistic dimensions is a task in which theory and practice meet.

Let me now single out three interrelated concepts, important to a theory of sociolinguistic description, which have the same property of enabling us to cut across diverse cases and modes of reporting, and to arrive at basic relationships. One such concept is that of verbal repertoire, which John Gumperz has done much to develop.[12] The heterogeneity of speech communities, and the priority of social relationships is assumed, and the question to be investigated is that of the set of varieties, codes, or subcodes, commanded by an individual, together with the types of switching that occur among them.

The second concept is that of domains of language behavior, which Joshua Fishman has dealt with insightfully in his impressive work on *Language Loyalty in the United States*.[13] Again, the complexity and patterning of use is assumed, and the focus is upon "the most parsimonious and fruitful designation of the occasions on which one language (variant, dialect, style, etc.) is habitually employed rather than (or in addition to) another."

The third concept is that of *linguistic routines*, sequential organizations beyond the sentence, either as activities of one person, or as the interaction of two or more persons. Literary genres provide obvious examples; the organization of other kinds of texts, and of conversation, is being given fresh attention by sociologists, such as Harvey Sacks, and sociologically oriented linguistics, such as William Labov. One special importance of linguistic routines is that they may have the property that the late English philosopher Austin dubbed *performative*. That is, the saying does not simply stand for, or refer to, some other thing; it itself is the thing in question. To say "I solemnly vow" is to solemnly vow; it does not name something else that is the act of vowing solemnly. Indeed, in the circumstances no other way to vow solemnly is provided other than to do so by saying that one does so. From this standpoint, then, disability and ability with regard to language involve questions that are not about the relation between something else that language might stand for or influence; sometimes such questions are about things that are done linguistically or not at all.

These three concepts do not exhaust those that are relevant to the type of theory that is needed, and a number of scholars are developing related conceptual approaches, such as Basil Bernstein, Harvey Sarles, and others. But the three concepts do point up major dimensions: the capacities of persons, the appropriateness of situations, and the organization of verbal means for socially defined purposes.

In the context of interference, let me take up another aspect of communication relevant to work with disadvantaged children. I have so far not justified the scope implied by the word "communicative" in my title. Although I shall continue to focus on language, let me introduce one principle with regard to interference that does call for the larger perspective of communication in general.

Phenomena of intonation, tone of voice, expressive phonetic features, and other parts of paralinguistics; phenomena of body style, gesture, and other parts of kinesics; all that Edward Hall designates as the "silent language" and the "hidden dimension"; need only be mentioned to be recognized. Yet it is remarkable how easy it is for us to forget them. Cazden makes an important critical point, namely, that a common finding may easily be given two quite different interpretations. The example cited may be evidence of the point I now wish to make. Bernstein has interpreted a greater use of "I think" among higher-status subjects in terms of egocentricity-sociocentricity contrasting with "ain't it," whereas Loban has taken a like result as evidence of cognitive flexibility (grouping it with "I'm not exactly sure"). The question arises: did Bernstein's English subjects say "I think" (egocentric) and Loban's California school children "I *think*" (cognitive flexibility)? Clearly the import of data can not be assessed apart from the co-occurring set of intonational and expressive signals.

The question of communicative interference poses itself in two ways. First the problem of interference between differing sets of expressive signals. Of this there are many examples in education and the transmission of information, e.g., Steven Polgar reported some years ago that Mesquakie Fox children near Tama, Iowa, interpreted the normal loudness of voice and directness of teachers as "mean"-ness and as getting mad.[14]

Second is the problem of interference with regard to relations between co-occurring codes within a single message. The principle of concern here can be expressed as an instruction: *"Find out where the information is."* A child is making use of a set of modalities, as he or she communicates and interprets communication, and only one of them is discursive language. One of the essential features of Bernstein's model for restrictive and elaborated types of codes is that the grammatical and lexical restrictiveness of the first type is accompanied by intensified perceptual activity with regard to other cues of subjective intent, such as the paralinguistic. (I may mention that I have found Bernstein's model very useful cross-culturally.) In such a case the two parties to a communicative exchange may be putting their main information in different places, and likewise looking for that of the other in different places. The situation is further complicated by what the late Dutch linguist A. De Groot called "the law of the two strata," namely, that when the discursive and the expressive import of a message conflict, the latter signals the real intent. Quite possibly some teachers are not reading their students at all, and some children are reading their teachers all too well. In any case, a theory of competence is needed that is to be of much help in assessing an array of signals and a battery of functions, such that what is signaled lexically in one case may be signaled with expressive intonation in another, and so on. The theory of competence cannot be limited to the referential use of language.

Here indeed is the point at which the sort of theory of competence one needs must depart more decisively from the orientation of the sort of theory first discussed. When one takes into account the full set of functions served in speech in relation to the means diversively organized to serve them, one's starting point and orientation both shift. A linguistic theory in the narrow sense, insofar as it deals with use, looks out from language: structure precedes, functions follow. A theory in the broad sense looks in at language in the contexts of its use: functions guide, structures follow.

Such a broad theory of competence is essentially sociolinguistic. As such, it makes three assumptions:

1. Each social relationship entails the selection and/or creation of communicative means considered specific and appropriate to it by its participants.
2. The organization of communicative means in terms of social relationships confers a structure that is not disclosed in the analysis of the means separately.
3. The communicative means available in a relationship conditions its nature and outcome.

These three assumptions are rather simple and obvious, but to take them seriously is to define an area of linguistic investigation that is almost wholly unsystematized and theoretically little understood. The first assumption is that a social relationship gives rise to a use of communicative means that distinguishes it. Now it is probably a sociolinguistic universal that the speech of men and women can be distinguished in every society. Yet articles on men's and women's speech are few; but they are also very revealing. They deal with men's and women's speech when markers of the distinction intrude themselves into the ordinary analysis of the language. For the vast majority of societies where the markers have not so intruded, we are largely ignorant.

The fact is evidence of the second assumption: the way communicative means are organized in terms of a social relationship is unlikely to appear unless one begins with the social relationship, then looks for the means.

The third assumption is perhaps the simplest, the most obvious, and for some reason, the most resisted by some linguists. Stated colloquially, with reference to language it says that what people have to work with affects what they can do. In it lies the heart of the element of truth in what is often called the Whorfian hypothesis. Partly the question is one of performance, as brought out by Cazden:

> When we shift . . . to the difference between the speech of a middle-class child and a lower-class child, however, we aren't looking at the total of what is available in language as a set of symbols, but only at what is actually used by certain individuals at the moment of framing an utterance.[15]

To a large extent, the question is also one of competence, a competence that is in part an individual matter (cf. Sapir, "every individual's language is a distinct psychological entity in itself") and in part a matter of social group.[16] Each child in a classroom has a competence definable in terms of what is normally and habitually available to it for utterance and comprehension, a competence partially unique to it, largely shared and predictable in terms of its social origins and experience, and never identical with that of a dictionary, a grammar, or an ideally fluent speaker-listener.

With regard to disadvantaged children, the goal of an integrated theory of sociolinguistic description would be to guide accounts of the range of settings, function, and means, and their interrelationships, acquired by the children. Of these the school setting would be one, but not the only one; and the major purpose would be to place the school setting in the context of other settings, so as to delineate the true communicative abilities of the children and to show the extent to which the performance in school settings was not a direct disclosure of their abilities, but a product of the interference between the system that they bring and the system that confronts them; or a setting simply largely irrelevant to the direction their abilities and competence otherwise took. In part the problem is one of a conflict of values and of perceived interests.[17] Indeed, since the beginnings of stratified society and the use of writing, it has been characteristic of much of mankind that a desired or required linguistic competence has stood over against men, as an alien thing, imposed by a power not within their control. Even in the simplest case, of course, sociolinguistic competence is achieved along specific lines and not merely released. In the complex circumstances of our own society, it is hard to see how children can be expected to master a second system, complementing or replacing their own, if the process is not perceived as intrinsically relevant, or enjoyable, preferably both (here, compare Mead's discussion of literacy in this volume).

Much more needs to be said and done with regard to the conceptual content of sociolinguistic description, regarding interference and competence. In other writings I have outlined schemes for the "ethnography of speaking," or "ethnography of communication," together with some notes and queries about children's acquisition of language; I shall not go further into that here,[18] rather let me sketch what might illustrate a practical framework for the use of a sociolinguistic description.

As Edmund Gordon has stated, it is hardly our task to say what the goals of the disadvantaged should be. If one prime consideration is to be chosen, it is probably that of jobs. From this standpoint, a rough scale can be defined in terms of the concepts of repertoire, domain, and routine. For each one asks how many and what kind, moving from the minimal to the maximal requirements for the use of a more-or-less standard set of speech habits. For purposes of the scale, the single concept of a fluent speaker is replaced by a rough division into *fixed, flexible,* and *fluent* (or *facile*) use.

	REPERTOIRES	DOMAINS	ROUTINES
Fixed			
Flexible			
Facile			

The minimal competence (lowest rung of fixed) could be characterized as the use of a single routine in a single domain without the need for switching within one's repertoire. Additional considerations might be that the channel be writing, thus permitting revision and correction somewhat at leisure, and that the demands on the one part of the repertoire be of the transactional or restricted code sort. Today jobs of this sort are probably taken care of mostly by form letters, or, in the vocal sphere, by recordings, to be sure. Perhaps the need only to receive and not to send, might be added to define the minimal rung.

The maximal competence (facile) could be characterized as the use of multiple routines in many domains with a facility at switching between parts of one's verbal repertoire, both sending and receiving.

Medial competence (flexible) could be defined in terms of the empirical situation, if some intermediate set of needs and abilities with regard to routines, domains, and repertoires can usefully be recognized.

Some such scale could be used to conceptualize and analyze the requirements of situations, such as types of jobs, the capacities of persons, and the aims and levels of a program of training.[19]

What sorts of interference may occur, and what sorts of learning and change may be required, cannot of course be postulated in advance. Sometimes the question will be one simply of dialect markers, of the social rather than the referential or expressive information called for in the situation.

(My own quite unrealistic preference would be to leave dialect alone, inso-far as markers are all that is involved.) Sometimes the question will be one of added skills in the use of syntax or narration; and so on.

(Ultimately I should hope that a concern for language use might get to the aesthetic and clarifying and truth-telling roles it plays in our lives, and that we might someday have a conference on the ways in which middle-class and verbally fluent individuals are deprived. A critique of the use of language among the (educationally and socially) advantaged would indeed not be hard to mount, and there are even some who argue that a complete withdrawal from the ordinary uses of language is under way in rebellion. But no government is about to spend much money to get its functionaries to use language in a more satisfying, beautiful, clarifying, or truthful way.)

Let me conclude by summarizing the way in which a concern with language use among disadvantaged children fits into the present stage of linguistic theory.

First, it is of course not mandatory that the term "linguistic theory" be used in one particular way. If one wishes to reserve "linguistic theory" for the narrower sort of competence, then "sociolinguistic theory" will do for the broader sort of competence. What is essential is that concepts of the nature of language and its use not be preempted in the name of "linguistic theory" by a narrow view. The understanding of language use involves attention not only to participants, settings, and other extralinguistic factors, but also attention to purely linguistic phenomena, and the discovery and statement of new features, organization, and relationships in the data of language itself, when viewed from the more general perspective of social relationships. What is essential is that conceptions of speakers, listeners, and competency, take into account as quite normal in the world the situations of diversity of codes; see the child as acquiring and indeed, achieving, narrowly linguistic and broadly sociolinguistic competence together.

In this regard a sociolinguistic theory is not a departure from past linguistic insight. The narrow theory earlier discussed has known how to *reculer pour mieux sauter*. It has found in Wilhelm von Humboldt, and more recently in Otto Jespersen and Edward Sapir, instances of fresh in-sight into the structuring of language which it wishes to renew and to capitalize. Sociolinguistic theory is in an analogous position. In von Humboldt it finds not only a generative conception of rules, but also a concern with the individual worlds created in and through language; a concern not only with universals, but also a concern with the particulars in which they are embodied; a concern with the infinite capacity of man that also implies the determinate form such capacity requires for realiza-tion in each person; an understanding of human nature, the human essence, as not so much a state of being, as in each case a unique existential achievement.[20] In Jespersen it finds a grammarian who de-

voted himself to universals, productivity, and to understanding mankind, nation, and individual from a linguistic point of view. In Sapir it
finds a pioneer of structuralism, the autonomy of linguistic form, and
proper insight into phonology, who also urged that:

It is peculiarly important that linguists, who are often accused, and accused
justly, of failure to look beyond the pretty patterns of their subject matter,
should become aware of what their science may mean for the interpretation of
human conduct in general. Whether they like it or not, they must become
increasingly concerned with the many anthropological, sociological, and psychological problems which invade the field of language.[21]

There is under way now, I think, a shift in emphasis (almost a shift
in axioms) in linguistics. The shift is partially completed, and the work
with disadvantaged children may help to bring it to completion. The shift
can be illustrated by means of a 2 x 2 table, which on the vertical dimension distinguishes language structure and function, and which on the
horizontal dimension distinguishes the study of a single language (or community) from a comparative perspective:

	SINGLE CASE	COMPARATIVE
Structure	a	b
Function	c	d

Historically, the emphases of linguistics were with regard to the structure
of a single language (a), find the *invariance* (i.e. discover within the flow
of speech these entities that were unchanging and so characteristic of any
speaker). With regard to structures comparatively (b), find the *diversity*
(for each language would have a unique system of invariants). With regard to functional aspects in a single case (c), assume *diversity*, and the
variation of *parole* (and assign anything that interferes with the invariance
and system of structure to this category). With regard to functions comparatively (d), assume *invariance* (i.e. that the functions of language are
universal so that all languages are functionally equivalent).

Currently emerging are a contrary set of emphases within linguistics.
With regard to the structure of a single language (a), the researcher
should find the *variation* (i.e. it is no longer assumed that the same structure
is manifesting itself identically in the utterances of every speaker). With
regard to structures comparatively (b), find the *invariance* (what is unchanging among all languages). In short, the relationships of emphasis
are reversed as is well established in the new interests in social dialect,
linguistic varieties, styles, and levels, on the one hand, and in the different
approaches to the universals of language on the other. The rest of the new
set of emphases, reversing the former set, is only coming to be realized:
with regard to functional aspects of a single case (c), find the invariance
(i.e. the sociolinguistic system); with regard to functions comparatively
(d), find the diversity (i.e. take the functions of language, or of a language,
as problematic for any given group).

It is precisely with regard to these last two sectors that the problems of the study of disadvantaged children and the needs of theory converge. The understanding of sociolinguistics systems as a basis for handling the interference between them, and the nonidentity of the functioning of language in different social groups are problems common to both. Perhaps this common interest can help end the division between linguistic theory and the concrete, existential human world, the world of actual human relationships, that has dogged the study of language for so long.

NOTES

1. Noam Chomsky, *Aspects of The Theory of Syntax* (Cambridge: The M.I.T. Press, 1965), p. 3.
2. Explanations of such terms as "tagmemic" will be found in Dell Hymes, "Linguistics: The Field," *International Encyclopedia of the Social Sciences*, David L. Sills, ed. (New York: Crowell Collier & Macmillan, 1968), vol. 9, pp. 351–371.
3. A continuity with more recent American structural theory is seen in the concern with what linguistics is taken not to include, as reflected in attitudes toward words that tag the external. In the heyday of Bloomfieldian linguistics "meaning" and "mentalism" were "dirty" words; today, for some, "context" is.
4. Leonard Bloomfield, "Literate and illiterate speech," 2 *American Speech* (1927): 432–439; reprinted in *Language in Culture and Society*, D. Hymes, ed. (New York: Harper & Row Publishers, Inc., 1964), p. 395.
5. Courtney B. Cazden, "Some Views on Subcultural Differences in Child-Language," 12 *Merrill-Palmer Quarterly*: 185–219; 191.
6. William Labov, "Stages in the Acquisition of Standard English," in *Social dialects and language learning*, Roger W. Shuy, ed. (Champaign: National Council of Teachers of English), pp. 77–103; 102, n. 12.
7. Cf. Labov on the priority of subjective evaluation over performance in social dialect and process of change, pp. 84–85.
8. Cazden, "*Subcultural Differences in Child-Language.*"
9. Labov, pp. 77, 91–92.
10. Dell H. Hymes, "Functions of Speech: an Evolutionary Approach," in *Anthropology and education*, Frederick C. Gruber, ed. (Philadelphia: University of Pennsylvania Press, 1961), pp. 55–83; 65–66.
11. William A. Stewart, "Urban Negro Speech: Sociolinguistic Factors Affecting English Teaching," in *Social Dialects and Language Learning*, Shuy, ed., pp. 10–18; 11, n.2.
12. John J. Gumperz, "Linguistic and Social Interaction in Two Communities," in *The ethnography of communication*, John J. Gumperz and Dell Hymes, eds., 66, no. 6, part 2 *American Anthropologist* (December 1964): 137–153.
13. Joshua A. Fishman, *Language Loyalty in the United States* (The Hague: Mouton and Co., 1966), pp. 424–438, 428.
14. Steven Polgar, "Biculturation of Mesquakie Teenage Boys," 62 *American Anthropologist* (1960): 217–235, 220.
15. Courtney B. Cazden, "Sociocultural Differences in Child-Language," p. 190.
16. Edward Sapir, "Language," 9 *Encyclopedia of Social Sciences* (New York: Crowell Collier and Macmillan, Inc., 1933), pp. 155–169; cited from *Selected Writings of Edward Sapir*, D. G. Mandelbaum, ed. (Berkeley and Los Angeles; University of California Press, 1949), p. 23.
17. Labov, pp. 96–99, discusses opposing value systems in the New York speech community.
18. Dell Hymes, "The Ethnography of Speaking," in *Anthropology and Human Behavior* (Washington, D.C.: Anthropological Society of Washington, 1962), pp. 13–53; "Introduction: Toward Ethnographies of Communciation," in *The Ethnography of*

Communication (Washington, D.C.: American Anthropological Association, 1964), pp. 1–34; "Linguistic Aspects of Cross-Cultural Personality Study," in *Studying Personality Cross-Culturally*, Bert Kaplan, ed. (New York: Harper & Row, Publishers, Inc., 1961), pp. 313–359.

19. Labov distinguishes six levels of the acquisition of spoken English. His sixth, *full range*, would be maximal with respect to switching within repertoire and among domains, but perhaps admitting degrees with respect to routines. His fifth level, *consistent standard*, seems to define a medial area of some flexibility short of complete facility.

20. Ernst Cassirer, *The Logic of the Humanities*. Clarence Smith Howe, trans. (New Haven: Yale University Press, 1961), pp. 19–26, discusses Herder, Goethe, W. von Humboldt.

21. Edward Sapir, "The Status of Linguistics as a Science," 5 *Language* (1929): 207–214. 214 (the concluding remark)

ETHNO-PSYCHOLOGICAL AND PRECULTURAL

4: *Early Childhood Experience and Later Education in Complex Cultures*

MARGARET MEAD

Education in a complex society may be seen as merely an extension of the educational process found in simpler societies, but taking longer, requiring more specialized institutions, and involving progressive absorption into wider or narrower segments of the total society. Or it may be seen as involving, from the very start (from the moment that a rattle is put into an infant's hands, or a set of alphabet blocks is spilled on the floor) a set of assumptions that are different in kind from education in a primitive society. Both approaches have their uses. By taking the former, Hart (1955) and Yehudi Cohen (1964) have been able to point out striking correspondences between the treatment of the prepubertal and pubertal young, and the initiation ceremonies and educational experiences to which they are subjected. I have used the same approach in discussing such questions as the way in which children learn sex roles or control of impulse (Mead, 1930, 1931d, 1935). It may be said that where we are concerned with character formation—the process by which children learn to discipline impulses and structure their expectations of the behavior of others—this cross-cultural approach is very valuable. It provides insights into such subjects as conscience formation, the relative importance of different sanctioning systems, sin, shame and pride, and guilt, and into the relationships between independence training and achievement motivation.

It may be argued that the younger the child, the more we are concerned with educational processes that are universal and of fundamental importance throughout life, and least imbued with the specific cultural differences that distinguish a Frenchman from an Egyptian, or an Eskimo from a Bushman or from an American. All infants must be weaned, but only a certain number will ultimately be asked to master calculus or a dead language. All infants must learn to respond with enthusiasm or apathy to adult incentives, but only a certain number, in identified countries and at particular periods, will come to care about the controversies between Stoics and Epicureans, or between fundamentalists and contextualists. So it has been fashionable in many areas in which the relationship between child development and later character has been studied, to concentrate on uniformly present experiences, and to ignore the subtler and more difficult problems of what as well as how the child is learning.

Take, for example, the question of reward and punishment. It is relatively easy to characterize systems of child rearing as using either reward or punishment in certain distinguishable proportions. The reflections of this learning can be followed in later life, and differences can be demonstrated in the school performance of children who act out fear of being wrong, as compared with those who actively seek rewards for being right. Such reflections can also be recognized later in the conformist behavior of the civil servant—secure unless he makes a positive mistake—and in the freer behavior of the politician who must perform in some positive manner if he is to be rewarded by re-election. It is upon the recognition of identifiable sequences such as these that constructs such as David McClelland's (1953) achievement motivation are built.

LITERACY

But we may ask instead what happens if we stress what a modern society requires its new members to learn, rather than start with the relationship between early disciplines and later learning. For purposes of study, we would then juxtapose two societies—one that required that children learn to read and the other that did not. We would not consider learning to read in terms of motivation, of who taught the child his letters, or whether, while learning, the child had his hands smacked, or had honey put on his tongue. We would say, instead, that learning to read involves first the idea that such a thing as reading exists, that artificial marks that are small, regular, identifiable, and recurrent have meaning. We would note that when someone who can read looks at one book, he utters a particular series of words, while if he looks at another book, he utters a different series of words. Children often learn this elementary fact by associating sequences of words with pictures, and "read" by reciting a memorized sentence that goes with a particular picture. They may then move to the over-all "look" of the sentence—whether it is long or short, or contains a certain number of capital letters. The child who does this is not learning to read, but is, in fact, learning an early form of reading badly. He is dependent upon past experience and upon the extraneous and irrelevant likeness between the contours of words but is skipping the stage of learning that is the essence of reading—the arbitrary correspondence between symbols and sounds.

So one child may learn, depending upon the kind of home in which he lives, that there are many, many books, that the pages of each yield different materials, and that if he can learn to decipher these pages he will have a new experience, as compared with another child who learns to repeat, from minor clues, a sentence that an adult has read to him. This fundamental piece of over-all learning is probably determinative of whether individuals will be literate or nonliterate, no matter how much schooling they are exposed to. The history of developing countries—in which education is imposed, often in a different language, on people who own no books and read no newspaper—has demonstrated how it is possible to make a people formally literate, able to read and write simple information, decipher signs, and keep lists and records, although they never read, in the sense that they pick up a written object of unknown content. Sometimes, children from nonreading homes may learn by accident, later in life, that reading is a way of opening a window to something new. These individuals experience a tremendous sense of freedom and enlightenment, comparable in freshness but often greater in intensity to the experience of a child who for the first time reads something new by himself. Elementary education geared to establishing literacy but not reading ability in people who are thought of as "the masses" or even "the people," carries with it a continuation of what the child has learned at home. It strengthens the concept that reading is simply saying what you know is there (for example, whether today is Monday or Tuesday, or if it is the first or the second of the month) instead of being a way of finding out things you don't know, or of reading a new story with an end you don't know.[1]

One of the familiar phenomena of the American scene in the post World War II years, is the terrible boredom that reading parents feel toward Dick and Jane, the reader based on the simple expectation that learning to read is learning to reproduce correctly only what is in the reader.

A terrible degeneration accompanies the shift from teachers who read to teachers who do not read. It is often found in developing countries, as missionaries are phased out in favor of native speakers who never read but can teach competently enough from a text. Teachers who read can

[1] Those who have not learned to read fiction as children may be dangerously uneducated, unable in later life to exercise the discipline that separates fact from fantasy in the practical world.

teach children what reading is about; teachers who have not learned to read but have only learned to be literate, cannot do this.

So we may usefully compare the infant in a primitive preliterate home, the infant in a literate but nonreading home, and the infant in a reading home. The infant in the primitive home never sees any event that suggests that there is a substitute for the spoken and heard word. If his father wants to send a message to his brother-in-law in the next village, someone has to go and tell him. If it is important to know whether a debt consists of forty dog's teeth or only of thirty, there is a lengthy debate with supporting evidence, and the matter is likely to be clinched by the dictum of whichever participant is most respected or known to have the most accurate memory. There is no way to go back to the event in question except in memory, and people's memories differ. Whether the child will learn that an event actually did occur, and that different people give different versions, some more accurate than others, or simply that the world consists of claims and counterclaims that are designed to promote the purpose of one person rather than another, depends upon the particular culture. This may seem a very small point, but it is perhaps not an accident that those people whose interest in relating past events is simply to validate present purposes, may, when writing comes to them, use it for forgery rather than for records. In contrast, those people who have been deeply concerned over establishing the actuality of an event, take delightedly to the possibilities of script that can provide them with accurate records and cross-checks on the process. This difference between regarding script as accurate and reliable, and regarding it as something to be manipulated, reflecting as it does much earlier attitudes—recurs at many levels of the use of records. It is seen, for example, in the fundamentalist approach to the Scriptures, which is based on an excessive reverence for the written word among people who themselves could read but did not write. It is seen in other peculiar manifestations, such as the willingness of otherwise well-trained scientists to believe that a film, in which they are dependent on the experimenter to identify the subjects, nevertheless is convincing proof that something occurred.

So, in the primitive home, into which the idea of script will penetrate with conquest and community development programs, are already a series of underlying expectancies that will partly shape the ways in which reading and writing will be learned. One of these expectancies will be the amount of curiosity that is cultivated within the particular sociocultural setting. If there is a strong interest in the strange and the unknown, then the groundwork is laid for looking at pictures and later reading books about that which is not known. Or one may find the society in which there is strong genealogical interest. Where writing is done by individuals it is used primarily to preserve the history of the family, the only photographs in which people are interested are those of family members. The intermediate position in which pages of *Life* magazine are pasted sideways on the wall to cover a crack, or as meaningless decorations, are active preparations for the rejection of reading. Probably the single picture pasted sideways is more threatening to the future literacy of children in the family than the differences in abstract and concrete thinking being so heavily emphasized today. The picture pasted sideways means that the symbolic nature of position in space is ignored, and also very often that even the representational quality of the picture is ignored; it becomes a bright red splotch on a gray wall.[2]

The first introduction of a primitive people to script may come in a variety of ways. A government official may come into the village and try to take a census. As people repeat their names, he writes down their responses, often with only the most faulty approximations. But still, since people remember things such as the order in which they gave their names, they can recognize their names the next time the official comes. At this point, another essential piece of learning may occur. Writing is seen as a way in which people can get the better of you, know who you are, relate your past actions to the future, check on whom you married, how many children you have, and where you live. In New Guinea, natives almost invariably responded in this way to attempts at census-taking by the government. It became fashionable to have a "government name" that was used for no other purpose, and that people remembered only with the greatest difficulty from one governmental visit to the next. Instead of records being considered as a way in which one becomes securely placed in the world, so that over a period of time one's identity becomes firmer and more unassailable, record-keeping is thus turned into a hostile act. This response of the illiterate to the record-keeping abilities of the powers that be is reflected at a higher level in current attitudes toward a central computer. Such concern is constantly expressed as a fear that knowledge of who you are will only be used to do you damage. In New Guinea, the response means that electoral rolls are almost impossible to compile, that savings bank accounts lie dormant because the depositor has not claimed them—in fact, has often forgotten the name under which they were deposited—and that individuals who need treatment for leprosy or tuberculosis may either go unidentified or receive double doses of treatment.[3]

[2] We may ask whether the present popularity of the kind of pop art in which pieces of newspaper are cut into decorative shapes is not a rebellion against the arbitrary nature of script.

[3] It has been fashionable to discuss such attitudes toward one's name as "primitive magical thinking" and those who do would assimilate the fear of their written name to fears of what others can do to them through waxen images. But it is perhaps more useful to simply consider whether first encounters with reading and writing are experienced as ones in which other people have power, or you have power (compare the essay by Thomas and Wahrhaftig in this volume). If the more salient is power in the hands of others, then protective measures may follow. This may also be reversed as when relief clients learn that an ability to produce long sets of dates and figures gives their claims an appearance of verisimilitude. The client who has learned to rattle off a

On the other hand, a first experience with writing may be brought by missionaries. If the missionaries refer their power and superior wisdom not to lists of the natives' names, but to lists of other peoples' names and deeds, then the power of the book, as compared with the power of the handmade list or record, can become salient. The aspiring young native will also want to learn to read that book. Indeed, his ability to read it aloud, to read different things from different pages, will give him prestige among his nonliterate fellows. He comes among them clothed in a mantle of external and higher authority, conferred by books that he can vocalize and they cannot. The prestige of all sacred texts, read by the elite, memorized by the humble, and in cases where religion is transplanted from one language group to another, often "read" in the sense of being pronounced without respect to meaning, can be referred to this experience in which the one who reads has power not shared by those who do not.[4]

The ease with which literacy can be spread, among the children of immigrants or within a class or group to which education was previously unavailable, is partly explained by the obvious power that educated children acquire over their uneducated parents. Any association of reading or writing with increased autonomy and authority can be made attractive. This was so even where the parents were themselves literate, like shtetel Jews. As soon as he was literate, a boy could argue with the elders and be treated with respect, and thus he was permitted the verbal release of aggression which physically had been restrained since childhood. "And the love of learning was born" (Zborowski, 1955).

If we shift from the consideration of a primitive people experiencing script for the first time to children learning from their immediate surroundings what script is about, we find that early learning may be equally determinative. What is a book? One of many, standing on shelves, one of many kinds—some read by Daddy, some by Mommy, some by older siblings, some recent presents, some heirlooms, and some read by Mommy when she was a little girl. What is a book? Something that Daddy is writing and you mustn't disturb him or he won't get that chapter finished. What are those long shiny pieces of paper with printing all over the back that Mommy gives you to draw pictures on, but she says are part of Daddy's book. Why did grandmother look so stern when you knocked that book off the table, and why did she start talking about the way your dead grandfather felt about books? How does writing your name

---

set of dates without any concern as to their accuracy will in due course believe that his investigator saves time by fabricating his record.

[4] One of the puzzles of the modern world is the failure of the African peoples south of the Sahara to adopt script, a failure that has severely compromised the speed with which they can avail themselves of civilization. But if one remembers that they were offered the memorizing type of learning of the Moslem world in which neither innovation nor imagination was encouraged and the record-keeping of the trader and slaver, when they themselves had highly trained and highly trusted memories, this failure becomes more explicable

in the front of a book make it your book? What does "dedicated" mean—so that this book, which is dedicated to you, is somehow more yours than any other book, but nobody reads it to you because you aren't old enough? What is the difference between books with pictures for children and books without pictures for grownups? Why don't grownups need pictures to tell them what Little Red Riding Hood looked like? What tells them? What is a dictionary, and why are Daddy and Mommy always having a kind of fight that ends with one of them going and getting a dictionary, and one looks pleased and one looks angry? What is an engagement book, and what is an address book, and what is the difference between the telephone book Mommy made, and the big one that is printed? And what is printing? How do they make so many copies of the newspaper that are all alike, and yet there is only one copy of each book in the house? Why, if someone gives you a second copy of *When We Were Very Young* does Mommy say, "Oh, we have that; we'll give it to Jimmy?"

For the child in the home of those who not only read but also write books, a book becomes something that is made by the kind of people you know. A book is something that you yourself might write. In fact, you can begin now, folding pieces of paper together in book form and covering them with imitation letters. Or if you are a little older, write the beginnings of a story, labeled "Susan Lane, her book." Children from such homes passionately enter into reading. If they have difficulties, it is because they have serious problems of eye coordination, or deep emotional difficulties, or occasionally because they have gotten so far ahead of themselves that the discrepancy between what they can read and what they can write is unbearably frustrating. Such children have no image of a house that does not contain books, of an adult who does not often have a book in his hand, or of an individuality of which books are not a part. The hazards here are hazards that come from the overevaluation of books. The child whose eyes coordinate more slowly may become frightened and his parents may share his fright. "Maybe he isn't going to read" is a statement almost equivalent to "Maybe he isn't going to be human." The child who wants to learn, but who is held back because his parents have been warned not to attempt to teach their children prematurely, may give up. The bright moment passes, never to be regained. But attitudes toward the importance of reading have been established for good or ill, long before the child goes to school.[5]

It will be by careful detailed ethnographical study of different kinds of homes, of which the two quoted represent extremes, that we should be able

[5] The importance of a library, either a very large private library, or a public library, is the sense it gives a child that there are more and more new and different books to be read. Ownership of a few books, and no use of libraries and no books in their parents' library, means that children learn that reading is essentially a self-limiting and terminable part of life summed up in the wry joke, "She has a book."

to chart, and correct for, children's earliest learnings about reading and writing. Inevitably, experience will be diverse and defective with respect to the goals held up by a society in which reading is absolutely essential. In addition to the kinds of broad learnings that have been sketched in here, there will be many idiosyncratic miscarriages: children to whom letters or numbers come to have a magical significance, children who learn to read secretly and so become unintelligible to those around them, and children who block completely on part of the symbolic process. But these individual early sequences can only be fully identified, allowed for and treated, if the broader cultural outlines associated with class and occupation, region and religion, are better known.

ABSTRACT THOUGHT

Much of the current discussion of the relationship between types of thinking displayed by school children in the United States, which distinguishes between abstract and concrete thinking, lacks comparative perspective, and so fails to take into account many significant dimensions. However, when the various explanatory schemes for the development of thought that have evolved within one culture, or that include material from other cultures taken out of context, are subjected to comparative scrutiny, the kind of links between early childhood experience and type of thinking that individuals will display as adults can be distinguished in outline, however lacking we may be in detailed research on their implications.

Whether one follows the classical outlines of Binet (1916), the original schemes of Piaget (1926)—with their inclusion of Lévy-Bruhl's (1923) armchair use of primitive materials, modified in the late 1950s in confrontation with living cross-cultural material—(Piaget, 1950; Tanner and Inhelder, 1960)—or whether one follows the developmental schemes of Gesell and Ilg (1943), it seems clear that we must take into account when, from whom, and in what way children encounter such types of thinking, as, for example, the Binet interpretation of proverbs, the Piaget demand for a recognition of the conservation of matter, or the Gesell-Ilg recognition of mathematical pattern as a recurrent spiraling capacity. Every intellectual capacity that is later tested by achievement, test, or observation is intimately linked with early childhood experience, with the level of education of parent or nurse, with the structure and furnishing of the home, with the content with which the members of the family and the neighborhood are preoccupied, and with the availability of the apparatus and technology on which abstract thought is dependent.

The child who is cared for in infancy and early childhood by individuals of a lower level of education than the child will later be expected to reach, faces a different educational situation than one who is reared from infancy by parents who represent the same level of education to which the child is expected to aspire. Whether it is an explanation of time or space, money, or the telephone, or a recognition of the child's attempt to search for some generalization among dissimilar objects, the highly educated parent or surrogate will meet the child on a different level than will the educated nurse, child nurse, or peasant grandmother. Where the educational level is lower, crude, or folk, concrete explanations may be given that will coexist in the child's mind and interfere with his later learning required by the school. This situation is further complicated by the relative intelligence of nurse and parent, which need not be proportional to their educational level. If the nurse is actually more intelligent, but less literate and less widely experienced than the parent, the child may develop considerable confusion about modes of thought. If the nurse or grandparent is able to draw on a folk level of thinking, rich in imagery and metaphor, while the parent represents the first generation of schooling—arid, disassociated from his or her primary learning—this may lead to the kind of repudiation of the intellectual life in which poverty and immediate existential experience are opposed to the hypocrisy, or aridity of formal learning.[6] The importance to the total character structure of the child, of the nurse who taps a different cultural level, has long been recognized, but the educational consequences for thought remain unexplored. But it surely accounts for the superior achievement of parent-reared children who come from families with several generations of high achievement. They are exposed to highly abstract thinking from earliest childhood as contrasted with (1) children reared by nurses with low levels of literacy; (2) those who grow up with a lower level of thought at home than that encountered in church and school; (3) those who grow up in homes where no abstraction is ever made, and who in many cases are taught by teachers who came from similar homes, and who have only attained a schoolroom acquaintance with educated thought.

High intelligence occurs in all social strata and every ethnic group. A few individuals from primitive tribes or severely disadvantaged groups have risen to great intellectual distinction. But emphasis on these conspicuous exceptions has obscured the equally significant fact that the absence of a nurturing environment stunts and stultifies the mind of a child so that in most cases high natural intelligence is never realized. Early contact between young children and highly intelligent, highly educated adults is the best means we have yet devised for giving children a chance to escape the limitations imposed by uneducated parents and limited homes. This was evidenced in the striking contrast between the style—as expressed in pos-

---

[6] Sartre's analysis of his repudiation of his grandfather's pretentious and unscholarly intellectual life gives a detailed account of the effect on a child of exposure to a type of intellectuality that he feels cannot be respected and must be repudiated (Sartre, 1964)

ture, gesture, expression, and responsiveness—of the infants reared in Anna Freud's (1943) special residential home for children during World War II, where the children were cared for and taught by highly educated refugees, and that of children of the same class who were cared for by lower-class adults with limited education.[7]

But the failure to make finer discriminations than rural and urban, educated and uneducated, colored and white, professional and nonprofessional, rich and poor, is likely to obscure the issue, especially in the United States. In some ethnic groups—notably Eastern European Jewish groups—parents in the poorest homes, with the simplest occupations and very little formal schooling, may still provide a premium on thinking and exegesis that supports the child in school. Even before he enters school, the child learns the rudiments of analytical thought. On the other hand there are homes in which the father's highly paid occupation and specialized education is never made manifest, or where the children are left to the care of unintelligent and uneducated nurses. In such homes the children are more handicapped than those in a very simple home, where the Bible is read with reverence, and the preacher is expected to discuss Scripture like an educated man. When we are dealing with large populations or with whole ethnic groups in the midst of transition, or with large urban immigrant groups with a given background, it may often be possible to establish some regularities. Such regularities can be discerned in the contrast between the adaptation of Japanese and Chinese immigrant children in California, or between the intellectuality of Eastern European and Middle Eastern Jewish children on the East Coast of the United States. But any attempt to generalize without research into the specific group is dangerous. What we need is more basic research on the one hand, and more devices for assaying the quality of preschool experience on the other.

The consequences of the differences, in the intellectual tone and interest of those who are most in contact with a small child, involve a variety of factors, some cultural, some idiosyncratic, and some familial. On the cultural level it is possible to work out in some detail the consequences for later learning of living in houses constructed without benefit of any precise measurement, without clocks or calendars, or even toys that embody some of the principles on which education is postulated. The house built to specifications—the fine machine tool, the clock and calendar, the thermometer and barometer, the compass and the blender, the thermostat and the television set—all carry a set of messages that can be absorbed in early childhood and later transformed into an interest in mathematics and computers. This can be so even when there is no adult in the home capable of explicitly fostering a child's interest in abstraction. Similarly, the city child learns from plants that mother keeps for show, or father keeps to impress the neighbors, or from herbs

[7] This statement is based on visits to residential nurseries through the United Kingdom in 1943.

growing in the window box, things about a part of the universe that he would not otherwise experience. The regularities in the homes of any group of children can be analyzed for these mute messages that equip them, long before they enter school, for receptivities far beyond the level of the background from which they come. All this learning will be enormously reinforced if at least one adult in the home understands and explains a short-circuit, or the principle upon which the thermostat operates. But the artifacts that are the products of science nevertheless carry their own teaching: the child who comes from housing built on the basis of explicit geometrical knowledge makes a different order of discovery of geometry than the child who comes from a circular thatched dwelling, or from a crazy, sagging hut made of broken pieces of tin. In turn, the child who comes from a squatter's town built partly of thatch and partly of fragments of tin that have been shaped to recognizable geometrical forms learns still something else about pattern as being independent of materials.

Conversely, it is possible for homes to so smother children in words and high-level generalizations that their ability to work from direct perception of shape and size and material may be permanently impaired. High levels of verbal precocity may accompany very rudimentary understanding of basic physical and physiological relationships (Newman and Krug 1964; Parens and Weech 1966; Weisberg and Springer 1961; Wieder 1966).

It should be borne in mind that each of the situations with which I have dealt may occur on a cultural, societywide basis. They may be characteristic of particular families, and therefore, incongruent with the over-all cultural emphasis. They may even be attributes of one individual within a family who gives the young child some extraordinarily deviant and unorthodox intellectual exposure. When the familial or individual style deviates from the wider style, the educator has still another element to cope with—the unexpected language of particular children that render them incomprehensible, unpredictable, and maladjusted in the school-room with its standardized expectations.

LANGUAGE LEARNING BEFORE SCHOOL AGE

During the 1920s it was argued that whatever difficulties children had on entering school, because they came from homes where a foreign language was spoken, would be eliminated by the third grade. The most significant attempt to refute this argument was a study of bilingual and monolingual children, in which the effects of a type of bilingualism associated with different contexts such as home, school, and play, were shown to be reflected in later school achievement. The design of this study has since come under criticism; there are still no definitive studies on the subject

(but see the studies summarized in this volume by Cazden-and-John).
However, from related fields, there have come some suggestive observations
that should be considered.

Jakobson (1941) has assembled evidence to show that the way in which
a language is learned by an initial dichotomizing of a large unstructured
repertoire of sounds, which are then progressively elaborated into a
structured system, can be found to be repeated in the loss of the
mastery of speech that occurs in traumatic amnesia. This study suggests—
and the suggestion is supported by observations in other fields—that
children learn the phonemic structure of their language at a very early age.
It may be hypothesized, although there is no evidence yet in support,
that certain fundamental morphemic generalizations are also learned early,
and that fundamental ways of viewing the world, with contrasts between
durative and punctuated action and with an insistence upon sources of
information and matters of this sort, are also learned within the first three
or four years of life. At present, it seems probable that the ability of the
child to learn other linguistic and thought patterns is not so much a
question of the interference of the latter pattern by the earlier one, as it is
of the conditions of learning the two patterns. If two or more languages
are learned, either sequentially or simultaneously, but one is the language
of play and the other the language of discipline; if one is taught within the
intimate environment of the home and the other in the more demanding and impersonal environment of school; if one is a language that is
spoken by all the members of the child's environment, and the other
spoken only by servants, or only by parents, or only by teachers; then the
learning of the two patterns will be affectively weighted, and the learning
will be of a different sort.

When, for example, a Spanish-speaking child is taught English by a
teacher whose mother tongue is Spanish, and who has only a classroom
mastery of English, the situation is profoundly different from the case in
which a child is taught English by a native English speaker with a good
idiomatic knowledge of Spanish, or by a teacher who speaks no Spanish at
all. It seems likely, but it has never been properly studied, that if the
mother tongue is a dialect in which literacy is never attained, rather than
a literate language in which literacy is first obtained, the results for the
child's subsequent use of language will be very different. The success of
the Colonial Dutch in teaching literacy and languages in Indonesia was
based upon teaching literacy in the mother tongue, followed by literacy
in Malay (the Indonesia *lingua franca* in the Netherlands Indies), followed
by Dutch taught by native speakers, followed by English, French, or
German taught as another formally mastered European language, by
Dutch native speakers. Here a sequence of teaching had been developed
that was severely mutilated when the school system was revised, and
the Dutch dropped out. English teaching deteriorated markedly when the
Dutch step was removed and Indonesian teachers were asked to go directly

from Indonesian—a second language related to their own mother tongue—
to English, a language that they had learned as a second European language from Dutch native speakers.[8]

Experience of this sort suggests that it is most important to explore
the relationship between different kinds of language learning and to
identify breaks and continuities in the sequence within which different
versions of the same language, or different languages, are learned. The most
significant situations may well be those in which significant adults in the
child's world do not share a knowledge of the different varieties of speech
with which the young child has to cope; different degrees of identification
of these versions may be most important. For example, children who
speak a dialect, identified and labeled as a dialect, in a country such as
France or Germany or Italy, may have parents who speak the dialect at
home, but use the standard language in all formal and public situations.
Such children may be far less handicapped than those who speak a version
of the language that is treated not as a dialect with an identifiable style
of its own but simply as class-typed, or regionally- or ethnically-typed, as
in lower-class urban English in the United Kingdom, "bad English" in
the English-speaking Caribbean, or the typical Southern rural Negro
Americans in the United States. If the mother tongue is treated as an
inferior version of the standard language, rather than as a dialect, movement becomes much more difficult between the phonemic, morphemic,
and cognitive structures of the two forms, the home language and the
school language (compare the discussion of these points by Hymes in this
volume).

When, as is so often the case, the teacher has an inadequate grasp
of the standard language and can only operate within a formal school
context, the children with class-typed or race-typed speech are deprived
of any formal grasp of the differences between the two forms. On the other
hand, the teacher who is a native speaker of the standard language cannot
recognize that the prevalent "mistakes" in grammar or spelling or thought
found among children whose home language is "poor English" or "bad
English" are, in fact, intrusions into the standard speech from unrecognized
dialect.[9]

[8] Based on exploratory fieldwork in 1957–1958, in Bali, under NIH Grant No.
M-2218.

[9] I am indebted to the fieldwork of Rhoda Metraux, in the Caribbean, for my
understanding of the significance of the failure to identify Caribbean dialects as dialects, and to a brief visit to her field site in Montserrat, W. I., during the summer of
1966 for an opportunity to listen to the sliding relationships between standard English
and an almost completely unintelligible dialect, indulged in by both native dialect
speakers and native English speakers born on the island, with minimal consciousness of
the way in which they handle equivalent utterances. (NSF Grant to AMNH, No.
MH-07675-04.)
Fieldwork in the village of Peri, among the Manus speaking people in 1964 and
1965, where an Australian teacher, without a knowledge of either Manus or the Neo-
Melanesian *lingua franca* (pidgin) was teaching English, gave me a further opportunity

Experience therefore suggests the importance of making as articulate as possible the varieties of a language or of different languages that a child learns as an infant, as a toddler, in nursery and preschool, in elementary school, college and university. Such articulacy would include a detailed study of the various types of mother tongues, recognized dialects, recognized dialects associated with illiteracy and low prestige, unrecognized versions of the standard speech, standard expectations among the nonstandard speech speakers of what the standard language is like, divisions of experience that are learned in each language, counting, body parts, names for bodily functions, recitation of dreams, fantasy, disciplined logical thinking, authoritarian moral dicta, sacred scriptures, and poetry. Complementary to such an analysis, we will need the language style of the standard language and such contrasts as the Dutch emphasis on learning to *speak* foreign languages rather than on learning to listen; the Chinese emphasis on learning to read a cross language script and to *hear* different languages while speaking them imperfectly, and the contrasts among ways of learning English, Spanish, Russian, and German spelling. Of particular interest would be the consequences of the older and later German experiences, in which a teacher was accustomed to correct for local dialects and still teach the children to spell as they spoke, and the postwar experience when (owing to the wartime dispersal of populations throughout Germany) this was no longer possible.[10]

Similar interesting comparisons could be made of the ways that children progress in learning a standard language that is not their mother tongue —for example, between the Soviet Union where a Russian-speaking teacher may be faced with a group of children with a common foreign language, and the United States where, in cities like New York, the teacher may be faced with children speaking several mother tongues as well as unrecognized dialects of English.

Detailed analysis of some of these situations should yield a set of early childhood deutero-formulations of the order of: "Real speech is how we speak at home; THEY speak and insist that I learn to speak in another way that has less reality." "Different people of the same kind speak different languages; it will be necessary to learn them all." "Different people of different kinds, some of higher or lower status, or greater or lesser warmth, speak different languages, learning these languages must include these extralinguistic differences."

There are, of course, the much more extreme cases of children reared in foreign countries who learn to speak their nurses' language, but whose

to compare the children's progress in English and the problems they encountered, with the progress of Manus-speaking children on Balowan, in 1953, with a native English-speaking teacher who also spoke fluent Neo-Melanesian. (1953, Admiralty Island expedition, grant from the Rockefeller Foundation to the AMNH; 1964 and 1965, NIH Grant No. MH-07675-02-03 to the AMNH.)

[10] This material was a by-product of the analysis by Rhoda Metraux (1955) of a large sample of Anderson Story Completion Forms written by German children.

parents do not. When these children are removed to their country of origin, the original nurse-tongue may be completely suppressed, only appearing as grammatical or phonemic intrusions, or under conditions of extreme amnesic stress, while providing a background for unrecognized cognitive confusions. Even more extreme are the cases in which children, after having learned to speak, are adopted across a complete linguistic, cultural, and racial border, and are required to learn the new language from foster parents who know nothing of their mother tongues—as with Chinese, Korean, or Vietnamese war orphans adopted at the age of two or three in the United States.

Such deutero learning may be very potent in determining children's later ability to learn, to think in the abstract terms that are presented in the second, standard language. Access to their unconscious creativity is also affected. On the other hand, if these deutero learnings can be identified and articulated so that the mother tongue or the nurse tongue is treated with dignity as having equal reality standing with the standard language, much of the damage of such weighted compartmentalization can probably be avoided.

It will be particularly important to explore the later effects on the thinking ability of the coexistence of two languages: an infant or child language that remains rudimentary and undeveloped, unused since childhood, and a standard language that is reinforced with literacy, literature, and disciplined thought. The state of teaching the deaf in the United States is a case in point. American teaching of the deaf has until very recently repudiated the use of sign language, and insisted that deaf children be taught lip reading. The sign language, a language that uses many condensations for morphemes in addition to a manual alphabet, has continued to be used as a disapproved subversive form of communication among deaf children. Since it is not taught by competent and self-conscious teachers, as it is, for example, in the Soviet Union, dialects grow up; the deaf can easily recognize the great variety of divergent forms characteristic of sign language in the United States. But as the children do not connect the sign language with literacy, and no attempt is made to relate it systematically to standard English, it remains essentially the language of preliterate nursery years. In the Soviet Union, the use of a manual language coexists on formal terms with lip reading, reading, and writing, and very small children demonstrate an impressive mastery of thought and language.[11]

But the situation of the deaf is only an extreme and dramatic example of what happens when any form of communication, including the modalities of touch, taste and smell, is developed in childhood and left un-

[11] Unpublished field work on teaching of the deaf in the United States, by Rhoda Metraux and Margaret Mead, and in the Soviet Union by Margaret Mead. NIH grant to AMNH Factor in Allopsychic Orientation in Mental Health. (NIH Grant No. M-3303.)

recognized and undeveloped by later formal teaching. Many cultures, including the highly literate versions of our own, depend upon using such separations to dramatize the difference between intimate and informal and distant, impersonal, and formal relationships. As a result, the uncultivated, preliterate modes of early childhood become the modes of communication within marriage, often carrying with them as unrecognized baggage, the unbridled fears and hopes and fantasies of early childhood, so that records of the intimate life of highly cultivated people contrast astonishingly with their level of sophistication and humanization in less intimate contexts (Hall, 1959; Ruesch and Prestwood, 1950; Gorer, 1963; Frank, 1956; Wiener, 1966; Birdwhistell, 1959, 1962).

Remembrance of such earlier forms of once efficient and now disallowed communications has many repercussions in learning situations at the beginning of school. In establishing a nursery school in a Southeastern city in the early 1940s for White children who had had Black nurses, it was found necessary to bridge the gulf from home to school, by including in the nursery school staff, a warm Black woman who fed the children to counterbalance the young White teachers who stood to the children for a different affective style.

It is probably impossible to overestimate the extent to which languages are the carriers of different kinds of thought. Quite aside from the resolution of the adequacy of the Whorfian hypothesis about the relationship between language and thought, the simple fact that more or less cognitively disciplined, socially hierarchical, or emotionally toned kinds of speech are used by the same individual, puts a burden on the transfer of learning. In the extreme case, the multilingual individual who has "lost" his or her mother tongue through migration or adoption may experience extreme hiatuses in his thinking processes. Such an individual may be denied all access to poetry as a form, or be unable to move easily through different levels of consciousness, or through different kinds of imagery. The sorts of imagery associated with primary process thinking—the figures of speech of classical rhetoric—may become so disturbed that little or no congruence remains between image and word. This is the case of a great deal of American slang where the visual image is lost in favor of an inexplicit motor image.

SEX AND TEMPERAMENT

Another conspicuous area of significant early childhood learning comes in the way a child experiences within the familial group cues to styles of intellectual behavior that are sex typed. Sex identity is imposed on children from birth; different terminology, different tones of voice, and different expectations all reinforce and elaborate underlying biological differences. Ways in which the world is to be perceived or represented may be so deep that when given pencils or crayons, children who have never drawn will nevertheless be sharply differentiated by the time they are five or six. Boys, for example, may draw scenes of activity from real life; girls draw patterns for cakes or clothing. Both style and content are conveyed to children very early, together with permission or prohibition about experimenting with styles of behavior culturally assigned to the other sex.

There is also great divergence in such cultural styles. In one culture, the small girls may be permitted to behave like boys, even in their stance and posture, as in Manus, where significantly the girls have taken to schooling as readily as the boys before puberty; their capacity to learn interrupted only by different expectations at puberty. In contrast, among the Iatmul, early childhood experience places the boys with the girls, with mothers as the first models; only in late childhood is a male model superimposed on a female model. But in Bali each child is firmly assured of his or her sex identity, reared from earliest childhood to differentiated behavior, and individual children are given permission to experiment with the behavior of the other sex.

As a child learns its sex identity, it learns its appropriate cognitive style, and arrives in school with deeply ingrained expectations of what learning will be about. When the cultural style is rigid and extremely incongruent with the realities of human abilities, disturbances in the ability to learn are inevitable. This is so because of the child's already fixed sex identification and belief, such as that mechanics or mathematics are masculine and art is feminine, and because the teachers, as part of the same culture, reflect the same sex-typed expectations. Children whose abilities deviate sharply from normal expectation experience great difficulty in learning. This is exacerbated if, within the family, a child's proclivities for some sex-typed form of intellectual or artistic behavior is not only deviant from the cultural norm but also reinforced by temperamental similarities with the parent of the opposite sex. If a boy is both musical beyond the expectation for his class and region for male behavior, and has a musical mother with whom he identified, the complications are doubled. The school can help break down these very early, obdurate learnings, particularly if the school system presents at every stage both male and female models in sufficient profusion so that the child's earlier arbitrary learnings will be questioned rather than perpetuated. But small sensitive responses in early childhood to the cognitive style of the parents of the same and opposite sex can provide one of the often seemingly inexplicable blocks to learning, or a pathway of unusual facilitation, as when a certain high school provided an unusual number of good science students, all of whom went to the university from which the science teacher—also a first-class athlete—had come. As in other cases, knowledge of the cultural style, by class and region, can facilitate teaching in school. Where the learning capacities of a particular child are complicated by idiosyncratic learning, additional analysis is required.

Finally, it is important to recognize that preschool children may be learning ways of dealing with life that are radically opposed to the expectations on which the school system is built. The American school system is based upon the belief that children should and will accept more and better education than their parents had. (The parent who insists that what was good enough for him is good enough for his children has been treated as a gross reactionary.) Such institutions as the Parent-Teachers Association are postulated on the parents' enthusiastic support of this position, whether it is reflected in the pride with which the first report card is exhibited, or in the foresight with which the parents enroll a child at birth for a particular school or college. Each piece of infant learning, mastery of a new skill, learning to count, or reciting a nursery rhyme or the alphabet is greeted in this model American household as a precursor of achievement that will eventually outstrip that of the parent. The child's learning is never begrudged; the child who suffers is the child whose early achievements do not promise such later educational success.

This is the model—one based on the style set up by hopeful immigrants from older societies who emigrated of their own accord to find better opportunities for themselves, and particularly for their children. Our whole educational system has been postulated on this style (here, see the essays in this volume by Green and Khleif). It was, therefore, with a terrible shock that Americans woke up, in the late 1950s, to a recognition that for some 30 million or more Americans there was no such expectation. The enthusiasm, bred of immigration to a wider and more open world, has died among those who failed generation after generation to make the grade. It had only a fitful life among those who had not been immigrants out of self-propelling hope, but who had been brought here as slaves, or pushed here by desperation and starvation within their own borders, or who were slowly reduced to despair as their traditional ways of life became less and less congruent with modern American life. In such families achievement is not rewarded. The child is not gazed upon as one who will go further than his father but instead is clutched or pitied, loved or rejected as part of the misery, poverty, deprivation, or grudgingly accepted low status that his parents, grandparents, and great grandparents have known, and from which they have no genuine hope of escape. This is the child who is a dropout from the first day of school. Deeper than the marks of a different intellectual style, of a failure to grasp the meaning of literacy as access to new experiences, and deeper than the learning that comes from the content of the home and from the cues given by sex and temperament, is the mark laid upon the small preschool child by his parents' expectations of his achievement. It is this cultural factor that we are just beginning to appreciate and allow for; it is this deep block to achievement with which programs such as Head Start are attempting to deal. Without seriously coming to grips with this discrepancy between a school system built for the first generation of aspiring immigrants and pupils who are the product of many generations of low expectation and despair, we will not be able to reconstruct our schools so as to provide the type of education that will be needed in the coming world.

But the reconstruction will need to provide ways through which children from whom little is expected may learn to expect much. It will also need to rescue those children—equally the victims of our one-way convictions of progress—from whom too much is expected and who are therefore branded as failures. Instead of a single-track notion of education from which those with the "wrong" cultural backgrounds were automatically excluded, and within which those with the "right" social backgrounds were often severely punished, we need to construct a system in which all sorts of lateral movements are possible, as some of the children of rural migrants become poets and physicists, and some of the children of lawyers and physicians and bankers become first-rate automobile mechanics or hospital orderlies. To accomplish this, the school needs to be more explicitly geared to compensate and balance, to take advantage of and when appropriate undo, the enormous strength of preschool experience.

New York, 1966.

REFERENCES

Ariès, Phillipe
    1962 Centuries of childhood: a social history of family life. New York: Alfred A. Knopf.
Bateson, Gregory
    1942 Social planning and the concept of deutero learning. In Science, philosophy, and religion, second symposium, Lyman Bryson and Louis Finkelstein, eds. New York: Conference on Science, Philosophy, and Religion, pp. 81–97.
    1955 A theory of play and fantasy. Psychiatric Research Reports, 2:39–51.
    1956 The message "this is play." In Group processes, Bertram Schaffner, ed. New York: Josiah Macy, Jr. Foundation, pp. 145–242.
    ——— and Margaret Mead
    1942 Balinese character: a photographic analysis. New York: New York Academy of Sciences; reissued 1962.
Berkowitz, Leonard, ed.
    1964 Advances in experimental social psychology, vol. 1. Influence of Culture on Cognitive Processes. New York: Academic Press.
Bernstein, Basil
    1960 Language and social class. British Journal of Sociology 11:271–276.
    1961 Social structure, language and learning. Educational Research 3:136–176.
Binet, Alfred
    1916 The development of intelligence in children. Baltimore: Williams and Wilkins, Inc.
Birdwhistell, Ray L.
    1959 Contribution of linguistic-kinesic studies to the understanding of schizophrenia. In Schizophrenia, an integrated approach, Alfred Auerback, ed. New York: Ronald Press Company, pp. 99–123.
    1962 An approach to communication. Family Process 1:194–201.

Bloom, Benjamin, et al.
  1965 Compensatory education for cultural deprivation. New York: Holt, Rinehart and Winston, Inc.
Bruner, Jerome S.
  1966 Toward a theory of instruction. Cambridge: Harvard University Press.
Bryson, Lyman, Margaret Mead, Rudolf Arnheim, and Milton Nahm
  1960 Conditions for creativity. *In* The creative mind and method, Jack D. Summerfield and Lorlyn Thatcher, eds. Austin: University of Texas Press, pp. 105-111.
Cohen, Yehudi A.
  1964 The transition from childhood to adolescence. Chicago: Aldine Publishing Company.
Dart, Francis E., and Panna Lal Pradham
  1967 Cross-cultural teaching of science. Science 155:649-656.
Deutsch, Martin
  1965 The role of social class in language development and cognition. American Journal of Orthopsychiatry 35:78-88.
Entwisle, Doris R.
  1966 Developmental sociolinguistics: a comparative study in four subcultural settings. Sociometry 29:67-84.
Erikson, Erik H.
  1958 The syndrome of identity diffusion in adolescents and young adults. *In* Discussions on child development, J. M. Tanner and Bärbel Inhelder, eds. London: Tavistock Publications, Ltd., pp. 133-167.
Ferguson, Charles
  1965 Directions in sociolinguistics: report on an interdisciplinary seminar. Social Science Research Council Items, 19:1-4.
Frank, L. K.
  1956 Tactile communication. Genetic Psychology Monographs 56:209-255.
Freud, Anna, and D. T. Burlingham
  1943 War and children. New York: Medical War Books.
Fromm, Erich
  1951 The forgotten language. New York: Holt, Rinehart and Winston, Inc., reprinted 1962, Evergreen E47, New York: Grove Press, Inc.
Gesell, Arnold, and Frances Ilg
  1943 Infant and child in the culture of today. New York: Harper and Row Publishers, Inc.
Goldman-Eisler, Frieda
  1958 Speech analysis and mental processes. Language and Speech 1:59-75.
Gorer, Geoffrey
  1963 The life and ideas of the Marquis de Sade. N226, New York: W. W. Norton Company, Inc.
Hall, Edward T.
  1959 The silent language. Garden City, New York: Doubleday Co., Inc., reprinted 1961, R204, New York: Fawcett Publications, Inc.
Hart, C. W. M.
  1955 Contrasts between prepubertal and postpubertal education. *In* Education and Anthropology, George D. Spindler, ed. Stanford: Stanford University Press, pp. 127-145.
Hebb, D. O.
  1949 The organization of behavior. New York: John Wiley & Sons, Inc.
Hymes, Dell H.
  1962 The ethnography of speaking. *In* Anthropology and human behavior, Thomas Gladwin and William C. Sturtevant, eds. Washington: Anthropological Society of Washington, pp. 13-53.
Jakobson, Roman
  1941 *Kindersprache, Aphasie and allgemeine Lautgesetze.* Uppsala, Sweden: Almqvist and Wiksells.

Kaplan, Bert, ed.
  1961 Studying personality cross-culturally. New York: Harper & Row, Publishers, Inc.
Lesser, Gerald, et al.
  1965 Mental abilities of children in different social and cultural groups. *In* School children in the urban slum, Joan I. Roberts, ed. New York: Hunter College (Project True), pp. 115–125.
Levinson, Boris M.
  1960 Subcultural variations in verbal and performance ability at the elementary school level. Journal of Genetic Psychology 97:149–160.
Lévy-Bruhl, Lucien
  1923 Primitive mentality. Authorized translation by Lilian A. Clare. New York: Crowell-Collier and Macmillan, Inc.
Luria, A. R., and F. I. Yudovich
  1959 Speech and the development of mental processes in the child. New York: Humanities Press.
Lynd, Robert S., and Helen M. Lynd
  1929 Middletown. New York: Harcourt Brace Jovanovich.
  1937 Middletown in transition. New York: Harcourt Brace Jovanovich.
McClelland, David C.
  1961 The achieving society. New York: Van Nostrand Reinhold Company.
————, et al.
  1953 The achievement motive. New York: Appleton-Century-Crofts.
Malinowski, Bronislaw
  1948 The problem of meaning in primitive languages. *In* Magic, science and religion and other essays. Boston: The Beacon Press, pp. 228–276.
Mead, Margaret
  1926 The methodology of racial testing: its significance for sociology. American Journal of Sociology 31:657–667.
  1927a Group intelligence tests and linguistic disability among Italian children. School and Society 25:465–468.
  1927b The need for teaching anthropology in normal schools and Teachers' Colleges. School and Society 26:466–469.
  1928 A lapse of animism among a primitive people. Psyche 9:72–77.
  1929 South Sea hints on bringing up children. Parents' Magazine 4:20–22, 49–52.
  1930 Growing up in New Guinea: A comparative study of primitive education. New York: William Morrow & Co., Inc.: reprinted 1962, Apollo A58, New York: William Morrow & Co., Inc.
  1931a Education, primitive. *In* V, Encyclopedia of the Social Sciences, Edwin R. A. Seligman and Alvin Johnson, eds. New York: Crowell-Collier and Macmillan, Inc., pp. 399–403.
  1931b The meaning of freedom in education. Progressive Education 8:107–111.
  1931c The primitive child. *In* A handbook of child psychology, Carl Murchison, ed. Worcester, Mass.: Clark University Press, pp. 669–686.
  1931d Two south sea educational experiments and their American implications. *In* Eighteenth Annual Schoolmen's Week Proceedings, March 18–21, 1931. University of Pennsylvania School of Education Bulletin 31:493–497.
  1932a The changing culture of an Indian tribe. New York: Columbia University Press; reprinted 1966, Cap Giant 266, New York: G. P. Putnam's Sons, Inc.
  1932b Contrasts and comparisons from primitive society. Annals of the American Academy of Political and Social Science 160:23–28.
  1932c An investigation of the thought of primitive children, children with special reference to animism. Journal of the Royal Anthropological Institute 62:173–190.
  1935 Sex and temperament in three primitive societies. New York: William Morrow & Co., Inc.; reprinted 1963, Apollo A-67, New York: William Morrow & Co., Inc.

1937 Cooperation and competition among primitive peoples. New York and London: McGraw-Hill Inc.; reprinted 1961, BP123, Boston: The Beacon Press.

1940 The student of race problems can say. . . . Frontiers of Democracy 6:200–202.

1942a And keep your powder dry. New York: William Morrow & Co., Inc.; reprinted 1965, Apollo edition A105, New York: William Morrow & Co., Inc.

1942b Educative effects of social environment as disclosed by studies of primitive societies. *In* Environment and education, E. W. Burgess, ed. Chicago: University of Chicago Press, pp. 48–61.

1946 Professional problems of education in dependent countries. Journal of Negro Education 40:346–357.

1947a Babies in primitive society. Child Study 24:71–72.

1947b The implications of culture change for personality development. American Journal of Orthopsychiatry 17:633–646.

1947c On the implication for anthropology of the Gesell-Ilg approach to maturation. American Anthropologist 49:69–77.

1949 Male and female. New York: William Morrow & Co., Inc.; reprinted 1955, NP369, New York: New American Library.

1951a The impact of culture on personality development in the United States today. Understanding the child 20:17–18.

1951c The school in American culture. Cambridge: Harvard University Press.

1952 Some relationships between social anthropology and psychiatry. *In* Dynamic psychiatry, Franz Alexander and Helen Ross, eds. Chicago: University of Chicago Press, pp. 401–448.

1953 Cultural patterns and technical change. Paris, Unesco; reprinted 1961, MT346, New York: New American Library.

1954a Cultural discontinuities and personality transformation. Journal of Social Issues, Supplement Series, No. 8: 3–16.

1954b Research on primitive children. *In* Manual of child psychology, 2nd ed., Leonard Carmichael, ed. New York: John Wiley and Sons, Inc., pp. 735–780.

1956 New lives for old: cultural transformation, Manus 1928–1953. New York: William Morrow & Co., Inc.; reprinted with a new preface 1966, Apollo A124, New York: William Morrow & Co., Inc.

1957 Toward more vivid utopias. Science 126:957–961.

1958a Changing teacher in a changing world. *In* The education of teachers: new perspectives. Washington: National Education Association of the United States, pp. 121–134.

1958b Why is education obsolete? Harvard Business Review 36:164–170.

1959a Closing the gap between the scientists and the others. Daedalus, Winter: 139–146.

1959b Creativity in cross-cultural perspective." *In* Creativity and its cultivation, Harold H. Anderson, ed. New York: Harper & Row, Publishers, Inc., pp. 222–235.

1960a Adaptation to change, Participant in panel discussion. The social environment. *In* Man's contracting world in an expanding universe, Ben H. Bagdikian, ed. Providence, Rhode Island: Brown University Press, pp. 90–101.

1960b High school of the future. California Journal of Secondary Education 35: 360–369.

1960c Participant in discussions on child development: a consideration of the biological, psychological, and cultural approaches to the understanding of human development and behavior: proceedings of the fourth meeting of the World Health Organization, 4 Study group on the psychobiological development of the child, Geneva, 1956, J. M. Tanner and Bärbel Inhelder, eds. London: Tavistock Publications, Ltd.; New York: International Universities Press, 1960.

1961a Gender in the honors program. Superior Students (JCSS) 4:2–6.

1961b Questions that need asking. New York (Columbia University): Teachers College Record 63:89–93.

1962 A creative life for your children. Washington: Department of Health, Education and Welfare, Children's Bureau Headliner Series No. 1.

1963 Socialization and enculturation. *In* Papers in honor of Melville J. Herskovits, Current Anthropology 4:184–188.

1964 Continuities in cultural evolution. New Haven: Yale University Press; re-
     printed 1966, Y154, New Haven: Yale University Press.
1965 The future as the basis for establishing a shared culture. Daedalus, Winter:
     135–155.
——, and Frances C. Macgregor
1951 Growth and culture: a photographic study of Balinese childhood. New York:
     Putnam's Sons, Inc.
——, and Martha Wolfenstein, eds.
1955 Childhood in contemporary cultures. Chicago: University of Chicago Press; re-
     printed 1963, P124, Chicago: University of Chicago Press.
——, and Rhoda Metraux
1957 Image of the scientist among high-school students: a pilot study. Science 126:
     384–390.
——, and Elizabeth Steig
1964 The city as the portal of the future. Journal of Nursery Education 19:146–153.
Metraux, Rhoda
1955 The consequences of wrongdoing: an analysis of story completions by German
     children. In Childhood in contemporary cultures, Margaret Mead and Martha
     Wolfenstein, eds. Chicago: University of Chicago Press; pp. 306–323; re-
     printed 1963, P124, Chicago: University of Chicago Press.
Miller, Daniel R., and Guy E. Swanson
1965 Social class and motoric orientation. In School children in the urban slum,
     Joan I. Roberts, ed. New York: Hunter College (Project True), pp. 188–199.
Newman, C. Janet, and Othilda Krug
1964 Problems in learning arithmetic in emotionally disabled children." Journal of
     the American Academy of Child Psychiatry 3:413–429.
Neisser, Ulric
1962 Cultural and cognitive discontinuity. In Anthropology and human behavior,
     Thomas Gladwin and William C. Sturtevant, eds. Washington: Anthropologi-
     cal Society of Washington, pp. 54–71.
Parens, Henri, and Alexander A. Weech
1966 Accelerated learning responses in young patients with school problems. Journal
     of the American Academy of Child Psychiatry 5:75–92.
Piaget, Jean
1926 The language and thought of the child. New York: Harcourt Brace Jovanovich.
     reprinted 1960, Meridan M10, Cleveland: World Publishing Co., Inc.
1950 Psychology of intelligence. London: Routledge and Kegan Paul, Ltd.; reprinted
     1963, Patterson, N.J.: Littlefield, Adams & Co.
Ruesch, Jurgen, and Gregory Bateson
1951 Communication: the social matrix of psychiatry. New York: W. W. Norton
     & Co., Inc.
——, and Welden Kees
1956 Nonverbal Communication. Berkeley: University of California Press.
——, and Rodney Prestwood
1950 Communication and bodily disease. In Life stress and bodily disease, Harold G.
     Wolff et al., eds. Baltimore: Williams and Wilkins, Inc.
Sartre, Jean Paul
1964 The words. New York: George Braziller, Inc., reprinted 1966, Crest T883,
     New York: Fawcett Publications, Inc.
Spindler, G. D., ed.
1955 Education and anthropology. Stanford: Stanford University Press.
Swanson, Guy E.
1960 The birth of the gods: the origin of primitive beliefs. Ann Arbor: University
     of Michigan Press.
Tanner, J. M., and Bärbel Inhelder, eds.
1957–1960 Discussions on child development, 4 vols. New York: International Uni-
     versities Press.

Useem, John
    1963 Notes on the sociological study of language. Social Science Research Council Items 17:29–31.
Vygotskii, Lev S.
    1962 Thought and language. Cambridge: Massachusetts Institute of Technology Press.
Weisberg, Paul S., and Kayla J. Springer
    1961 Environmental factors in creative function: a study of gifted children. Archives of General Psychiatry 5:554–564.
Werner, Heinz
    1964 Comparative psychology of mental development, rev. ed. New York: International Universities Press.
Whiting, Beatrice
    1950 Paiute sorcery. New York: Viking Fund Publications in Anthropology, No. 15.
Whiting, John W. M.
    1961 Socialization process and personality. In Psychological anthropology, F. L. K. Hsu, ed. Homewood, Ill.: Dorsey Press.
———, and Irvin Child
    1953 Child training and personality: a cross-cultural study. New Haven: Yale University Press.
Whorf, Benjamin L.
    1947 Science and linguistics. In Readings in social psychology, Theodore M. Newcomb and Eugene L. Hartley, eds. New York: Holt, Rinehart and Winston, Inc.
    1950 Time, space and language. In Culture in crisis, Laura Thompson, ed. New York: Harper & Row, Publishers, Inc., pp. 152–172.
Wieder, Herbert
    1966 Intellectuality: aspects of its development from the analysis of a precocious 4½ year old boy. Psychoanalytic Study of the Child 21:294–323.
Wiener, Harry
    1966 External chemical messengers. I. Emission and reception in man. New York State Journal of Medicine, 66:3153–3170.
Williams, Thomas R.
    1966 Cultural structuring of tactile experience in a Borneo society. American Anthropologist 68:27–39.
Wissler, Clark
    1923 Man and culture. New York: Crowell Collier and Macmillan, Inc.
Zborowski, Mark
    1955 The place of book-learning in traditional Jewish culture. In Childhood in contemporary cultures, Margaret Mead and Martha Wolfenstein, eds. Chicago: University of Chicago Press, pp. 118–149; reprinted 1963, Phoenix P124, Chicago: University of Chicago Press.

5: *On the Importance of the Study of Primate Behavior for Anthropologists*[1]

SHERWOOD L. WASHBURN

My own interest in the study of the behavior of the nonhuman primates has been focused primarily on the understanding it affords of the evolution of man. If one accepts the theory that selection has been the guiding force in evolution, then the biological history of a species must be viewed in terms of the behaviors that made the success possible. A wide variety of techniques and lines of evidence is useful in determining the interrelations of animals and in charting the course of evolution, but interpretation of the reasons for the survival of populations must be sought in their behavior. While the evolutionary approach is useful and offers insights that can be obtained in no other way, interpretation of the course of evolution is always controversial and fraught with speculation. This is especially true in the case of the primates; for example, present estimates of the length of time that the human lineage has been separate from that of the apes vary from 5 million to 50 million years.

The major importance of the study of the behavior of the nonhuman primates does not, however, depend upon any detailed agreement on evolution—it provides a series of contrasts that allows us to see man in better perspective. Just as the nature of one culture or social system is illuminated by comparison to another, so the biosocial nature of our species is brought into perspective by comparison, especially by comparison to the monkeys and apes. In making the comparisons, it should be remembered that the purpose is to understand the biosocial nature of Homo sapiens. For example, the study of the communications systems of monkeys and apes shows how remarkably different language is from non-linguistic systems, but will not help at all in analyzing the differences among languages.

From the point of view of research or of teaching, the study of the social systems of monkeys and apes has certain great advantages over the

[1] Prepared for the National Conference on Anthropology and Education sponsored by the American Anthropological Association, May 1968. I wish to thank David A. Hamburg and Phyllis J. Dolhinow for their advice and help in the preparation of this paper. Supported by a research grant from the National Institutes of Health (No. MH-08623).

study of human culture and society: the behavior is not concealed by houses or clothing, the small size of these groups provides a perspective on the activities of the entire group, and observations frequently can be supplemented by experiments. The initial field studies provide the basic behavioral information. Comparisons of different species suggest interpretations of the significance of the behaviors and, finally, the interpretations can be tested by planned experiments. Ideally, a study begins with the investigator's familiarizing himself with the behavior of the species in the laboratory; second, field observations of a free-ranging group should be carried out with as little disturbance to the group as possible; third, the observer can then check his guesses about the factors influencing behavior by changing the group's behavior through feeding, by the use of drugs, or by altering the social structure. Lastly, the study returns to the laboratory for detailed observations and controlled experiment.

When the whole range of observational and experimental data becomes available for a number of species of primates, it should be possible to develop a model for behavioral research that is more comprehensive than anything presently known. Part of the importance of the study of the behavior of nonhuman primates lies in the possibility of developing such a model for the analysis of behavior, taking full advantage of comprehensive field work and laboratory experiment.

Certainly the most important implications of the studies of the behavior of the nonhuman primates for our understanding of man lie in the future. The long and intensive field studies are a recent development, and it is frequently difficult to determine whether the apparent differences in behavior are real or are the result of sampling or observer bias. For the remainder of this paper, I would like to discuss several topics that are illuminated by contrasting man with the other primates.

WORLD VIEW

Man thinks that what he sees and feels is reality, and anthropologists have been particularly concerned with showing the extent to which these perceptions and feelings, are affected by culture and society, by the individual human being's actual experiences. But this perceived reality is also determined by biology, and it is by no means easy for the human being in a given sociocultural system to see the relative contributions made by biology and experience to his perception of the world. In discussing differences in vision, for instance, it is not enough simply to talk about stereoscopic vision as opposed to monocular vision, with its minimum overlapping of the visual field, and it is difficult to stress adequately the importance of color vision in providing a possibility of a richer view of nature. We are even more bound by our biology than we are limited by culture, and it is hard for us to internalize the notion that our naïve view of the world is a product of the interaction of a uniquely human biology with the external world.

A discussion of sensory input soon reveals that man is not at all unique in his sensory equipment. The sense of smell is much more highly developed in most mammals; many birds have more efficient eyesight; many mammals (rats, dogs, bats, dolphins) can hear sounds of much higher frequency. Man's great adaptive advantage lies in his brain and in the behaviors that it makes possible.

The most important adaptive ability made possible by the brain is language, and the study of the communication systems of the nonhuman primates shows the immense gap that separates man from his nearest living relatives. Human biology makes it easy for man to learn one, or even several languages, and to acquire enormous technical vocabularies with relatively little effort. But even the most minimal linguistic competence lies beyond the power of the monkeys and apes who cannot be taught to talk because they lack the biological base for such learning.

Attainments of such things as a human world view, acquisition of skills, and culture are clearly dependent on the human ability to name, to recall the past, and to consider the future. The adaptive importance of these capacities can be seen distinctly if we consider the communication systems of the nonhuman primates that are socially important but do not have the functions of human language. The comparative approach to the study of language stresses the biology of learning and the adaptive function of what is learned (note the recent reorientation of linguistic theory described by Hymes in this volume).

The human world view assumes the importance of choice and, particularly in academic circles, the importance of self-conscious choice. Yet the brain only makes self-conscious choice possible in situations that have been of adaptive importance to the species. For example, an individual may choose to drive a nail with a hammer and, with practice, may perform this action skillfully, but he has no idea of which muscles, joints, or nerves are involved in the performance of this task. Most of the details of the event are unknown to the person performing the action, and hundreds of scientists are still trying to learn more about how such an action is ordered and controlled by the brain. A person is conscious of his actions and their immediate consequences but not of most of the events occurring in the body that make those actions possible. The adaptive advantage of conscious choice is that it permits a variety of behaviors based on past experience and, through language, knowledge of the experiences of others. Adaptive advantage is translated into differential selection among organisms in the evolutionary process, and so, over the long run, the biological bases of choice, and the actual choices that are made, are functionally related to the environment of the species.

The biological limitations on choice can be shown by experiments on readily available animals, and through direct observation the student may gain an appreciation of his own nature. He may therefore come to view science as a continuing effort to extend the content of the self-conscious part of the world. Input is no longer limited by the senses directly, and processing is no longer limited by such factors as immediate skills, the brain, and tribal tradition.

THE SOCIAL SYSTEM AS AN ADAPTIVE MECHANISM

As mentioned in the introduction, the societies of the nonhuman primates may be viewed in their entirety, their behavior richly sampled, and experimentally analyzed. For example, the nature and importance of the mother-infant relationship may be seen in the field and analyzed in the laboratory. Both kinds of information are essential to our understanding. In the laboratory one cannot see the mother-infant problems that arise when the mother is running full speed or leaping from one tree to another. But in the field one cannot determine the relative contributions of the various factors determining the mother-infant relationship nor the consequences of separation. I believe that data from both field and laboratory offer the student of behavior insights into the nature of the social system that cannot be obtained in any other way. Theories can be immediately tested and long-continued controversies avoided. For example, the importance of early experiences for man has been debated for many years, but this issue has been greatly clarified by experiments with monkeys.

Comparisons of the social groups of monkeys and apes clearly show that the differences are adaptive and are dependent upon biology and learning. Comparisons of the groupings of such forms as gibbons, patas monkeys, and hamadryas baboons show how differently one-male groups may function, and how differently the basic biology of these species expresses itself in social and ecological adaptation. Similar accounts of langurs and chimpanzees might further enrich the comparative data. The comparisons show the importance of the biological nature of the actors in determining the social system, and the social system as the adaptive mechanism that permits the survival of the individuals. The problems become biosocial, and this model can then be used in approaching human problems.

Some illustrations will show where this method differs from that of traditional anthropology and the kinds of discussion that it generates. Basic information is needed as to what the animals do over the period of a whole day. Obviously sleep is a major problem and the sleeping patterns of vervets, patas, hamadryas, and chimpanzees show that this major adaptive problem has been solved in several different ways. These data can lead to a discussion of the importance of predation or of the anatomy and physiology of sleep. The differences between sleeping-sitting and sleeping-lying and the consequences for anatomy, the brain, and social groupings may be suggested. The study of the evolution of sleep, REM state, and dreams offers rich insights for further research. Studying sleep can develop an awareness of what it is to be human: by comparison with other primates, by considering the adaptive importance of the behavior, by watching common animals, and by noting some physiological factors. Sleep is particularly useful for developing two fundamental themes. First, since reliance on common sense is quite inadequate, the techniques of science are necessary to help in understanding an activity such as sleep, which is a daily occurrence.

Moreover, the subject of sleep may be used to show that what might appear to be a simple problem is in reality complex. The duration of the sleeping period is related to activity by night or day, to the time necessary for feeding, to predation (not in general, but the specific local predators), and to circadian rhythms. And there are many questions—why is the human cycle so adaptable? Is this as an evolutionary consequence of the use of fire by our ancestors, or is it a by-product of the greater importance of the cortex? Does evolution account for the existence of so much individual variation in the need for sleep?

Sleep is an example of an activity which, observation shows, takes a great deal of time. Many other such activities will be immediately revealed by observation of the daily round of activities. Walking, feeding, resting, and group life consume many hours every day, and the differences from one species to another offer opportunities for interpretation through comparison and experiment. Mother-infant relationships, play groups, and communications are frequently seen. Behaviors such as dominance, bluffing, and aggression vary with different species and with such factors as social structure and crowding. Such indications of positive affective behavior as grooming are seen frequently. Mating may occur throughout the year or may be seasonal and may vary from frequencies that are so low that observed instances are rare (gibbon and gorilla) to very high frequencies in even quite small groups of baboons or chimpanzees. Starting with simple observations, there are ample data to develop a functional view of society, which includes both biological and social factors.

Although it is best to begin with the common, frequently occurring events, rare events may be of great importance in revealing functions of behavior that would otherwise be missed. The contrast between the behavior of patas, vervets, and baboons when confronted with a predator is manifested in three quite different social structures—all vervets flee, and therefore must be near trees; while female and young patas freeze in the grass, the single adult male pata runs off as obviously as possible, thus decoying the danger from the group; the male baboons confront the danger. Such situations demonstrate how the biology has meaning only because of its function in a particular system. A patas monkey that ran toward a cheetah would be caught and a large baboon that tried to hide in the grass would die.

Although these escape patterns are biosocial, they are not simply instinctive, a mechanical reaction to danger. A baboon that confronts a cheetah flees from a lion. Moreover, in areas in which baboons have been shot at, baboons run down the trees and flee from man on the ground. In this sense, the behavior of every group is unique, and whether the animals resist or flee, either into the trees or on the ground, depends upon the previous experience of its members.

From the field observations, comparisons, and experiments some generalizations may be derived with implications for the understanding of human behavior:

Through evolution each species is so constituted that it easily learns the necessary adaptive behaviors.

These behaviors are pleasurable to the members of the species and are practiced in play.

Fears are easily learned and hard to extinguish. This is highly adaptive, provided that the fear-producing situation is correctly appraised.

Exploration takes place primarily when animals are well fed and secure.

Juveniles see all aspects of adult life and practice all phases of life.

Late juvenile and subadult males cause more disruption than any other class of individuals.

Early experience is so important in forming the basis for abilities that the interaction of the developing individual with the environment at this time may have permanent consequences.

This is not the place to attempt a complete catalog of possible generalization, and it should be stressed that these are not rigid conclusions or laws. They are intended to be topics that are worth discussing to determine what kinds of additional information are needed if they are to be applied to man. For example, the studies of the nonhuman primates suggest that it is the preschool years that are the most important educationally, that the process of education should be fun, and that adult life should be understandable to the child. Any such conclusions might be reached by direct studies of man (for example, see the essays in this volume by Mead and Goodman). But what the studies of the nonhuman primates should do is to raise problems so that the student can learn what it means to be human and to become aware of the implications of human biology and of the interrelations of biology and a social system. I believe that the extension of the comparative method to these small, nonlanguage societies offers many insights, and that, as the field studies become more and more experimental, it will be possible for us to see man in a far better perspective.

SUMMARY

The primate studies demonstrate the importance of understanding the relation of the biology of the actors to the social system. They show the essential relation between the system and the development of the abilities of the actors. They show the profound importance of interpersonal bonds. The brain of an infant monkey, or of a human being, is not a *tabula rasa*: it is the organized, driving seat of abilities offering opportunities, posing problems, and setting limits. The biological potential must be nourished by a mother, developed by peers, and related to society. Each phase of this combined emotional-intellectual development may be analyzed experimentally in the societies of monkeys and apes, and the costs and problems of biosocial development will ultimately be fully understood.

Even now, some conclusions may be stated that I think will stand the test of time. This highly adaptable, emotional, social creature we call man learns best in the early years through emotionally rewarding interpersonal bonds, later through clearly visible, socially important objectives. In education, discipline is no substitute for play. A system that substitutes examinations for life cannot expect to produce organisms that are adapted to the problems of life. The field studies show the relation of organisms to society in simplified form, but, in spite of the vast differences in culture, the fundamental biosocial differences may not be so great. A man's personality is still the product of genes and a very small world. Emotions still drive the human actor, and the price for not understanding man's nature and culture is not only the extremes of riots and war but also a tradition-bound educational system that frustrates the inmates. If man did not have a profound capacity to adapt, youth would have revolted long ago. The cry for reform comes not only from the ghetto but from all we know of primate nature.

SOCIAL
AND INSTITUTIONAL

6: *Handle with Care: Necessary Precautions in the Anthropology of Schools*[1]

HARRY F. WOLCOTT

During those infrequent occasions when anthropologists have gathered to discuss formal education, an outside observer might find himself wanting to ask: Is this the way anthropologists approach other settings in which they study human behavior, or does a discussion of schools evoke a different kind of response? The purpose of this paper is to suggest some crucial ways in which anthropologists *do* fail to apply the methods and perspectives of their discipline in the study of schools in contrast to the more analytical stance that characterizes their approach in other settings.

The title of this paper reflects the essence of the caution—or admonition—that is the message herein: handle the educational setting with care. This is not, however, a request for special treatment. "Handle with care" is a reminder to anthropologists to treat school settings with the same care that they use in their inquiries into human life in settings with which they are less familiar.

Lest this discussion appear to be only a cautionary one in which anthropologists begin to look like the "bad guys," two additional aspects of the relationship of anthropology to schools are also included. One is a brief review of some recurring problems in anthropological fieldwork.

[1] Grateful acknowledgment is expressed to Charles Frantz and George Spindler for their critical reading of earlier drafts of this paper and to Norman Delue for editorial assistance with the present version. The author also wishes to acknowledge the support of CASEA, a national research and development center established under the Cooperative Research Program of the United States Office of Education, during a portion of his time devoted to the preparation of this chapter.

Although the problems identified are not unique to the anthropology of schools, they warrant a critical examination of their effect in the educational setting on both the anthropologist and the educator, for these problems can impose significant restrictions on the oft-touted potential of the anthropology-education liaison. The other aspect is an identification of some possible unrecognized benefits that may accrue to anthropology in making increased use of the schools as research settings. Whether the potential of such benefits can be fully recognized will, of course, reflect the handling of schools in previous encounters with anthropologists.

The impetus for writing this paper came to me as a result of attending the National Conference on Education and Anthropology in Miami Beach, in May 1968. Although my comments extend well beyond the parameters of that meeting, the conference provided both the provocation for the ideas expressed here and a field setting for obtaining illustrative examples of some of the problems in the anthropology of schools. The reader must realize, however, that the proceedings have been drawn upon selectively in order to illustrate the points I wish to discuss. The responsibility for providing a more complete account of the proceedings of the conference has been assumed by others (Gearing 1968).

NECESSARY PRECAUTIONS IN THE ANTHROPOLOGY OF SCHOOLS

The major precaution contained in these remarks has already been made explicit in the title and in the introductory comments: the anthropologist working professionally in any formal educational setting should take substantially the same stance, particularly in terms of careful observation and inquiry into human behavior as it really is, that he adopts in other field settings. The discussion in this section deals with some specific ways in which schools have been or can be subjected to "rough handling" by anthropologists. The list is brief but bold; it is intended as a precautionary note, not an indictment. There are anthropologists who have been extremely sensitive to one or another of these points, but there are probably few who have been sensitive to them all. Indeed, as Anthony Luria suggested during the meetings, we might well look at the hostility of anthropologists toward formal education as a source of data about both anthropologists and schools.

1. Although a rapidly increasing number of anthropologists have evidenced interest in schools, relatively few anthropologists have actually done fieldwork in them. Yet anthropologists belong to a discipline in which fieldwork has traditionally been a prerequisite both to personal validation and to professional commentary. The immediate problem of having so few anthropologists engaged in fieldwork in schools is magnified by the

fact that they have not been reluctant to render opinions and advice on educational matters. This they do both in personal roles and, in curriculum matters, as professional consultants. That anthropologists should take an interest in, or render opinions on, school matters is certainly a right they have as parents, citizens, and anthropologists—but they have an obligation to their audiences to clarify whether they are speaking as informed social scientists or in some other role—not infrequently that of an angry former inmate or zealous reformer. It is unlikely, for example, that the prominent anthropologist who stated in a national teachers' journal that the educator's task is to "join knowledge to loving-kindness in himself and in his pupils" could provide data in support of his statement, regardless of how noble his intent as a humanist. Yet it was his prominence as an anthropologist that obtained him his audience and, presumably, lent an aura of scientific authority to his comments.

Those anthropologists who accept roles as curriculum consultants take a further step by actually intervening in the system. That they respond to requests for assistance, and that they maintain a reserve about their role in curriculum planning, is at once commendable and suspect. The dilemma was illustrated by the comments of an anthropologist at the Miami Beach conference (May 1968) who said at one point in the proceedings, "I don't know anything about school systems," and yet reported later, "We've just finished writing a unit for high schools." When confronted with the implications of the first statement in terms of the second, he explained that in the development of the curriculum unit he had acted only as a subject-matter specialist. Yet here, if in very minor relief, is a problem that in other contexts has often perplexed anthropologists: does one hire out his expertise if he finds himself unclear about, or in opposition to, the goals of his employer? Is an anthropologist justified in acting as a consultant if his covert purpose is to induce change into a system prejudged by him to be in need of it? The broad question involved deals with the ethics of intervention. The problem deserves the same consideration in the school setting that it customarily receives in other contexts.

2. A second type of rough handling occurs as a consequence of making references to schools as though they were a single, monolithic structure. One would expect social scientists to make references to "American schools" with the same caution used in making statements about "American culture." Yet one can find anthropologists making global statements about "the school" that suggest a lack of awareness of both the real differences among types and levels of schools and, equally important, of differences perceived to be important by the students, parents, teachers, administrators, and others whose lives are affected by them.

The problem of treating schools as a monolithic structure is not rampant in the anthropological treatment of schools, but neither is it unknown. Since anthropologists are committed to the study of small and specific communities rather than to entire institutions, their *professional* pronouncements about schools should customarily reflect such boundaries. To the extent that their *personal* pronouncements reflect the same concern with specific cases, anthropologists may find their educator audiences more receptive to their views.

3. Those who regard schools monolithically then proceed to derogate the educative efforts of the schools by assuming them to be dysfunctional unless proven otherwise. Such an assumption creates a bias that detracts from the researcher's usual commitment to assess how schools function rather than to attempt to evaluate whether they "really" accomplish anything. It may be a revelation for a researcher to discover after his first extended period of observation that "the schools aren't as bad as I thought," but such a conclusion provides schoolmen with little new insight. *Don't assume*

One example of this "assumption of dysfunction" at the Miami Beach conference appeared in an all-encompassing comment by a participant, "Everyone agrees, as we did yesterday, that the schools are doing a poor job." As far as I know, we had *not* agreed. The task of social science research in schools is not to prejudge them as bad (or even as good), but rather to help school people and others to see and analyze what does go on in schools. One test that we might use in any discussion of the anthropology of schools is to substitute a comparable social institution or process and to inquire whether the treatment we would accord that institution is comparable to our treatment of education. In a conference on anthropology and law, for example, I assume that attention would be drawn to questions of process—what the system is and how it operates—rather than arguing whether judges, lawyers, the courts, the prisons, or even the prisoners are good or bad. The dialogue between anthropology and education labors under a handicap as long as educators have reason to assume that they are on the defensive or that every educator is to be held accountable for all the shortcomings of all the settings in which education has been institutionalized. *avoid treating each different*

4. The fourth caution concerning rough handling deals with the problem of according different treatment to different statuses within schools. In preparing a brief review of the literature in anthropology and education recently (Wolcott 1967a) I found few studies in which teachers or school administrators received either relatively compassionate or at least dispassionately analytical treatment, and I found fewer studies in which pupils and parents, particularly ethnically different ones, did not receive special, almost "underdog," treatment. The type of treatment accorded different statuses suggests that educators and their pupil- and parent-clients are viewed with different sets of lenses. The set of lenses for looking at teachers and administrators draws attention to the static aspects of long traditions and unfortunate stereotypes. Exceptions are treated as outside the real sample: "We did find *one* good teacher in our study, but. . . ." Parents and pupils are viewed in terms of dynamic qualities

suggestive of action and change, restive toward their present status, or unwitting victims of an oppressed condition. The schools seem always to be "out of joint."

One aspect of this rough handling perplexing to the educator is that anthropologists often appear to ignore the fact that they themselves are teachers. It might serve some advantage if anthropologists interested in formal education would acknowledge more explicitly their kinship within the extended family of educators (as evidenced, for example, by two volumes concerned with the teaching of anthropology, Mandelbaum, et al. 1963). Teacher receptivity both for cooperating in field work and for utilizing anthropological research would certainly not suffer through efforts to recognize common purposes, for there is a persistent belief among teachers that no one can understand the dynamics of a classroom unless he himself has been "on the firing line." Similarly, anthropologists might resist the temptation to treat teachers too severely or to over-generalize about them if they referred occasionally to teachers as "we" instead of "they," even though they maintained their primary identification as researchers. Perhaps Jules Henry's comments and observations about the public schools, penetratingly painful though they were, have commanded an attentive audience among educators because Henry acknowledged (1955, p. 189) that he was a teacher and a part of, not apart from, the social system in which teachers function:

I would like to add that while the data used here place teachers in an inglorious light at times, I intend no fundamental criticism of teachers. I am a teacher myself, and though I am aware of many of our shortcomings, I am conscious also of the degree to which our profession has become the scapegoat of those who would place the blame for our contemporary desperation on teachers. Teachers, parents, and children can rarely be better than the social system of which they are a part.

Even those anthropologists who deny their own roles as teachers cannot afford the luxury of badly handling some statuses within the school's system. At least they cannot do so without jeopardizing their own possibilities in fieldwork and threatening the possible success of future work by colleagues. My own introduction to fieldwork was in studying the contemporary education of a group of Canadian Indian children (Wolcott 1967b). In that setting it was apparent from the very nature of the problem that the teachers and officials of the Indian Affairs Branch would inevitably emerge as the culprits unless I made a conscious attempt both in the field and in writing to treat everyone with objectivity. (It has been observed, moreover, that one can be objective without necessarily being neutral.) Dealing specifically with my problem of what to say about the majority of teachers who have served in the Kwakiutl schools, I received this cogent bit of advice in a personal communication from anthropologist Helen Codere: "The real issue, I suppose, revolves around the fact that if anthropologists are known to specify derogatory things about even your own worst enemy, you wonder mistrustfully whether they might do the same to you." There is no reason to assume that every piece that anthropologists write about schools will be patient and understanding, and there is no way to ensure that anthropologists will always be objective. Both anthropology *and* education stand to benefit, however, if instances of prejudicial handling can be shown to be only instances rather than customary treatment.

5. The problem of doing fieldwork *in one's own society* rather than in a strange and foreign one suggests a final precaution. The universal nature of schooling in American society makes this problem universal for anthropologists, for while they may have avoided prolonged exposure to retirement communities, street corners, relocation centers, or Indian reservations, the very fact that they are anthropologists assures a long and thorough contact with formal education. Achieving a competent anthropology of American schools is complicated by a twofold problem: one, having to make the obvious obvious; and two, recognizing what it is that the observer does and does not know of his own culture.

The problem of "making the obvious obvious" is that the novelty that characterizes the entry into a new field setting has probably been eroded for the anthropologist embarking upon a study in the schools by some twenty to forty years of participation in a variety ranging from Sunday Schools to seminars, and for a variety of subjects from phonics to functionalism. The tendency of anthropological accounts to dwell on differences hints at the difficulty of observing, recording, and reporting on shared aspects of behavior where anthropologists and subject hold similar expectations (see the footnote by H. S. Becker to the paper in this volume by Wax-and-Wax).

The anthropologist may find it difficult to force into consciousness such "obvious" data as the fact that boys and girls at school use different rooms for toileting, that a school is administered from an office, that instructional supplies are separated from maintenance supplies, that desk and table heights change with pupil size but doorknob and window heights do not, and so forth. Imbued with school culture though he may be, the anthropologist brings some unique qualifications to observing in schools. These qualifications may include formal training in techniques of observation. They *should* include fieldwork in cross-cultural settings—a fairly good case can be made for insisting that cross-cultural experience be a prerequisite to an ethnographic study in one's own culture. Furthermore, the anthropologist's professional commitments to observe behavior as it *is* (the schoolman is often preoccupied with what *should be*) and to see individuals as interacting members of cultural systems, enable him to unmask assumptions, "discover" hypotheses, and identify paradoxes or unanticipated consequences in the attainment of institutional goals that the educator might never become aware of on his own.

Merely because he is interested in the study of culture, however, is no reason to assume that the anthropologist's professional activities have perforce led him to any great understanding of his own cultural system. This caution has been sounded before (Spindler 1955, p. 20).

The anthropologist's experience with small and relatively integrated societies sometimes gives him an extraordinary naivete about the complex relations in our own society—a society he himself may have escaped from—into anthropology. He fails to see complications and looks for integrating features, consistencies, and values where there are none. And as a consequence he may make outlandish pronouncements as to what educators should or should not do.

By simply calling attention to this problem, I may not do anything to alleviate it, although the problem may become acute if anthropologists continue to turn more of their attention to studies within their own society. The true caution, to carry through with the analogy of this commentary, is that the educator should realize that sometimes the rough handling he gets is because no one knows any better.

II. SOME RECURRING PROBLEMS FOR ANTHROPOLOGISTS CRUCIAL TO THE ANTHROPOLOGY OF SCHOOLS

Under four major headings in this section I have identified problem areas that pervade the work of the cultural anthropologist in any setting but are especially important in the anthropology of schools. The problem areas are (1) gaining entree and maintaining rapport, (2) reporting back, (3) acquiring prestige and status in anthropology and education, and (4) explicating method. Although these problems do not have perfect solutions, more will be gained by addressing them directly than by ignoring them in the hope that they will go away. There is no reason why a discussion of these problems should not provide the basis for a useful dialogue between anthropologists and educators.

Gaining entree and maintaining rapport: The term "public," used as an adjective, carries a connotation of availability and access; the very point of having public museums, public libraries, or public parks is that one does not need to obtain permission to enter them. Public schools, as those who endeavor to do research in them are repeatedly reminded, do not interpret their obligation to be public in the same way. No simple formula serves as a guide for gaining access to schools from the outside. In communities where schools are under stress, the entrance to any specific school may be physically guarded by administrators, police, pupils, parents, teachers, or community demonstrators, and not unlikely by some combination of these, each partially on guard against the others. But such drama obscures the fact that outsiders never have automatic rights of access to schools anywhere, and that in many school districts even a demonstrator may be more welcome than a researcher.

A researcher is scrutinized by the subjects of his research in relation to the kind of information he seeks. The resistance of school systems to large-scale, nationally recognized and federally funded research projects only hints at the extremes of resistance an anthropologist might expect to encounter in requesting access to a school district for the intensive study that characterizes his discipline.[2] A field-study approach in the schools can become *more* threatening as it proceeds, since the constant surveillance over a long period of time and the lack of an explicit statement of research purposes may put the researcher at odds with a public-relations-conscious school administrator. In my own field study of the elementary school principalship (Wolcott 1970, n.d.) I was not excluded from an administrative gathering in the school district until the twenty-fifth month of the project. On that occasion, however, so many reasons were offered by the superintendent of the school district rationalizing why I should not be present that I expressed surprise that permission had been granted for the study in the first place. He replied that he wished it had not.

Whatever the reasons, there appear to be at present whole categories of schools reluctant to undergo anthropological treatment. In this volume Murray Wax notes:

My own experience indicates that the decision to investigate a school system may trigger all manner of adverse reactions from a power elite and that these reactions can travel surprisingly far, quickly and emphatically.

Among professional groups such as educators, where members tend to exhibit a great sensitivity to differences in hierarchical status, it is important for the fieldworker to recognize and to try to assess what effect the level at which he enters the system will have on the information he is able to obtain. Researchers easily become overidentified with school administrators, for example, because administrators maintain formal control over entry into schools. A glowing endorsement from the Superintendent of Schools or the Dean of the School of Education may be a handicap in beginning a study of student or teacher subcultures. Yet, it also may be the only way.

Inadvertently, the researcher in schools may find himself overidentified with the administration in another way. The techniques most frequently used by fieldworkers in the collection of descriptive data—observing, note-taking, inquiring, and probing—are similar to the formal data-gathering

[2] Consider, for example, the 1966 survey of educational opportunity, the "Coleman Report," in which complete data were obtained for only 59 percent of the sample of 4,000 U.S. public schools. Although authorized by Congress and initiated by the U.S. Office of Education, the survey reportedly "was met with suspicion and slander in many communities, and school systems in several major cities refused to participate" (Nichols 1966, p. 1312).

techniques that administrators and supervisors use in the preparation of evaluative statements of school personnel for purposes of promotion and tenure. It is difficult not to look officious when carrying a notebook into a classroom; it is even more difficult not to look like an evaluator or supervisor while taking notes during a classroom lesson. It is important to realize that schoolmen, especially teachers, are often extremely sensitive to being the subjects of observations, and that their previous experiences with observers may be associated with unpleasantness, anxiety, and even hostility.

A related problem, and a more familiar one to the cultural anthropologist, is whether anyone in a system has the authority to "volunteer" the cooperation of subordinates for participation in research. Like tribal leaders in a host of other settings, school administrators have been known to promise more cooperation than they could deliver. Official sanction by the headman is a customary prerequisite in conducting field research, but enlisting the cooperation of subjects only *begins* there.

Reporting back: Perhaps there was a period dominated by "hit-and-run" anthropology, a time when the fieldworker felt no anguish about publishing his research account of a group of people he had studied. The conditions of such an approach assume (1) the subjects of the study are unlikely ever to see the report, and (2) it does not matter anyway because the fieldworker never intends to return to or confront his subjects again. Certainly such conditions do not characterize contemporary fieldwork, even when conducted in relatively isolated and distant settings (Barnes 1967, p. 205):

> Books find their way far into the bush and if they are not always well understood they are easily misunderstood.

With the enthusiasm for interdisciplinary studies evident in education today, anthropologists express concern for the possibility that even the wildest of conjectures shared only among a group of intimate colleagues may find its way prematurely into the domain of education. What use do educators make of the "findings" of anthropology? What constitutes a "finding?" During the Miami Beach meetings caution was expressed several times about the kind of implications that might be prematurely drawn by educators from what were only intended as conjectures and questions. This is part of the problem of feedback and the diffusion of information between disciplines.

Feedback is more than an ethical problem in fieldwork. It becomes an urgent problem in the immediate relationship between observer and subject. No researcher in a natural setting ever achieves the role of the completely unobtrusive observer. His very presence, his attention to some aspects of behavior more than others, his casual probes—everything the observer does calls attention to some aspects of behavior to the exclusion of others. Every incidence for calling attention has the potential for causing anxiety, self-consciousness, and even changed behavior on the part of his subjects. Overreacting is an obvious way to provide observer inter- ference and feedback, but underreacting can have the same effect by the *failure* to laugh, to ask, or to appear interested.

One can anticipate certain almost inevitable questions during a field study in the schools. At least once the fieldworker must be able to answer the question, "Why did you choose us?" Not unlikely he will confront a protoanthropologist or two among his educator subjects and will hear, "I took a few anthropology courses myself, so you can level with me. What are you *really* here to study?"

The field researcher characteristically attempts to minimize feedback and to hold himself aloof as part of his stance as a scientist. In the edu- cational setting, this stance may be admired intellectually but it will not necessarily be rewarded. Unlike the native informant who may find it sufficiently satisfying to have an eager audience for his stories and legends, and who at best may only want to know "How is it with your people?" the educator-subject couples his academic interest in the intellectual and never-ending processes of research with an impending sense of urgency regarding the need for immediate action. The pupils continue to arrive everyday; the school cannot declare a moratorium on its efforts and wait for a research report. Wherever the researcher decides to burrow in, those who have to carry the responsibility for programs and pupils are going to beset him with their need to know NOW. "How are we doing?" "What *should* our role be?" "How would *you* handle this?" The anthropologist who hears the pleas of educators to help them with their problems may find it exceedingly difficult to heed Solon Kimball's caution against the proclivity to conduct educational reform under the guise of educational research.

The anthropologist in the school faces other problems related to report- ing his findings, problems that can be especially acute if he accepts funding support from the educational establishment. One dilemma is that the anthropologist probably does not want the educator to tell him what the problem is for him to study. The problem that interests the educator may be only remotely related to the problem that the anthropologist identifies as the proper focus of his research. In this regard the educa- tional setting is subject to the same "frustration, misunderstanding, and lack of good communication between administrators and scientists" that Foster (1962, p. 241) reports to be characteristic of the history of anthro- pological participation in developmental programs. Explicit statements of mutual expectations might alleviate such misunderstanding or at least lead to more precise delimitations of rights and duties.

A second dilemma in reporting arises from the fact that the anthro- pologist has at least two rather different audiences immediately interested in his commentary, one audience composed of his fellow anthropologists, another composed of professional educators, each with a set of expectations that is in some ways antithetical to the other. Anthropologist Alfred G. Smith (1964) has used the terms "peers" and "patrons" to distinguish the two audiences and has called attention to their differing expectations. Among the expectations held by the patron groups Smith includes "a high ratio of explanation to information," value-oriented formulations presented in terms of good and better, and goal-directed explanations committed to future improvement, extending in some cases to the belief that the future determines the present. Peer expectations, by contrast, include a constant call for more data, a reluctance to include the study of values within the domain of scientific inquiry, and a preference for explanations in causes. The anthropologist will do well to recognize that his educator audience may expect a different kind of report from that which he customarily presents to his colleagues. Meeting the expectations of different audiences is not resolved, however, by simply preparing the report for the patron group immediately at hand. Anthropologists need also to be read and reviewed within their own ranks, a need that they sometimes fail to allow for in accepting consultant roles.

Acquiring prestige and status in anthropology and education: Professionally trained anthropologists are a relatively scarce commodity. They find themselves in a seller's market, not constrained by professional overcrowding in their choices of problems. In choosing research problems they can heed motives of personal interest or reflect on the relative status assigned by their colleagues to differing arenas of inquiry along with such pragmatic considerations as sources of funding.

Those anthropologists who are interested in using schools as settings for research activities are usually caught in a cross-fire of competing demands on their time from variations in their own wide-ranging interests as well as the variety of their professional commitments. As one anthropologist recently commented to a group of educators, "Anthropologists have so many and such widely varied interests among themselves that it is a wonder they ever talk with others like educators." Aside from the general lack of trained anthropologists to meet the opportunities confronting them, there are some special problems in the relationship of anthropology and education which, although not unique only to this interdisciplinary liaison, are critical enough to warrant review here, for they tend to serve as factors militating against the more rapid development of anthropology and education as an area of major interest among anthropologists.

One factor is that education is an "applied" field. Anthropologists, like most social scientists, show a deference to problems and appointments in "basic" rather than in "applied" research. The relatively few journal articles dealing with anthropology and education circulated among their colleagues have appeared mostly in *Human Organization,* a substantial journal but one heavily weighted toward problems in applied anthropology. As for articles on anthropology and education appearing in the prestigious

journal of basic research, the *American Anthropologist*, except for a few
book reviews, one brief exchange (King 1964), two articles dealing with
conceptual styles of school children (Hill 1964, Cohen 1969), and a discussion about teaching anthropology to ninth graders (Bohannon et al.
1969), an observation (Spindler 1955, p. 15) made several years ago
continues to hold true today:

> Edgar L. Hewett's articles "Anthropology and Education" (1904) and
> "Ethnic Factors in Education" (1905) in the *American Anthropologist* were
> the first and almost the last contributions of their kind in that journal.

A second militating factor is the questionable legitimacy or prestige of
education as an intellectual discipline. I have heard anthropologists comment that they and their colleagues have an aversion to "hyphenated"
fields, yet there seems to be no aversion to such combinations as medical
anthropology or legal anthropology. Perhaps the problem is not so much
that anthropologists are loath to study education but that educators,
unlike doctors or lawyers, expect anthropologists to join actively with them
in research rather than merely to make themselves available as subjects
of the research of others. Anthropologists prefer to *study* other groups,
not to join them.

The fact that educators (as well as a handful of sociologists and psychologists) have joined anthropologists in contributing to the developing
body of literature in the field of anthropology and education has helped
to create a noticeable increase in organizational activity and academic
interest in this special field (cf. the rapid development of the Council on
Anthropology and Education subsequent to the annual meeting of the
American Anthropology Association in 1968). These educators are primarily researchers whose initial commitment is to education but whose
inquiries have drawn them into association with anthropological methods
and perspectives. Their efforts have provided both payoff and problem
for the field of anthropology and education. The payoff is that they are
successfully drawing upon their own (sometimes limited) anthropological
training to bring relevant approaches and new perspectives into educational research. They present a problem because no one, anthropologist or
educator alike, is quite sure who—or what—constitutes sufficient anthropological sophistication to be acceptable as a professional in this field.
These educators-cum-anthropologists search for terms by which to describe themselves: educational anthropologist? anthropologist of education? anthropologically trained educator? and for terms to describe their
field of endeavor, from Montessori's "pedagogical anthropology" to today's
educational anthropology, ethnopedagogy (Burger 1968), educanthropol-
ogy (Brameld and Sullivan 1961) or anthropology *of, in,* or *and* education.
Individually their unsure status seems neither to have hindered their efforts
nor detracted from their results, but collectively their presence serves as
evidence of an unresolved dilemma in establishing criteria for assessing

eligibility and/or competence in anthropology and education if it is to become a legitimate cross-disciplinary field.

Explicating method: The word "method" did not make its way into the discussions at the Miami Beach meeting until the next to last session. At that time someone made a cautious recommendation that although we "probably are all using the same methods," it might be a good idea to make these methods explicit. Anthropologists by tradition have seldom been explicit about their research methods; viewed against some of the "powerful" methods that characterize the physical sciences, or some experimental and statistical laboratory techniques, their reticence may have seemed understandable. George Spindler once dismissed (1955, p. 13) the idea that there existed a set of esoteric methods used only by anthropologists and especially relevant to educational research in a single sentence: "As for methodology, it is doubtful that many clear claims to contributions can be made by anthropology, other than in a devotion to informants and informal participant observation." There are, however, compelling reasons at present why the methods used by anthropologists, whether unique to their discipline (e.g., genealogical, linguistic, or "formal" ethnographic methods) or shared by other social scientists (e.g., participant-observation, interviewing) need to be reviewed carefully and critically for educator audiences.

Educators themselves can take the responsibility for conducting much of the research needed in their field. It is ingenuous to fail to recognize the large number of people engaged today in educational research, the resources at their command, or the level of research scholarship that can be attained. However, the corollaries of holding educators responsible for conducting the bulk of educational research are that they must be competent with the methods they are using and that they must be able to recognize when the methods of one or another discipline are appropriate for the problems at hand. Actually they need more than this, they need a validating footnote for embarking upon studies utilizing relevant nonexperimental research approaches like those characteristic of field studies, or for lending moral support for conducting in-depth studies of single cases instead of confining all their efforts to monumental surveys and rigidly designed experiments. Education research has been so dominated by a pigeon-and-probability persuasion that educators sometimes ignore their intuition and common sense in their approach to the real problems of schools. They need to hear (as in the essays in this volume by Leacock, Horton, Henry, Wax-and-Wax) that one way an anthropologist would find out what goes on in a school or classroom is to go observe it—day after day after day.

Although few educational researchers ever have the opportunity to extend their own research experience into radically different societies, they do not lack the opportunities for extensive *in situ* observation, and they do not lack the necessity for doing enough unstructured observing to be able to put their own work and the role of formal education into broad perspective. They do need opportunities to review anthropological field methods to understand exactly what the limits of each method are and when each may or may not be appropriate. Like cultural anthropologists, educational researchers also need to review which of the traditional field methods developed essentially for describing small preliterate societies in strange lands are appropriate for describing and analyzing contemporary societies in familiar urban settings.

III. WHAT THE SCHOOLS CAN DO FOR ANTHROPOLOGY

Handled with care, the schools have provided and will continue to provide some important benefits to individual anthropologists and to anthropology as a discipline. Several such benefits are described in this concluding section.

Audience: Educators provide a receptive patron audience and an important market for the products and services that anthropologists provide. There are other such audiences for anthropologists, but like any special group this one has some distinct advantages. Educators are eternally eager and interested to hear the pronouncements of any social scientist who will address himself to their problems; those anthropologists who have answered requests to lecture or to conduct workshops for teachers may have felt at times that they have opened a Pandora's Box of speaking and teaching invitations. An anthropologist somewhat at odds with his own culture and new to audiences of teachers may find rather heady wine in their masochistic tendency toward self-effacement (cf. Landes 1965, pp. 19, 193–196); hopefully he will not limit his efforts to castigating teachers and administrators simply because they have come to expect it in the past.

The fact that the financial resources available to the educator audience for both research and teacher training did increase so dramatically in the past decade certainly served to increase the popularity of education as an arena for research. Even within anthropology circles there were accusations that some anthropologists had "sold out" to high bidders rather than to high purposes, and that others could be "bought" when the price was right. There is no doubt that patron audiences with fat purses are occasionally going to be bilked; anthropologists themselves will have to aid in monitoring and identifying inadequate performances.[3]

Anthropology continues to hold a small but significant place in teacher-training programs and in graduate schools of education. If it exists at all,

[3] The now terminated "Culture of the Schools" project might provide an interesting starting point for critical examination. How and why did it come into being? What were its objectives? What were the outcomes?

however, the chair designated for the anthropologist on the faculty of education is usually an empty one, for even where the place is recognized, the position goes unfilled. In the absence of professional anthropologists to take an active part in the training of educators, a growing body of specialized literature can be drawn upon as an alternative to accomplish this purpose. The interest and receptivity of the book market for such material is illustrated by the appearance of four publications since 1955 with essentially the same anthropology and education title (Spindler, ed. 1955; Gruber, ed. 1961; Kneller 1965; Nicholson 1968). Teachers and in-service programs have recently been recognized as special audiences for preparing introductory statements about cultural anthropology (Pelto 1965; Sady 1969). Two new and complementary monograph series have recently been inaugurated, one to provide case studies of the educational process in a variety of cross-cultural settings (Spindler and Spindler, eds. 1967), and the other addressed to a wide variety of topics under the broad rubric of anthropology and education (Kimball, ed. 1968). Increasing attention continues to be given to the writings of anthropologists both in educational journals and, especially, in the ubiquitous collections of readings prevalent in the field of education.[4] Whether in literature or in person, the essential contribution of anthropologists in the training of teachers and administrators is directed to fostering their sensibilities as observers of the influences of the various cultural systems that are brought together in the formal setting of the school.

As discussed earlier, the methods of ethnographic field research are also receiving more attention in education research (cf. Sindell 1969). It seems inevitable that anthropologists will be invited more frequently to train educational researchers in relevant field methods. One of the recommendations growing out the the Miami Beach conference was that plans be developed for a summer institute to give concentrated research training in the field of anthropology and education for both anthropologists and other researchers. Educational researchers have already anticipated this training need and have conducted a research training seminar, "Anthropology Field Methods in the Study of Education," offered in conjunction with the annual meetings of the American Education Research Association in 1968 and 1969.

Field sites: There are reported to be almost 90,000 elementary schools and more than 30,000 secondary schools operating in the United States today. Even if only a fraction of these institutions are amenable to anthropological research, here is a vital source of field site possibilities for research and for the training of researchers. The schools, of course, have

---

[4] In this regard, it is interesting to note how frequently the same few anthropologists, and even the same few articles, appear in anthologies in education. Spindler (1955, p. 18) called attention to this phenomenon fourteen years ago and, except perhaps for the addition of his own name and that of Jules Henry, the list of favorites he identified remains substantially unchanged: "Kluckhohn, Mead, Benedict, Davis, West (Carl Withers), and Warner are cited in great disproportion to all others."

always been around; from time to time anthropologists need to be reminded of them. The prognosis for future research in anthropology is that there may be a decline in the opportunities to conduct research abroad and an increase in research inside the nation and into contemporary and pressing social problems (Franz 1968; pp. 8–12). While schools are special kinds of human institutions, and while they do present special problems for researchers (cf. Khleif 1969), their great number and wide distribution, their sometimes-receptiveness, their links with the communities and subcultures in which they are located, and their constantly changing membership all serve to make them attractive sites for research into human behavior.

Their very proximity to departments of anthropology should make schools especially attractive as research settings. The life of the college professor can make inordinate demands on personal time, and many an anthropologist who thinks of himself as an active ethnographer of the human scene may in fact be drawing on rather limited opportunities for fieldwork during his own lifetime. In this regard I recall a recurring feeling I had whenever I encountered the anthropologists on my own campus while I was engaged in fieldwork for my study, "The Ethnography of a Principalship" (Wolcott n.d.). For all the exotic or at least distant places they cite among their area specialties, most of them were limited at the time of our encounters to the research potential of their offices or the library. My field site, by contrast, was only a few minutes drive from the campus.

Cultural processes in schools: Schools are not only geographically convenient but are particularly appropriate settings for research in cultural processes in certain ways:

Schools provide access for learning about American society and for identifying some of the paradoxes that inevitably occur between real and ideal values in specific cultural settings. Education reflects culture, and American public education reflects American culture. Yet one cannot be oblivious to observations such as Willard Waller's comment years ago (Waller 1932) that the schools are "museums of virtue," or to the fact that one does not get an adequate portrait of American society by studying American schools. The schools reflect and teach a *selective* set of American cultural attitudes and beliefs rather than a cross-section of them (see Khleif's essay in this volume). Thus the schools provide a laboratory for the study of the conscious attempt to select and to transmit a limited and idealized set of cultural norms, as well as opportunities for studying the institutional handling of value conflicts and of shifts in value patterns. Central as this idea of a selective and sometimes goal-defeating process of cultural transmission is to understanding either American society or American public education, few writers have described and analyzed elements of it from an anthropological perspective.

Schools provide a setting for the study of culture conflict and of the domination and submission of various subcultures. Where the school operates with ethnic minorities who are not oriented toward the pervasive and oft-indicted "dominant middle-class values," the school provides a field site for observing both the problems and consequences of cultural conflict (see the essays in this volume by Thomas-and-Wahrhaftig, Henry, Wax-and-Wax). The schools in such settings can be studied as an acculturative agent; sometimes school people are quite explicit about taking roles as acculturators. Conversely, from the perspective of the pupils in school, acculturation warrants consideration as an educational variable.

By his attention to what and how the individual learns to become a functioning member of his society, how he becomes "enculturated," the anthropologist necessarily takes a broader view than the schoolman of "learning," and of the conditions under which learning takes place. Enculturation perhaps ultimately is *the* dynamic aspect of culture, for it is in the process of incorporating new members into a group that shared and patterned ways of behaving become distinguishable from idiosyncratic ones. "Every teacher, whether mother's brother or Miss Humboldt of Peavey Falls, reenacts and defends the cultural drama as experienced" (Spindler 1955, p. 14). Education, then, is central to culture viewed as a process. The anthropologist's attention to all the cultural influences that shape the role of the child (cf. Kimball 1963) can provide provocative data for the educator. It is also the central stuff of cultural anthropology (as evident in the essay by Cohen in this volume).

School systems provide excellent arenas for studying topics of special interest to cultural anthropologists, such as status and hierarchy, male and female roles (e.g., the feminine setting in which early formal education occurs), modes of reward and punishment utilized in the classroom system of social control, processes of recruiting and socializing new pupil and teacher personnel, and the consequences of formal instruction, both anticipated and unanticipated. In chapter 1 of this volume, Murray and Rosalie Wax describe one such process to which we might draw attention, the process by which young persons are "transformed" into teachers. The importance of the period of time between the beginning of student teaching and the conclusion of the first year of teaching in the public schools has been recognized as a period of intense socialization in which anthropological models from other settings (e.g., rites of passage, cultural compression) might provide a valuable analytical perspective (cf. Frantz, ed., 1967).

Because the problems faced by school people are current and pressing, their questions provide the anthropologist with the opportunity to apply his analytical lessons in terms of real and immediate problems, and to extend his understanding in the interest of promoting human welfare. If anthropologists are going to work increasingly within the context of their own society, school studies will provide opportunities for adapting, developing, or testing methods that are suitable for the study of complex societies and for studying subcultures within the institutionalized settings. Sherwood

Washburn alluded during the Miami Beach meetings to the possibilities for developing new and "experimental" methods in anthropology through the work of anthropologists in schools, methods at once more powerful than some of the traditional methods of cultural anthropology (e.g., comparative methods) and more relevant as a basis for making policy recommendations affecting the lives of many children.

Finally, for the anthropologist interested in cultural dynamics, the schools provide a remarkable but not often recognized opportunity for the study of stability in the face of change. How and why do schools manage to remain so similar and so unchanging in spite of the impact of forces for change in the social environment surrounding them? What is the nature of the cultural "ballast" that so effectively stabilizes the educational institution?

Anthropologists have an unusual opportunity at present for studying an instance of cultural dynamics in the high school by observing the diffusion and assimilation of the new curriculum materials developed by their own Anthropology Curriculum Study Project. In this instance the anthropologists have a precise record of the material as initially introduced. After a few years, which of the curriculum materials developed will have remained intact as originally developed? What will have been dropped, what will have been adapted? As the materials are diffused through "generations" of teachers and students, will they eventually come to look more, or less, like other social studies materials?

But this is only one aspect of change, and perhaps curriculum changes are not the best processes to observe in order to study stability and change within the formal educational setting. Anthropologists could also address themselves to broader questions of persistence regarding the organization of schools. What accounts for the persistent ways of organizing pupils and teachers? What accounts for the tendency of the educational "establishment" to seek out innovations and then to literally smother rather than nurture them? Here is an aspect of formal education that has received almost no attention from anthropologists, yet the process of schooling presents a remarkable laboratory for the study of change and the resistance to change.

Even if the relationship between anthropology and education remains as tenuous as it has seemed in the past, there continue to be benefits to be gained from the bond that does exist. The same assumption that has provided a basis for previous conferences and for the meeting at Miami Beach underlies this paper: anthropology and education have something relevant to say to each other; each discipline will fare best in that continuing dialogue by recognizing the other's integrity as well as its limitations.

REFERENCES

Barnes, J. A.
    1967 Some ethical problems in modern fieldwork. *In* Anthropologists in the field,
         Jongmans, D. G. and Peter C. W. Gutkind, eds. The Netherlands, Royal Van
         Gorcum Ltd.
Bohannon, Paul, Merwyn S. Garbarino, and Earle W. Carson
    1969 An experimental ninth-grade anthropology course. American Anthropologist
         71:409–420.
Brameld, Theodore and Edward B. Sullivan
    1961 Anthropology and education. Review of Educational Research 31:70–79.
Burger, Henry G.
    1968 Ethno-pedagogy: a manual in cultural sensitivity, with techniques for improv-
         ing cross-cultural teaching by fitting ethnic patterns. Albuquerque, New Mexico:
         Southwest Cooperative Educational Laboratory, Inc.
Cohen, Rosalie A.
    1969 Conceptual styles, culture conflict, and nonverbal tests of intelligence. Ameri-
         can Anthropologist 71:828–856.
Foster, George M.
    1962 Traditional cultures: and the impact of technological change. New York: Harper
         & Row, Publishers, Inc.
Frantz, Charles
    1968 The current milieu and the immediate future of U.S. anthropology. Washing-
         ton, D.C.: American Anthropological Association, Fellow Newsletter, May.
——, ed.
    1967 Proceedings of a conference on anthropology, education, and the schools. Wash-
         ington, D.C.: May 19–20. 18 pp. Mimeo.
Gearing, Frederick O., ed.
    1968 Proceedings: the national conference on anthropology and education. Wash-
         ington, D.C.: Program in Anthropology and Education of the American An-
         thropology Association. 323 pp. Lithographed.
Gruber, Frederick C., ed.
    1961 Anthropology and education. Philadelphia: University of Pennsylvania Press,
         The Martin G. Brumbaugh Lectures in Education.
Henry, Jules
    1955 Culture, education, and communications theory. *In* Education and anthro-
         pology, George D. Spindler, ed. Stanford, Cal.: Stanford University Press
Hill, Shirley
    1964 Cultural differences in mathematical concept in learning. American Anthro-
         pologist 66:201–222. Special Publication, Transcultural Studies in Cognition.
Khleif, Bud B.
    1969 Issues in anthropological field-work in schools. Paper presented at the annual
         meeting of the American Anthropological Association. New Orleans, Novem-
         ber 21.
Kimball, Solon T.
    1963 Cultural influences shaping the role of the child. *In* Education and culture:
         anthropological approaches. George D. Spindler, ed. New York: Holt, Rine-
         hart and Winston, Inc.
——, ed.
    1968 Anthropology and education (a series). New York (Columbia University):
         Teachers College Press.
King, A. Richard
    1964 Comments on Jordheim and Olsen's use of a non-verbal test of intelligence in
         the Pacific Islands Trust Territory. American Anthropologist 66:640–644.
Kneller, George F.
    1965 Educational anthropology: an introduction. New York: John Wiley and Sons,
         Inc.
Landes, Ruth
    1965 Culture in American education. New York: John Wiley and Sons, Inc.

Mandelbaum, David G., Gabriel W. Lasker, and Ethel M. Albert, eds.
  1963a The teaching of anthropology. American Anthropological Association, Memoir 94.
  1963b Resources for the teaching of anthropology. American Anthropological Association. Memoir 95.
Nichols, Robert C.
  1966 Schools and the disadvantaged. Science 154:1312–1314.
Nicholson, Clara K.
  1968 Anthropology and education. Columbus, Ohio: Charles E. Merrill Publishing Company, Foundations of Education Series.
Pelto, Pertti J.
  1965 The study of anthropology. Columbus, Ohio: The Charles E. Merrill Social Science Seminar Series.
Sady, Rachel Reese
  1969 Perspectives from anthropology. New York (Columbia University): Teachers College Press.
Sindell, Peter S.
  1969 Anthropological approaches to the study of education. Review of Educational Research 39:593–605.
Smith, Alfred G.
  1964 The Dionysian innovation. American Anthropologist 66:251–265.
Spindler, George D.
  1955 Anthropology and education: an overview. In Education and anthropology, George D. Spindler, ed. Stanford, Cal.: Stanford University Press.
———, and Louise Spindler, eds.
  1967 Case studies in education and culture (a series). New York: Holt, Rinehart and Winston, Inc.
Waller, Willard W.
  1932 The sociology of teaching. New York: John Wiley and Sons, Inc.
Wolcott, Harry F.
  1967a Anthropology and education. Review of Educational Research 37:82–95.
  1967b A Kwakiutl village and school. New York: Holt, Rinehart and Winston, Inc.
  1970 An ethnographic approach to studying school administrators. Human Organization 29.
  n.d. The elementary school principal: notes from a field study. In Education and cultural process: approaches to an anthropology of education, George D. Spindler, ed. Holt, Rinehart and Winston, Inc. forthcoming.

7: *Comments on the Science of Teaching*

PAUL GOODMAN

In a sense there cannot be teaching at all, since learning must start from the learner's intrinsic interests and needs, which provide the energy for the Gestalt of what is learned and assimilated as second-nature. Because of this, Carl Rogers denies that there can be teachers at all, although people do learn.

Attempts at teaching—either to provide "motivation" or to provide experience not meeting intrinsic needs—can be positively harmful. Children learn to speak excellently where no formal attempt is made to teach them, but parents and peers provide a milieu of the code that will be picked up by the child because of his own predispositions. On the other hand, the teaching of reading in many cases seems to prevent the learning of reading, and in the majority of cases it results in the development of superficial reading-skill and wooden writing. Most normal children, not in an underprivileged urban milieu, would probably pick up the reading-and-writing code anyway by the age of nine or ten, without formal teaching (here, compare Mead's discussion in this volume).

To learning, the child brings: exploring, questions, aping, taking part, coping, and sociability. "Teachers" can meet the child by answering questions, making the environment fairly safe and copable, making it authentic and relevant to the child's life, providing good personal models, and being sociable.

There is no need at all for a preset "curriculum" in the elementary years (to age twelve); trying to meet the child's developing interests is sufficient. The important task is not to motivate but to avoid discouraging the child's intrinsic motivations.

TYPES OF "TEACHING"

1. Training—processing—instruction (in the sense of Skinner's operant conditioning):

This is a process of excluding all alternative motion or motive (by isolation or punishment) that does not lead to the programmer's goal. Suffering inevitable defeat in his own desires, the subject identifies with the experimenter and temporarily takes on his motions.

Such conditioning is labile, and as Kurt Goldstein has demonstrated, is lost at any negative reinforcement. This kind of learning should be contrasted with that which becomes "second-nature" and is never lost, e.g., riding a bicycle.

Most successful examination-passing is to be interpreted as follows: the real-life situation of the student is the need to pass; what is "learned" is a means to this end, and is forgotten as soon as the need vanishes.

a) Sometimes incidental learning occurs during the training, when the program happens to touch upon an intrinsic need. My hunch is that very many people who have really learned to read and write did so by being processed in the code during the first grades, and then really learned to read with their own books at their own pace and according to their own interest (again, compare Mead's presentation of a similar view in this volume).

b) Processing can also look like learning when it meets the intrinsic need to don the social uniform and be like the others.

2. The most natural kind of learning is an objective interest in a real enterprise. The "teacher" in this case is really providing an apprenticeship.

In my opinion, at the secondary level (high school), the best method of "teaching" cultural subjects would be to provide many small real enterprises, such as television and radio stations, scientific labs, design offices, local newspapers, little theaters, and the like in which adolescents would serve apprenticeships according to their choice, with an option to change from one enterprise to another.

In this kind of learning, energy is provided by the desired worth of the product and by the animation of cooperation. The primitive integrated community is an example.

3. The teaching of professions is a further stage of the same master-apprentice method. Here the teacher must make a special effort to help the young apprentice, for the subject-matter is too complicated to be simply picked up in the course of carrying on the enterprise.

Why does the professional make the effort? Noblesse oblige, erotic attachment to the young, and a wish to have his own professional identity continued in the profession. As Veblen said, contact with the young in this sense keeps the professional undesiccated and relevant to new problems.

Mother cooking and helping the small child make a small pie. A humanist explaining his appreciation of a poem.

4. *Guru* as teacher. The Guru (e.g. Frank Lloyd Wright) confronts the young with his own reality, concerns, and prejudices, as fact. He is a source of power in the environment. The student's energy to learn in this confrontation is the fascination of the real, and his own confusion needing integration.

The guru seems to put up with the student either for erotic reasons or out of a hostility to anything different from himself; that is, he needs to proselytize.

a) A milder form of the same method of teaching-learning is teacher as model, where the student grows by temporary identification, and the teacher has the satisfaction of showing off.

A good deal of good teaching is just providing entertainment.

5. Different from the guru is the negative-reality provided by the *maieutic* (Socratic midwife) method, or psychotherapy. Here the therapist-teacher maintains his own reality like the guru but severely limits his power to his own ego-boundary, and the student or patient is strengthened in his own integration.

The energy of the teacher in this situation seems to come from a need to have allies in the political, cultural, or moral Republic. He wants a world of plural free centers in which open exploration can occur, so that he too can transcend himself.

The (Socratic) means is often shaming, whereby the student expresses himself freely, and finds that his expression is not acceptable in the universal Republic, but his potential self is respected so that he is encouraged to integrate himself.

6. The Saint or Nurse finds fulfillment precisely in the creative growth of the other. This is a kind of *agape*, or perhaps the gardner's love of growing things.

Teaching as service; Sylvia Ashton-Warner is a good model of this kind. Progressive education in general is on this theory: it puts things in the child's way that the child is (guessed to be) reaching toward.

a) Good academic teaching is a species of this serviceable kind: the teacher is really living, and fulfilling himself, in memory, in repeating the great moments (e.g., St. John's of Annapolis). He is a servant of history and civilization.

(No doubt, also, much of the energy for the psychotherapist in maieutic teaching is to use the process as a bridge to his own past [so Socrates is trying to "remember" the courts of Jove]).

b) Second-rate academic teaching is a perverted version of this type. There are several bad variants:

(1) Trying to impose on the student a theorized schedule of development. (Martin Deutsch's Head-Start theory, with its revival of "transfer of training." So often Piaget.)

This soon becomes operant-conditioning: an abstract school-environment is imposed on the youth in which they cannot cope intrinsically, and must meet the extrinsic schedule. Typically: it is believed that children first learn monosyllables like "cat" and "rat"; but indeed *Tyrannosaurus Rex* is to a child just as much a word as any monosyllable.

(2) A bad variant at the level of higher education is the notion of the "well-rounded academic syllabus" with its required subjects; rather than relying on the acquisition of well-rounded learning by the branching out of intrinsic interest.

8: *The Art and Science of Teaching*

FRANCIS A. J. IANNI

The title of this paper epitomizes both the essential dichotomy of the educational process—the science or theory of instruction as contrasted to the art or practice of teaching—and the two different levels of scholarly interest in the study of the teaching process here, the distinction being between the structure of what is taught and how we go about teaching it. Both the theory of instruction and the structure of the disciplines have received far more scholarly interest and concern in recent years than has the art of teaching or any new insights into pedagogy. In fact, they may have received far more interest than they deserve. The cognitive psychologist, for example, having sated himself on learning theory, has—almost in the manner of the anthropologist running short of exotic cultures discovering modern American society—begun to systematize a theory of instruction that is a companion to learning theory. Still crude and untried, still more a series of propositional theorems than a comprehensive theory, this beginning at least gives some comfort in knowing that some competent people are at work. At the same time, one of the more recent of the many "revolutions" in education—the reform of the curriculum—has attracted the attention of the university scholar who, joining with his colleagues in physics or mathematics or in music or the social sciences, has attempted with varying results to improve the course content of what is taught in the schools. Where the community of scholars has shown the least interest, however, is where the educationist has shown the need for most help: in the analysis of the instructional process as a transmitter and amplifier of culture and in the role of the teacher within the social system of the school. Let me just point to a few problems in each of these areas and suggest some possible interests for further discussion.

THE ANALYSIS OF THE INSTRUCTIONAL PROCESS

One of the important steps still to be accomplished for the study and the practice of teaching is the development of a theoretical framework that both transcends the behavioral elements of the act and recognizes the cultural context within which it occurs. A few examples:

1. If we rule out, for the moment, the many correlative studies of intelligence and family background or child-rearing practices and personality, little systematic study appears to have been given to the child-rearing antecedents of cognitive behavior and even less to the development of teaching strategies based upon such knowledge. And yet, if we consider learning as essentially an exploration of alternatives, and one of the functions of teaching as the economizing of random activity in such choice, then any attempt to encourage such exploration through the art of teaching must take into account the fact that the propensity to explore is heavily conditioned by the cultural context within which it takes place. That is to say, every culture produces predisposing factors that develop or inhibit the child's drive to explore and to consider alternatives. An adequate pedagogy, then, must understand these factors and develop an instructional strategy that builds upon or vitiates the predisposing factors.

2. The present mood of so-called diagnostic teaching which places strong emphasis on the individualization of instruction posits certain optimal conditions for instruction: specifically (a) that the teacher should operate within a system that identifies and exploits the antecedent experiences and encounters that predispose a child to learn; (b) that the information to be transmitted must be based on a careful structuring of knowledge that is optimal for comprehension and presented in the properly programmed sequence and, *finally* (c) that the system must comprehend the nature and pacing of rewards and punishments. Here again the cultural context becomes a critical if largely overlooked factor. Obviously, such cultural elements as the degree of intellectual stimulation the child receives from his family, the value the society places upon learning, and the richness of the cultural environment will all structure his predisposition to learn. Again, the structure of knowledge and the mode of presentation are heavily dependent on the complexity of society. In technologically primitive societies, instruction of the young most often occurs by actual performance of the activity to be taught; frequently, no effort at instruction is made, and the child is expected to absorb the requisite knowledge just by repeated exposure to the activity as performed correctly in its natural context. In modern society, on the other hand, most instruction of the young is by a recitation of abstract principles detached from context, e.g. the pupil does not witness the political process in operation but is offered a formal outline of governmental structures. In the same way, he is taught the abstract structure of the solar system although he may never have observed any of the planets through the smoggy skies. Finally the numerous examples of cultural differentiation of rewards and punishments are as obvious intraculturally from class to class as they are cross culturally. It would seem that these examples are regional as well.

3. One of the great pedagogical inventions of the new education—as great now as when it was invented in the days of Socrates—is inductive

teaching. As important as the inductive approach seems to be in the teaching-learning sequence, there are certain obvious problems it presents as a model for how a society should proceed to transmit its culture to the young. Given the limited amount of time available for learning in modern society and the vast amounts that could profitably be learned, there must be some emphasis placed on economies of time and effort. Not everything can be learned inductively, nor is there time to try. We may yet bless the computer as a resource for the presentation of general rules and of that which must always be taught by rote. Even so, it would seem that as knowledge expands we must increasingly face the companion questions of "What shall be taught and to what end?" and "What information has become technologically and culturally obsolete and should be given lower priority or perhaps not be taught at all?"

Schools are not random associations of teachers, students, and administrators but rather are well-ordered systems having a well-defined institutional structure and normative system (note the discussions by Horton and Leacock in this volume). Schools are part of a well-articulated institution that has an existence apart from the church, and even the state. As in any organic structure, all of the parts must be understood before any of the parts can be systematically developed. If we consider that the school consists of four major domains, the students or learners, the instructors or teachers, the materials taught or the curriculum, and the environment within which all of this takes place—the spatial and temporal arrangements within the school; the "administrative climate;" the ways in which teachers and pupils are deployed; the traditions, customs, and folklore of that school that make it different from others—if we consider all of these factors then we are looking at the school as a social system that becomes amenable to the same kinds of structural analysis as any other social system (Wax-and-Wax make a similar point in their essay in this volume). Most of our study to date, however, has centered on the learner as part of this system and in recent years on what is being taught in that system. Let's consider the teacher as a part of the organizational structure for a moment. Three examples will suffice.

1. For the moment accept all of the characterizations of the school as a series of cubicles into which the children and the teachers file every day and in which the teacher must assume an essentially custodial role. Further, let us not argue with the obvious fact that role conflict is a constant and aggravating part of every teacher's daily life: where she is, for example, told to be creative, and yet is given neither the time nor the space within which to even think how she might go about this; and where she is commanded to be innovative while remaining the fountainhead of the traditional values of the society. Let us accept all of this and then ask what would be necessary to change the teacher so as to make her into the perceptor, tutor, analyst, and mother we would have her be? I hasten to say I don't know the answer, but I do suspect that what we are really

dealing with here is much more than changing the job-description of the teacher or giving her a private office and time to think and plan, or even firing every teacher in the country and replacing them with inspired amateurs, scholars, businessmen, or even with a tree and a swimming pool, or computers. Rather we are dealing with a complete redefinition of what and who the teacher is and, more importantly, of what teaching should be in a particular social system. Either in spite of, or because of, the emphasis of the curriculum reform movement, the schools tend to teach subjects and no longer teach children. Any such redefinition of the role of the teacher must not only relate the teacher to the social system of the school but must come to grips as well with the extirpation of learning from the action that takes place in the general society, and thus question the very existence of schools.

2. The preparation of teachers is a second area that has been left to educationists with less than happy results. Here again, in the interest of economy let us dispense with any disciplined approach to the question and accept the proposition that what has been lacking in the preparation of teachers is that illusive quality that is at once the mark of the true professional in any field and the most austere of all mental qualities—the sense of style. Style in art, style in literature, style in logic, style in science, and style in teaching all have fundamentally the same quality— an admiration and a striving for the direct attainment of a foreseen end, simply and without waste. As in art, archaeology, or culture history, however, style in teaching can best be understood as a manifestation of the culture as a whole, what Meyer Schapiro has called the "visible sign of its unity" and "the inner form of collective thinking and feeling." The paradox here is that while the Enlightenment came at least partially as a reaction against scholasticism, we continue to expect the school and the teacher to foster enlightenment without any understanding of it. The elements of style in teaching as well as in learning their relationship to the culture and how one goes about instilling a sense of style in teachers are all questions still to be answered.

Finally, there is the question of the role of the teacher in the transmission of cultural values. Is the teacher to be the objective purveyor of knowledge or does he have a defined role to play in acculturation? The general materialization of Western culture and the high value placed on techniques have seen education progressively degenerate into instruction. Remember that *instruction* is the process of putting information into the person—it literally means "to build into," whereas *education,* in the sense of the Latin word from which it is derived—*educere*—"to lead forth—" connotes much more responsibility for socialization. The social function of education, formal or informal, in any society is to introduce the youngster to the founding myths and rituals that bind together those who share a common practice and doctrine and to shape their personalities to conform to certain ideal types. The introduction of the teacher into this process of socialization at increasingly earlier ages and with a broader social range of children in modern societies requires attention to the twin questions of who explicates the values and how society determines that they are being properly taught.

All of these questions remain to be answered and each of them has an urgency for being answered. In a deep sense they are all part of that wonderful yet maddening characteristic of American education and of the culture that has produced it—the faith in a process rather than in any particular product or attained result. As a colleague of mine recently observed, social problems in Europe lead to revolutions, whereas in this country we attempt to solve the problem by introducing a new course into the curriculum. Until we understand the art as well as the science of teaching, more courses are hardly the answer.

PART II

Schools in Modern
Urban Society

9: *Citizenship or Certification*

THOMAS F. GREEN

[handwritten annotation: male white children get 3 yr. of Schooling — Jefferson]

I

In the past eighty years or so of American history at least two important transformations have occurred in the role and conception of schools and schooling. The first developed when the conception of educating the public became closely linked to public school education so that the education of the public tended to become coextensive with the conception of public schools. Thomas Jefferson argued that "if a nation expects to be free and ignorant in a state of civilization, it expects what never was and never shall be." While this remark is often taken to express the fundamental necessity upon which the American system of public schools rests, it also expresses the conviction that whatever else education may accomplish, its fundamental purpose is political. The most basic contribution of education is in the formation of a democratic public; its most important goal, the development of citizens. But not even in his famous proposal to the Virginia legislature did Jefferson express the belief that formal education would become the primary instrument in the education of the public. By way of public schooling, Jefferson proposed to offer three years of grammar school for "every white child of the Commonwealth," more advanced education for some of the more promising ones, and free higher education for a very select group, which he referred to as "the natural aristocracy." That is not as extensive a proposal for public schooling as we might expect from a man who believed so strongly in the political importance of educating the public.

For Jefferson, the most fundamental function of education was defined in relation to the formation of a civic body, but he clearly distinguished between education and schooling. The basic skills transmitted through the common grammar school were to be the necessary prerequisites rather than the definition of one's education. Thus schooling, though necessary, was less important in educating the public than was participation in the polity and the economy. Political participation and a free press, were to be the primary means of educating the public. Not even for the generation of Horace Mann did the demand for mass education imply mass schooling over increasingly extended periods of one's life. Schooling and education were not synonymous. "Education" was the more comprehensive term and was tied directly to the formation of a civic order.

In the same light consider the underlying function of education in the American encounter with immigrant groups. The "common school" undoubtedly played a significant role in the process of assimilation. Mass education was required to reduce the dangers of cultural pluralism. The function of the common school was, among other things, to tone down cultural differences and equip the immigrant with a historical memory that would allow him to find his identity as an American. This educational goal was pursued through many kinds of schooling at different age levels, but it was never intended to include mass schooling over extended periods of time. The process of assimilation, was aided, moreover, even at the outset, by the fact that participation in the economy and the polity often required the immigrant to shed some of his distinctive behavior in favor of what was more functional in American society. And so, not even in the process of assimilation was the mass education of the public focused in mass schooling. It was assumed throughout that, quite apart from schooling, there were many ways of securing an education, many agencies of education, and a variety of paths to dignified adult status and full-fledged membership in the public body. A richly diversified pattern of educating the public was understood to exist, and schooling was but a small part of it.

The first significant shift in these assumptions occurred, or at least became evident, in the first two decades of the present century. John Dewey, for example, clearly recognized that education and schooling were not the same thing. He argued that all of life is educative in the sense that every experience has consequences in developing habits and, therefore, in bringing pattern to the release of human impulse in action. Some experiences, however, can be miseducative because they tend to develop patterns of habit that are restricting rather than liberating. They tend to minimize the subsequent capacity of the child to respond appropriately to a changing environment. The only proper solution, he thought, was to develop the habits of intelligence and the habits of reflection, which alone are sufficient to adjust the pattern of human action to changing circumstances without limit. Education was growth, and whatever tended to limit the capacity to grow was miseducative.

Dewey's complaint was that many of the agencies of deliberate education were not doing their job. The process of industrialization had contributed to the decay of the family, and education offered by the church was either ineffective or inherently damaging in the process of developing people who would participate in a democratic society. Neither these institutions nor the press, unions, neighborhoods, or shops were effective in educating properly; another institution would be required to take on their educative functions. It became almost a folk assumption that this institution should be the school. It was Dewey's view not that the school played too large a role in the education of the public but that its role was too narrow. He did not deny that there were other forces for education, but he turned constantly to the school as the best hope for assembling the educational resources necessary for the preservation of a democratic public.

On this view it became increasingly difficult to separate the education of the public from the institutions of public shooling. The function of schooling was no less political in conception, no less directed toward a civic ideal, but the role of schooling in education was greatly expanded. Jefferson's assumptions concerning the political necessity of educating the public were retained, but in achieving those ends, the sphere of the schools and schooling was greatly expanded. This represents a substantial shift in emphasis.

The second transformation in the conception of schooling was more radical. It was also more recent, and for that reason alone is more difficult to define and will require more extensive exploration. The fundamental point is that as the role of schooling in the education of the public is expanded and institutional differentiation proceeds, the schools may come to take on not simply enlarged but entirely different responsibilities. As the importance of the schools grows, their actual social function may be transformed. Moreover, as such a change occurs, it would not be unexpected if the course of social development were to outstrip the ideology that is intended to provide the rationalization for schools and schooling. The traditional rationalization, although continually appealed to, would no longer reflect what is actually done in schools and through schooling. It is precisely this kind of transformation that has occurred in American schools and in American society. At least that is the thesis I wish to explore.

Let us recognize, to begin with, that education, wherever it is found, is always concerned with three fundamental functions. Education is always concerned with (1) socialization, (2) cultural transmission, and (3) the development of self-identity in the individual. These functions, of course, overlap, but I think it well to treat them as being conceptually distinct. By "socialization" I mean to focus on the structural aspects of society and the process of inducting the young into the adult roles of the society structurally defined. (Compare Cohen's discussion of this term in this volume.) By "cultural transmission" I mean to emphasize the value component of society and the process of learning, adopting, and adapting the beliefs and values that provide some rationalization for the social norms and practices that the child learns. By "the development of personal identity," I mean to focus upon two fundamental but discriminable requirements of education. The first is the demand for some meaningful participational roles in a contemporary community, and the second is the necessity for a sense of identity in some historical community. It seems to me a proposition in no need of demonstration that whatever schools exist, they should be the institutions through which society deliberately seeks to advance the social functions of education. That is simply to say that schools should be educational institutions. Whatever their role may be, it must be defined in relation to these educational purposes (although Murray and Rosalie Wax seem, in their contribution to this volume, to regard this as an issue for research rather than definition).

The scope of formal schooling was relatively small in the mind of Jefferson and was not greatly enlarged in the assimilation of the ethnic minorities because the social functions of education could be satisfied in other ways than by formal schooling. The process of socialization did not require extensive schooling. Adult roles in the polity and the economy were readily accessible through other means, even to those with common or elementary education. Self-identity through some vocation could be achieved without extensive formal preparation; and cultural transmission, being frequently regional and ethnic, was accomplished through a myriad of local arrangements, folk clubs, trade associations, Sunday schools, and national celebrations such as Independence Day. Extensive schooling was simply unnecessary in such a society in order to satisfy the functions of education.

But we no longer have that kind of society. We are passing from an industrial to a technological society, from a rural to an urban society, and from an individualistic to a corporate and highly organized society. The process of socialization is different. The role of cultural transmission does not occur with the same clarity, and the path to a clear historical and meaningful contemporary identity is not as easy. Now the adult social roles defined in the economy and the polity are heavily loaded with technical prerequisites, and the satisfaction of those prerequisites requires extensive schooling. Consider an example, which is in many ways paradigmatic. Not long ago, Governor Rockefeller of New York State vetoed an act of the state legislature that would have required a college degree as a prerequisite for obtaining certification as a mortician. Had he allowed the act to become law, then access to the position of mortician in the state would then have been unavailable to anyone except through prolonged formal schooling. Again, it was once possible for a young farmer, for example, to "read law" under the supervision of an attorney and then, through examination, gain admission to the Bar. Abraham Lincoln did not have a law degree; he read law as a clerk. This path for entrance into the profession, however, is now virtually closed. "Reading law" now takes the form of schooling undertaken in the pursuit of a law degree. Schooling is becoming an increasingly pervasive path in the process of socialization. Not even by joining the Army can one avoid the necessity for schooling as the means of gaining access to adult social roles in American society.

The point I wish to stress is that under these conditions, the actual social functions of schooling became transformed. Schooling was an important part of the process of developing a democratic society, but it was only a part, one among many alternative paths to adult social roles. Now it has become very nearly the *sole* path for gaining access to full-fledged adult membership in American society. The result is that the schools have had to assume the heavier burden of certain functions that were previously accomplished in other ways. Schools have had to assume a heavier share in the task of certifying, sorting, and selecting, the self-conscious process of determining who will assume which kinds of positions in the work force, and who will receive which forms of higher education.

The impact of this change is perhaps most vividly seen in the so-called "dropout problem." It seems to me a sobering fact that prior to 1950 there was no dropout problem in the schools of this country, not because everyone finished twelve years of school but because we did not define the failure to do so as a problem. There were youngsters who left the formal school system, but this was not viewed as a serious matter because there were other ways available for a person to develop his powers and to demonstrate his capacities. A dropout from school did not mean in any sense a dropout from society; the term "dropout" is a fairly recent addition to the vocabulary of education. It does not reflect an increase in the number of youngsters who fail to finish high school. In fact the proportion of students who fail to finish twelve years of school is probably less now than ever before. The use of the term to designate an important social problem thus reflects a profound shift in our conception of schooling and in our understanding of the social functions of the schools. "Dropping-out" can become a problem only if we adopt the view that the fundamental function of schooling is to meet the "man-power needs" of the economic and military institutions of our society (and note Seeley's rejection of this model in his comments in this volume). The failure of students to complete their education through high school did not, in fact, become defined as a problem until the school system began to be widely viewed in this way. In short, the growing authority of the schools to perform the function of certifying and sorting has transformed a school dropout into a dropout from society. Failure in school has become one way in which society has learned to say to many young people that they are simply no good.

The important point, however, is that the schools have been made to assume a greater share of the recently enlarged tasks of certifying, sorting, and selecting personnel. Equally important, this change has brought with it a corresponding transformation in the assumptions by which we understand the purposes of schooling. An emphasis upon the certifying function has led to a deemphasis on the political function. The purposes of schooling have tended to be defined less in relation to the formation of a body politic, less in relation to a civic ideal, and more in relation to the "manpower" demands of our economic and military institutions. In short, if there is a degree of tension between the concept of schooling for citizenship and schooling for certification, then the American schools have tended to move away from the former in favor of the latter. This constitutes a truly radical departure from the assumptions about the function of schools held either by Jefferson or by the leaders of the Progressive Movement such as Dewey. It means in effect that the connection between public schooling and the education of the public is broken.

It might be argued that I have provided a distorted view of the transformation of the role of American schools. The assumption by the schools of a greater share in the tasks of certifying, sorting, and selecting and a lesser share in educating the public is simply the result of a transformation in the economic structure of American society, and is a consequence of the schools reacting appropriately to a transforming job structure in society. The number of unskilled jobs is declining and the available adult roles increasingly require technical skills that can only be acquired through schooling, and schooling, moreover, carried on over expanding periods of time. Hence, schooling through high school is a necessity, not because the schools have made it so, but because the nature of the economy, objectively viewed, has made it so.

No doubt these observations are true *in some sense* and *to some extent*. But the vital question is "In what sense and to what extent are they true?" Doubtless our society does require more education in order for people to effectively participate in it. But where is the connection between that fact and the conclusion that it must require more formal schooling? The fact is that there is not, and *in principle* cannot be, any close correlation between the actual technical skills acquired through school and the specific technical prerequisite for any particular job. There cannot be a very close relation between the skills required for a particular job and a high school or college diploma. In fact, what is increasingly required in American society is a diploma, a proper note of certification and not a particular set of capacities developed in school. And what that diploma attests to in fact is not a specific set of abilities but a certain measure of dependability, acquiescence, and plasticity of personality—the capacity to take directions and to be punctual. These are important qualities to develop for participation in the economy, and a diploma or certificate from a school is evidence that they have been developed. But this, which the schools *do* certify, is not a new thing; it does not result from the increasingly technical prerequisites for jobs in the American society.

Whether the actual fulfillment of adult roles in modern America in fact requires more extended schooling is a highly debatable point. It seems to me to be doubtful but many people believe it to be true, and if they believe it to be true, however erroneously, it will turn out structurally to be so. If a garageman believes that a good mechanic must have a high school diploma, or a banker that the duties of a teller require a college education, then the fact that their beliefs are mistaken is no comfort to a young person seeking either of these jobs without a diploma or degree. He must return to school not to acquire the necessary skills but to acquire the certification essential in order to gain access to a role where his skills can be displayed. The school in this sense functions as a sorting and certifying agency for admission to adult roles. This function of the schools is not a consequence of the growing demand for technical skills in the economy, but is rather a consequence of the way in which we have translated the demand for more education into a demand for more schooling, and have as a consequence transformed the role of the school from an institution for the education and development of a civic body into a certifying agency for economic and military purposes.

This, then, is the second and more radical transformation in the conception of schools and schooling. We began with the assumption that the education of the public was essential because we are a democratic society. Schooling had its role to play in this process, but the purpose of schooling was defined primarily in civic terms. Then through time the role of the school in the formation of the public was enlarged although it was still related to a civic ideal. Finally, we have managed to expand the role of the public schools to a virtual monopoly in determining access to adult roles in American society. In the process the civic function of the public schools, their political role in the education of the public, has atrophied. This development and its significance may be a consequence of other changes in our society, more fundamental and profound changes in the very conception of the public and of politics. In view of these more fundamental changes, it is an open question whether the schools can really turn from a concern with certification to a more explicit and forthright concern for citizenship.

II

The idea that schools and schooling should be directed toward the formation of a *public* is a troublesome notion. The concept of a public, or civic body, is one of those fruitful ideas at the same time central to the tradition of social thought and amenable to endless change. It is an idea both pregnant and equivocal. And, so, when it is said that education must be a public affair, what public is it that we have in mind? What do we mean by "public"?

The idea of a public is troublesome, not only because it is so illusive, but because it has received so little direct and sustained attention. There are certain resources upon which we can draw, but they are perhaps most notable for their inadequacy in contemporary America.

There is, for example, the *polis* of Aristotle, the space where the heads of families met as equals under no other necessity than their common agreement to speak and to act together. The public in this sense was synonymous with a political body, and membership in it required participation in the affairs of that body. Membership in the public was indistinguishable from being a political agent and was indispensable to being a human being. Aristotle's famous principle was not that man is by nature a social being but that he is by nature a political animal; not that man is by nature simply gregarious, or that he happens to live in the presence of others, but that he is by nature a member of a civic body. The opposite of "public" in this sense would be "nonpolitical" rather than "private." Typically in the ancient world the power of the head, the *patria potestas*, was without limit. Relations in the family were, by definition, relations among unequals, and so the affairs of the family fell outside the public not because they were private but because they were nonpolitical. The public then was a political body, and education could be conceived in no other context than as the preparation for entrance into that body of "free and equals." It was natural that both Plato and Aristotle should deal with education within the context of a concern for citizenship, and that they should both see the exercise of citizenship as being inseparable from the cultivation of both civic and human *arete*. Education was at once both technical and moral and at the same time civic.

Though the ancient *polis* remains for us a kind of haunting memory of what we might mean by "the public," it cannot, however, constitute the model of what we mean by that word in discussions of "public education" and "public schools." In the modern city, and certainly in the nation state, to say nothing of a worldwide or regional "family of nations," there is precious little to remind us of the public in the classic sense. Where is the *res publica* in a modern city, such as Chicago or New York? Both Plato and Aristotle, as well as others in the ancient world, recognized that the *polis* must be small because it must be intimate and face to face. Indeed that was the problem of Rome: how is it possible to govern an empire on the model of the *civitas*? A public cannot in principle be expanded beyond limits permitting a meeting of free and equals and a verbal exchange among them. Insofar as it provides one model for the meaning of "public," the *polis* is more closely related to a public defined by the concept of community than a public defined by the concept of society.

The model of *societas* is that of a social relation founded on contract, a kind of agreement, the result of will, serving sometimes the temporary and sometimes the more durable needs of men. A contractual relation, however, is like a promise. It is something one can enter and from which, therefore, one can be absolved. The concept of "society," or *societas*, was frequently based on the idea that men may be bound together by a "common" interest. But, the word "interest" is a metaphor, which be longs admirably to the conception of the public as *societas*. For an interest (*inter est*), understood literally is that which is between two men. It may be understood as that which in coming between them either separates them or joins them. Between the North American continent and Europe stretches the Atlantic Ocean. Does it separate the continents or unite them? It depends upon one's point of view. From one perspective the ocean is surely an uncluttered highway that connects the two. The point of view of *societas* is that of separate men who are bound together by a kind of common interest or common fate. But that which unites them, which is between them, is of a different order from kinship or blood, common religion, or long and mutually acknowledged historical loyalties. The latter factors are more of the nature of *communitas*, for they bind men in a public, a brotherhood as opposed to a partnership even when their interests are divergent. The point is well expressed by Tönnies when in *Community and Society*, he writes,

The theory of the *Gesellschaft* deals with the artificial construction of an aggregate of human beings which superficially resembles the *Gemeinschaft* insofar as the individuals live and dwell together peacefully. *However, in Gemeinschaft they remain essentially united in spite of all separating factors, whereas in Gesellschaft they are essentially separated in spite of all uniting factors.*[1]

The classical *polis* does not provide a useful image from which to build a modern understanding of the "public." The ancient *res publica* is not much better. Both are essentially political conceptions and the modern understanding of public is not. The latter term, moreover, calls to mind the conception of the legal organization of the public, namely, the state, and that is not what we mean by the public. The notion of a national society, with its historical relation to social contract theory and the Roman *societas*, is too large and indefinite, too much connected with the idea of polity, and too likely to admit many publics in a society without seriously coming to grips with the term "public" at all.

If we are to understand the meaning of "public" in our discussions of "public" education, "public" schools, and the education of the "public," then part of what is needed is some symbol of *the public* that is adequate to express and to evoke the needed social commitment of our time. What we seek is some formulation of the idea of "public" so that through the process of education men may find it believable that they are in some sense "united in spite of all separating factors." In that respect our understanding of a public must bear some of the marks of *Gemeinschaft* or *communitas*. Such a symbol cannot be discovered in the mere fact that from time to time we are prompted to associate with one another around some common interest. Nor can it be found, as Cicero would have it, in some "common agreement concerning what is right." The public must contain disagreement. An adequate symbol of public life must transcend mere interest

The kind of thing that is wanted is perhaps best displayed in that panoply of symbols surrounding the Hebrew notion of "the people." When the *Bar Mitzvah* declares "I am a Jew," the memory of a long history of belonging to a people or a public is called forth, which transcends differences of interest, geographic boundaries, and economic and political distinctions. But the important point about this illustration is that what constitutes the public, what evokes its consciousness in people, is not a shared interest or an agreement about what is good. It is rather a common memory transmitted through a set of shared symbols adequate to communicate that membership. And what is even more important, this conception of a public does not establish any solid division between what is public and what is private. Membership in a public in the Hebraic sense is not set over against membership in a family. It is in no way confined to political affairs or civic affairs, and yet it leads to participation in the shared life of a people.

That is the *kind* of thing we see in the Hebrew notion of "the people." It suggests that what is required for the education of the public is a conception of the public and some way of communicating that conception so that the public is seen to extend back into the past and forward into the future. One of the functions of educating the public is to assist in forming a self-identity not only through participation in a contemporary community but also through memory of some historical community. It is one of the decisive points at which the social function of certification obfuscates the educational issues; for when it is the primary function of schools to sort and certify, they must be concerned with modernity above all else, and the necessity to form the kind of memory that establishes a person in some public is likely to go not only unrealized but even unrecognized.

There are, of course, alternative ways of understanding the idea of a public, approaches that rely less than the Hebrew view on the effects of a common history and shared mythology. Perhaps the most sustained and direct attack on the idea of the public is to be found in that most neglected of Dewey's writings, *The Public and Its Problems*, in which Dewey directly sets out to answer the question "What do we mean by the public?" His answer rests neither upon the idea of a common interest nor upon the idea of contract. Neither does Dewey suggest that the existence of a public stems from the existence of a state nor from the way the state is organized. He points out instead that among the transactions that occur among men are some whose effects do not extend beyond the lives of those immediately engaged, and others whose consequences reach far beyond those immediately concerned. Here is the germ of the distinction between public and private. In the latter case, when the consequences of an act go far beyond those directly concerned, it takes on a public character, whether, as he puts it, "The conversation be carried on by a king and his prime minister or by Catiline and a fellow conspirator or by merchants planning to monopolize a market."[2] A public then is constituted by *all* those who are in fact affected for good or ill by actions. Dewey says, "Those indirectly and seriously affected . . . form a group distinctive enough to deserve a name. The name selected is The Public."[3]

This view has several consequences. In the first place, it follows that the existence of a public is a question of fact. It is not something that needs forming as much as it simply needs recognizing. There are at least two ways in which a public may fail to be recognized. In the first place, it may fail in self-recognition. For example, those whose lives will be seriously affected by the location of a school may be unaware not only of how the decision will influence them but also of the fact that it may touch them at all. Hence they may remain an inchoate public, lacking self-consciousness. They are, according to Dewey, a public, nonetheless, and potentially an articulate public. On the other hand, a public may fail to be recognized by those who are responsible for acting. Hence, the school authorities may fail to recognize those who are touched by their actions, or they may simply ignore them. This is a fairly accurate description of the relation between the public and school officials during the recent controversies in New York City over the control of I.S. 201 and P.S. 36–125. What was for a long time an inchoate public in Harlem has become what Dewey calls a concerned public, but the decisions of the school authorities often appear to be made without reference to that concerned public. Public decisions are then seen as removed from the public, as being in no way expressive of the concerns of the affected public. In any case, the point is that a public is defined by the actual consequences of actions taken. A concerned public arises when people are aware of the consequences of those actions.

In the second place, Dewey's view implies that there are many publics. Presumably, there are as many publics as there are consequential issues calling for action. Here it should be observed that a public in Dewey's sense is not confined to people who have a *common* interest, or the *same* interest in some issues. A public contains people who have divergent or even conflicting interests. Hence, the public defined in many current school controversies, such as those so publicized in New York City, includes not only parents and children, but also teachers and other professionals, political representatives, business associates, and many others who see their interests as divergent and who are differently persuaded. The fundamental political task is to bring into some comprehensive whole not only the diversity within each such public but among various publics that may come into existence.

From within this framework of thought, important things can be said about educating the public and education for public participation. To begin with, the existence of a public is for Dewey a matter of fact and not a result of education. But what is often needed is the transformation of an inchoate public into a concerned and articulate public, and that does require education. One must learn how it is that decisions *do* touch one's life. If we were to introduce a distinction of Gilbert Ryle's between "knowing how" and "knowing that," between skills and information, then we can say that the creation of a concerned public requires a great many kinds of "knowing that"—knowing that such and such decisions are pending, that they are likely to have such and such consequences, that they are likely to be made by such and such persons or offices, that one has certain rights to information relevant to these decisions, and so forth. But participation in a concerned public is also likely to require many kinds of knowing how—knowing how to exercise one's rights, how to make information widely available, how to influence those in authority, how to conduct meetings, how to contact allies, and so forth. The point is that education of the public for that kind of participation is heavily laden with instruction in the exercise of skills. For preparation for citizenship it may become less important to be right and more important to be effective. It may be that the good man is not in demand if he be good for nothing. In short, education of the public tends to more closely resemble technical education, civic action becomes tied to a kind of technical reason, and civic problems to technical problems.

It is impossible to overstress how extensive a transformation these remarks imply for the traditional American views of civic and moral education. Within Western moral theory, three fundamental metaphors have tended to guide our understanding of moral education. On the one hand has been the image of man the giver of law, the legislator. From that perspective the basic moral question has been "What is right?" That is the central question in the theory of duty. The second metaphor has been the image of man as the searcher for and creator of value. From this point of view the crucial question is always "What is the good for man?" This was the basic question that guided the utilitarians of the nineteenth century to search for the underlying principle of value and is also a strong element in Greek ethics. It is the view of moral theory that takes as fundamental the problem of value. The third guiding metaphor has been the image of man the artist, and from this view, the crucial question in the moral life is not what is right or what is good, but rather what is fitting. This is the central focus of the moral sense theorists and is a strong element in the Greek conception of *hamartia*, the notion that life is an art, that it requires the cultivation of *techne* or skill. These are quite distinct though related approaches to the topics of ethical theory.

The American experience, however, has been strongly influenced by the character of life in the New England town and on the frontier. The prevailing moral understanding has been strongly shaped by religious tradition and in particular by Puritan influence with its strong focus on the theory of duty, and a corresponding rejection of a life based upon prudence alone. In short, the focus has, for the most part, been on what is right and good, and relatively less upon what is prudentially wise, effective, and efficient. But in the world of modern America, more highly organized, more urban, more technologically oriented, it may be precisely these latter features that must prevail. In the setting of urban life, the most fundamental moral and civic question may turn out to be not what is right or good but *what is happening*—to one's neighbor and to one's self—and *how*, by what *techne*, something can be done about it. One's duties to his neighbor may be unchanged, but the context in which they are discharged is greatly changed. They are more likely to be referred to as the business of some institution, some agency, or some public body, such as the police, hospitals, schools, or churches. To discharge one's duties to his neighbor in this sense becomes much more a matter of skill and efficiency. The moral agent becomes much more the public agent. He becomes a man with a particular set of skills, the man who is able to "read the signs of the times," determine what is happening, what can be done about it and by what means, when action can be taken and when it cannot, and with what permanent and what temporary gains. This is a much stronger element of prudence, effectiveness, and public involvement than Americans have been accustomed to associate with the conception of a moral agent. It is a view strongly reminiscent of the traditional moral metaphor of man as an artist, but it would be better in the American context to view it as the model of man the technologist.

The problem is too difficult to deal with in detail within the limits of this essay, but one might hypothesize, nonetheless, that it is precisely this transformation in the social context of civic and moral action that has made the concept of "responsibility" so important in the modern world. It is astonishing to note how little mention is made of responsibility in the Western tradition of moral thought. As far as I can determine, there are only two paragraphs in all of Aristotle's writings that deal with this concept, and those have to do with the problem of identifying the conditions for free choice. They do not deal with responsibility in the sense in which moderns understand it. As far as I am able to determine, the term itself, or its equivalent, does not figure at all in any of the writings of the classical moralists. One will search in vain for any treatment of the idea in the utilitarians of the nineteenth century. In Emile Durkheim's lectures on moral education, in many respects the most mature expression of his thought, the idea of responsibility does not enter at all as a fundamental category of moral conscience. The idea of duty is there, but that is not quite what is meant by the modern "ethic of responsibility." To the best of my knowledge the notion that "responsibility" might be placed alongside the concepts of "right," "good," and "fitting" as a fundamental moral category is a distinctly twentieth-century idea.

As far as I can determine, H. Richard Niebuhr's book *The Responsible Self* is the first major work of moral theory to make the moral concept of responsibility more fundamental even than the ideas of the right, the good, and the fitting. He understands responsibility to be quite literally the ability to respond to what is happening in a network of public relationships. His thought is based upon the ideas of George Herbert Mead, but the significance of his work is that he interprets moral behavior in the context of a public in the modern sense and sees the moral agent as possessing a certain kind of civic skill. He sees the responsible self as a kind of moral technologist, the possessor of a technical conscience, no different in kind, however, in his public and private life. The responsible self is able to respond to acts of love and intimacy and return them as well as he is able to respond to the acts of public officials on public questions. Niebuhr's conception of the responsible self is the conception of a man who lives and acts within a public in the sense in which Dewey intended, and yet it is not a view of moral agency that sets up any hard and fast dichotomy between the social skills required in public life and the capacity to respond in the intimacy of one's private associations.

Such an approach to the nature of civic education might provide a means of preserving the unity of the Hebrew view between public role and private life. It is heavily laden with the political connotations so central in the classical view of the public. It also places a premium on the cultivation of the necessary social skills that are so functional a requirement for life in modern urban societies. But the sphere of intimacy is very limited in the urban setting, and the social skills essential for participation in the public may nonetheless be exercised in relation to a narrowly circumscribed image of who is one's neighbor. What is at the same time crucial and also omitted from these suggestions is any means of representing and communicating in the process of education the kind of social commitment that transcends temporary interests and is the basis for a social concern that extends beyond one's immediate public in Dewey's sense. In short, the education of a public requires an image of the solidarity of men in a public sufficient to evoke a social commitment of the suburbanite in the solution of the problems in the city, and a social commitment of the rich to the poor, of the religiously diverse to the service of those who do not share their peculiar history or their uniquely defined community. What is demanded for the modern education of the public is a symbol of the social commitment so necessary in our day, a vivid image of how it is that we are united in spite of all divisions, a conception of the public that bears the marks of *communitas* in the midst of urban technological society but that at the same time does not involve us in the nostalgic return to the small, spatially limited community of New England or the frontier.

It does not seem to me in any sense obvious that this goal is attainable in a society whose schools are structurally and culturally devoted to the task of selecting, certifying, and sorting. The social skills essential for participation in the public might well be strengthened in such a system of schools, because such schools place a premium on the capacity of the student to learn to take the long view and to manipulate the school establishment so as to get the "proper certification." But it is extremely doubtful, in my mind at least, that such a school system can properly turn its attention to assist young people in interpreting their lives, and to vividly transmit the necessary civic mythology essential for the formation of a public. If there is some tension between certification and citizenship as the fundamental function of education, it must be most poignantly evident in the struggles of young and old alike to meaningfully interpret their lives and their place with others in some kind of public. In this sense, the most fundamental problem of modern education is anthropological in the classic sense.

1. *Community and Society*, Charles Loomis Jr., trans. and ed. (New York: Harper Torchbooks, 1963) p. 64 (Italics added).
2. John Dewey, *The Public and Its Problems* (New York: Holt, Rinehart and Winston, Inc., 1927), p. 13.
3. Ibid.

10: *The School as a Small Society*[1]

BUD B. KHLEIF

This paper is intended as an introduction to the anthropological study of the public schools. I explore a variety of approaches that may provide working hypotheses for the conduct of fieldwork within the schools. I hope that these may be useful in providing new viewpoints for the observation of old institutions, and throughout I focus on potential spots of tension and conflict in the inner workings of the public schools.

TOWARD AN ETHNOGRAPHY OF PUBLIC SCHOOLS

How are public schools related to the rest of American society? I propose the following:

1. It can be said that whatever is sociologically important happens in the school, that the school is a miniature society. For one thing, the sociology of education is but a study of the issues and achievement of American democracy (here, note Green's discussion of education and citizenship).

2. Perhaps the most constant thing about human affairs is change; hence, equilibrium in a social system—regardless of its theoretical boundaries—is but a case of constant change (homeostasis). In this regard, following Robert E. Park, we can define society as a group of competitive groups that are only temporarily in balance. Each new generation of a group tries to ratify its treaty with the remainder of society (see Seeley's essay in this volume).[2] This applies to regions such as the North and South in the Post-Reconstruction era; to ethnic groups such as the Irish, who, from the nineteenth-century condition of "No Irishmen Need Apply" signs on the Yankee stores in Boston succeeded successively in electing their own men to be Mayor of Boston, Governor of Massachusetts, and President of the United States; to such sociological minority groups as women—who, through the suffragette movement, obtained the right to vote (the Nineteenth Amendment in 1920) and are now organizing themselves to achieve much more; to academic pursuits, such as sociology and anthropology, which have become acceptable university disciplines; and to "emergent professions"—such as school-teaching, social work, library

science, and nursing—which are currently engaged in raising their status. In essence, society itself, as well as its component parts, is but a treaty between unequals and—in the long range of human events—is subject to modification. Society in whole and in part continues to be governed by a temporary elite, a minority group that defines other groups and whose self-definition itself is based upon the ascription of inferiority to other groups. In this sense we can see that society is but a *negotiated order*[3]—that is, a bargain—and that "status politics," "the capacity of various groups and occupations to command personal deference," is an on-going process that permeates society.[4]

3. We can apply the notions of "negotiated order" and "status politics" to the building blocks of social structure, that is, to institutions. An institution may be defined as a processing-plant for people and skills, as a guardian of integrative symbols in society, or to follow William Graham Sumner, as a set of functionaries formally established to deal with the person at various junctures in his life.[5] In other words, the daily business of institutions is socialization—the family, the school, the church, the factory, and the prison. (Here I am not concerned with definitions of institutions that portray them as disembodied "norms" or "needs" but with institutions as social systems.) Quite often, educators talk lyrically of small-town America where, in their words, "the home, the church, and the school" were equal in power, complementary to one another, and mere aspects of one another. But we can say that a major shift has occurred in the distribution of power among this trinity of institutions, with the school, in many cases, emerging as the most powerful of the three. It can be said that the school has become the major socializing agency in the culture, the chief institution for bringing up a new generation. The school cares for more children than are found in other institutions and keeps them for a good deal of the day and for a number of years. The school has assumed a multitude of functions; in neighborhoods where the traditional influence of the home and the church is not strong, and in communities characterized by rapid physical or social mobility, the school has become a major stabilizing force in the life of the child.[6]

The Federal programs of human reclamation have focused on the school as the setting in which a great number of individuals can be immediately and conveniently reached, which bespeaks of the rapidly emerging influence of the school. Moreover, schoolmen themselves are currently engaged in competitive status-politics; they have acquired experts on grantsmanship, new personnel whose sole function is to try to obtain a larger slice of the Federal financial pie and thus enhance educational power.

4. In this new shift in the balance of power among traditional institutions there has been an interinstitutional acculturation. For example, whereas the church nowadays uses secular methods for staying in business, the school uses sacred terminology in its functions. Listening to a principal

speaking in an assembly before the whole school and stressing individualism, democracy, good work-habits, and the like, we would think that we
were hearing a minister addressing his congregation. The point is that
there has been a shift in the sacred-secular dichotomy in society, that
society can be viewed as a process, and that the school, although officially
a secular institution, quite often performs a sacred function. In a sense,
school-teaching can be considered a religious occupation.

5. Now if we look at a lower level of phenomena, we can see that the
school system itself can be regarded as a treaty between unequals and
that it is permeated with status politics. For one thing, a school system
can be viewed as a source of jobs for particular ethnic groups.[7] For example, one who had any contact with the Boston Irish or were interested
in doing fieldwork in the Boston schools, would be smilingly advised by
the school people that he ought to meet the "only non-Irish principal in
the school system!" In addition, women as a sociological minority group
are rarely appointed high school principals and none of them can become
school superintendents. The same is true of Blacks: if we look at the
national picture we find that very few Blacks are appointed as school
principals, and, in mixed Black-White school districts, no Blacks are
superintendents. In Chicago, where the school population is 53 percent
Black, it was not until November 1968 that a Black was finally appointed
as an *assistant* superintendent. Men's status politics and Whites' status
politics dictate the distribution of job rewards and influence the educative
process.

6. (a) The school itself, not only the school system, can also be seen
as a treaty between unequals, as a group of competitive groups. There one
finds the teachers and the taught, the administrators and the administered,
the rulers and the ruled. Willard Waller has characterized the chief
aspect of interaction in the school as being ceremonious fighting between
functionaries and clients.[8] Jules Henry, John Holt, Edgar Friedenberg,
Murray Wax, Solon Kimball— among others—have described the public
school as a rigid bureaucracy run for the convenience of the administrators,
not the students:[9] Peace in the hallways, law and order in the classrooms,
written corridor-passes for the student before he can walk down the hall
to the library or the toilet, and the label of "cultural deprivation" flung
at students by some teachers who can themselves be perhaps more truly
described as "culturally deprived." As Erving Goffman says, "What is
prison-like about prisons is found in institutions whose members have
broken no laws."[10] Patients, prisoners, and students—persons for whom
services are organized—have no voice in the operation of hospitals, jails,
or schools; if they do, it is only as token participation; their committees
and councils are carefully controlled.[11]

(b) In the school, the principal himself may be regarded as a foreman,
mediating between the school system's central office and his school, and
among parents, teachers, counselors, and pupils. That seems to be the core

of his job, although educational literature in its emphasis on what a principal should be rather than what he is, often depicts him as an instructional leader spending most of his time in the "supervision of instruction" even of postprobationary teachers and in creating a Sunday-school world for "lay participation."[12] In particular, as every school observer knows, the principal is especially wary of those central-office personnel—often officially designated not as supervisors or inspectors but as subject-matter "consultants" and "coordinators"—who (to use an old-fashioned terminology) go to and fro in the hope that knowledge would increase but who actually constitute a large corps that can be called "maintainers of the system." These "consultants" essentially carry news to the central office and engage in informal as well as formal evaluation of principal, teachers, and pupils. School systems—with their scattered units that are administered as if they were citadels or tribal reservations—are run, perhaps more than any other institutions, on the basis of politics and gossip; the principal, for all practical purposes, must be a master of public relations and an expert on controlling gossip networks.

(c) It can be said that in our society, public-school teaching is a thankless job; the teacher acts not only as an instructor but also as clerk, accountant, policeman, recreation leader, embattled soldier, and mother-confessor. She is to be, as her trade-journals enjoin her, omnicompetent and omniscient.[13] Hence, the dropout rate among teachers is quite high (technically called "teacher turnover"—only kids supposedly drop out; teachers only turn over).[14] In the flight from the classroom up the educational ladder, there are perhaps three avenues: a job as a school administrator, counselor, or research assistant at the school system's research department. School administration, in the form of the principalship or of being a curriculum expert at the central office, tends to be more accessible to men than to women, which, among other things, leaves women to do the spadework of the school system (nationally, about 80 percent of the public school teachers are women). Counseling is a more lucrative avenue with an office of one's own, a coffee-break to take whenever desired, and being invidiously regarded as a sort of psychologist or low-level psychiatrist! Hence, we find an increasing number of school teachers going into counseling, especially beginning school teachers for whom their two to three years of teaching experience was obtained only to satisfy a job requirement for school counseling. We also find that in some school systems, nonprivileged ethnic groups are increasingly going into counseling: French-Canadians, Italians. and rural WASP's in New England for example. Working in research in the school system is a very limited possibility—only large school systems have a so-called research department whose chief task seems to be the routine administration of achievement and IQ tests (which are in a sense, a form of latter-day magic) or "casing" the salary-scale for teachers across a five-county radius. That is, of course, nonresearch. In addition, professors of education with federal grants usually tend to employ their students rather than provide fulltime jobs for teachers who are anxious to do research.

7. An institution, like a person, has a career. The Dame School of the nineteenth century developed into a Normal School, then into a State Teachers College, then into a State College, then, in some cases, into a State University, e.g., Western Illinois University at Normal, Illinois. Currently, teachers are most often trained at a state teachers college (e.g., North Adams State, Massachusetts), at a small private or state college (e.g., Western College, Ohio, or San Jose State, California), at a department of education in a small university (e.g., University of New Hampshire), or at one of those large warehouses called Colleges of Education (e.g., at Boston University, Columbia University, or the University of Kansas). There are still vestiges of the old order, the two-year school, e.g., Perry Normal School in the heart of downtown Boston. The development of the teacher-training institution and the kind of academic union-cards it offers (M.Ed. or Ed.M., and Ed.D.) may be indicative of who goes into teaching and who stays in it.

As Richard Hofstadter has pointed out, education as a discipline was cut off from the intellectual tradition of the university essentially in 1911 when the so-called Committee of Nine, composed mainly of vocational school principals, stressed that the objectives of education were not to be high-brow or intellectual, that is, concerned with the cultivation of the mind in the humanistic tradition, but practical, that is, concerned with vocational training and "citizenship." Later in 1918, the NEA formally adopted these objectives in a report issued, called the "Cardinal Principles of Education."[15] Ever since that time, education has been under the thumb of psychology; this alliance has given impetus to the large achievement and IQ-testing industry that we now have. It is only recently that the isolation of education has been broken; nowadays there is some cooperation between sociologists, anthropologists, and educators.

It should be remembered that at the turn of the century the country was flooded with poverty-stricken immigrants who came in large groups and necessitated a redefinition of the old settlers and raised educational issues. Educators at that time found a new function—the civilizing of immigrants. Thus, the schools gave emphasis to practical arts and to what was called "citizenship" or "Americanization" but which meant "civilizing." Indeed, in many a New England town that has a school building that had been built around 1900 and is still in use, one finds an inscription in big block letters carved at the very entrance: "Dedicated to Citizenship." The point is that group immigration was drastically curtailed by an act of Congress in 1924, that although the second and third generations of poor immigrants have now been quite middle-classized and McWASPicized (McWASP is middle-class, White, Anglo-Saxon, Protestant)—some have indeed run for the presidency and vice-presidency—the occupational literature of educators continues in large part to be salvational in character and permeated with the theme of civilizing immigrants. Obviously, the civilizing mission that school teachers are bent on is not ended, for nowadays those to be civilized are *native* strangers: geographically mobile pupils and lower-status Blacks and Whites—dwellers of urban and rural appalachias.

Whereas school teaching used to be an *ad hoc* occupation for people on their way to becoming lawyers or anthropologists, entry nowadays has become more difficult; school teachers tend to be, by and large, career teachers.

Ever since the rise of mass education, the country has needed functionaries who are not as literate as the other university graduates and has been willing to meet them half way, that is, grant them a modified form of the B.A., M.A., or the doctorate. James Conant has described the watered-down or dried-up shells of subject-matter called education courses.[16] Everett C. Hughes and David Riesman, among others, have emphasized the dame-school orientation of teachers and the omnicompetence expectations that still prevail in the teacher's work.[17] Whereas some writers have maintained that nationally public-school teachers tend to be drawn from the lower middle-class, others have maintained that there is now an increasing number of bona fide middle-classmen among them, that is, people who have been second-generation American middle-class.[18] School teaching, it can be said, has been a traditional avenue for the social mobility of the peasantry, of both "urban villagers" as Herbert Gans calls them, and of rural ones.[19] This is, of course, not to discount those people of nonrural background or of middle-class origins who do go into teaching. The important thing to remember is that a considerable proportion of teachers continue to be converts to the middle-class—Poles, Italians, Irishmen, Blacks, and fifth-to-eighth generation heretofore socially immobile "old stock." Perhaps public-school teaching with its multifarious duties and low occupational status can, to a considerable extent, be only performed by converts to the middle-class, as indeed, some schoolmen themselves have asserted.[20] What is sociologically or urban-anthropologically important about this notion is that the instruction of the young, of the new generation, being in part entrusted to converts, ensures, among other things, that competition and achievement continue to be zealously institutionalized in the school, and that those who transmit cultural values are themselves paragons of middle-class virtues. That the public school, as a middle-class institution, is partially manned by converts ensures the perpetuation of middle-class orthodoxy. No society could ask for better "cultural cops" than converts, and in this lies both the public schools' achievement and limitations! (Hence, the "stupidity" that Henry discusses in his essay "Is Education Possible?")

METAPHORS AND PHRASES

What kind of place is the school? Educational literature tends to eulogize it as a unique institution, but obviously this is not so. There are similarities between institutions, for example, in the way they are governed. In a system of checks and balances, public institutions tend to be governed by laymen and run by professionals. Schoolboard members are not invariably the most "educated" in the community (pity the school superintendent whose board is composed exclusively of ex-teachers!)[21] The same can be said of colleges, hospitals, and prisons, whose board of trustees are not the most educationally, medically, or criminologically trained. Church trustees are not invariably the most ardently pious or ministerial either; they represent, like other trustees of public institutions, the more respected and stable elements in the community. This means that educational and other institutions are kept "within the bounds of cost, intensity, and kind that the community . . . can stand and will support," that people who are hired to perform cherished services are kept in check, and that the institution continues to be responsive to the dominant elements in the community.[22] (But see Horton's essay in this volume.) If schools tend to be run by professionally trained middle-classmen, then their boards of trustees tend to be predominantly upper middle-class.[23]

For putting the school within the context of institutional networks in society, a variety of metaphors and descriptive phrases have been employed:

1. As indicated earlier, institutions are processing-plants for people and skills; their chief business is socialization. If socialization is regarded as coterminous with life, then it can be seen that the church, the clinic, the factory, the college, and the prison also engage in socialization, into meeting the person at various contingencies in his life and determining his identity.

2. Institutions, as Bronislaw Malinowski has indicated, have a synthetic rather than a unitary function.[24] What is churchlike about the school? What is familylike about it? What is factorylike, hospitallike, and prison-like about it? In some schools, e.g., some slum schools where children are deliberately trained in social amenities as boys lining up outside the classroom to wait for girls to enter, learning to pour tea and serve cookies elegantly—the public school could be regarded as a finishing school or a sort of family. In schools where there is an emphasis on production, the endless test-battery-scores and marking business make the school resemble a factory. It is as if teachers were employed on a piece-work basis and—as expected—would resort to rate-busting. On the other hand, some schools do seem like little hospitals, with "special adjustment rooms" (as they are called in some places in the Middle West) for emotionally disturbed

pupils. Some of these schools, because of recent Federal or private grant funds, often operate as if they were a Rogerian theological seminary. As for what is prisonlike about the school, in some upper middle-class schools, children—because of overcrowded cafeteria facilities—cannot talk while eating their fifteen-minute lunch; because of the rule of silence, they develop an elaborate nonverbal system of communication as if they were inmates of a prison or a Tibetan convent. Some slum schools are run as if they were day jails; maximum security is enforced constantly by teachers, principal, and school counselors. In a sense, the school could be studied as a part of the larger socioeconomic system and viewed as a "complicated machine for sorting and ticketing and routing children through life."[25]

3. The school, as W. Waller maintains, is a "museum of virtue."[26] The dichotomy between the idealized world of the child and the realistic one of the adult is institutionalized in the school.[27] Lower middle-class teachers who, as Riesman maintains, had missed being trained in poise, turn it into a big industry, a zealous quest for the all-rounded and colorless personality.[28] It is as if the mass media never existed or never trained pupils in manners and morals.

4. Schools, as Émile Durkheim points out, are guardians of the national character.[29] Teachers train children in terms of an ideal client, a person suited to what the dominant group in a society likes to see produced.[30]

5. Schools, as Peter L. Berger has said, are churches for drilling children in the religion of democracy.[31] The perceptual sphere of children is narrowed down to focus only on the history, that is, the official mythology of a particular society and a particular social class.[32] In this sense, we can see that stupidity or self-serving ignorance is, as Jules Henry has shown (both elsewhere and in this volume), institutionalized in the school.[33] That ethnic groups in America, as part of their status politics for social mobility, had to clean up the textbooks and ask to be included in the study of American history is not taught in school, nor in college for that matter.[34]

6. Schools, as William Graham Sumner has emphasized, teach the predominant orthodoxy of society, not the full range of beliefs and values in society.[35]

7. The school is not only an academy but a place in which the pupil acquires an identity. He is told there what he should do and get, and hence, what he should be.[36] There he learns to make out, to work the system. How a child is turned into a pupil, how a boy is turned into a man under school auspices, and how a girl is turned into a woman would be— as suggested by Wax-and-Wax in their essay in this volume—a worthy object to study in sociology and urban anthropology.[37]

8. Lastly, the schools can be regarded as a political arena for special-interest groups who are bent on social mobility, that is, as job monopolies for occupational as well as ethnic groups.[38] The way schools are run ex-

emplifies the notion that what is true about society at large may also be true about the school as a small society, namely, that it is a group of competitive groups.

SUMMARY AND CONCLUSION

In linking the public school with its social context and with other institutions, this paper has been guided by Robert E. Park's tripartite notion of society, namely, that society at large is composed of competitive groups, that these groups form a temporary balance or treaty, and that this treaty continues to be changed by new generations of groups, both ethnic and occupational. We have asserted that Park's notion could be directly examined in a smaller setting—an institution, that it cuts across both the school and society, and that the school itself can be examined as a configuration of society. We have maintained that what is macrosociological outside the school is microsociologically magnified therein, that the public school is a small society writ large.

In America, because of successive waves of immigration, particular ethnic groups have tended to supply public-service institutions with both functionaries and clients at different times. Part of the tension between social workers and socially-to-be-worked-on clients, as between teachers and those-to-be-taught, is that most often the client class has not been administratively represented in service and welfare-dispensing bureaucracies. In some instances, clients have no spokesmen; in others, spokesmen are champing at the bit because of the inferior staff-status assigned them. Hence, especially in large school systems, we find that ethnic and educational problems tend to be synonymous. Because of its vulnerability to local pressures, Burton Clark has termed the school an "accommodating institution."[39] This can be perhaps more clearly seen in terms of Park's formulations, for Park saw human collectivities essentially as ecological systems whose competitively cooperative elements are balanced against one another and regarded society itself as a patterned accommodation.[40]

Implicit in this paper is a further issue, namely the nature of American society as expressed by such concepts as a "melting pot" and "cultural pluralism." As is well known, both concepts are idealized versions of reality, a consummation devoutly to be wished. What has often taken place, as this paper suggests, is not so much a "melting pot" as a quietly seething cauldron, not so much "cultural pluralism" as cultural particularism within a framework of competing ethnic identities, and that nowhere is this issue better exemplified than in the way public schools are run. Society is such stuff as dreams are made on (to borrow the phraseology of Shakespeare's *Tempest*); the way these dreams are interpreted is at the core of an anthropology of the public schools.

In this paper, no fundamental distinction has been drawn between sociology and anthropology, especially when it comes to a fieldwork look at our public schools. In the perspective of the Chicago school of sociology (R. E. Park, E. C. Hughes, H. Blumer, and their students), the sociologist is defined as an anthropologist of his culture. (In this sense, "urban anthropology" is but a delayed form of sociology.) One assumes that to understand what goes on in the schools, one has to pull back from the school's culture in order to examine the unobvious things that lie behind the obvious, that is, one has to take the role of the stranger and try to decipher what the natives of the situation take for granted.

Whereas, in general, anthropologists have been fond of gathering detailed accounts of remote places, they have tended to take American society for granted. But perhaps, as Georg Simmel says, the far is near.[41] There is enough of the exotic in American society to make it a worthy concern of anthropology. As Waller has remarked in his study of public schools, "it is not necessary for the students of strange customs to cross the seas to find material."[42] The familiar is but a special case of the unfamiliar.

NOTES

1. Revised version of a paper read at the annual meeting of the American Anthropological Association, Seattle, Washington, November 21, 1968. I am indebted to Murray L. Wax and Marion Pearsall for helpful comments.
2. Robert E. Park and Ernest W. Burgess, *Introduction to the Science of Sociology* (Chicago: University of Chicago Press, 1921), p. 665. Cited in E. C. Hughes, "Race Relations and the Sociological Imagination," *American Sociological Review* 28 (December 1963):882.
3. For discussion of "negotiated order," see Anselm L. Strauss, et al., *Psychiatric Ideologies and Institutions* (New York: The Free Press, 1964), pp. 146–153, 373–377.
4. Richard Hofstadter, "Fundamentalism and Status Politics on the Right," *Columbia University Forum* 8, no. 3 (Fall 1965) :22.
5. William G. Sumner, *Folkways: A Study of the Sociological Importance of Usages, Manners, Customs, Mores, and Morals* (New York: New American Library, #MT-297, Mentor Books 1960), pp. 61–62.
6. Bud B. Khleif, "A Socio-cultural Framework for Studying Guidance in Public Schools," *in* D. Landy and A. M. Kroll, eds., *Guidance in American Education III: Needs and Influencing Forces* (Cambridge, Mass.: Harvard University Press, 1966), p. 174.
   Some colleagues, such as John Singleton, have contended that the family, peer group, and mass media are important socialization agencies on an equal footing with the school. It can be asserted, however, that in our complex *Gesellschaft*, our technologically advanced society with its high rate of social and geographic mobility, the public school—among deliberately established institutions rather than informal groupings or media—continues to exert a singularly comprehensive influence across social class, religious denomination, nuclear families, and age groups. The school has acquired many of the functions of the extended family, a cultural corrective perhaps to some of the deficiencies and problems of intact yet isolate, cracked, or broken homes.
7. See Jason Epstein, "Black Power in the Schools: The Politics of School Decentralization," *New York Review of Books* 10, no. 11 (June 6, 1968):26–32.

8. Willard Waller, *The Sociology of Teaching* (New York: Russell & Russell, 1961), p. 109.
9. See, for example, (a) Jules Henry, *Culture Against Man* (New York: Random House, Inc., 1963), pp. 283–321; (b) John Holt, *How Children Fail* (New York: Pitman Publishing Corporation, 1964), pp. 165–181; (c) Edgar Z. Friedenberg, *Coming of Age in America: Growth and Acquiescence* (New York: Random House, Inc., 1965, pp. 27–50; (d) Murray L. Wax, et al., *Formal Education in an American Indian Community*, SSSP Monograph (Supplement to *Social Problems* 11, no. 4 (Spring 1964):79–101; and (e) Solon T. Kimball, "Cultural Influences Shaping the Role of the Child," in *Education and Culture: Anthropological Approaches*, George D. Spindler, ed. (New York: Holt, Rinehart, & Winston, Inc., 1963), pp. 268–283.
10. Erving Goffman, *Asylums: Essays on the Social Situation of Mental Patients and Other Inmates*, #A-227 (New York: Doubleday Anchor Books, 1961), p. xiii.
11. Kimball, "Cultural Influences Shaping the Role of the Child," p. 268.
12. See, for example, Paul B. Jacobson, et al., *The Effective School Principal* (Englewood Cliffs, N.J.: Prentice-Hall, Inc., 1956), pp. 105–109, 306–315.
13. For a cogent paper on the manifold duties of public school teachers and their quest for omnicompetence, see David Riesman, "Teachers amid Changing Expectations," *Harvard Educational Review*, 24 (Spring 1954), pp. 106–117.
14. See (a) W. W. Charters, Jr., "Survival in the Teaching Profession: A Criterion for Selecting Teacher Trainees," *Journal of Teacher Education*, 7(1956), pp. 253–255; (b) W. W. Charters, Jr., "Research in Teacher Mobility," Cambridge, Mass.: Center for Research in Careers, Harvard Graduate School of Education, publication no. 27, March 1964, Mimeo.; and (c) F. Lindenfeld, *Teacher Turnover in Public Elementary and Secondary Schools*, Circular No. 675, OE-HEW, Washington, D.C.: Government Printing Office, 1963.
15. Richard Hofstadter, *Anti-intellectualism in American Life*, #V-317 (New York: Vintage Books, Random House, 1966), pp. 332–337.
16. James B. Conant, *The Education of American Teachers* (New York: McGraw-Hill, 1964), pp. 73–111. See also (a) J. D. Koerner, *The Miseducation of American Teachers* #A-771, Baltimore: Pelican Books, 1966); and (b) Martin Mayer, *The Schools*, #A-331 (New York: Doubleday & Company, Inc., 1963), pp. 461–474.
17. (a) Everett C. Hughes, "Education for a Profession," *The Library Quarterly* 31, no. 4 (October 1961):339; (b) Riesman, "Teachers amid Changing Expectations," pp. 107, 109, and 113; and (c) Hofstadter, *Anti-intellectualism in American Life*, p. 310.
18. See, for example, (a) Wm. Lloyd Warner, et al., *Who Shall Be Educated?: The Challenge of Unequal Opportunities* (New York: Harper & Row, Publishers, Inc. 1944), pp. 98–105; (b) Riesman, "Teachers amid Changing Expectations," pp. 107 and 109; (c) Hofstadter, *Anti-intellectualism in American Life*, p. 311; (d) Blanche Geer, "A Statistical Study of the Class Origin and Social Participation of Teachers," unpublished Ph.D. dissertation (Baltimore: Johns Hopkins University, 1956); (e) R. Dreeben, "Social Stratification and Guidance," in *Guidance in American Education II: Current Issues & Suggested Action*, E. Landy and A. M. Kroll, eds. (Cambridge, Mass.: Harvard University Press, 1965), p. 19; and (f) W. L. Warner, et al., *Social Class in America: The Evaluation of Status*, #TB-1013 (New York: Harper and Row, Publishers, Inc., 1960), p. 28.
19. I am indebted to Forbes O. Bryce for perceptive observations on the educational mobility of rural Yankees and other groups. Cf. Herbert J. Gans, *The Urban Villagers: Group and Class in the Life of Italian-Americans* (New York: The Free Press, 1962).
20. Unpublished fieldwork notes by the author, 1964–1966, *passim*.
21. E. C. Hughes, "The Study of Institutions," *Social Forces*, 20 (March 1942):307–310.
22. Hughes, *Social Forces*, p. 309. See also B. B. Khleif, "A Socio-cultural Framework for Studying Guidance in Public Schools," pp. 176–177.
23. Cf. W. W. Charters, Jr., "Social-Class Analysis and the Control of Public Education," *Harvard Educational Review* 23 (1953):268–283.
24. Bronislaw Malinowski, "Culture," *Encyclopedia of the Social Sciences*, 4 (1931):

626. Cited in E. C. Hughes, "Instituitons," in *Principles of Sociology*, A. M. Lee, ed. (New York: Barnes & Noble, Inc., 1955), p. 228.

25. Warner, et al., *Who Shall Be Educated?*, p. 49. On the work of school counselors in processing and sorting students, see the study of Aaron V. Cicourel and John I. Kitsuse, *The Educational Decision-Makers* (Indianapolis, Indiana: Bobbs-Merrill Company, 1963), pp. 6, 9, and 15.

26. W. Waller, *The Sociology of Teaching* (New York: John Wiley & Sons, Inc., 1932), p. 40. Cited by Miriam Wagenschein, "Reality Shock: A Study of Beginning Elementary School Teachers," unpublished M. A. thesis, Chicago: Department of Sociology, University of Chicago, 1950, p. 6. Waller amusingly remarks that "women teachers are our Vestal Virgins" and considers the teacher as "the carrier of certain supermundane values."

27. Francis L. K. Hsu, "Structure, Function, Content, and Process," *American Anthropologist* 61 (October 1959):796–798.

28. Riesman, "Teachers amid Changing Expectations," pp. 112 and 114.

29. Emile Durkheim, *Moral Education: A Study in the Theory and Application of the Sociology of Education*, trans. E. K. Wilson and H. Schnurer (New York: The Free Press, 1961), pp. 3–4.

30. Howard S. Becker, "Social-Class Variations in the Teacher-Pupil Relationship," in *Education and Society*, W. W. Kallenbach and H. M. Hodges, Jr., eds. (Columbus, Ohio: Merrill Books, 1963), pp. 231–244.

31. Peter L. Berger, *The Noise of Solemn Assemblies: Christian Commitment and the Religious Establishment in America* (New York: Doubleday and Company, 1961), pp. 65 and 69.

32. See Henry, *Culture against Man*, pp. 320–321.

33. J. Henry, "Stupid Textbooks: Education for Stupidity," *New York Review of Books* 10, no. 9 (May 9, 1968):20–26.

34. See (a) Nathan Glazer, "America's Ethnic Pattern: 'Melting Pot' or 'Nation of Nations'?" *Commentary* 15 (April 1953): 401–408; and (b) E. Digby Baltzell, *The Protestant Establishment: Aristocracy and Caste in America*, #V-334 (New York: Vintage Books, Random House, Inc., 1966), pp. 277–293.

35. Sumner, *Folkways*, pp. 521–523. On public schools as social hatcheries for middle-class values, see Marie Syrkin, "Don't Flunk the Middle-Class Teacher," *New York Times Magazine* (December 15, 1968), pp. 32–33, *et seq.*

36. Goffman, *Asylums*, pp. 173–188.

37. For commentary on the Waxes' paper, see *Proceedings of the National Conference on Anthropology and Education*, Fred O. Gearing, ed. (Washington, D.C.: Program in Anthropology and Education, American Anthropological Association, November, 1968), Mimeo., pp. 136–140.

38. See (a) Jason Epstein, "Black Power in the Schools: The Politics of School Decentralization," *New York Review of Books* 10, no. 11 (June 7, 1968):26–32; and (b) J. Epstein "New York School Revolt: The Brooklyn Dodgers," *New York Review of Books* 11, no. 6 (October 10, 1968):37–41.

39. Burton R. Clark, *Educating the Expert Society* (San Francisco: Chandler Publishing Co., 1962), p. 41.

40. See R. E. Park, *On Social Control and Collective Behavior*, selected papers edited by R. H. Turner, #P-275 (Chicago: Phoenix Books, University of Chicago Press, 1967).

41. Cf. Simmel's essay on the stranger, in *The Sociology of Georg Simmel*, K. H. Wolff, ed. and trans. (New York: The Free Press, 1964), pp. 402–408.

42. Waller, *The Sociology of Teaching*, 1961 edition, p. 103.

11: *Is Education Possible?*

JULES HENRY

We come together when a continuing world crisis has erupted in an expanding war in Southeast Asia; when the extreme vulnerability of our economic system has appeared once again in a loss of purchasing power, a serious slump in the stock market, and an expanding deficit in our balance of payments; when the prestige of the United States is low, although its power is vast; when the Black thrust toward equality threatens entrenched White status; when our cities are becoming too oppressive to live in; and when the defeat of school bond issues, refusals to increase local school taxes, and a savage fiscal attack on the University of California testify to the continued reluctance of Americans to recognize their educational obligations.

Crisis and calm, feelings of vulnerability and strength, determine how one thinks about education and what one does about it. The word "education," however, is so abused by the bureaucracies that have taken possession of it that it is easier to discuss our problem in terms of the idea of enlightenment. This automatically takes our problem out of the colleges of education and casts the discussion in a framework in which all efforts to understand may be examined.

Enlightenment, the process of testing the assumptions of a culture, usually leads to such questions as, "Is our form of political economy the best and the only moral one?" "Does my life have meaning?" "Is goodness always rewarded?" "Is our form of marriage really the best?" "Are Whites really the superior race?" "Is it right to be rich when others are poor?" and so on. There is no enlightenment unless the conventional answers to these questions, and many others like them, are constantly examined, and there can be no education unless there is enlightenment. Any so-called educational endeavor that does not do this is doing no more than tooling up for conventional occupations.

The question then arises: In our present world situation, is enlightenment possible? Since 1917 almost a third of the earth's surface and a third of its people have developed political economies radically different from our own. These are the peoples who have already become socialist; meanwhile, other millions wish to become socialist. The emergence of a new socialist humanity has been accompanied by the disappearance or extreme

weakening of many capitalist powers, to the degree that, feeling be-
leaguered amidst the diminishing strength of its allies, the United States,
according to former Secretary of Defense Robert MacNamara,

> has devoted a higher proportion of its gross national product to its military
> establishment than any other major free-world nation. This was true even
> before our increased expenditures in Southeast Asia.
> We have had, over the last few years, as many men in uniform as all the
> nations of Western Europe combined—even though they have a population
> half again greater than our own.[1]

The rise of socialism and the doubling of the number of violent
revolutions since 1958 (also according to MacNamara) has left the United
States with such an extreme feeling of vulnerability that one wonders
whether it can tolerate enlightenment, for enlightenment always involves a
reexamination of our basic assumptions about political economy.

Since 1939 the central position of armaments in the American economy,
the fact that the arms industries are its "balance wheel," as one presi-
dential commission has stated; the fact that the balance wheel has become
the pivotal gear, growing in importance each decade with our fears, is now
taken for granted, because the fear has become domesticated. We are like
those Africans among whom schistosomiasis is endemic, so that they think
bloody urine is normal; or like the Kaingáng Indians, whose teeth are so
rotten they wondered whether mine were real.

When we ask, therefore, under what conditions is enlightenment possible, realizing that it seems possible only when fears are few while our own
are numerous, we must wonder about our own possibilities.

With such general considerations in view, I shall examine educational
problems under the following headings: Political Economy, the Gross
National Product, War, The Historic Necessity of Stupidity, The Occupational System, Leisure, Vulnerability, Narrowness, and Education of the
Deprived.

Political economy: The citizens of any national society must be taught
to believe that their form of political economy is the only satisfactory
existence. In our own society this is accomplished not only through verbal
deprecation of other types of political economy but, especially in the
lower grades of school, by presenting educational materials as if decent
human existence occurred only in our type of political economy. Elementary arithmetic, even the new mathematics, is presented in narrow middle-
class settings. All of this restricts the possibilities of enlightenment.

Gross national product: At no point may anything be taught that might
interfere with the gross national product. This means not only that materials suggesting the possibility of an austere life, or one dedicated to
materially unproductive activity, must be excluded from or muted in
curricula, but also that people must be portrayed as spenders. Clothes
designers must surely have been employed to develop illustrations for
current elementary school readers, for when the Dick and Jane series tells

about the activities of the same family in a succession of stories, the entire family is wearing a different and attractive set of clothes in each story.

War: School does not interfere with the idea that all wars fought by the United States are just. Nothing must be presented that suggests that we could have done anything to avoid war, or that war is an unthinkable solution to contemporary problems. Pious sighs over the horrors of war have always been permitted, and sundry generals quoted, but little insight is given into war's causes, into American responsibility, into the general human responsibility for entertaining the possibility of war, or into the possibility of our citizens having the right to reject the bellicosity of our statesmen. Since the most important thing for a child to learn is that the United States must always have freedom to choose war when it pleases, nothing can be taught to dim this view. We cannot, for example, teach that violence is the last resort of even madmen, that a population has a right to voice its fierce objection to war, or that hostility in the face of the possibility of universal bloodshed is unconscionable.

Education for docility is the first necessity of a civilization oriented toward war, and a danger of enlightenment is that it undermines docility and replaces it with courage. One of the many paradoxes of modern warfare is that it exploits docility to train killers.

The historic necessity for stupidity: Throughout history, whether among the so-called civilized, or so-called primitive societies, people have had to be taught to be stupid. For to permit the mind to expand to its outermost capabilities results in a challenge to traditional ways. Hence the paradox that while man is intelligent he must also be trained to be stupid, and that a certain amount of intellectual sabotage must be introduced into all educational systems. It is better to have a somewhat stupid population than one trained beyond the capacities of the culture to absorb intelligence. It is clear that teachers with incisive minds, willing to take their students along all possible logical pathways, willing to entertain all intelligent questions, are a danger to any system. Hence, all educational systems must train people to be *un*intelligent within the limits of the culture's ability to survive. That is to say, there seems to be a decisive range, on the one side, where, if a people are too *stupid,* the culture will fall apart, and, on the other side, if they are too *intelligent,* the culture will also fall apart. The cutting points of this range are where the upward curve of intellect meets the downward curve of culturally necessary stupidity.

Common controversies in education revolve not so much around what students should know, and how they should learn, but how stupid we can permit them to be without wrecking the country and the world. In education for stupidity a fine line must be drawn between teaching the child how to make obvious inferences and letting him make inferences that are too far-reaching for comfort, between training him to see the validity or the truth of a proposition in plane geometry and teaching him to perceive the fraudulence of a proposition in advertising, political economy, international relations, and the like. Teaching a child to think has obvious perils, and for this reason has always been a delusive goal of education in our culture. In our culture, nobody can be taught to think, for example, where private enterprise, war, or the gross national product might be threatened.

Socialist countries, of course, have *their* forms of socially necessary stupidity. The fruit of stupidity is invulnerability, for, when one has been rendered too stupid to penetrate an issue, he can only follow the crowd, while the crowd always follows that which is popular and that which it thinks to be safe, even though that often leads to perdition. In any culture stupidity pays off in the social and political areas over the short run. This being the case, there can be little inducement to being intelligent, because intelligence leads to separation from the crowd and the crowd wants only to be safe from criticism and to have a good time.

This situation confronts the teacher at the college level in the "stone wall" effect: students who will not discuss, who will not object, who will not examine, and who are likely to become withdrawn and morose if forced to it by a determined teacher. For years, what most of us have encountered in the university classrooms are rows of moving hands that obediently wrote down whatever was said, and we never needed to worry about voicing the most radical or eccentric opinions because these merely went into the notebooks, along with the algae, ions, historic places, dates and names, equations, and the dates of the next test.

Occupational systems: The occupational system in any culture has inexorable requirements because jobs must be filled if the culture is to survive, and in our culture the fundamental outlines of the occupational system are congruent with the economic system and with the requirement of the gross national product. The occupational system is a fixed reality, like the sky, and this is true the world over. It follows that our educational system cannot enlighten regarding the possibilities of the soul, but must train children to fit the available jobs and teach them resignation to the occupational categories of the census bureau.

Children must be taught to accept the idea of fixed occupational niches and be so instructed that the freshman's question, "Philosophy is interesting, but what can you do with it?" will never become absurd. The question, "What am I doing with my life?" is the enemy of the question, "What job can I get?" The occupational system requires that the question, "Is this what I really want to do?" should not rise into consciousness, for it is an iron law of culture that to the degree that education touches on occupation at all it must not permit the question to exist. Culture as a system of thought must exclude dialectical opposites, for when these are permitted to enter consciousness, they shake a culture to its foundations. The dialectic, however, is a magic quern that grinds out its contradictions no matter where it is; so that socialist countries, where the quern presumably came to rest forever, now have to cope with it, too.

Leisure: Nowadays since there is much talk about leisure, it is necessary to say a few words about this tired subject. For the average person, leisure is the time left to him after he has stopped working for pay. That is to say, for the overwhelming bulk of the labor force, from lathe operators, shippers, riveters, and truck drivers to switchboard operators, secretaries, nurses, teachers, doctors, and so on, the main issue is what to do with themselves when they are neither getting paid for doing their jobs, nor engaged in learning trades, as in schools.

It is obvious that no use of this time can be tolerated that will interfere with our political economy, the gross national product, or with stupidity, and that, therefore, there can be no education for enlightenment after hours. Fishing, boating, bowling, cabinet making, sexual flirting, and fixing-up-the-basement can be engaged in because they help maximize the gross national product, but painting (as an art) and reading not only make very minor contributions, as compared to the others, but too much reading of philosophy, history, and the like can be threatening to the system for this may bring enlightenment.

People who have been through our educational system, however, will not use their leisure for anything but fun and games. It must also be borne in mind that an educational system that trains people for enlightening activities during their leisure would threaten the occupational and even the class structure. If too many people, on the basis of leisure-time learning, were to start changing their occupations, considerable instability would be introduced into the occupational structure and hence into the class system. Hence there is a fundamental contradiction between the idea of productive leisure on the one hand and the maintenance of our present political economy on the other.

Vulnerability: There is no more vulnerable white collar group than educators. For the most part without unions—subject to the whims of principals, superintendents, boards of education, and local parent organizations—elementary- and high-school teachers stand unprotected at the bottom of one of the most extended pyramids of power in the country. Hence they are in no position, even should they desire, to teach anything that might challenge the cultural features of which I have spoken. What I have said applies equally to so-called higher education, for there we see that educators are, on the whole, untroubled by problems of academic freedom, because, having come through the mill, they have divested themselves of dangerous thoughts, so that they have, on the whole, no freedom to worry about. They are self-imprisoned without knowing it. What would they teach that is unconventional? In my own discipline there are some brave men who have spoken in public against the war in Vietnam, but anthropology as an academic discipline is more innocent of dangerous thoughts than the late Pope John. What has become invulnerable also becomes rigid, because life has become safe. Thus invulnerable people are frozen, no longer because of fear alone, but because, by the miracle of the dialectic they have come to feel so protected. Why venture out? Since invulnerability is thus a self-reinforcing system, it acts as an immovable obstacle to enlightenment.

Education must be narrow, it must not ask questions such as, "Does life have meaning?" "What is meaning?" "What is the purpose of social life?" "What is the place in life of compassion, solicitude, wisdom?" "Is there such a thing as profundity, or as doing something with my life?" "Is there a *world* history?" "Is one country's richness a function of another's poverty?" "Is my country best?"

It is clear that broadening the questions asked would also question our political economy as presently constituted. A general examination of the question of meaning in life by the whole population would immediately drive the Dow Jones Index through the bottom because people interested in the question would not play the market.

The culturally deprived: In this segment of the population, the question is not quite as I stated it in the preceding paragraphs, for the culturally deprived, the most degraded of the Black poor, have to be brought up from the abyss before they can focus on the issue of enlightenment. That is to say, for this group the first order of business is a basic tooling-up to achieve a higher standard of living and equality with Whites. The ghetto child has to be removed from his situation of misery at the present time, and the only way to do this is for him to master the educational materials presented to him in school. In these circumstances it is inevitable that he will support a system that helps him, and thus be less interested in enlightenment.

Many technical problems still must be solved in upgrading the Black child. For example, although Project Head Start results demonstrate that deprived children can indeed be given a head start in the preschool years by special training, follow-up studies indicate that it may not do much good, because the children start to lose ground anyway as soon as they enter the formal educational system. Something happens to the ghetto child either at home, in the peer culture, in the school, or in all three, that undercuts whatever strength he may get from Head Start.

Finally, I wish to modify somewhat what I said earlier about the ghetto child. Although technical beefing-up and protection against destructive environmental forces must be in the forefront of his education, somewhere along the line the Black child has to be enlightened about the anti-Black power structure, and how to fight it. Knowledge of this structure cannot be picked up simply by being a ghetto Black, any more than knowledge of the White power structure comes simply from being White. Its complexities need teaching. Black children need to know how, a century after emancipation, they are neither free nor equal, and how they are denied equal protection under the law, and equal opportunity. They need to have an exact analysis of the processes whereby, in their case, it has been possible for Whites to act as if the Constitution did not exist.

In conclusion, I repeat that all cultures must introduce some intellectual sabotage into education. Some might argue that since, in the present stage of evolution, man is unable to develop a social system that will not make millions miserable, organized society would be impossible if everybody were intelligent because they would see through all shams, and social organization is impossible without sham. Others might argue that if the scales were lifted from the eyes of all, the hands of all might be against all, for each would see that the other is a liar. Some might urge that since man is incapable of constructing a system without massive flaws, it is better for children to be unable to perceive them.

However, I see no evidence that nature has set a certain pace on the clock of evolution so that our brains will be regulated until such time as, having constructed a utopia, men may look the truth in the eye without murdering their neighbors. This being the case I see no choice but to seek enlightenment and introduce it into education.

Although education is the most safely armored bureaucracy in our culture, no armor is without chinks. We must plan and we must use every device of which we are capable; we must hammer at supervisors and teachers; we must lobby among legislators; we must beseige publishers in the interest of enlightenment. We must find ways to breach the walls of fear and self-service if we are to avoid repeated economic misery and world war.

NOTE

1. From the text of MacNamara's address before the American Society of Newspaper Editors, as reported in *The New York Times*, May 19, 1966.

12: *Toward a Philosophy of Education Given the Crisis in Mass Education in Our Times: Some Disconnected, Inconclusive, Thematic Remarks*

JOHN R. SEELEY

A "philosophy of education," in the traditional sense of a rather fixed, extended, and useful set of principles, by which to guide educational practice has become far less attainable and/or useful. Beyond a narrow statement of a few principles at a high level of generality, any further attempt at elaborating a philosophy soon flies in the face of what we know to be the case.

The case is trivialized by being subsumed under the worn rubric of "rapid social change," since this makes us assimilate to it to some increase in the rapidity with which the familiar-feeling processes of, say, the nineteenth century, occurred. It is one thing to drive along a road that is getting considerably bumpier; it is another to scheme for passage along a road that is characterized by periodically recurring car-length chasms.

What we now have, or are on the brink of having, is a situation in which society, persons, and appropriately perceived problems are, in their most important respects, radically transformed not merely from generation to generation but from semigeneration to semigeneration or faster. Thus, whatever was appropriate education—with reference either to content or method—for the high school or college student of ten or fifteen years ago is no longer appropriate and may well be countereducative, today.

Nor do I mean this in the relatively trivial sense that curriculum (and method) must be "updated," because the logistical growth of knowledge has added a great deal and has shown much to be in error. By itself, this might be coped with, although probably only by making it possible, palatable, and required for all teachers to become half-time students. (This, in turn, would require a radical alteration in the character-structure and reference-group of many, if not most educators; as of the social organization and reward system of many, if not most, schools; but even these are relatively easy.)

I mean that each successive wave of "students" (and hence also, ultimately, of teachers) is so radically different, that the crucial problems in and for education are ever radically fresh. What might be called system-properties fade into insignificance as problems in comparison with historic properties, properties of radical novelty on both sides as *this* tribe of teachers—1940, 1950, 1960, 1970—faces *that* tribe of students. Of course something may be said of intertribal intercourse, but it will not carry us very far toward any effective parley.

What is different in each wave strikes very deep (as well as shallow). It is a commonplace, I think, of therapeutic practice to say that today we hardly ever encounter the classic forms of hysteria (*la grande hystérie*) that formed so large a part of the problems confronted by Freud. That— two to three generations—is a large bite of time. My strong impression is that today we are witnessing equivalent changes by decades: that children born, say ten years apart, are quite differently brought up in several senses.

Differently brought up, in the sense that the very character-structure is significantly altered: the degree of and balance between shame, guilt, and anxiety; the characteristic and preferred defenses and defense systems; the amount, source, and locus of internal conflict; the preferred resolution or maintenance modes, intrapersonal and interpersonal; the libidinal invest-ments in fantasies, and internal and external, familial and nonfamilial objects of love and hate; the self-image, general (what it is to be a person) and particular (what it is to be me); the ego-ideal, and the very vision of the place and function of an ego-ideal, and the investment appropriate therein; even, more radically, attitudes toward what it is to be neurotic, or hung up, and hence what the problem is, and hence the mobilization and disposal of energies for various uses. In addition are the significant changes by decade, at nonsuperficial levels, in definitions, cathected defini-tions, of what it is to be a man as opposed to a woman, and what is the normative, desired, and desirable degree of difference between them, and the desired nature and use of the bridges that are to span the differences desired and educed.

But it is not only that the formative experiences are different in their bearing on the, in a sense "mute," character structure, but that, *pari passu,* given certain conditions, the personal and shared consciousness of what is afoot (including the awareness of historicity rather than systemicity) changes rapidly, both in degree, and in what it is that is grasped. Thus both the "social structure" and the "culture" of the successive waves of persons are sufficiently different to raise all the questions of communication across cultural barriers, not in the old-fashioned sense of difficulties of understanding between those who are "there" and those who are not yet there, but in the new sense of communication between two cultures, one of which does not prefigure and the other of which does not prepare for the one being confronted. The "cultures" of the successive waves are not early and late stages of the same thing but presumedly are viable alterna-tives, indeed, alternatives that are intended to prevail. Indeed, if there is a succession, it is in temporal reversal: the older trying to guess at and readapt their culture to what they take to be the emerging shape of that of the young. And perhaps for the very good reason that it may indeed represent an enhanced appreciation, a more adequate understanding, and a larger, as well as a more generous, grasp.

Each generation is thus a regeneration of, in effect, novel personalities, in a substantially disjunct culture, supported by a society (rather than, properly, a subsociety), and this makes for two other novel circumstances in the setting of the educational problem. First, the preferred method of *divide et impera*, of dealing by choice with predominately competitive, "atomic" "individuals" (as described by Wax-and-Wax in this volume) is quite unavailing. And second, one cannot count upon as motive the tradition in which one is drawn forward by the believed-in excitements and enlargements of "the next stage," presented and modeled by one's just-next-elders in sight. What has to be looked to is the development and enhancement of the culturally immanent logic and resources of each wave, so that some considerable insight, inventiveness, and social and creative competence is called for, in place of what was *given* for earlier, luckier educators.

The essential source of this continuous discontinuity is not at all the technology (if by that we mean the means whereby material goods are produced), nor the resultant rapid alteration of the conditions of production, as the term is ordinarily intended. The primary source of such dizzying lack of "cultural lag," is social science itself, and its offspring— using that term to represent the fairly reliable "feedback" man has brought into existence to report, albeit partially, with tremendously increased rapidity and penetration, on what it is that man is doing to man, and what man is and is becoming as a consequence.

Feedback is really a misleading image, since the social and psychological beliefs are either constitutive of the society (of that which is social) or the medium in which the society exists, as community (according to Dewey) exists in communication. (Here, contrast Green's discussion of Dewey and "community" in this volume.) Thus a person, growing up, especially *ab initio*, on a different psychological theory (taken as within the compass of self-evident common sense, and unquestioned assumption) is in a profound sense a different person. And if we allow for the double impact of parents themselves differently brought up employing in each decade quite different child-raising methods (while simultaneously conveying disjunct messages consciously and unconsciously, by word and gesture) even as the child is caught up in his peer and public life in yet another set of authenticated gospels of ultimate things, we should expect, as indeed we find, far-reaching fundamental differences in the children. And as such facts become themselves the subject of authenticated and accredited report, and hence the new nucleus of the unexamined common sense, felt and known presumptions as to what it is to be a person—or child, adolescent, adult, parent, and the like—the problem of "intergenerational communication" makes ecumenical conferences look like child's play, as indeed they may turn out to be.

Now to return to the eternal as the necessary context to and constructed framework for the temporal or historic. Formal education in Western society has been under—has been taken to imply—two rather radically different major mandates. One heads up in what in the modern jargon is called "manpower procurement." The object is, as efficiently as possible, to cut, pare, trim, shape, and package people to fill what are aptly called "slots"—indeed, the human "products" are subsequently "slotted-in," with as little "wastage" as may be. The slots are taken as given, and the alleged justification for the procedure is "the needs of the society"—whatever that foolish but conclusive phrase may mean. These alleged social needs are set over against what underlies the other mandate; variously, the needs or rights of "the individual." (In case of conflict, the second, it is assumed, must yield to the first.) Thus "the task of education" is to hack away at the child until he fits into at least one of the predetermined shapes, while attending to "his needs" (both the natural ones, and presumably the ones growing out of the routine surgery being performed upon him) by the provision of counseling, football, clubs, gripe sessions, an air of personal interest and warmth (despite the overarching scheme of man-manufacture) in the classroom, and so on.

In the better schools and colleges some further attempt at reconciliation may be made: more commonly, by taking a more relaxed view of what "society" requires, and then assuming that what is good for society is good for you; more rarely, very rarely indeed, by proceeding on the assumption that what is good for you is good for society. The formulation is still incorrect, but it carries the burden of the more humane and sensible impulses.

The manpower-procurement model cannot be considered an eternal constraint that limits education in an industrialized society. Insofar as it was a constraint laid upon, not a mandate for, education, it has as its historic locus the point between abysmal poverty (when such things must be left to take care of themselves) and the period of mountainous affluence (when such things may and should be so left). Since we are in or on the verge of the latter condition, while we are increasingly obsessed by the thinking appropriate to the former, let me turn to the true task of an education appropriate to the times.

The tasks of a formal education proper to our time and the future are to see to (sometimes only to tend to, to watch over) the coemergence of: mind, self, and society (George Herbert Mead's Trinity) and history and culture; and not merely their coemergence, but their enhancement or "building up." The term "building up" is, perhaps, and perhaps necessarily, vague enough, but the sense intended is not that in which a building is built up toward a foreknown and preselected plan, but rather the sense in which a symphony, a poem, a good love-affair, or a good life builds up toward an ever-open, potentially ever self-capping of culminating non-conclusion.

It must be evident that such a building up—coemergently, again, of mind, self, society, culture, and history—cannot proceed as it has done in the past when, even under circumstances of relatively rapid social change, the theme as it were dominated the variations. Within rather narrow—certainly narrower—limits, the main lines of the play, the main dispositions and roles of the players, the balances between act, agency, and scene could be educatedly guessed at, the historic tasks or necessities were enduring and virtually self-evident, or seemed so. All were sufficiently given that while the educator might even then not properly fully fashion the emergent, he might "train him up" to a very high point and safely leave him to continue therein. Our problems are not like that.

What we must now vitally lead or encourage the child to discover is the particular intercept of his history with history in general, the history in which in one sense his history is caught, and in the other sense, which en-folds it. What he needs to understand in all particularity is "Who am I?" "Who are we?" and, "In what act am I with them—are we—engaged?"

And by "understand," we cannot mean know about, for in reference to such subject-matter merely to know about is to mistake, to put down, to disvalue, to destroy. Understanding that permits and furthers and de-velops the undertaking only grows out of the undertaking in and by a full engagement. Thus discovery flows out of commitment, which it enlarges, clarifies, and alters. Such community as is needed to make tolerable the risks alike of commitment and its examination, and the dialectic growth that these in their interpenetration give rise to, flows at one level out of the identity of common commitments, or their com-plementarity and mutual support, or—most thinly, perhaps—out of the bare communality of intelligent commitment itself.

What is additionally difficult under the new circumstances is that the context for the process is, as already indicated, one of radical cultural differences over less-than-a-generation intervals. And not only cultural differences but the virtual facing by one society, namely "ours," of another, namely "theirs." The image of "teaching" will hardly serve any longer, but one must proceed as with another society—very delicately. For, when members of two alien cultures confront each other, and their societies are not at war—hot or cold, overt or covert—the mandate upon each side is to explore the other in a tender, respectful, collaborative, and perhaps, mutually elaborative and enriching relation. Indeed, the enterprise in-dicated begins to bear some relation to what social research ought to be—the exploration in mutuality by people who are different, of the sources, meanings, values, "causes," and consequences of their differences, with a view to learning from each other, in love and reason, whatever it may be empirically discovered is of value to either or both.

Not only is it clear that action, committed action (is there another kind? perhaps I should have said highly and deeply and broadly committed action) is going to be and ought to be central for and in education (especially for the proximate historical period), but it seems clear also that what might be called activism is and is going to be central.

Activism as it presently appears is something far better and more sensible than its name implies. It is in actuality—and I commend it—a short- and long-run intertwined alternation in education between education in a posture of militance and a state of dispersion on the one hand and, education in relative quietude, receptivity, and (geophysically as well as psychologically) concentration on the other.

Also foreseeable, I believe, is a period of relative permanence for a new location of the balance or new constitution of the mix as between "realism" and "romanticism." The present (and foreseeable) "wave of the future" demands great realism with reference to past and existent stages, together with great romanticism with respect to futures and with regard to present means to bring such futures out of the alternative options.

Lastly, the demand for "integration" everywhere takes a new importance and a new turn of meaning. What is to be integrated, in a serious sense not left out, moves steadily toward the inclusion, both with reference to the world within and the world without, of all that is there to be taken count of. But the integration sought is no longer—either within persons or between them, or within groups or between them—an integration by melting-pot, nor an integration by and under a hierarchical scheme of values or social units or disposition, nor a mere treaty-state of "separate but equal." It is an integration of the sort that characterizes a good conversation, or a valued social relation in which distinctness (not separation) is preserved, but something that is common and valuable is built up—not over against and superior to and eliminative of what is distinct, but in constant dialectical relation to it, so that each is ever the ground for the other.

What all this calls for by way of organization, new relations, new methods for education—as well as new social context for it and appreciation of it—I leave for another time. But I suggest much of it is before us and around us (perhaps in a primitive state) on the campuses of the high schools and the higher high schools we call "universities," of our nation. What is peripheral and resisted needs perhaps only to be made central and cherished to embark us on a bright—or brighter—beginning.

MASS EDUCATION:
RESEARCH REPORTS

13: *Theoretical and Methodological Problems in the Study of Schools*

ELEANOR B. LEACOCK

I

To study schools with a view toward making recommendations for change brings one directly against a fundamental methodological dilemma. The need for evaluation and comparison of "better" and "worse" teaching and learning situations suggests that data must be codified and quantified. However, the teaching process is still not sufficiently understood for us to be able to select its significant features for quantification and comparison. As Wax-and-Wax contend in their essay in this volume, attempts to do so have only obscured the complexity, and hence the reality, of the teaching situation. As a matter of fact, the recent entry into the field of educational research by anthropologists, with their generally relativistic and holistic viewpoint, has accompanied the disaffection with the results of traditional social psychological research methods that attempt to isolate and test for the effects of rather narrowly defined aspects of teacher behavior.

As an example of this disaffection, Richard C. Anderson noted the inconsistencies among some forty-nine experimental studies of "authoritarian" versus "democratic" teacher behavior. Anderson concluded that a shallow conceptualization of leader behavior was in great part responsible for the inconclusiveness of the findings. Whether labeled teacher-centered—learner-centered, dominative—integrative, or supervisory—participatory, the idea according to Anderson was the same, and the conceptualization inadequate. What was needed before successful teacher behavior could be described, he stated, was the availability of "a satisfactory body of knowledge about learning in social situations."[1] Similarly, in a study of 301 teachers recommended as unusually good, to see what they might have in common, Philip Kraus found that for descriptions adequate for the purposes of analysis, a structured check list had to be abandoned in favor of thumbnail sketches of each.[2] Another research team, Kounin, Gump, and Ryan, pointed out the inadequacy of working with teacher personality ratings of the standard types. They stressed the complexity of the classroom process, and the differential effect of a teacher action, according to the child to whom it is directed, both as it affects the child himself, and as it influences other children.[3]

In view of such considerations, as anthropologists enter a field that has been characterized by a highly quantitative orientation, they should not become defensive about the use of traditional field methods for work in the schools, nor be caught up in the recent tendency in the social sciences to consider quantification as virtually synonymous with scientific method. A great many "field trips" are needed in a wide variety of schools, and with a variety of focuses, to yield the descriptive data necessary for posing generalizations about formal schooling and its results. It is all too often forgotten that quantification is secondary to detailed, intensive description and analysis of single entities, and that such analyses yield the basic materials with which science builds. Quantification can be no more than a shortcut for making generalizations and comparisons, or for isolating consistent relationships. Although it can demonstrate the frequency of presumed correlations, or give clues as to which of them may be more significant, it cannot of itself define cause and effect—quantification and correlation are not of themselves analysis. Traits believed to be significant should be counted, of course; this is a mandatory part of description. But the fetishism of the chi-square, with the possibility that, for example, the substance of highly meaningful incidents or episodes may be lost because of their infrequency is another matter.

This statement immediately raises the question, on what, if not frequency, does one base an assumption about significance? The answer, of course, is that one makes such assumptions according to the theoretical framework within which one approaches a study, and according to the kinds of questions that one is trying to answer. I think it is necessary to recognize that the American educational system is the socializing institution second only to the family (if it is not equal to it) and that a primary function of schooling, therefore, is to train children for their adult roles according to the major social-economic variables in our society, class and race. Thus the general character of a school—its "culture," so to speak—follows in great part from the neighborhood it serves, and this general atmosphere is more relevant to understanding what children are learning in any given classroom than the personality of the individual teacher.

In the research on schools I am about to describe, the charge was to analyze the complex subsumed under the terms "social psychological processes in the classroom," and develop new insights about better and worse teaching situations.[4] As the basis for understanding the context within which teachers function, I propose an initial study of classrooms in four schools representing differences in income and race, and hence schools in four neighborhoods: lower-income Black, middle-income Black, lower-income White, and middle-income White. This may seem to be a perfectly obvious choice to other anthropologists, particularly in view of the recent history of clashes over the schools and over educational policies. Some years ago, however, and in a setting in which social psychological studies of teaching style had been usual, the choice called for justification. Focusing on an individual teacher contradicts the simple fact that children will continue to learn, or not learn, from a succession of different teachers in the same school. Furthermore, children in one school will, as a group, consistently learn more, the same, or less than children in another. In relation to the "buck-passing" between the community and the school as to whether it is the neighborhood and family or the educational system that is primarily responsible for educational failures of children in low-income communities, the interplay between the two is clear. However, the active role of the school in socializing children for their class and race roles, and the different expectations for different groups of children, as built into the entire school system, and as consistently conveyed to children, has to be taken into consideration as a fundamental proposition to be explored.

A teacher is not simply interacting as a "personality" with the "personalities" of the children but is operating in a clearly defined situation, in one part of an educational system. It is within the context of established practices and expectations that teachers stabilize their roles and functions. We know a fair amount about the way teachers are both selected and select themselves for schools where they "fit." If the fit is not good, a teacher either learns to adjust and conforms to accepted school practices to some acceptable extent or leaves. Thus, in any one school, teachers develop remarkably similar attitudes toward ways of working with a given group of children, in spite of their personality differences, and in spite of always notable exceptions in those striking individuals who consciously refuse to "go along."

I considered Robert Merton's "self-fulfilling prophecy" (in *Social Theory and Social Structure* [New York: Free Press, 1957]) an important concept to remember when formulating research plans, and I was interested to explore in detail its enactment in the classroom. The influence of teacher expectations upon children has subsequently been well illustrated by Rosenthal and Jacobson's study, *Pygmalion in the Classroom: Teacher Expectation and Pupils' Intellectual Development.*[5] These researchers demonstrated the operation of the self-fulfilling prophecy with regard to children that the teachers were led to understand were likely to "spurt" ahead during the school year. Although the "spurters" were randomly selected, they did show a higher achievement gain by the end of the year than the other children. Some of the most remarkable gains were made by Mexican American children, including a boy whose IQ score gained 45 points, moving from 61 to 106, and a girl whose IQ score moved from 88 to 128.

A central theoretical concern in my own study, however, was to avoid the implication that the classroom is a mold, casting all children in the same impression. I wished to study the means whereby in this, as in any other social situation, a variety of alternative roles are structured for children. Some of these are relatively obvious. For instance, "fast" and "slow" children, compliant and rebellious children, withdrawn children, and so on, are accepted and expected by a teacher, who assesses a classroom in such terms during the opening days of the school term. Some children will already have been discussed with previous teachers, and will have reputations as bright, dull, helpful, or naughty children. Classroom gradients will vary, so that a child identified as "bad" in one group might be closer to the normative expectation in another, and a much more rebellious child will play the role of the "really bad" boy or girl.

We were particularly interested in seeing how the constellations of roles varied from classroom to classroom and what contrasts there were in the association of behaviors, attitudes, and expectations. For example, was it true that a quick, capable, and highly achievement-oriented child is more likely to be teacher-favored as well as peer-favored in a middle-income school than in a lower-income school? Is there, as a result, more concordance, and hence less conflict, between school achievement and other goals? We did incidentally find suggestions of this, although the converse did not automatically follow. It was not the most rebellious children who were peer-favored in the lower-income schools, rather it seemed to be those whose rebelliousness was more under control. How such differences are built into classroom structure through a teacher's management techniques, as well as attitudes toward and goals for the children, was a focus of our study.

II

Data-collection procedures included teacher and child interviews, as well as classroom observations. The teacher was interviewed twice, once before, and once after the observations, and in the second interview she was asked whether she had any comments to make about the observation sessions.[6] The schedule was direct and straightforward, and did not employ the personality-type questions of psychologically oriented questionnaires. We respected the fact that teachers had goals they were trying to attain and with which we should be familiar, and focused the interview on teaching aims and methods. We did, however, concern ourselves with teacher values as the more meaningful way to handle significant material that is generally included in the category, "personality." Several questions about different kinds of children in the classroom were included in the interview, and during the second session, the teacher was asked about any children who had not been mentioned during the first. The objective was to have some material on every child in the classroom, and on this we based a rather detailed and intensive analysis of the teachers' covert, as well as her overt, attitudes toward the children and expectations for them.

The child interview was also straightforward, although quite short. We asked questions such as, What kinds of things do children do that the teacher likes, that she dislikes? What does she do when she likes or dislikes something? What do the children learn at school, like at school? What would they miss if they did not attend school (sometimes receiving the answer from lower-income children, "lunch")? We asked about school in relation to the child's future goals. The children's stated occupational goals by and large reflected the occupational levels of their parents, although many of the lower-income children spoke of going to college, a well-defined goal for our society as a whole. However, their understanding of the steps toward college and the precise relation between it and occupational preparation was not clear. We also asked some sociometric questions, in order to examine teacher-favored versus peer-favored children in relation to role definitions.

Our observations were fairly brief, namely three periods of an hour and a half each. Yet the depth and richness of the material was such that it seemed sufficient for framing responses to the research questions we were asking. A number of studies have demonstrated a high reliability for the analysis of teacher performance from relatively brief periods of classroom observation. The fact that teachers might have tried to show only their best behavior to the observers—and did not "holler" at the children as loudly as might have been indicated by the interviews with the children themselves—did not seriously affect the analyses of their basic styles. Indeed, the very fact that they might be exaggerating what they felt to be most desirable behavior, even brought out the contrasts more sharply.

Two observers worked together in a classroom, one concentrating on the teacher, and the other on the students. The two records were then combined, affording highly detailed running accounts of classroom life. Each observer had a seating plan, so that all teacher statements about or to every individual child could be recorded. It was central to our design to see how a teacher differentially allocated her rewards or reprimands and to see how different children experienced different aspects of both her teaching and management style. We also attempted to obtain, in as much detail as possible, particularly value-laden incidents, and clearly goal-defining statements or directives.

The research team included people with teaching as well as research experience, and, for the analysis of teaching style, we drew in other teachers, as well as teachers of teachers. In order to avoid the unhealthy results that accompany the bureaucratization of research, all team members participated in the study at all levels—the formulation of research design and techniques, the actual collection of data, and at least the preliminary analysis of materials.

In developing methods of analysis, we attempted to work with both quantitative measures and significant observational units—one could think of them as "key" incidents—without losing the explicit content of the latter. We examined the record in detail, rating and analyzing the teacher's academic techniques along a number of dimensions, such as the value content of curriculum materials in relation to the children's background and general experiences. In examining classroom management, we dealt both with formal structural aspects, the stated rules and routines, and with informal or indirect aspects, that is, what the teacher responded to or ignored, and how, to whom, and for what she meted out her approval and disapproval. A major focus was always on the goals being set for the children (either to accept or reject), and the expectations being communicated. For example, after coding all of the questions, directives, or statements that the teacher addressed to an individual or to the class, we compared the number of those concerning the curriculum with that of those concerning behavior, to see what the relative importance of each was to the teacher. However, this relationship turned out to be less relevant to the value placed on learning than the total number of remarks concerning curriculum made by the teacher in a three-hour period, and the number of remarks per child in the classroom.

We collated profiles on each child in a classroom, including material on how he saw himself and how other children saw him, both in descriptive terms and as sociometrically favored or disfavored, as well as how the teacher saw him and how he emerged in observational materials. We included a count of all teacher statements to the child in the observations, and whether these were positive, negative, or neutral, as well as a scoring of her attitude toward him as revealed in her interview. We arrived at the latter score by coding each mention of the child in the interview with his teacher as either positive, negative, or neutral—a rather complicated procedure, since a teacher can say something generally positive about a child, but with a derogatory inference, or something negative in a supportive and accepting way. The picture that emerged of what the teacher actually valued in the children, which could then be matched against the children's views of each other, was an extremely rich one. We subjected it to quantitative analysis for clues on role constellations in the classroom and also used it to fill in the picture of teacher values as developed through collated incidents and value-laden statements from the observational records. None of this was very neat, nor did we consider that we had arrived at definite answers about the study of classrooms, but we did feel that the attempt to combine "objective" or quantitative and "descriptive" or qualitative materials had proved to be productive.

III

The results of our research concurred generally with the plethora of critical material on our educational system. Although all of the teachers whom we observed were experienced and competent by public school standards, much of their teaching was extremely poor. Moreover, while better teachers were at least clear and organized in the exposition of their material, their own educating was a one-way process. They had not mastered the techniques for achieving true involvement of the children in learning, and there was little understanding of how to relate material to where children are at any given point. The Deweyan concepts that are employed to one extent or another in private progressive schools (and now being rediscovered as "new" ideas in programs for more successfully educating lower-income children) are obviously not made real to public school teachers in their training courses. It also became clear that Deweyan principles cannot be applied where a child's experiences and capacities are not respected.

The findings on which I want to elaborate here, however, relate to the total socialization process as it is enacted in the classroom. We observed some children who were learning *in spite of* poor teaching, and, in another school, others who were *not* learning *because of* poor teaching. What appeared to be crucial was the general expectation of the teacher for the children's performance, as school life actively reinforced out-of-school differences arising from the children's social position according to their class and race. The similarities between the second and fifth grades in the same school, and the contrasts among schools were so striking, and so in accord with what we know of class and race roles, that it appeared that our classrooms had been selected on the basis of how well they paralleled social differences.

The middle-income White classroom almost parodied the world of the much-discussed organization man, replete with its committees and commissions. In the classroom, initiative was encouraged and rewarded, but only to a certain degree, or along certain lines. It was fascinating to observe the point at which authority, in the person of the teacher, intervened, and the sensitivity (or "other-directedness") with which the children looked to her for cues as to how far they could go. Some examples, humorous, and yet at the same time dismal, illustrate the relationship between teacher and children in this and other classrooms.

During the second-grade spelling lesson, the children were spelling "fish," and the teacher asked how many liked fish. Scattered hands were raised, and the teacher pressed the point, saying, "Those who like fish, stand." At this, all but six stood, and the teacher said, "I'm sorry you are not all standing. I am sorry, since fish is good for you." At this, another child slowly and uncertainly shoved himself up from his seat, but one girl near the observers snapped her eyes resentfully. The teacher closed this part of the lesson by asking the children to list different kinds of fish for their homework. Later, when reminding them, she said, "With the fish, I hope you will list the fish I like. I will tell you tomorrow." There was a rising whisper in the class, "Tuna . . ."

A contrasting incident in the lower-income, all-Black second grade shows the children's lack of interest in teacher preferences—*but in the context of an episode in which the teacher had summarily rejected a child's long and enthusiastic account of a personal experience.* The lesson was on transportation, and the teacher asked if any children had been to an airport. Many raised their hands, and the teacher called on a boy who gave a full account of watching various airplanes land and take off. The characteristic response of the teacher in the middle-income White classroom to such expositions was, "Oh, how wonderful," or "Isn't that nice" (academically meaningless, perhaps, but at least accepting). However, in this case, the teacher responded not to the child, but to her own curiosity, with the implication that all was not quite right. "Who took you?" she asked, making no reference to the content of his talk. "Day Care," he responded, which, with a "How nice" from the teacher, ended the incident. Shortly thereafter, the teacher remarked to the children, "You know, I've never been on an airplane," and continued, after a stagey pause, "What is something that Mrs. M. is going to do very soon?" There was no response from the children.

Material such as this made us realize how oversimplified is the assumption that a major difficulty for lower-class children in school is identification with its "middle-class values," in comparison with middle-class children who readily identify. In classroom incidents, such as the one previously described, one could observe the teacher directly negating a child's enthusiastic recounting of experience, and the children responding in kind. This was made all the more clear in this classroom, since the teacher was friendly and the atmosphere pleasant. The main drawback of this learning environment was that it lacked real educational goals for the children. Indeed, this enabled the atmosphere to be relaxed and amiable—there were no real demands on the children to achieve. By the fifth grade in the same school, the children had become much more apathetic. They gave the impression of rather patiently sitting through the day. We came to understand that flatness and boredom are more characteristic of classrooms in Black neighborhood schools than the jazzed-up features deduced from the "blackboard jungle" stereotype.

The fifth-grade teacher in the Black lower-income school stated discipline, not learning, or even "social adjustment," to be her primary aim for the children. When asked what she felt to be the main thing the children should be getting out of school, the teacher answered, "First of all, discipline. They should know that when an older person talks to them or gives a command that they should respond; they should listen." Yet she was not authoritative as a person, but was instead friendly and accepting of the children, who were allowed considerable freedom in the classroom. Her conception of her role, which paralleled the "boss" the children would be taking orders from in their adult life, was indicated by the classroom structure. When a child gave a report, it was the teacher who questioned him. By contrast, the White middle-income fifth grade had an elaborate committee and class leader structure. When a child reported, another child led the session and asked for questions and discussion from the floor.

The minimal educational goals in the lower-income Black fifth grade were further revealed when a count was made of all questions or responses about the curriculum that the teacher addressed to individual children. The number was markedly lower in this classroom than in any other, both absolutely and relative to the number of children. Furthermore, the ratio of positive to negative responses by the teacher to the children's work was one to three, while the lowest ratio in any other classroom was one to one. Usually it was two or three to one. This ratio is more than a simple function of whether an answer is correct. A wrong answer can be evaluated "positively," with a remark such as, "You're close to it," and a correct answer can be derogated. In the classroom we are discussing, a child wrote an arithmetic example on the board, writing the correct answer, "45." "45 what?" the teacher said. The child answered, "45 cents." "Show me that it's 45 cents," said the teacher. "It doesn't look like 45 cents to me. It just looks like 45." In and of itself, such a remark has little significance. As a recurrent type of statement, however, in conjunction with low goals for the children and little intellectual stimulation, it become part of a consistent and undermining trend.

Classroom atmosphere in the middle-income Black school differed sharply from that which I have been describing, and along lines one might guess if one considered the differing social expectations for the two groups of children. Children in the middle-income school were being groomed for heavy competition in a relatively hostile middle-class world, which meant, as James Baldwin has commented, their being the most scrubbed and polished group in our society. They were being asked to be better than best, more controlled than the most disciplined of their White rivals. "Now you have had many compliments," the teacher said to the fifth grade, as they were getting on line, "but I think we need to stop once more and ask, is this the *best* we can do?" However, the children were also being taught. We observed some of our best technicians in this school. I use the term "technician," because they were effective in getting across a specific body of material to the children, and in drilling them, in a consistent and businesslike manner. Their teaching was, however, limited as far as real education is concerned.

When the "middle-class" neighborhood of this school, with its single family houses set in small lawns, changed from White to Black, the principal had refused to allow the school to be categorized as "special service." She stated it would prejudice the children's chances for entrance into the better junior high classes. In order that academic standards would not decline, she had tightened the control and organization of her academic program. For instance, a "single track" system for reading had been instituted. Each entire classroom read together, and at precisely 11 o'clock children changed classrooms to read with others at their level. As a result of the principal's attitude, morale had remained high, and there had been no acceleration in the rate of teacher turnover. However, the rigidity of the classroom atmosphere was such that we wondered about the cost to the children's individualities. Yet the children were being effectively prepared to compete for positions in a specific and narrow social slot; they were being fitted for their social role.

The atmosphere in the lower-income White classrooms was rather amiable, and, as in the lower-income Black school, related to the lack of strong pressure on the children to achieve. Teaching standards were higher, however, and teachers were more supportive. As a matter of fact, the school was developing a more "middle-class character" during the period of our observations. A decision had been made to keep the neighborhood from "going down hill," a middle-income project was being built, and the school district was rezoned to segregate the growing Black and Puerto Rican population. (We discovered that, in spite of the hue and cry about bussing, school districts are still largely zoned to segregate.)

These brief remarks indicate the kinds of things looked for, and the methods used, in studying four schools that contrasted by class and race. The extent to which they relate to the differential training of children for different positions in our society renders it naïve to think that it is only necessary to discover "correct" methods for teaching lower-income children in order to improve their education. Instead, what becomes apparent is that the total institutional structure of the school must be examined for sources of change.

NOTES

1. Richard C. Anderson, "Learning in Discussions: A Résumé of the Authoritarian-Democratic Studies," in *Readings in the Social Psychology of Education*, W. W. Charters, Jr., and N. L. Gage, eds. (Boston: Allyn & Bacon, Inc., 1963), p. 160.
2. In an informal report on a project published as "Skillful Teaching Practices in the Elementary Schools," Board of Education of the City of New York, *Curriculum Bulletin*, 1961–1962 series, no. 12, 1961–1962.

3. Jacob S. Kounin, Paul V. Gump, and James J. Ryan, II, "Explorations in Classroom Management," in *Readings in the Social Psychology of Education*, W. W. Charters, Jr., and N. L. Gage, eds.
4. Conducted at the Bank Street College of Education with the support of a grant from the National Institute of Mental Health. The full report is published as *Teaching and Learning in City Schools: A Comparative Study* (New York: Basic Books Inc., 1969).
5. Robert Rosenthal and Lenore Jacobson, *Pygmalion in the Classroom: Teacher Expectation and Pupil's Intellectual Ability* (New York: Holt, Rinehart & Winston, Inc., 1968).
6. All of the teachers were women.

14: The Interplay of Forces in the Development of a Small School System[1]

DONALD HORTON

Most of us have some acquaintance with the schools from having gone through them ourselves, or perhaps from helping to guide our children through them. Our recollections, however, concern individual schools, not school systems, and it is the system with which we must usually deal when we are proposing new educational programs or undertaking extensive research in the educational field. Then we not only need to know something about the structure of the system, which is of course much more complicated than that of a single school, but also to arrive quickly at some understanding of the dynamics of the system, of the changes that are going on, and the direction in which the system is moving. For this we need the aid of a conceptual model or, more likely, a number of models for different kinds of systems. This paper represents the first stage of an attempt to develop a model of this type on the basis of a study of a suburban school system.[2]

Within the limits of a short paper I can introduce the subject only in outline. The course of the system will be described here in gross terms as a product of transactions among and within four powers: the school system itself, the local community, the government, and the educational world. Since the base is a single case-study, my presentation will consist partly of an abbreviated account of actual events, arranged to suggest general processes, and partly of generalizations from these data where I feel that established theory or common knowledge would justify it.

[1] Paper prepared for presentation at the annual meeting of the American Orthopsychiatric Association, Washington, D.C., March 1967.

[2] The study was conducted mainly through participant observation and interview. It was part of the Schools and Mental Health Program of Bank Street College of Education supported by grant 3M-9135 from the National Institute of Mental Health, U.S. Public Health Service. The fieldwork was carried on during the years 1961 and 1962, and was supplemented by research on the previous history of the system and occasional contacts since that time.

THE COMMUNITY AND SCHOOL SYSTEM
OF BROOKVIEW

The public school system referred to serves a suburban, residential community of a population of between 30,000 and 50,000 in the New York City area, which will be referred to as Brookview. The system was chosen for research not because it was considered to be representative of all systems of this size but because it was reputed to be a "good" system, well supported by a community of moderate means, and was, therefore, judged to be a favorable location for certain educational innovations to be introduced in one of its schools by other members of the Bank Street College staff.[3]

For our purposes, the most significant demographic facts about the community are that its population is rather evenly divided between blue-collar and white-collar families; the class spread is narrow—there are few very rich or very poor families and the average income is close to the county median. Catholics, Jews, and Protestants each constituted about a third of the population in 1960–1961. A majority of the Catholic children attended parochial elementary schools but went on to the public high school. The number of Blacks in the community was insignificant. Tensions associated with class, religious, and ethnic differences operated within the Brookview community and school system, but the problem of racial integration had not begun to arise.

The population of Brookview had been expanding rapidly since the middle 1940s; by 1961 it had nearly reached the limit set by available land, given the prevailing custom of building single family houses on individual plots. In the decade from 1950 to 1960, as the population increased, there were upward shifts in the medians of age, education, and income.[4] There is some evidence that the Jewish population increased more than the Catholic and Protestant populations during the decade. The town was becoming larger, more middle class, more prosperous, older, and more Jewish. These and related changes contributed to the kinds and energies of the demands made upon the educational system by community groups.

The Brookview public school system consists of several elementary schools, two junior high schools, a comprehensive high school, a central

[3] The sociological study on which the present paper is based was intended to provide a perspective on the structure and dynamics of the system for the participants in the educational project. Invaluable assistance in the field study was given by Harry Gracey and June Greenlief and, in the analysis of data, by Carla Drije.

[4] Comparison of the census figures for 1950 and 1960 shows a higher proportion of college graduates (up 18 percent) and fewer with eighth grade or less education (down 25 percent), a 29 percent increase in the number of persons 65 or over, and an increase in families with incomes of $10,000 from less than 10 percent to nearly 35 percent of all families

administrative office, and a nine-member board of education. Three board members are elected each year for a three-year term. School budgets and bond issues are submitted to the electorate for approval.[5]

THE DYNAMICS OF THE SCHOOL SYSTEM; TRANSACTION AND COMPROMISE

I have suggested that the development of a school system (that is, an American public school system in the 1960s) can be understood as a product of its transactions with the local community, the educational world, and government agencies. In a transactional model, of course, each of the tributary systems is subject to a similar analysis, and it is only by arbitrary choice and simplification that we describe the internal structure and dynamics of one as an integral system, while treating the others only in their partial connections with it. In this perspective, the object system is seen as a self-directed and self-motivated organization whose course of development is influenced in various ways through its interdependence with the external world.

It is a familiar observation that organizational personnel tend to defend their organization against demands for change made by "outsiders." They develop an internal program and mechanism of regulated change that to some degree is autonomous. They try especially to initiate and regulate in their own interest those changes in definitions of the aims and functions of the organization as may be required by changes in environing systems, and to devise and control the structural innovations that may be called for by changed functions. In school systems the critical processes of developmental control include the reformulation of educational goals, planning for curriculum innovation, and "staff development." These self-steering processes are protected by claims of professional authority, collegial solidarity, rejection of lay "interference," and other defensive mechanisms.

On the other hand, the school system, like other organizations, may be subject to coercion by external agencies such as the legislature and the courts, which may impose unwanted regulations and obligations, against which the defense mechanisms are ineffective, especially since the school system is itself, legally, an instrument of the state government.

Between the poles of completely autonomous and coerced change (both

[5] It should be said that this degree of citizen participation in school affairs is not typical for the country as a whole. Although election of board members is common, occurring in 87 percent of all systems, according to the N.E.A. (National Education Association, *Research Bulletin* XXVIII, no. 2 (April 1950):58; and see also *NEA Research Memo*, 1966–19 (August 1966), only 28 percent submit the budget to the electorate (13 percent in a town meeting, and 15 percent by ballot). It may be presumed that in other kinds of systems the forces we are concerned with operate in other and less public ways.

of which may be more theoretical than actual) lies a wide zone in which proposed changes are negotiated between the personnel of the system and the spokesmen of external groups, particularly those of the local community, whose financial, technical, and political cooperation is needed to keep the system in action. The structural changes that are agreed upon represent compromises between the demands of the staff, following the logic of their own system, and the demands of the outside agents. There is doubtlessly great variation in the extent to which compromises involved in organizational change involve conflict and the reconciliation of con- trary interests, but conflict is so pervasive that it seems justifiable to assert that organizational change typically includes a political element. Political processes are as characteristic of the internal dynamics of the organization as are its interchanges with the milieu; what we have called autonomous change may involve an intraorganizational form of "change politics." In a more developed model, the relations between the internal and external politics of organizational change would be considered; however, in this paper I wish to view the development of the Brookview system in the large, as a product of the transactions in which its own program of development is modified in response to the demands of community groups, governmental agencies, and educational organizations. I shall have to disregard the internal processes through which the policies and strategies of the school system itself were arrived at.

TENDENCIES IN THE DEVELOPMENT OF THE BROOKVIEW SCHOOL SYSTEM

As one looks at the development of the Brookview system, it is apparent that four basic trends can be distinguished: (1) an enlargement in size, (2) an elaboration of structure and functions, (3) an intensification of the basic educational work, and (4) an upgrading of positions. By "enlarge- ment" I mean an increase in the numbers of schools and other facilities and in the number of employees; by "elaboration," I mean an increase in the variety of positions and units within the organization, accompanying further differentiations of tasks and functions; by "intensification," I mean changes in task performance that are regarded by the personnel them- selves as "improvements" or "enrichments" of performance, but that might be defined neutrally as representing an increase in the demands made upon pupils and teachers—demands for more work, at more sophisticated levels, at earlier ages, for example; and by "upgrading" of positions I mean attributing professional status to them, increasing the degree of autonomy in work allowed teachers, and increasing their remuneration. All four tendencies are described here involve expansion in some sense.

These expansionist forms of development follow consistently from the logic of the system itself:

Enlargement is a necessary response of the organization to an increasing pupil population. During the period from the mid-1940s to 1960, for example, the people of Brookview invested approximately $9 million in new school buildings and equipment. A concomitant increase in staff and materials was reflected (along with the effects of inflation during those years) in an increase in the annual school budget from $500,000 to $4 million. Elaboration of structure and intensification of activities both appear to follow from two principles, one ideological and the other organizational. Ideologically, the Brookview system is committed to a highly individualistic form of education, in which a unique pattern of "developmental needs" is postulated for each child, and it is believed that the educational process should be adjusted to this pattern in a way so as to "maximize" each child's "learning potential" and "creativity." This aim is far from being achieved, but the educators press toward its accomplishment. The ideology of extreme individualism implies an ever-decreasing class-size and increased provision for tutorial relations and practices, with an accompanying increase in the ratio of teachers to pupils (although the optimum conditions are not known).[6] A correlative increase in individual psychological testing and in counseling or therapy is also implied; a higher minimum level of educational training and psychological sophistication of teachers; a premium upon graduate training and continued in-service training; and a demand for experimentation with new contents and new forms of the educational enterprise.

The organizational principle to which the system responds is that of occupational specialization. When specialists are introduced into a system they tend to push for the addition of others like themselves, or complementary to themselves in function, partly in order to more fully achieve the aims of the specialty and partly to strengthen the position of the specialty within the system. In Brookview, for example, during the past decade school psychologists, librarians, and counselors had been introduced and there were recurrent demands for an increase in their numbers on the grounds that more of them were needed to do an adequate job according to the standards prevailing in the educational field.

What we have called "upgrading" is in large part a result of a drive for professional status on the part of lower-ranking occupations, and for increased professional privileges and rewards on the part of the already recognized professions. The drive for professional status goes hand in

---

[6] These tendencies appear to be approaching their logical limit in the new programs for the education of culturally deprived children. According to an NEA analysis ("Class Size in Elementary School," *NEA Research Bulletin* 43, no. 4 (December 1965:106): "The focal point in this new educational movement is the individual child. . . . In some extreme cases a single pupil may constitute the full load of a specially trained teacher and in many other instances the service of a teacher will be limited to a small group."

hand with specialization and aims at raising the level of prestige and salary of each specialty, in competition with others, and in increasing occupational autonomy, especially as against control exercised by laymen either in the organization or in the community. For example, the school nurses in Brookview were demanding to be put on the same professional salary schedule as the teaching staff. There were recurrent requests for additions to the staff and facilities of the audiovisual center. The Teachers' Association was becoming increasingly aggressive in demanding a greater share in the making of decisions within the board of education, professional autonomy in such matters as development and enforcement of a professional code of ethics, and an ever-rising professional salary schedule.

THE EDUCATIONAL WORLD

Although the specific demands for expansion arise within the system itself, they are encouraged and given form by influences from the educational world, a complex of educational associations, teacher training and research institutions, publishing enterprises, accrediting and regulatory agencies, and governmental advisory bodies and commissions; all of which are in turn linked with the universities and other institutions of the intellectual establishment. The local school system has many connections with this world, the most important of which is the participation of its professional personnel in their respective state and national associations. The associations and the training institutions (supplemented by the publishing industry) provide the main channels through which modifications of educational standards and practice are made known and advocated, thereby influencing local systems to intensify their educational programs. The associations also have a unique role in advocating and supporting the demands for occupational advancement of their members by providing formulations of aims and suggestions of strategy to be used in drives for occupational benefits and enhancement of status. They supply the statistics that enable the members of any local system to compare their occupational benefits with those of other school systems, and to play the competitive game in which a boost in salaries or benefits in one system is used to press the boards in other systems to meet or surpass it. There is a continuous stimulation and steering of educational innovation, of the occupational differentiation that accompanies innovation, and of the professional claims that grow with both.[7] Although these claims may be partly reduced and modified by the administrators within the system, they

[7] The educational world, of course, interprets and transmits large-scale societal demands. At the time of our fieldwork, the post-Sputnik demand for the intensification of science and mathematics training was still strong.

are eventually passed on and become an element in the pressure of the expanding system against the local community.

THE LOCAL COMMUNITY

Innovations in the system bear differentially upon a community consisting of numerous categories and groups of people who stand in different role-relationships with the educational system—as citizens, voters, taxpayers, businessmen, political leaders, and as parents (to name the most important). These roles may be separated or may overlap in various combinations. For our purposes we might make a crude distinction between *personal* and *impersonal* relations with the schools. The most significant personal relationship, that between school and parents, also creates a direct link between the school and these parents in their other roles as, say, taxpayers and voters in school-board elections. Taxpayers and voters without children, or whose children attend nonpublic schools, perform important functions in the cycle of school-community interchanges, and yet lack the personal contact and involvement of the others.

Innovations in the system have different meanings and entail different obligations for these two categories; for those with no children in the schools, innovation means an increase in annual taxes in return for intangible future benefits to the welfare of the community as a whole; for those with children in the schools there may be immediate benefits in addition. In some cases a special group of parents will benefit, for example, the parents of brain-damaged children when special classes are instituted for their education; or the parents of "bright" children who are afforded accelerated programs; in other instances, for example, an expansion of library resources, all parents will, in theory at least, receive a benefit. But the changes are not necessarily seen as unalloyed benefits, even by parents, since some innovations may involve new and unwelcome obligations. The introduction of new programs oriented toward college entrance may encourage an interest in college education on the part of students whose parents do not welcome this interest. The introduction of psychological services may mean that parents are pressed to learn a new way of looking at children's conduct; they may also be asked to reexamine their own conduct and to redefine their parental responsibilities; and some may find their traditional patterns of family life under attack. Or, if the parents do not feel that the pattern of their relations with the school has been affected directly, they may resent the special attentions and services being given to others. In any case, they may weigh any given innovation unfavorably against its money cost.

SOCIAL CLASS INFLUENCES

Such calculations of immediate and future personal benefits and costs are also affected by social class perspectives in which the nature and desired ends of education are defined differently. Nearly everyone in Brookview would agree that every child should "achieve his maximum potential," but the full implications of this slogan appear to be especially congenial to the outlook of the most highly educated, the upper-middle-class professionals and intellectuals, whose own success is seen by them as depending upon intellectual competitiveness and self-discipline, inventiveness and personal style; the small businessmen, whose "service club" speeches extol competition, seem to be more concerned in practice that their children learn the values of teamwork and conformity appropriate to the corporation office; the blue-collar class, on the other hand, with its limited perspectives on the personality and educational requirements for success at higher occupational levels, is likely to be unconvinced of the need for more intensified or extended education, and inclined to resent having its tax money spent for the college preparation of other people's children.

The blue-collar workers also seem most likely to resist the claims of the school people to professional status and salary levels, regarding school teaching as a soft job that ought not to pay unmarried women more for what appears to be part-time work than male family heads for fulltime work in the factory. It is not uncommon to find blue-collar workers who view all of those organizations as inherently corrupt and self-serving and who assume that the school administrators are lining their pockets in some way with the taxpayers' money. Among the storekeepers who regard themselves as representatives of the business world, it is often assumed that the schools are managed inefficiently by men who have no "business sense." Among the elderly, there is a tendency to believe that "an education" more elaborate than they received fifty years ago is unnecessary.

RELIGIOUS INFLUENCES

Cutting across and modifying or intensifying these general class perspectives run the influences of religious ideology. In particular, the ortho-doxies of fundamentalist religions and their associated nationalistic pieties, especially strong in the blue-collar and lower-white-collar classes, make these groups receptive to charges that the psychological services of the schools are meddling with parental authority, and indeed with the founda-tions of belief, and they are alienated by the unorthodox ideas and unconventional behavior that seem to result from "modern" education.

The extent to which organized religious groups influenced educational affairs could not be established without an intensive community study. Church intervention is generally regarded as highly improper, and, although there was much private gossip on the subject, public reference to it seemed to be subject to an absolute taboo, even in the heat of election controversy, as if merely to mention religion would be regarded as evidence of prejudice. Such intervention as came to our notice was chiefly a matter of church leaders advising their followers with respect to their vote on the budget and recommending preferred board candidates. Private advice of this kind was reported from most denominations. Jewish congregational leaders were generally reported as favoring the expansionist trends of the school system whereas the Catholic leaders were said to oppose them, and the Protestant churches were divided. We could not determii.e how much influence these leaders had. Voting patterns showed that the budgets tended to be supported most strongly in areas where Jewish residents predominated, and defeated in Catholic areas, but it was impossible, in this type of analysis, to separate religious affiliations from the class and income factors with which they were associated.

THE EDUCATIONAL-POLITICAL SYSTEM

The state law governing the educational system of Brookview provides three means by which the community may act to control the development of the system: the election of board members, a referendum on the annual budget, and referenda on bond issues for the acquisition of property and expansion of the physical plant.

In these elections the community passes judgment on the adequacy with which the system has performed its functions and makes decisions on the proposals of the administrators for changes and innovations in its structure and performance. Into the annual debate are fed the arguments for and against the current state and direction of the system that arise at the various crucial points where the educational process affects the interests and values of subgroups of the community. The organizing of this decision has become, in Brookview, the work of an informal educational political system that stands outside of, and is only remotely connected with, the official politics of municipal and state government. The law provides merely that properly qualified citizens may register and run as candidates for the school board, and during the 1940s candidates presented themselves in this "independent" way. In the 1950s a political association was organized to support the physical expansion program of the school system by mobilizing a favorable vote on bond issues and budgets and electing candidates who favored the plans for expansion. Opposing candidates still ran as independents. In the 1960s, as the opposition to the continued development of the system increased and hardened, an opposition group was organized, and a typical bipartisan system emerged. As might be expected, this political dichotomy tended to polarize the educational issues: a liberal party tending to synthesize the various demands from the community and from within the system itself for elaboration and refinement of the system and a conservative party resisting this trend on the basis of an amalgam of the currents of criticism and discontent.

In general, the Conservative party appeared to receive its basic support from the low-income people, predominantly blue-collar workers or elderly pensioners, and in religion either Roman Catholic or Protestant fundamentalists. The large Italian group played a prominent role in this party. The Liberal party typically received its support from middle- or upper-middle-class Protestants and Jews of higher income and education. The political associations received informal support from many of the local organizations—churches, service clubs, and patriotic and cultural societies—but these generally operated in the background because it was considered somewhat illegitimate for them to participate in "partisan" politics of any kind. In particular, the churches are under the official taboo of separation of church and state. In this more-or-less behind the scenes mobilization of political forces, the school people have the advantage of their connections with the PTA organizations, which, in Brookview at least (apparently not so in Harlem), are identified with the professional staff of the schools and are led by people imbued with the educational culture who have become, as it were, quasiofficial participants in the system.

CONTROL OF THE SYSTEM

The vote on the school budget is the climax of an annual cycle of development of educational plans in which the school administration, led by the superintendent, works out its compromises with the various factions of the board of education. Control of the board through a majority of members is an even more substantial basis for power over the system's course than is a party's success in the budget referendum; and a sympathetic administration is still more reliable, because it is more permanent than control over the board. The political struggle, therefore, inevitably involves control over the appointment and tenure in office of the superintendent. It also follows that the farther down into the system the control of the dominant party extends, the more it can affect the proposals of the staff with respect to organization and program. If the superintendent is similarly inclined, the control is exerted through him and follows the constituted lines of authority; but if he is antagonistic, the dominant party may try to dislodge him, or to reach his staff directly, or both. But it cannot reach the staff and exercise control of the internal phases of program development without violating the line of privilege that separates the administrative sphere from the policy-making sphere, and without affronting the organized professional staff.

Under the most favorable conditions, the relations among board, superintendent, and staff must be equivocal since they depend upon an understanding of their respective functions that appears to be a product more of custom and the intrainstitutional power struggle than of legal authority. The notion that the proper role of the board is to determine policy, of the superintendent to recommend and administer it, and of the technical staff to execute was thought of by many people in Brookview as an assignment of responsibilities having the force of an elementary constitutional separation of powers; but in fact the state statutes bestow upon the board almost unlimited power and responsibility over every detail of the educational process. What authority the board delegates to the superintendent appears to be less a matter of legal requirement than a matter of mutual agreement, supported by customary expectations, and by the limits of what the administrative and technical staff and their supporters would accept. Consequently, the distribution of functions depends to a considerable degree upon a largely tacit bargain with the board that may be relatively stable in some circumstances, but quite unstable in others. It appeared to us that the teaching staff in Brookview, in its drive for increasing professional autonomy, was attempting to change the terms of the bargain in its favor by slightly reducing the powers of the superintendent, and by substantially reducing the powers of the board. This movement came into head-on conflict with the drive by the conservative board members to reassert lay authority over the system and to resist the expansion of program and costs. Both forms of aggrandizement of power operated to diminish the power of the superintendent who stood between the two parties.

INTERVENTION BY PROFESSIONAL ASSOCIATIONS

During our two-year period of observation, the conservatives succeeded in defeating a budget and in electing additional conservative members to the board: the board was then balanced, four to four, between conservatives and liberals, with a ninth member holding the balance of power and shifting from side to side. For several actions on courses of study and staff appointments the conservatives gained decisions that were interpreted as invasions of the prerogatives of the professional staff, and this served to increase the militancy of the professionals and their leaders in the teachers' association: moreover, after the first superintendent's resignation, the temporary absence of a superintendent brought these leaders into direct confrontations with the board.

During this ominous period, the backing of the local school people by their outside educational organizations played a significant and, on occasion, decisive role. For example, a representative of the state teachers' organization participated in the strategy meetings of the executive committee of the teachers' association in its conflict with the board; and at the climax of an attempt by the board to introduce changes in the high school curriculum without the approval of its principal, the board was forced to back down by a threat of loss of accreditation by the regional accrediting agency. Thus, in the critical moments, when it appeared that community interests were overriding the professional staff and reducing its autonomy, the educational world with which it is allied, and from which it receives its ideological direction and moral support, became an active agent in resisting local power.

THE ROLE OF GOVERNMENT

Government, the fourth major participant in the Brookview educational field, was relatively unobtrusive during our fieldwork and we have not attempted to study its role in any detail. The state government established the ground-rules of the local organization and its procedures—especially economic and political. It prescribed and supervised a complex accounting procedure to guarantee the safe custody of the taxpayer's money, and an equally complex procedure to guarantee honest elections; it provided for the licensing of school personnel and assured them various safeguards and benefits; but it had relatively little to say about the standards of education or the internal operations of school systems except to promulgate minimum curriculum requirements emphasizing patriotism and good citizenship. In short, the state's role appeared to be the traditional role of government in the market place under a laissez-faire economy: to guarantee minimum standards, order, and fair play in what it assumed to be an essentially local and competitive enterprise.[8]

Perhaps the most important thing to be said about this fourth factor in the educational scheme of things is that the government's role is one of the usually unseen and taken-for-granted constraints that prevent the educational-political conflicts from getting out of hand and destroying the functional coherence of school system and community. It embodies, in a way, the taken-for-granted agreements and expectations to which all members of the community assent—the agreement that public education is a necessary function of the community, and that it has to be effected at something approximately the standards set in American society generally.

[8] The role of the national government had begun to be foreshadowed in small ways such as in grants of money for upgrading science teaching, but given the absence of minority groups and of slums in Brookview, it will probably be some time before the more recent expansions of the national government's role will become significant there.

The parties are able to quarrel safely only because they are already united on these premises.

Yet the state government also exerts a long-range inflationary pressure on the local system as it gradually falls in line with the movements of the educational world—periodically raising mandatory minimum salaries for teachers, increasing minimum fringe benefits, recognizing and licensing new specialities, and generally consolidating professional gains. The equilibrium it protects moves on an upward course.

THE BATTLE OF EDUCATIONAL EXPANSION

The discussion up to this point may be summarized by saying that the general course of development emerging from the transactional network that we have outlined has been one of generally uninterrupted expansion in the size, range of services, and organizational complexity of the educational system, led by the demands of the professional staff, supported by the advice and, at critical moments, the active intervention of the professional associations, looked upon favorably (or at least not interfered with) by the state, supported by a political coalition of local citizens, and opposed by a coalition of approximately equal power.

We may surmise that Brookview reached a critical point in this expansion when it began to be apparent, probably in the mid-1950s, that the educational cost curve was not leveling off, as many must have expected and hoped for, as population growth began to reach its limits. The extent to which growth was increasingly a function of the ideology and interests of the professional staff and of their educational world rather than of the pressures of increasing enrollment must have been gradually revealed. In 1956, for the first time a proposed school operating budget was disapproved; the budget was again defeated in 1961, to the accompaniment of a bitter political struggle that led to the resignation of the then superintendent. In 1965 the budget was again defeated and the new superintendent, who was hired in 1963 to restructure the system, resigned in 1966. The struggle over whether the system should be stabilized or as its defenders would say, "move forward," continues unabated.

PROFESSIONAL POWER AND LOCAL AUTONOMY

In connection with the continuing political struggle there was (and still is) in Brookview an atmosphere of bitterness and reciprocal hostility that was damaging to the morale of the educational staff and to the unity of the town. Although the hostility of one side was answered by the hostility of the other, and so built up to periodic crises, it was the conservatives who typically initiated these attacks and who injected the emotional violence into educational controversy. Granted that the pressures of expansion bore especially heavily upon the religious sectarians by constantly raising the competitive standards and price of private education; and upon the lower classes because they served to advance a "middle classification" of education that might seem inappropriate in content and cost to these classes; and granted, too, that because of the superior organizing skills of the middle-class supporters of educational expansion, they more often dominated the board of education—nevertheless something seemed to be disproportionate and overdetermined in the opposition response.

In Brookview it was sometimes said that the emotional level of controversy about the school budget was high because the budget determines the only tax rate over which taxpayers have any control, and so they take out on this tax the resentment they feel about the intractable and higher state and Federal taxes. Perhaps this is so, but the exasperation of those who wished to reduce the school taxes seemed to be greatly increased by the fact that they appeared to be unable to do it, even during those periods when conservatives controlled the school board. The convergence of forces behind the expansion of the system was such that in spite of the appearance of local control, the community was limited in its power to affect either the content or direction of the system's development, although it is the community that must pay for it. The board could apply restraints to the budget, that is, to the rate of growth, but could not prevent growth entirely.

This condition is symbolized by the fact that in Brookview a struggle so bitter that it has driven two superintendents out of office in the span of five years has actually been concerned with differences on the order of a few hundred thousand dollars in budgets of five millions or more, sums proposed for relatively marginal forms of elaboration of the basic program such as a summer camp program, an expanded in-service training program, and so on. During the same period there has been a steady increase in staff and facilities, in salaries, and other costs. The determination of these basic costs is a product of forces that the conservative group in the community cannot effectively resist: the rising educational requirements of the labor market; the increasing national standardization of educational practices running with an increasingly uniform national culture; and these constraints reinforced by an increasingly aggressive coalition of national professional associations sometimes using the agencies of government as their instrument. Although the forms of local determination of the school system continue in effect, it would appear that local control is becoming something of a fiction. Aside from the economic problem that this creates for many of the local residents, it also represents a further and painful attack upon one of their sacred values, local autonomy, a value that appears to be increasingly anachronistic in the current era.

THE PROBLEM OF THE OPEN END

From the educators' point of view, the unending and often violent political conflict in which they were engaged in Brookview was a sign that too many people in the town did not "understand" or "appreciate" the meaning of "good education." It was often said that poor communication was at fault, and that if only the right means of communication could be found the troubles would disappear. But, in fact, even among the supporters of the expansionist policy some were concerned because the educators seemed either unable or unwilling to suggest that some optimum state of the system might be reached at some foreseeable time in the future. It seemed to us that, like other organizations serving other functions in American life, the school system is assumed by its leaders to be moving forward through an endless progression of improvements in quality as new discoveries of science and technology contribute to its infinite perfectability. Although there are some internal controls on its development, the system depends chiefly upon external resistance to set its limits at any given time. The resistance is a product of the competition among various agencies and institutions for limited community resources. Until a more rational procedure is available for the planning of community life, it would appear that a political struggle among the interested parties is a necessary condition of orderly growth of the educational system and of its adjustment to community needs, however much deplored this may be by the educators themselves.

15: *Rhetoric versus Reality: A Study of New York City High School Principals*[1]

ARTHUR J. VIDICH
AND CHARLES MC REYNOLDS

New York City high school principals are living out the tensions of the "crisis in urban education" in their occupational lives. Daily they confront the multiple forms of that crisis as their school populations change, as new factions make new demands, and as new issues and arguments are advanced that must be ideologically absorbed, refuted, or evaded. Principals are men on the defensive, confronting an educational world they neither made nor anticipated; it is not surprising that their model for the future as well as their defense against the present is their vision of the past.

The elements of this analysis are, then, (a) the changing reality of urban public education and its confrontation with (b) the principals' professional ideology and career expectations within (c) the limits set by their occupational (i.e., "structural") position. It is the conflict between reality and rhetoric that creates the principals' central dilemma; their response is a collective reworking and reaffirmation of their ideological position. They thus become defenders of the status quo at the very time that the maintenance of their claims to professional expertise and educational leadership requires them to respond creatively to the crisis that continually challenges them.

Since it is long experience rather than formalistic training that principals invoke as the source of their professional expertise, they have good

---

[1] The research on which this article is based was carried out under a grant from the U.S. Office of Education: Grant No. OEC 1–7–062727–2931, Project No. 6–2727.

The research for the following analysis consisted of extensive open-ended interviews with twenty-three principals plus a series of four seminars attended by a group of twelve principals during the 1967–1968 school year. Each seminar meeting was addressed by a speaker on a topic relevant to urban secondary education with ample time for discussion. Topics of the seminars were (1) What should be the role, if any, of the community in educational decision-making? (2) What is the future of integrated education in the New York City public schools? (3) What curriculum is appropriate for the urban secondary education of the future? (4) Who should pilot the future of public education in New York City?

Principals from different sizes and the various types of high schools (e.g. vocational, specialized, academic) were included as interviewees and as seminar participants.

reason to look to the past. This past experience formed their impressions of what a good school is, what a principal does, and what education means. Recent changes in the schools and in the principal's role are responded to with a mixture of regret and resentment. They see no academic training that can replace on-the-job experience, and the criteria used in selecting principals in other school systems—such as political favoritism or community popularity as a teacher or coach—are regarded by them as being obviously inferior to the exam-and-experience system by which New York principals have long achieved their positions. Standing as they do at the apex of a system of difficult exams and long service, they are proud of their achievements: they feel that the selection process does indeed get the best men. As a district superintendent stated: "They are very intelligent, very capable, well-informed, courageous, and articulate. They are an elite club with fierce loyalty to one another." This is an "elite" based on personal accomplishment proven in open competition ("Even the worst principal is a scholar in some field"); structurally they hold an elite position in the public school system—they are high school principals. Despite their protestations that they, like all humans, exhibit a wide range of personality types, occupational styles, attitudes, and ideas, our interviews indicate a great deal of similarity among principals regardless of the type of school or neighborhood or length of service.

Most New York City principals are Jewish (estimated at "at least 80 percent" by the head of one of the major associations of supervisors) and most entered the school system as teachers during the Depression. As Jews they are likely to place a high cultural value on education and for these men in particular the value of education is obvious—it is both the content and prerequisite of their careers. Several principals revealed some conflict between their sympathy for the poor—especially Blacks—who need a chance to rise as they did, and their resentment toward that same group for not being as actively committed to, and respectful of, the value of education.

The Depression provided a bench-mark against which most principals can measure their financial success. In addition, the extreme competition for positions during the Depression years made success on the teacher's exam an academic distinction in itself. In interviews several principals mentioned the small number of applicants who had been accepted at that time and the severity of a competition that included men with master's degrees. Achievement in terms of this exam system legitimates the principals' feeling of personal accomplishment while it publicly establishes their credentials as superior administrators and scholars. Each stage of advancement in the system, from teacher to department chairman to principal, was earned through hard study and a good record on the job.

Additional interviews were held with others in the school system such as district superintendents, teachers, and students, and several public meetings at which principals spoke were attended.

Chidingly, a district superintendent reminded his audience of principals, "We got where we are by being good boys and girls." Their proven ability in academic competition plus their long experience in the schools provide the principals with the sense that they possess the technical, esoteric knowledge (unavailable to the layman) that justifies their claim to professional status.

Yet, these very exams are acknowledged (somewhat evasively) to be of little relevance to the demands of their jobs. Since on the written parts the point spread tends to be rather narrow, only a few points assume great importance in ranking the examinees. Study courses are available that are taught by men familiar with past exams. In addition to written and oral exams, the candidate's job performance is evaluated and here good record-keeping is essential. He must have documentary evidence of how, as a department chairman, his conferences with teachers helped them to "grow." Obviously, this kind of system does not encourage and reward the innovative or the critical individual, but to say this is not to say that it does not select competent men. Rather it reminds us that competence is oriented almost entirely toward mastering the tasks, the definitions of problems, and the rhetoric of the established system. And the exam system is of course administered by men who are a product of it: the Board of Examiners.

In consensus with the official rhetoric in American society, principals take for granted that "education" and "achievement" mean the acquisition of middle-class demeanor and skills symbolic of the academy. The desired student is polite, respectful of authority, and "motivated," that is, he accepts school-learning as important. The corresponding model of the desired school is a smoothly functioning organization in which teachers teach and students "achieve." Neither the rationale of the school nor the authority of its staff is questioned. The best students carry their education further by going to college, while the remainder have been prepared to make a decent living and live decently. Those who fail or lose interest know and accept that it is their own fault and proceed quietly to take their appropriate place in the job structure. Although academic subjects must be watered down for the less able, yet even in the worst school, pride can be taken in those few who have been "reached" and helped, and are thus candidates for college. The rest are exposed to as much academic education as can benefit them. This model holds for vocational high schools as well as academic high schools. The teaching of vocational skills rather than academic subjects holds an inferior value within the system. In the hope that some of their better students will be able to go on to community colleges, even vocational schools have "college bound" programs. The vocational schools have been attacked, however, as being "dumping grounds" for minority group students thereby excluding them from academic opportunities and from real occupational opportunity.

The middle-class model of what education is and what a school should be is most clearly expressed when lower-class and nonacademic students are discussed:

> What harm is there for a child to have to use decent language, dress decently, and sit in an orderly classroom? Is that middle-class? Well, I say what's wrong with it?

Describing a meeting of the High School Principals' Association, which was addressed by Frank Reissman on the subject of the "culturally deprived child," a principal remarked with some indignation:

> Following his talk one courageous soul asked for an example of the virtues of the lower class which he claimed weren't being recognized and he suggested their wonderful use of language and verbal expression. But their wonderful language is full of four-letter words that have no place in the classroom! How can you encourage them to use language like that? Why, we'd be the first to be criticized if we did!

The meaning of "educational achievement"—defined in practice by scores on standardized tests—has rarely been opened to question and debate even by those militant Blacks most critical of the school system. They are critical of the schools' failure to teach Black children so they can advance to middle-class jobs; *what* they want taught is basically the same things that the schools teach to White middle-class children. As the guardians and trustees of that definition of education and as the presumptive experts in transmitting it, the principals ought to be favored men. For the issue then becomes one of assessing the blame for the schools' failure to make this definition of education a viable reality for a lower-class Black clientele. Defenders of the system say the lower-class child fails to learn; the critics say the schools fail to teach.

The high school principal of the past, at least from the perspective of the present, was a dignified, erudite, and slightly distant figure, autonomous in authority, and respected both inside and outside the school. In both respects the principals of today feel cheated. Within the school their freedom of action has been narrowed by the teachers' union and the increasing bureaucratization of the school system. Outside the school they feel subject to continuing attacks from many critics including disrespectful and sometimes openly hostile attacks from members of "the community."

The recognition of the UFT as the representative of the New York City school system's teachers in 1959 has led to important changes in the day-to-day performances of the principals' roles. When interviewed the principals consistently remarked that the union contract has seriously encroached upon their prerogatives within the school. Through the establishment of formal rules regulating teacher-administrator relations and the establishment of grievance procedures, the chapters of the UFT offer their members protection from administrative harassment, arbitrary decisions, and favoritism. While principals tend to see the union as having "done a lot of good" they resent the imposition of these formal rules on their dealings with the teaching staff. In their eyes, these rules tend to reduce their relations with the staff to a simple employer-employee relationship rather than one of "professional cooperation." Because of the elaborate grievance procedure, it is now difficult to remove an incompetent teacher and usually troublesome even to give one a low rating since any charge must be fully explained and documented if challenged. Matters that in the past were handled informally—such as helping students after school—are now either incorporated into funded programs or formally regulated with the effect being that teachers tend to work only for time paid by contract. Assignment of teachers to school duties for which teaching time is reduced must now be advertised within the school and periodically rotated, with appointments of applicants determined by seniority rather than "ability." Staff meetings are limited to one forty-minute meeting per month (found by one principal to average twenty-three minutes of actual meeting time). The union thus presents itself as a source of constraint and, occasionally, a means of harassment as teachers have collectively gained in power vis-à-vis the administrators.

Since the union negotiates its contract directly with the Board of Education, and representatives of supervisors are not directly involved, principals must live with a contract they have not negotiated. Moreover, in these negotiations the supervisors are themselves employees. Consequently, their place in the hierarchy is akin to that of "middle-management": while they have considerable authority within the schools themselves, they have but little within the system that maintains the schools. In order to gain additional strength and largely in response to the establishment of the teachers' union, the Council of Supervisory Associations was formed as a spokesman for the common interests of the various principals' associations, department chairmen, and assistant principals. It successfully lobbied for the passage of a state law requiring automatic pay increases for supervisors proportionate to those attained by teachers. This, of course, has led to union resentment since the supervisors have not joined the union in its efforts, including several strikes, to receive pay increases.

In addition to the union, principals see the increasing bureaucratization of the school system as a threat to the prerogatives of the past. Assignment of teachers and substitutes is controlled and regulated by central headquarters subject to the provisions of the union contract. An unstable teacher population, with a high turnover in schools that in the past had only the problem of replacing those retiring, has resulted from the increasing enrollments since World War II and the corresponding teacher shortage.

Until recently, the New York City high schools were directly responsible to their own functionally autonomous unit, the Division of High Schools. Although this unit still exists, administration of the high schools has been "decentralized" so that all except the "special" high schools (e.g.,

High School of Music and Art) are now under the authority of the local
district superintendent for whichever of the city's thirty school districts
the high school is in. At the time of our study this change seemed to have had
little practical effect since the district superintendent's office tends to be only
an intermediate transmission point for directives and reports between the
central office and the high schools. In principle, however, it represents a
concession by the Board of Education to "community pressures" and
demands for "local control." Since the high schools often draw students
from across district lines, principals regard the policy as impractical and
functionally irrational.

The local school boards are at present appointed by the Board of
Education and have only an advisory function. The local board visits
each school at least once a year but, except in three experimental districts,
it lacks even the power to hire the district superintendent. None of the
principals interviewed saw his local board as a threat or an interference
in the performance of his duties. Several principals, however, expressed
annoyance that the local district superintendent, although cooperative, was
not a high school man and could hardly be expected to know and understand their problems.[2]

Although the principal has some freedom in shaping his school's
curriculum and choice of personnel, the school budget and the allocation
of new personnel are controlled by the central bureaucracy. The work the
principal does is administrative; few are directly engaged in aiding, super-
vising, and rating classroom teachers. Although most say the real job of
the principal is the improvement of classroom instruction, principals are
much more likely to be involved with such activities as the managing
of a large cafeteria, the sophisticated scheduling that is needed to make
full use of an overcrowded school, the collecting of information and
preparation of reports for supervisors, the arbitrating of problems in discipline and of conflicts in organization, and the representing of the school
to its publics. Mainly, the principal is responsible for providing an organizational setting adequate for classroom teaching. Staff, students,
materials, time, and space must all be properly allocated for the efficient
and routine transmission of knowledge and skills from a staff of perhaps
250 to a conscript mass of 3,000 to 5,000 students daily. Although educational ends are pursued, the principal's time is monopolized by the
press of immediate managerial imperatives:

What is most important from where I sit in the principal's office is that the
entire philosophy of the high school principal is changing. It's very different
from what it used to be. At one time we considered ourselves educators. I
think the problem is much too complicated, the organization is much too vast,
the ramifications are too great, the partners in the enterprise are too many for
us any longer to serve as educators. It seems to me that the changing role of

2 By 1971 this statement had become out-dated, as local boards were elected and
had the power to hire district superintendents. The high schools, however, remained
under the authority of the Division of High Schools.

the high school principal is to move from educator to administrator, and I think this is what is happening in the high school picture. With 4800 children in my school and 245 teachers, with 50 or 60 new ones coming in each year, with a mass input of community decision and policy making, with the selection of staff, with the multiplicity of building improvement, of purchasing and so on, the high school principal doesn't have much time left for the educational process.

Despite the encroachment on his prerogatives and the pressing demands of managerial problems, the principal is still a key figure in the school, exercising considerable authority and responsibility. The principal is the key to the "personality" of a school, a vague amalgam of efficiency and morale that one can presumably sense upon entering a school. Although no one could define what general qualities make a "good" principal, all felt it was easy to recognize one—he "does the job effectively." He may be democratic or authoritarian, casual or formal, friendly or aloof, but none of these styles is in itself necessary or sufficient to define the "good" principal. He must be "effective," the implicit criteria being efficiency and orderliness of school operation, good staff morale, and good relations with his various publics.

Of all his publics, the principal has control over only the students. He tends to respond to students administratively—they exist for him either as statistics or as problems. Figures reporting attendance, dropout, and suspension, as well as group reading and achievement scores, go into the "paper-profile" of the principal's school at headquarters. Disciplinary problems reach the principal only as the last step in a series of authorities from teacher to department chairman to "dean" or administrative assistant. The principal thus stays remote from the routine measures necessary to organize daily work and control the students. In a "difficult" school pupil control may be an overriding concern: fights among students, disrespectful gestures toward teachers, and general disorder may absorb a great deal of the staff's time and energy. In the ongoing struggle between staff and students, symbolic defiance by students, such as improper dress or hair length, are defined as major problems. Since order is the vital prerequisite for teaching, order and education sometimes become almost interchangeable terms. That the necessity for order may itself be a source of educational problems is rarely considered within the bureaucratic structure of mass public education.

Principals are very aware of the "bad press" the public schools have been receiving in books, press, movies, and television reporting. Several were pleased to take the interviewer through their schools to show him "quiet halls and orderly classrooms" in refutation of the disorderly "Blackboard Jungle" image. Since the authority and respect they believe to be their due are dependent upon a favorable evaluation by the public of the school system, they are sensitive to critics and they harbor some resentment because they have not been more adequately defended by the Board of Education. In their view, better public and press relations are a crucial need at this time and emphasis should be given to publicizing the achievements and merits of the New York City school system.

The problems underlying the "crisis of urban education" are not, of course, the creation of the educational critics. The "reality problem" that the New York City public school system confronts is made up of the following major elements: (1) a demographic shift in the city's population and in the school-going population, in both cases there being an influx of Blacks and Puerto Ricans and an outflow of middle-class Whites—the Whites moving to the suburbs or transferring their children to private or parochial schools; (2) the Civil Rights movement and its demands first for integrated education and currently for "equal educational opportunity" even if segregated; (3) the documented failure of the school system to educate lower-class Black and Puerto Rican children to "achievement levels" comparable to those of Whites; (4) a concomitant change in the job market whereby an education of at least high school level has become a requirement for all but the most menial jobs and of college level for better-paying white-collar employment.

Educational advancement is now the main avenue to economic opportunity. The increasing saliency of education in American society has paralleled the demands of Blacks for educational equality, demands given legal sanction and public legitimation by the Supreme Court decision of Brown versus Board of Education in 1954. Although the basic demand is for economic opportunity, the political battle has to a large extent been focused on the public schools which, since they are visible, local, and tax supported, are more vulnerable to criticism and available to politics than is the economic structure.

The central problem of the public school system in New York City and other major cities is the failure to teach the lower-class Black (and Puerto Rican) child. This failure, along with the demise of meaningful integration, has led to an increasing "politicization" of the school system, laying open to public view and political debate its role as an allocator of life-chances.

The professional educators whose careers are embedded in the present educational system, a system legitimated by many years of reasonably satisfactory operation, resent the intrusion of "politics" into their professional domain. They do not think of themselves as political men and they are not prepared by experience or ideology to engage in the hurly-burly of the political arena; their own "politicking" is more of the nature of bureaucratic intrigue. For principals the public attack on the school system and its organization is a threat of what might be called "incipient deprofessionalization." Their ideological defense against those groups accusing the schools of a failure to educate their children is a reiteration of the prerogatives of professionals and the need for public respect:

How can we stem the very unfortunate tide that is sweeping this city, and I suspect from my reading, other cities, in so far as community relations are concerned? I think we have a lot to blame on ourselves. We have, for example, as the only profession that I can think of, encouraged people regardless of their scholarship, to come in and sit down and give us advice on how to run a public school system. You don't see the legal profession asking the public, for example, to sit on the bench with the judge and give him tips on how to conduct a court case . . . and we say come on in, anyone can teach. Now, I think this is one of the things which has led us to our present lack of eminence in the community. I would say this—that one of the greatest problems we face, I think myself the greatest problem, is the loss of professional respect which high school principals once had . . . the high school principal then, I think, was a source of professional power, control, and advice primarily because he had the respect of the people in the community. We have somehow yielded that. I think part of the reason is our own timidity . . . And we have had a succession of Boards of Education which have been notorious for their lack of guts . . . I think it is true and fair to say that the successive Boards of Education have not acted—they have reacted to pressure and they have reacted to shouts and screams—when some show of educational strength and professional strength might have helped us in this situation.

Educators in the public schools are vulnerable since the school system that presumably renders professional services to its clients may in fact be experienced as an agency of domination and control more concerned with its own organizational requirements than the "needs of the children." In any case, the analogy between a massive organization run on public funds that forces its services upon captive clients and the freely chosen fee-paid legal or medical expert is a weak one. The school system of New York City cannot be entirely removed from politics; the decision to "keep education free of politics" is itself an eminently political one. At a time of openly expressed public discontent disrupting the previously untested consensus of public support, a claim for professional autonomy will be difficult to maintain. Should hospitals have as little success as schools, doctors too would face public criticism, questioning of their expertise, and demands that their professional autonomy give way to public (that is, political) accountability.

As managers (although not directors) of the school system, principals have responded publicly and politically through the High School Principals Association and the Council of Supervisory Associations. The latter recently initiated a successful lawsuit to prevent the experimental school districts from bypassing the civil service eligibility list of the Board of Examiners in the selection of principals. The June, 1968, Newsletter of the CSA stated that "The Executive Board believes CSA must become a powerful union with sufficient funds and manpower to protect its legitimate interests." It calls for personnel and funds to "provide sufficient manpower for publicity, community organization of supervision, prompt handling of grievances, organization of mass meetings and/or demonstrations, preparation of position papers with adequate research, and other similar services performed by active labor unions." The High School Principals Association received credit from the Schools Editor of the New

York *World Journal Tribune* (November 6, 1966) for acting with the United Parents Association and the Public Education Association to block a program proposed by the Board of Education for promoting integration through the establishment of "clusters" of comprehensive high schools:

While the Board was mulling the pros and cons of the comprehensive cluster controversy, the coup de grace was delivered this week by the High School Principals Association.

The principals' organization urged its members not to cooperate with the Board or the superintendent of schools in further planning of the comprehensive complex program.

In telling its members not to cooperate further in planning the program, the association charged that curriculum was being ignored, too much money was being spent and that the whole thing was conceived and was being carried out without consultation with principals.

The high school principals, especially in concert with other supervisory groups, thus have the capability of acting as a "veto group" blocking those policies that they believe to be hostile to the interests of its members. The ultimate rhetoric of justification, as with other groups having an interest in school policies, is the "needs of children." Each group politically involved in school politics and policy formation assumes or at least claims that those policies that are in its interests are also those best designed to promote "education" or to "meet the needs of the children." One finds, however, little or no discussion of those "needs" as a substantive issue. At the CSA convention held in May 1968, for example, where the theme was "Supervision in the Critical Years," the panel discussion topics were "Living with a Collective Bargaining Agreement," "Grievance Procedures for Supervisors," and "Selecting Leaders for Tomorrow's Schools."

In their ideological defense of the school system high school principals tend to claim that the system is much better than its critics allow. Statistics on integration or educational achievement are used to defend the accomplishments of the New York school system relative to those of other cities. The disproportionately large number of New York City students receiving national scholarship awards may be cited as proof of academic quality, while relative statistics on integration need only be compared in order to show that New York City has made a major effort in this direction:

We are not in a spiral of decline as far as I can see. We've just failed to solve the problem of the disadvantaged child. Not that we *just* failed—*we failed* together with every city in the U.S. But section per section of kids we've got statistics you can use by the thousands which show that the New York City system is still a good system and in many respects a superior system.

The admitted faults of the school system are blamed on the multitude of difficult problems confronting the school system. Chief among these problems are the children themselves, many of whom come from homes that the educators perceive as being not only disorganized and emotionally damaging but incapable of supporting the activities of the school. Parents demand that their children be educated yet the children do not respond to the curriculum and methods that are usually successful with academically motivated middle-class children. Other problems cited by principals are the lack of "leadership" by the Board of Education and the Superintendent of Schools, the loss of a White middle-class clientele that has been fleeing a growing colored population, the demands that the school be a welfare unit and agency of social change, the powerlessness of principals to correct the socioeconomic causes of social discontent, the lack of funds for buildings and materials, and the ignorance of "the experts" from whom they would like practical proposals for coping with school problems. In the face of these problems principals express frustration and helplessness:

The reason that the school has been challenged isn't so much that we didn't do the job well in the past . . . we did the job all right until we reached this problem of integration and of dealing with a new kind of student for whom the methods we'd developed weren't adequate. And they were not adequate for reasons well beyond the capacity of the school to deal with. They were not adequate, for example, because of the social structure in which our society lives. They were not adequate because of the restrictions of labor unions, the employment picture, the housing picture. And suddenly what happened to us was that instead of selecting our goals, which were purely and primarily educational goals in the past, we found that goals were suddenly superimposed upon us and we were told: "You're not just a school, as it were; you're not just teaching these new students what you've got, but you're going to be the vehicle whereby they're going to be launched as equals into our society."

Despite the many problems faced by New York City's high school principals, in our interviewing we were struck by their almost total absence of self-doubt or career regret. Apparently their defenses against inner doubt as well as outer attack are well developed and effective. They, of course, have tenure, which protects them from loss of their position or salary, but tenure can hardly be sufficient reassurance against anxiety about their performance. Were they to doubt the ideological basis of their authority—the rhetoric of education—the principals would face paralysis in carrying out the duties that keep their schools functioning smoothly. It is thus essential that they denounce all who challenge or attack the school system—those they quickly label as "enemies of the public schools" and respond to with anger, resentment, and often poorly concealed contempt. Professors of education are commonly typified as going into college teaching because they "couldn't control a classroom" and as having acquired their experience in school systems whose total enrollment is less than that of a large New York City high school. Their credibility as advisors to the practical` schoolmen of the system is thus opened to question. Educational critics are particularly resented (the more distant, the more resented) for telling principals how education and schools should be changed without saying how their ideas are to be implemented.

Most of the people who are presenting major suggestions for the improvement of the schools are people who deal exclusively in generalities. They don't know enough about the things to deal in specifics and I think this is one of the things we're suffering from in education these days—that there is no role for the practical schoolman. Everybody's an educator—the college professors, the professors of education, are sublime educators. Sociologists—they have the center stage. The people who work in schools are rarely consulted about anything. We're not asked . . . this to me is the basic fault which exists now so that we have school people arrayed against other people instead of really working cooperatively to solve problems. Everybody is solving our problems without asking what the problems are or what we think ought to be done about them: From the Civil Liberties Union to the Center for Urban Education.

Part of their defense is to immerse themselves in the immediate demands of the job. This tends to result in what might be called the "bureaucratization of the imagination." When asked what they would do if given unlimited power and resources, principals often respond with ideas for improving the bureaucratic functioning of the job as it is—"Well, I could use another administrative assistant" or "We need more telephones here." (Several, however, stated that the greatest need is for better teachers.) The kind of experimentation demanded by the failure to "reach" a changing student clientele does not appear to be psychologically available to principals regardless of the security of tenure and a rhetoric of educational leadership. To ally themselves with parents or community groups in an attempt to pressure the Board of Education for school improvements would require as a prerequisite that they accept and acknowledge criticisms of their schools and of the system. This in turn would leave them vulnerable to self-doubt, which they already feel when under attack, and would weaken the collective defenses and mutual support worked out among principals to hold the line against further encroachments on their position or any major change in the system. They will accept new programs that can be absorbed into the routine of the school; they will work with those community people who share the principals' side of school problems. In our research the only open expression of self-doubt and questioning occurred during a seminar attended by ten principals:

There's something that bothers me here. Can we be so right and everybody else so wrong that we have no supporters anyplace? Maybe we are looking at the thing a bit narrowly. I mean, what's wrong with the present situation? Why don't parents keep their children in the public schools? Why has the school system fallen apart? Is there a theory, a political theory here that there are evil-doers like the members of CORE and other organizations who are deliberately pulling the school system down in order to effect some political gains of their own? Is this the only philosophy we have? I'm a little puzzled by this. How could we have come to this pass if we've been so good? Now I've been in this business a bit longer than some of you here—in a difficult area all the time—and I've bemoaned some of the things that have been happening too, and it can happen to any of us in two minutes. It happened in the Harlems and in the Bedford Stuyvesants first. But I think we can look at this thing a little narrowly. I mean, if we stop and ask, "What's wrong?—Why has this pablum which has been handed out by CORE and the others been so readily accepted? Why have the other parents been silent if it's been such a patent fraud? Why have they responded by taking their children out of the public schools and parochial schools?" Let's be honest about this. What's wrong? In what way aren't we serving properly? We can't always take the position—and I think this is the reputation we've gotten in the CSA and the High School Principals Association—of always defending the status quo. Is there anything that anybody else has suggested about the organization of the schools, its curriculum, its reorganization, that we approve of? I've attended our Association meetings for almost fourteen years and we've always been "agin." Why have we always been the victims of the people in the community, instead of playing an active role? . . . Whether they've been mistakes on our part or mistakes on the part of the administration or the budget makers or whoever, I think our schools have left a lot to be desired and we have very often been defensive where we should have been taking the role of making changes initially and of taking leadership.

Such self-doubt would be a necessary part of an honest confrontation of the problems that might allow principals to come to terms with the predicament in which they find themselves. It probably would require them to become educators rather than administrators, innovators rather than bureaucrats, and would endanger the collective alliance that they have established with one another and other defenders of the established system. It would demand a respect for lower-class children and parents and an experimental attitude toward education neither of which was a prerequisite for advancement in their careers. At a time of social change, political conflict, and educational uncertainty, the principals are, and seemingly can only be, architects of the status quo.

REFERENCES

Gittell, Marilyn
    1966 Participants and participation: a study of school policy in New York City, Center for Urban Education.
Hughes, Everett C.
    1958 Men and their work. New York: The Free Press.
Levy, Gerald
    1970 Ghetto school: class conflict in a public school. New York: Pegasus.
Rogers, David
    1968 110 Livingstone Street: Politics and bureaucracy in the New York City schools. New York: Random House, Inc.
Weitz, Leo
    1960 The high school principal in New York City: a study of executive responsibility in theory and practice. Unpublished Ph.D. dissertation, New York University School of Education.
Wilensky, Harold
    1964 The Professionalization of Everyone? American Journal of Sociology LXX, no. 2 (September), pp. 137–158.

NATIONS AND ENCLAVES

16: *Education, Modernization, and the Process of National Integration*

HELEN ICKEN SAFA

The importance of national integration in the process of modernization is acknowledged by most students of social development. The process of "nation-building," as it is also popularly called, is seen to have both a material and an ideological component; that is, emphasis is given not only to the mobilization and development of the country's resources, but to the achievement as well of an ideological consensus that binds the people together in shared values and goals.

Education can play an important role in both the material and ideological components of the process of national integration. It develops the manpower resources of the country by providing new opportunities and new channels for upward mobility. In this way, human resources that may have been unproductive are mobilized and utilized for the country's further growth. From the ideological viewpoint, the school provides a common institutional system through which all children must pass and from which they derive a common set of symbols, values, and goals. Thus, they learn to salute the national flag and to sing the national anthem, and they acquire a vision of the past glories of their national heroes (compare Cohen's discussion of "Schools and States" in his essay in this volume). The school provides a framework through which a national ideology can be shaped and formulated, and then taught to a large segment of the society at an age when competing values have presumably not yet had a chance to take hold.

While schools are an important instrument for national integration—especially in the developing areas—education, like other mechanisms of modernization, may also widen the gap between certain sectors of the society rather than narrowing it. This can be most clearly seen in the advantage that urban children commonly enjoy in terms of schooling; since most schools, at least beyond the first few elementary grades, are located in towns and cities, rural children must go to extra expense and effort in order to receive more than a primary school education. The result can be observed in statistics from an underdeveloped country such as Haiti, where annual enrollment figures for urban and rural elementary schools differ by less than 10 percent (Dale 1959, pp. 49–63), while 87 percent of Haiti's population lives in rural areas. Similarly, all secondary, vocational, and commercial schools in Haiti are located in urban areas, which employ almost 90 percent of all professionally trained teachers (Dale, pp. 25).[1]

The educational advantage enjoyed by the urban versus the rural sectors of society is not the only disparity that may be accelerated by the modernization process. The decision to support secondary as opposed to primary education, private as opposed to public schools, or scholarships for university study abroad as opposed to development of an indigenous university, each tend to create an educated elite rather than raise the educational level of the public at large. Of course, where financial resources are limited, as in most underdeveloped countries, such decisions may be necessary and indeed, more suitable for the country's development plans. But it would seem that such an educational policy can only retard the process of national integration by widening the gap between the elite and nonelite sectors of the society. Silvert (1965, p. 12) has described the political implications of this "asymmetry of development," as he calls it:

> The obvious result is to impede consensus and the consequent legitimation of a single, coherent series of institutions, and thus to inhibit the generation of the public power that otherwise might permit the employment of massive force to impose a certain minimum compliance with modernizing behavioral norms despite opposing belief systems.

In other words, the asymmetry of development impedes the achievement of a common core of values and institutions upon which the legitimacy of public power is based; without this consensus the national government lacks the power to mobilize the country in accordance with modernizing norms so that the whole process of development is weakened.

Asymmetrical development widens the gap between the elite and the masses in a developing society. It means that the benefits of modernization accrue to only the elite (although that may be somewhat broadened in the process), while the subordinate elements in the society remain

[1] Statistics from other Latin American countries are comparable. Thus, according to the 1964 school census of Brazil, 80 percent of the children in urban areas were attending school and only 51 percent of those in rural areas. In Guatemala, rural elementary schools have only three years of instruction, and few pupils go beyond the first grade. In rural areas, the registered students represent 26 percent of those eligible by age compared to 77 percent in urban areas. (Secretaria General del Consejo Nacional de Planificacion Económico, *Programa de Educación para la República de Guatemala*, Guatemala, 1965, p. 3).

stagnant or, in terms of relative deprivation, their position may even worsen. Asymmetrical development would seem to be particularly true of "plural" societies, which consist of culturally differentiated segments usually divided along tribal, ethnic, linguistic, religious, or racial lines (M. G. Smith 1960, pp. 763–777; see also the discussion of the "out-of-it" groups by Thomas-and-Wahrhaftig in their essay in this volume). The cultural differentiation between the dominant group and subordinate elements in a plural society makes the process of national integration vastly more complicated, since it involves the establishment of common cultural norms as well as common institutions in the various sectors of the society. The elite group in a plural society may find it advantageous to maintain this cultural differentiation, since its power depends on denying access to avenues of upward mobility to those below. The national integration of plural societies often requires an overthrow of the traditional elite and its substitution by an institutional system that represents the subordinate elements and is justified by a new ideology. This is especially true of colonial societies where the dominant elite consists of a foreign power imposing its rule by force on the indigenous population.

However, plural societies represent a special case and in this paper we shall deal primarily with the problem of articulation between the nation-state and its constituent local communities in the society without marked ethnic or racial divisions. That is, we are less concerned with breaking down cultural differentiation between sectors of a plural society than with establishing channels of communication and mobility that will permit the free flow of people, products, and ideas between the national and local levels of any developing society. This is achieved not only by an increase in the power of the central government but by the development of national level institutions such as the market economy, political parties, labor unions, and education, which absorb all sectors of the society into an interlocking widening framework (Cf. Despres 1968, p. 14).[2] As Richard Adams (1964, p. 6) has pointed out for Latin America, the process of national integration is not simply the incorporation of communities within the national system but the incorporation and creation of other organizations such as labor unions and agrarian reform groups, which intersect with and form parts of communities and thus become devices whereby the national government can gain direct access to and control over local populations.[3] National integration in Adams' terms thus becomes a conscious attempt by the government to break down community

---

[2] Highly centralized governments may actually impede the process of national integration, as the Latin American experience has shown.

[3] Adams seems to view these institutions primarily as tools for control from above rather than for participation from below. Clearly both are possible, but it would seem that if national integration is used only as a device to increase the power of the central government, this can only accentuate the asymmetry of development discussed. We shall return to this point later.

bonds that inhibit communication and control from the larger political system.

Education is a powerful tool in this process. The school is the only national-level public institution in which all members of the society, theoretically at least, should spend some years of their lives. They may never join a political party, or serve in the army, or belong to a labor union, but most people, particularly in the younger age groups, have attended school. And this is becoming increasingly true as educational programs expand in the underdeveloped areas.

Therefore it is important that policy makers be made to understand the contributions that education may make to the process of national integration and to the development of a national ideology, based on a core of common values and institutions. We shall look at education as a nation-building institution, as a link between the national society and the local community. Yet to do this, we must begin with a thorough understanding of the process of national integration itself. What are the mechanisms by which the local community is tied into the national state? How is the shift from an inward orientation toward the local community to an outward orientation toward the nation-state reflected in the attitudes and behavior of the local inhabitants? What can be done to accelerate the process by which a self-contained, isolated peasant community becomes a full participant in the national society? In particular, what contribution can education make to the nation-building process? These are some of the questions that this paper will attempt to answer.

DEFINITIONS OF NATIONAL INTEGRATION

While most students of socioeconomic development agree upon the importance of national integration in the modernization process, the definitions of what constitutes a modern nation-state differ considerably. Usually these differences reflect the various academic disciplines that have been successful in the area and their respective emphases on one or another type of institution.

For example, the economists were probably the first to work in the development area, and they still continue to dominate the scene, both in terms of theory-building and field practice. Economists, and those influenced by them, have generally emphasized the growth of an economic infrastructure as a necessary component of the process of national integration. Thus, the establishment of a national currency and banking system; the development of trade, transportation, and communication; and even such modern institutions as the stock market are seen as contributing to the process of national integration. Because of the ready availability and identification of economic indicators and the considerable amount of research that has already been done in this area, it is not surprising that most quantitative measures of socioeconomic development rely heavily upon·these items.

Political scientists, on the other hand, emphasize the growth of a "participant society" as being indicative of the process of national integration (compare Green's essay in this volume). In their view, as long as a substantial sector of the electorate remains outside the national political system of the country, its members cannot be considered as full participants in the life of that society. Thus, political scientists focus on mechanisms that will broaden the base of political support in a country, such as the development of national political parties, the extension of the suffrage to nonelite sectors of the society, the percentage of the population voting in national elections, and the growth of government functions and services.

Sociologists and anthropologists are now only beginning to work in the area of social development, but their theories also tend to reflect their respective disciplinary interests. Thus, sociologists such as Leonard Reissman (1965, pp. 16–17) emphasize the growth of a middle class as a necessary component of the modernization process. National integration is seen as encompassing a change in the society's stratification system and a widening of the elite stratum of the society. Anthropologists, on the other hand, tend to emphasize a change in values or ethos as being indicative of the process of national integration. Thus, Clifford Geertz speaks (1963, pp. 153–154) of the "integrative revolution" as the "progressive extension of the sense of primordial similarity and difference . . . to more broadly defined groups . . . within the framework of the entire national society." That is, Geertz envisages the widening of primary group sentiments based on kin, religious, or linguistic ties to larger and more inclusive groups in the society (compare Cohen's essay in this volume).

Whereas these definitions of national integration differ in emphasis, they all point up the necessity of replacing traditional, local, "primordial" ties with a new identification with the nation-state. Karl Deutsch (1961, p. 494) comes closest to the meaning of national integration as used in this paper when he defines his theory of "social mobilization" as the "process in which major clusters of old social, economic, and psychological commitments are eroded or broken and people become available for new patterns of socialization and behavior." Yet most of these theories emphasize changes at the national level rather than at the local community level. Thus, the growth of a system of national trade or national political parties, or the shift in the social structure or value system of a society may all be conducive to national integration but they do not tell us what happens in the local community as it is subjected to these developments and absorbed into the national structure.

We shall observe national integration primarily from the viewpoint of the local community and shall primarily direct our attention to the changes that take place in the local community as it becomes more closely articulated with the national society. As communities come to play a more specialized role within the larger society, they in turn become more internally differentiated and more dependent on goods, services, and ideas from the outside. Local people begin to participate in institutions that cross community boundaries and bind them together in new forms of association and interest groups. Seen from this perspective, the process of national integration involves the loss of purely local community ties and the increasing importance of "broker" institutions that mediate between the local and national level of the society. How this process evolves will become clearer in the following section as we examine the theories of community growth and change developed by anthropologists.

STEWARD'S THEORY OF SOCIOCULTURAL LEVELS OF INTEGRATION

One of the first anthropologists to turn his attention to the concept of nation-building was Julian Steward, a scholar who enjoyed the distinct advantage of having worked in both primitive and complex societies— among the Great Basin Shoshone Indians of the American Southwest, and among the peasant and urban subcultures of Puerto Rico. From his work Steward derived a theory of sociocultural levels of integration along an evolutionary continuum, whereby territorially larger and more complex systems replace simple, localized systems (Steward 1950, p. 107). Thus, the traditional Shoshones had been organized simply into patrilineal bands, without any hierarchy or permanent chiefdom, whereas the complex society of Puerto Rico incorporated various regional subcultures whose people were interrelated through an intricate network of economic, political, and social institutions.

According to Steward (1950, pp. 107–108), the process of sociocultural integration does not consist merely of the incorporation of more numerous and diversified parts or communities, but in the growth of functional interdependence among these parts. In complex societies this functional interdependence is accomplished through special social groups, which Steward calls horizontal segments and through formal national institutions. Steward's horizontal segments consist of occupational, class, caste, racial, or ethnic groups that cut across localities and bind segments of communities into new, national subcultures. The formal, national institutions such as currency, banking, trade, education, the legal system, the army, and churches constitute the infrastructure that holds the society together at the national level (1950, p. 115).

It would be possible, therefore, using Steward's theory to trace the absorption of the local community into the national state by comparing the importance of formal, national institutions and these horizontal segments at two points in time: for example, Tepoztlán at the time of Redfield's and later of Lewis' study, or Middletown as studied by Robert and Helen Lynd in 1925 and in 1935. Similarly, one could compare two different communities in terms of their degree of involvement in a national structure by comparing the relative importance of national institutions and horizontal segments in these communities. There would be no question, for example, that Middletown would show far greater involvement with the national state than would Tepoztlán.

THE "BROKER" CONCEPT

Building on Steward's theory of sociocultural levels, Eric Wolf (1956) elected to emphasize the significance of the horizontal segments in the process of national integration. According to Wolf (1956, p. 1065), these "nation-oriented groups" follow ways of life quite different from that of their community-oriented fellow villagers. School teachers, policemen, or tax collectors are agents of national institutions and, as such, they act as mediators and interpreters between the national levels, on the one hand, and the local community, on the other. National integration thus proceeds from a "web of group relations which extends through intermediate levels from the community to the national level." That is, nation-oriented groups are the vehicle or channel through which a national culture and ideology is transmitted to wider and heretofore isolated segments of the society.[4]

The value of Wolf's approach lies in the fact that it focuses attention on relationships among groups operating on different levels of society rather than on the local community per se. As Steward (1950, p. 22) has pointed out, the anthropologist working in community studies has devoted too little attention to the extralocal influences to which the community is subject (Wax-and-Wax in this volume employ for this purpose the Redfield-Singer notion of "great tradition"). Wolf (1956, p. 1075) has coined the term "broker" to refer to those persons who mediate between nation-oriented and community-oriented groups. As he points out, brokers are often marginal men seeking political and economic power in the society.

----

[4] The distinction Wolf makes between nation-oriented and community-oriented groups can be compared to Redfield's folk-urban dichotomy (Redfield 1947). The *correctos* of Tepoztlán, as defined by Redfield, are also nation-oriented and lead less traditional lives than the *tontos*, their inward-oriented folk villagers (Redfield 1930, pp. 217–223). However, whereas Redfield saw the city as the focal point of change, Wolf places more emphasis on the nation-state (Wolf 1966, p. 11). Wolf argues that the city is merely the locus of power for most nation-states, which would help to explain why urbanization and the growth of state systems often parallel each other.

Thus, in Mexican history the brokers were neither the Indians living in isolated, largely self-sufficient rural communities nor the large landowners or *hacendados*, who held effective economic and political power and blocked the channels of communication and control from the local to the national level (Wolf 1956, pp. 1067–1073). The brokers in Mexico were marginal, largely landless men who with the development of the concept of private property bought into Indian communities and developed their farm land for cash-crop production through plow culture. Through the Mexican Revolution and the land-reform program, they succeeded in breaking the power of the *hacendado* and opening up channels of upward mobility, chiefly through the institutions of the political party. The result has been a great increase in the power of the national government, which now has direct access to the peasants through the *ejido* program, and the creation of a new nation-oriented political elite to replace the old, community-oriented *hacendados*.

THE CLOSED CORPORATE COMMUNITY AND THE "OPEN" COMMUNITY

Following Wolf's thesis (1955), "brokers" form an essential link between the local community and the national society. With the development of a broker class, there is a shift among the rural peasantry from what Wolf has called the closed corporate community to the "open" community, which is an integral part of the nation-state.

The closed corporate community, as defined by Wolf (1955, pp. 456–461), is characterized by a tightly knit internal structure that attempts by various means to shut off the influences from the outside world. Thus, the community restricts the sale of land to outsiders and in other ways (e.g. marriage rules) tries to prevent outsiders from becoming members of the community. The Westernized person is not looked up to as a model of modernity, but is ostracized as a deviant from the traditional way of life. The only involvement with the national economy is through intermittent day labor on *haciendas* and plantations and through a regional marketing system particularly geared to the peasant's subsistence economy. Thus, little cash flows through the community and whatever wealth there may be is never allowed to accumulate but is redistributed periodically through religious fiestas, the *cofradía* system, and mutual aid practices. In this way, pressure is brought to maintain everyone at the same, low socioeconomic level, or what Geertz (1956, p. 141) has termed "shared poverty." There are strong sanctions against conspicuous consumption; and superstition, witchcraft, envy, and gossip operate to maintain a close social control over community members.

In Latin America the closed corporate community is generally concentrated among subsistence peasants in the highland area but it can also be found in other world areas, and Wolf (1957) has compared Mesoamerican cases with examples from Central Java. Wolf himself has stated (1957, p. 8) that the closed corporate community is not limited to any culture area, but is the product of ". . . the dualization of society into a dominant entrepreneurial sector and a dominated sector of native peasants." This situation occurs most commonly under conditions of colonialism, where the foreign power acts as the "dominant entrepreneur" as was the case with the Spanish in Mexico and the Dutch in Java. However, the closed corporate community can also be found in many noncolonial under-developed countries characterized by what economists have called a "dual" structure (Boeke 1953).

Under the pressure of modern conditions the closed corporate com-munity is rapidly disappearing. Land scarcity is forcing the surplus popula-tion in these communities to seek other sources of income, and many migrate to the cities in search of better job opportunities. These migrants constitute a new type of "broker," introducing new standards, tastes, and values to the villagers left at home. This is particularly true where, as in Greece, urban migrants maintain frequent contact with their rural kin, despite changes in class position and ways of life (Friedl 1959, p. 31). Friedl has noted (1964, pp. 572–574), for example, that the peasants' occupational and educational aspirations are becoming more urban-oriented under the influence of these migrants and of other urban-educated elite living in the village; they now aspire to traditional professions in teaching, law, medicine, and the priesthood, with emphasis on a humanistic educa-tion, but have not yet caught up with the new urban trend toward education in the physical and social sciences and engineering, and toward work in industry and commerce. "Lagging emulation," as Friedl (1964, p. 570) calls this concept, thus "provides a mechanism of transition by which rural peasantries gradually become an occupational, nonpeasant segment fully integrated into a national culture and society." In other words, to use Wolf's terms, lagging emulation becomes a means of hasten-ing the transition from a closed corporate community to an open community.

My own data from a Puerto Rican shanty town (Safa 1968, p. 345) show how older urban residents may also act as brokers for newly arrived migrants by easing their transition into the urban milieu. In the shanty town, friends and relatives of new migrants help them to find a home and a job, to locate urban facilities such as the school and hospital, and to establish new social contacts in the urban area. In this way older urban residents hasten the incorporation of newly arrived migrants into the national urban structure of the society. The result is to reduce cultural differences, which could be maintained intact in the rural area, and to encourage the development of a new, national culture based upon uni-versally recognized values and standards. Seen in this light, migrants can be considered as an important tool in the process of national integration, which those who deplore the rush to the cities in the underdeveloped areas might consider.

Wolf (1957, pp. 13–14) lists other factors that contribute to the disintegration of the closed corporate community. He cites the inevitable inequality of community members resulting from crop losses, differential family size, and dependence on outsiders for credit. One could add the inequalities stemming from planned development schemes, which as we have shown, often tend to favor certain sectors of the society more than others. Thus, Berreman (1963) describes a community development program in an Indian village, where the benefits of increased agricultural productivity fell primarily to the high-caste Hindu farmers, at the same time alienating the untouchable artisan castes. Berreman also cites the failure of attempts at democratic decentralization through granting side powers to the village councils or *panchayats*, which were dominated by the local elite or high-caste groups. Here is a clear case in which the process of modernization has served to increase the power of the elite, even when the avowed aim of the program was the democratization of the village structure.

Kunkel (1965) has cited evidence from several Mexican community studies of the social changes consequent upon the absorption of small agricultural villages into the national economy, through mechanisms such as cash crops, wage labor, and importation of foodstuffs. Most of the changes are in the direction of greater internal differentiation, such as the breakdown of the *cofradía* system and compulsory labor, the sale of land to outsiders, and the instability of ritual kinship and extended family ties (Kunkel 1965, p. 444). Closer articulation with the national economy, in short, involves a loss of internal village cohesion and homogeneity and greater orientation outward to the larger society.

The peasant in the open community is forced to be more outwardly oriented than the peasant in the closed corporate community because he relies heavily on outside sources of credit to finance his production of cash crops. The risks attached to cash-crop production often spell downward mobility for both the peasant and his creditor, so that the open community is characterized by a repeated "circulation of the elite" not found in the stabile, subsistence economy of the closed corporate community (Wolf 1955, p. 465).

With the shift from the closed corporate community to a more open type of community, a change occurs in both the number and the nature of the broker relationship. The traditional subsistence farmer may be involved with a person of wealth and influence in a particular, highly personal relationship, usually termed a patron-client relationship (Foster 1963); these relationships tend to maintain the stability and status quo of the subsistence community. By emphasizing the superior nature of the patron as opposed to the inferior nature of his client, status distinctions in the community are reinforced and individual mobility is discouraged. The peasant in the open community, however, is usually involved in a series of such relationships and is rarely completely dependent on one person.

Thus, Silverman (1965) describes the historical changes in the nature of the broker or mediator relationship in a central Italian *commune* as the community moved from comparative isolation to integration into the national society. For centuries the Italian peasant, who worked the land on a *mezzadria* or sharecropping basis, looked to the landlord as his patron, to supply him with his material needs as well as to provide his only contact with the outside world. After the unification of Italy, landlords were supplemented by other professionals residing in the community such as schoolteachers, priests, and tax collectors, who in effect controlled economic and political relations with the outside world. The postwar period, however, signaled a new kind of relationship between the community and the larger society, with peasants beginning to participate directly in the national society and patrons being replaced by a variety of "diverse, competing intermediaries" (Silverman 1965, p. 292).

The brokers of the integrated, open community differ radically from the traditional patrons of an earlier period in that the former generally represent the extension of national-level institutions into the local community. They are schoolteachers, labor-union officials, political party representatives, and policemen, most of whom come from oustide the community and may not even be local residents. They should represent a mechanism for change and improvement in the local community, in contrast to the static nature of the old patron-client relationship. As Silverman points out (1965, pp. 280–281), the patrons maintained their power in the local community by their exclusive control over relations with the outside, and the modern "intermediary" has lost this exclusive function.

However, Wolf (1956, p. 1073) has argued that a comparable change in the nature of the broker relationship in rural Mexico has not substantially changed the life styles or life chances of the Mexican peasant. The Revolution of 1910 succeeded in breaking the power of the local patron or *hacendado* and in increasing the power of the national government by giving them direct access to the peasants through the *ejido* program. The Revolution opened up channels of opportunity to the nation-oriented but for most peasants ". . . the granting of *ejidos* tended to lend support to their accustomed way of life and reinforced their attachment to their traditional heritage" (Wolf 1956, p. 1073). Thus, the Mexican Revolution, and specifically the *ejido* program, strengthened the power of the central government but did not lead to increased participation and mobility for the average peasant at the village level.

It would seem, then, that the movement toward national integration does not necessarily spell increased participation at the local level. It may merely represent a change in the power structure, from a local elite to a national bureaucracy. The channels of communication established from the local to the national level allow the government to exercise greater control over the local population but do not necessarily allow this population greater participation in the national society. The powerless continue to be subordinate, but to a new set of rulers.

To summarize, then, the process of national integration signifies a loss in autonomy and isolation of the local community, and a growing importance of formal national institutions as well as of the special class of brokers who mediate between these national-level institutions and the local villagers. The shift from a closed corporate community to an open community is accompanied by the following.

1. There is a growing outward orientation on the part of the villagers, signified by the development of various kinds of "broker" relationships with persons in the outside world.

2. There is an increasing importance in the community of cash crops and other monetary institutions such as banking, credit associations, and national trade.

3. Changing standards and aspirations occur in such matters as occupation, education, prestige symbols, age and sex roles, and even attitudes toward time (see Friedl 1964), consonant with the standards prevalent among the urban, nation-oriented elite.

4. An emphasis is made on status and upward mobility, demonstrated through conspicuous consumption and wealth accumulation; and the loss of community solidarity formerly exhibited through the fiesta system, *cofradías*, communal land and labor, and the like.

5. There is a growing inequality of community members, which eventually leads to the development of a number of subcultures in the community besides the peasantry. The homogeneous, one-class peasant community is replaced by a heterogeneous, multiclass community composed not only of peasants but artisans, shopkeepers, white-collar workers, and professionals. With time, the peasantry itself is transformed into an occupational category and is no longer a distinctive subculture with values and ways of life it can call its own.

The movement toward internal differentiation at the village level would appear to be an inevitable outcome of the modernization process. Modernization acts as a selective device, whereby channels of mobility are opened to some and remain closed to others. Modernization does not necessarily ensure a higher standard of living for all the citizenry, and the symbols of progress—such as highways, steel plants, and new office buildings—may benefit only a very few.

If not carefully planned, modernization is thus likely to widen the gap between the elite and nonelite sectors of the society, leading to Silvert's asymmetry of development referred to earlier. National integration, however, depends to a large extent on closing this gap, and on giving subordinate elements in the society a greater voice in the decision-making process. Thus the effectiveness of national institutions such as political parties, labor unions, agrarian reform groups, and education, may be measured by the degree to which they accomplish this aim and truly represent new interest groups in the society. If they serve only to increase the power of the central government and to reinforce the traditional elite structure, then they are not likely to succeed in achieving national integration. National integration coupled with modernization should thus help to ensure the *distribution* of resources and rewards over a greater proportion of the population.

IMPLICATIONS FOR EDUCATIONAL DEVELOPMENT

What is the role of education in this process? Will educational development widen the gap between the elite and nonelite sectors of the society, or will it open up new channels of mobility to incorporate formerly subordinate elements of the society in the nation-building process? A great deal depends on the goals of the educational policy in each nation and the way in which these goals are implemented at the local level. Education may reinforce the existing stratification system or it may represent a vehicle for change, at the national as well as at the local level.

Perhaps the easiest way to see the relevance of education to the process of national integration is to take an actual example of a village school and examine the social consequences of its operations at the local level. Fortunately, Manning Nash (1965) has presented us with just such a case in his illuminating article on the role of village schools in the process of economic and cultural modernization. We shall extend Nash's analysis somewhat further by examining his data in the light of the theory of national integration developed here.

THE "CLOSED" VILLAGE OF AMATENANGO[5]

The village of Amatenango, Mexico, as Nash (1965, pp. 133–136) describes it, is a good example of Wolf's closed corporate community. Despite the work of the Instituto Nacional Indigenista and an *ejido* program in the community, villagers have but little interest in or contact with the outside world. Nash relates that nothing in the school curriculum implements the aims of the Indians, who confine themselves largely to earning a living in the village and getting along with their neighbors. The school, as an agent of the outside world, transmits an entirely dif-

5 Nash's article includes a description of two village schools in Burma, but we have restricted our discussion to the two Latin American examples.

ferent cultural tradition, alien to the villagers, and therefore has little impact on the community (compare the description by Wax-and-Wax of the relationship of school to Indians in the U.S.).

The school's isolation from the lives of the villagers of Amatenango is heightened by the alienation of the schoolteacher, the only *ladino* or non-Indian resident in the village. He has little to do with the village population and feels no identification with them. Consequently he cannot and does not act as a broker for the village; only a person with links to *both* the national and community level can serve in this role. It would seem that the only real brokers in this community are a few former graduates of a boarding school established by the Mexican government, all of whom have returned to reside in the village. These graduates now form somewhat of an elite in Amatenango, and hold top offices in the *cofradía*, the village's self-governing civil-religious hierarchy.

Nash (1965, p. 106) cites the successful example of these boarding school graduates as proof that education in this type of closed corporate community must be "withdrawn from community constraints" to have any effect on the villagers. As long as the school operates within the community setting, students are not free to open their minds to a new and different cultural tradition, and they must, therefore, be physically removed from the village for education to have any impact (here, contrast the views of Cohen and of Thomas-and-Wahrhaftig in this volume).

So drastic and costly a solution would obviously be unacceptable to most educational planners—as well as to most villagers. They would not want to see their children taken away to school at an early age and be deprived of their help at home and in the fields. To establish boarding schools on the elementary school level would clearly be costly because of the mass of children involved, and to limit this to a select segment of the elementary school population would only reinforce the elite base of the society. It would seem that only at the secondary school level might boarding schools become a feasible alternative, since the number of students involved is usually much smaller and they often require technical or specialized training that can be given most efficiently and economically in centralized institutions. Even this measure, however, will deprive the majority of peasant children of a secondary school education.

If boarding schools are not a viable alternative, what then can be done for the elementary school children of a closed corporate community such as Amatenango? It would seem that closer attention could be paid to the curriculum so that it bore more relationship to village life. Perhaps more emphasis could be given to Indian heritage and custom, to farming and other agricultural activities, and to sports and other recreational activities in which village children traditionally participate. The school could become a center of village life by serving as a meeting place for the *cofradía* and other traditional village activities and by participating in village fiestas such as the feast of the patron saint. Above all, members

of the community, adults as well as children, must be given a voice in forming educational policy, at least at the local level; they should participate in
the selection of the teachers, in determining curriculum content, and in
awarding scholarships and other honors. In this way, perhaps, the school
will be seen as an integral part of the local community and may become
a mechanism by which peasants begin to participate in the national
society. In this respect, the personality of the schoolteacher and his rapport
with the villager is, of course, extremely important.

Amatenango already shows several signs of change. The fact that the
boarding school graduates are looked up to as leaders in the community
is evidence that the value of education is recognized and respected. If
this were a completely closed community, these persons would be treated
as deviants. It is also important that these former students have remained
enough a part of village life, despite their superior education, to act as
mediators between the villagers and the outside world. As more villagers
recognize the prestige attached to this broker role and the benefits to be
gained from knowing how to deal with the outside world, the value of
education is likely to sharply increase.

THE VILLAGE OF CANTEL

The second community Nash (1965, p. 136) describes is located in the
highlands of Guatemala and is, by Wolf's definition, a far more "open"
type of community than Amatenango. Compared to the latter, the village
of Cantel numbers more persons and contains several subcultures in addition to the peasantry—particularly an important artisan class. Many of the
residents are also literate and bilingual. Above all, Cantel is the site of a
relatively large factory, which has opened up new job opportunities to the
villagers and provided them with new links to the outside world.

One index of the "openness"of Cantel is to be found in the occupational
aspirations of its schoolchildren. As Nash (1965, p. 137) points out, their
marked preference for artisan and specialist occupations shows a decided
break with traditional community roles and ties. Since most of these
occupations could not be exercised within Cantel, the children, in choosing
them, have indicated their willingness to risk their futures in the outside
world.

Nash found, however, that the older generation of Cantel were less
willing to undertake new occupational roles, which would involve leaving
the village and learning new skills. They were hesitant to risk their
investment in village life for an unknown return in the outside world. As
Nash (1965, p. 138) explains:

In local communities, the village school begins to instill different values
from those of the local community, but adulthood, the claims of mundane

life, the competition of the known with the unknown, and the absence of supporting institutions beyond the schools makes these values, in most instances, atrophy and disappear.

Nash has recognized an important policy implication for educational planners, namely the need for additional institutions to reinforce the values transmitted through the educational system. Peasants must see the utility of education in terms of new job opportunities, the ability to read a local newspaper or understand an official document, or of growing a better crop or selling more products at the market. They must participate in other institutions that instill a national ideology, such as the army, political parties, labor unions, land reform, and other development programs. Education alone cannot "open up" a community; it must be part of a holistic program that includes the improvement of trade, transportation, communication, and other mechanisms that link the local community to the outside world.

Nash (1965, p. 137) also cites the lack of government support as another reason for the failure of the schools in Cantel to act as major catalysts of change in the community. Here Nash refers not only to the lack of financial support—in the form of textbooks, teachers' salaries, and school buildings—but also to the lack of a clearly defined governmental policy for the incorporation of Indian communities into the national state. While the government would like the electoral support of these Indians, it fears that the growing political consciousness of this submerged majority may be turned against the government and used as a potential force to bring about major changes in the political and social structure of the society. Thus, as Nash (1965, p. 137) points out:

The schools are not seen nor used as catalysts in social change but are confined to transmission of the elementary skills, some patriotism, and some minor facts about history and geography.

In most developing countries the politicalization of a submerged sector of the population poses a major threat to the existing power structure of the society. As we have pointed out, effective political power is, in most cases, still concentrated in a small elite group, which is afraid of losing its historic privileged position in the society. Yet national integration cannot be truly achieved without broadening the base of political support. As Deutsch (1961, pp. 498–502) has pointed out, the process of "social mobilization" brings with it an expansion of political participation and increased demands for government services and expenditures. Thus the government must choose between safeguarding the rights of a privileged minority and broadening the stratum of its political support to incorporate all segments of the society within the national political structure.

If the government succeeds in winning the support of this new electorate, it can greatly strengthen its own political position. It can establish direct links with this rural population and thus subvert the power of the traditional elite. But to do so, the government must embark upon a bold new program involving a radical change in public policy and a rapid extension of government services. It must institute programs of tax reform, land reform, and welfare services, and it must modernize its educational system so as to serve the needs of this new electorate. By extending education and other services to this heretofore neglected population, the government can reach a much wider population than the small urban elite upon whom it traditionally depended for support. Not only must the government provide more services to these people but it must also open up channels of mobility that will encourage their participation in the national-level institutions of the society.

However, if the government chooses to ignore the demands of this potential political force and to confine its base of political support to a traditional elite, the school may serve essentially as a mechanism for maintaining the status quo in the society. As in Guatemala, the school will concentrate on traditional curriculum and teaching methods and fail to prepare its students for new roles in the outside world. It may act merely as an additional mechanism of control for the government, teaching students to accept the existing power structure by indoctrinating them with the inherent superiority of the traditional elite. Thus, only if the government adopts a conscious program aimed at radical social change and at the incorporation of all peoples into the national political framework, and sees education as an instrument of that policy, can the school serve as a nation-building institution.

SUMMARY AND CONCLUSIONS

In this paper we have attempted to trace the role of education in the process of modernization and national integration in developing societies. In line with Steward's levels of sociocultural integration (1950, p. 115), we have emphasized the importance of formal national institutions and special subcultural groups who mediate between the national and village levels. These "brokers," as Wolf (1956, p. 1075) calls them, help to "open up" a community to the outside world by establishing links between nation-oriented groups and their community-oriented fellow villagers. Eventually, as the community is integrated into the national state, it begins to lose its isolated, corporate character and to depend increasingly on the resources and services provided by the larger society. It also begins to exhibit marked integral differentiation as the modernization process places more emphasis on cash crops, wage labor, and the creation of new occupational groups in the community.

By way of summary, it may be worthwhile to repeat some of the principles developed in the course of this paper that help illuminate the role of education in the nation-building process. Four principles appear as the most important:

1. The Distinction Between Closed and Open Communities.

It should be evident from our discussion that education will have a very different impact in closed and open communities. The open community is likely to be more receptive to education, viewing it as a means of upward mobility and as a means of learning more about the larger society. Therefore, an initial educational development scheme in a developing area might well start with such communities, since the possibilities of success are much greater than in closed communities.

The closed community represents a far more difficult challenge to educational planners. The standard curriculum and teaching methods that work well in the open community may require considerable revision in order to have any impact on the students in a closed community. Some people argue that the very contrast with their traditional way of life will be more appealing than a gradual, evolutionary change, so that the best way to deal with these insulated communities is to assault them with the most modern techniques and innovations. This approach must be qualified, for in a program of planned educational change it is important to demonstrate respect for local traditions, to build upon the people's knowledge of their own local customs and institutions, and to develop their capacity to participate in the larger society. The school subjects all students to a common set of norms and values that helps to break down the plural nature of many of the developing societies. In order to adopt a more universalistic set of values, the closed community need not break completely with past tradition, but must widen its sphere of reference to include larger and more inclusive groups in the society. As Geertz (1936, p. 154) has pointed out, "The integrative revolution does not do away with ethnocentrism; it merely modernizes it."

But the virtue of a gradual, evolutionary approach in a program of planned educational change versus a radical, massive transformation is a tactical argument to be settled by educators through practice and experimentation. The important point to recognize here is the differential role of education in open and closed communities and the need to revise curriculum and teaching methods accordingly.

2. The Importance of the Broker Role.

The broker role emerges as being highly important in the process of incorporating village communities into the national society. In particular, educators should recognize how the school can promote the development of a broker class in the local community. The schoolteacher himself serves as one of the most important brokers in relating the community to the larger society. He is an agent of a national institution and he is usually an outsider born and educated in a different area of the country, and thus embodies a somewhat alien cultural tradition. By virtue of his superior education and official position, however, he is almost automatically a member of the local elite and as such, his attitudes and way of life are looked up to by local villagers as a model for their own behavior (Cf. Friedl 1964, p. 579). Thus, the personality of the schoolteacher and his rapport with the villagers are crucial factors in determining the success of programs of planned educational change in local communities.

Students also come to form part of the elite of these communities, and thus become the leaders who direct the pattern of change along certain lines. Graduates of secondary schools or other forms of higher education are often forced to leave the local community in order to occupy new positions in the larger society; but if they continue to maintain close contact with their home community, as in Greece, they help to relate this larger world to their former fellow villagers. If they remain in the community, the new concepts they have learned in school and the new social contacts they have made serve to establish new links between the local community and the outside world.

Education has been blamed for contributing to the exodus from the rural areas to the cities because migrants are often impelled to test their newly acquired skills in the urban area, which offers greater and more diverse job opportunities than the small rural community. In addition, education, simply by teaching students about the outside world, makes them anxious to see and know more about it. While this charge is probably correct, it is also true that when educated migrants come to the city they are better prepared to withstand the demands of a new urban way of life than those who arrive with no skills and no knowledge of how the larger society operates. Educated migrants adapt more easily and can contribute more to the development of a modern, industrial economy. However, should these migrants encounter the same frustration in the city that they faced in the rural area, they are likely to constitute an explosive political force aimed at making radical changes in the society. Again, the foresight of the government in anticipating these new demands and their ability and willingness to meet them is of prime importance.

3. The Need for Supporting Institutions in Addition to the School.

While education may serve as a vehicle for social change, it cannot operate in a vacuum. To be effective education must be part of a comprehensive development plan, even on the village level. It is totally unrealistic to set up a new school in a community and expect it alone to alter the villagers' way of life and outlook. Under these circumstances, the school either has no impact on the local populace or it too loses touch with the mainstream of national culture and becomes merely a mechanism for perpetuating the status quo in the community.

Education, like other mechanisms for effective change, must be linked to other institutions that give it meaning and value. If the school is to prepare students for new roles in the national society, there must be possibilities for these students to participate in that society through job opportunities, political posts, and access to the administrative structure. Villagers must become aware of the outside world through various channels in addition to the schools such as the mass media, political parties, labor unions, and agricultural cooperatives. Only through participation in a number of national-level institutions can villagers become fully integrated into the life of the national society.

4. The Importance of Government Support.

An effective policy of national integration relies heavily on government support. As Adams (1964, pp. 7–9) has pointed out, the impetus for the development and integration of local communities must come from the national level. It is the government that provides the techniques, implements, credits, and education on which development is based. Therefore, development on the community level presupposes some degree of development on the national level.

It is clear that communities cannot develop in isolation from the national society. For development implies closer articulation of the local community with the national society, through which villagers gain access to markets, systems of transportation and communication, and educational facilities. But community development is not a simple process of funneling down from the national level, as Adams would seem to suggest. Some "grass roots" development must take place for the community to be integrated into the national society. An isolated village of subsistence farmers has little need to be part of the national structure. As the village produces more—and so requires markets for its crops, credit to purchase equipment and supplies, and new agricultural techniques to augment its yields—its need and desire to become a part of the national society increases. It is true that the national government must supply these needs, but it does so in response to a demand emanating from the local communities.

All too often the process of national integration is seen merely as an extension of government control over a wider, heretofore isolated population. However, if this population is not given an active role in the new political order, then it remains as subordinate as before, and perhaps subject to new sources of exploitation. The process of participation must begin at the local level, with local people assuming greater responsibility over local institutions, which in turn link them into the national power structure. Thus, communities must be given greater control over their own destinies, even as they merge more closely with the national society. Otherwise, we are merely "pouring old wine into new bottles"; that is, we are using the vehicle of the modern nation-state to perpetuate a traditional, elitist power structure. As we have seen, this is a process in which education can play a vital role; it can enable people to play a greater role in the national society or it can maintain and reinforce existing inequalities.

REFERENCES

Adams, Richard
 1964 The Latin American community in revolution and development. Occasional publications no. 3, Center of Latin American Studies, Lawrence, Kansas: University of Kansas, pp. 5–10.
Berreman, Gerald
 1963 Caste and community development. Human Organization, 22, no. 1 (Spring): 90–94.
Boeke, J. H.
 1953 Economics and economic policy of dual societies: as exemplified by Indonesia. New York: Institute of Pacific Relations.
Dale, George A.
 1959 Education in the Republic of Haiti. Department of Health, Education and Welfare, Office of Education Bulletin no. 20, Washington, D.C.
Despres, Leo A.
 1968 Anthropological theory, cultural pluralism, and the study of complex societies. Current Anthropology 9:3–26.
Deutsch, Karl W.
 1961 Social mobilization and political development. American Political Science Review 55, no. 3 (September):493–514.
Foster, George
 1963 The dyadic contract in Tzintzuntzan, II: patron-client relationship. American Anthropologist 65, no. 6 (December):1280–1294.
Friedl, Ernestine
 1959 The role of kinship in the transmission of national culture to rural villages in mainland Greece. American Anthropologist 61, no. 1 (February):30–38.
 1964 Lagging emulation in post-peasant society. American Anthropologist 66, no. 3, part 1 (June):569–586.
Geertz, Clifford
 1956 Religious belief and economic behavior in a central Javanese town. Economic Development and Cultural Change, 4 no. 2 (January):134–158.
 1963 The integrative revolution: primordial sentiments and civil politics in the new states. *In* Old societies and new states, C. Geertz, ed. New York: The Free Press.
Kunkel, John A.
 1965 Economic autonomy and social change in Mexican villages. *In* Contemporary cultures and societies of Latin America, Dwight Heath and Richard Adams, eds. New York: Random House, Inc.
Nash, Manning
 1965 The role of village schools in the process of cultural and economic modernization. Social and Economic Studies 14, no. 1 (March):131–143.
Redfield, Robert
 1947 The folk society. American Journal of Sociology 52 (January):293–308.
Reissman, Leonard
 1965 Urbanization and education in the development process. Paper prepared for A.I.D. project on noneconomic factors in social development. Syracuse, New York: Syracuse University Center for Development Education.

Safa, Helen Icken
  1968 The social isolation of the urban poor: life in a Puerto Rican shanty town. *In:*
       Among the people: encounters with the poor, Irwin Deutscher and E. Thompson, eds. New York: Basic Books, Inc.
Silverman, Sydel
  1965 Patronage and community-nation relationships in Central Italy. Ethnology 4,
       no. 2 (April):172–189.
Silvert, Kalman
  1965 Social modernization: outline of a theory. Paper prepared for A.I.D. project
       on noneconomic factors in social development. Syracuse, New York: Syracuse
       University Center for Development Education.
Smith, M. G.
  1965 The plural society in the British West Indies. Berkeley: University of California Press.
Steward, Julian
  1950 Area research: theory and practice. Social Science Research Council, Bulletin 63.
Wolf, Eric
  1955 Types of Latin American peasantry: a preliminary discussion. American Anthropologist 57:452–471.
  1956 Aspects of groups in a complex society: Mexico. American Anthropologist 58:
       1065–1078.
  1957 Closed corporate peasant communities in Middle America and Central Java.
       Southwestern Journal of Anthropology 13:1–18.

17: *Indians, Hillbillies, and the "Education Problem"*

ROBERT K. THOMAS
AND ALBERT L. WAHRHAFTIG

INTRODUCTION

As anthropologists, our talents are best realized when we can deal with the institutions of human societies as expressions of viable communities of people dealing with their environment. It is not with the exotic aspects of "culture" with which we are concerned as much as with the processes of human viability. We are bound to see education as part of the general human process of socialization whereby young people are prepared to fit successfully into the internal environment of the community of their upbringing and into the external environment within which exists the total community of human beings of which they are a part. Schools, where they exist, are treated by us as a specialized institutional arrangement designed to accomplish some specified part of the educational process that related individual humans to their communally understood environment.

Although anthropologists have dealt sympathetically with the intricate and alien education given to the young of many distant societies, we still generally deal with such communities as a closed system—e.g., with a single African tribe, heuristically isolated. It is for this reason that so little anthropological knowledge has been transferable to the educational problems encountered by communities of people in the United States and by those who educate them. By virtue of this methodology, we are seldom equipped to do more than consult on the degree of fit between given educational institutions and the people of a given culture. To the extent that we become able to comprehend our total national society as the context wherein the life of small communities is enacted, we find that it is not the nature of the communities encountered within it that causes us to pause. We find that Yaqui Indians are Yaqui Indians, whether they live in communities in Tucson, Arizona, or Potam, Mexico, and Kickapoo Indians are Kickapoo Indians whether their communities are in Jones, Oklahoma, or Nacimiento, Mexico. Rather, the nation-as-environment presents us with new factors to consider. We are accustomed to dealing with communities where only famine, disease, or, perhaps, conquest constitute serious threats to communal viability. Now, when we turn our attention homeward, we must suddenly add to this list of environmental variables those threats to survival posed not only by urban civilization with its universal tendency toward dehumanization and alienation, but also by the centralization and stratification of power and technology in our national variant of urban society.

For the many tribal and folklike communities in our country today, our national expectation of social mobility, and our imposition of education as an instrument of mobility, are cardinal facts of the total environment. These are conditions for viability demanded of such communities by the increasing number of highly urbanized people who, as a corporate elite, guide our national destiny on the assumption that as individuals, through education, we can all learn to become successful participants in a national social system.

Within this environment, as within any other, we are only able to know how much and in what ways individual human beings learn by seeing how and with what success whole communities of human beings function in context. Only from this can we determine the effectiveness of the educational process. Anthropological research on schools and education is meaningful under these circumstances only to the extent that it is an aspect of research on the small community "in process." Research on the small community as it engages in the process of dealing with a national environment is reflexive; if our studies teach us nothing about our national social system, then we are learning nothing about the community, its educational processes, or its scholastic problems. It is the process of coming to terms with an environment that is causal of human action, and it is the defects in this process that are causal of human problems.

INDIANS, FOLK-WHITES, AND "THE SYSTEM"

Our own knowledge of Indians, folk-Whites, and their schools has been gained in the Ozark area of Eastern Oklahoma. Within this area we find all the ingredients of the American "educational problem" as well as most of the latest "solutions" devised to solve it.

Before 1907, this entire area was part of the Cherokee Nation. Today 12,000 Cherokee Indians live there, 9,500 of them in traditionally structured, small, Cherokee-speaking settlements. The educational level of these Cherokee Indians is one of the lowest in the United States and their dropout rate one of the highest. Of the adult Cherokees 40 percent are functionally illiterate in English. Approximately one in three heads of

Cherokee households in country Cherokee settlements cannot speak English. Cherokees attended their own schools for half a century and the school system of the State of Oklahoma for sixty years thereafter. Even so, the Cherokee community of eastern Oklahoma is one of the least educated in our nation.

Interspersed among the Cherokees are rural communities of what we shall call "folk Anglo-Saxons." Elsewhere in the United States these people might be called "hillbillies" or "Okies," but the terms are pejorative and do not match the local self-image. Most of these White families moved into the Cherokee Nation either as "intermarried Whites" or as illegal intruders during the 1890s. They were the restless, rootless seekers after opportunity who moved west from Arkansas, Kentucky, and Tennessee. Some have "made good" as the backbone of the local small-town middle class. Most are "just country folk," "respectable people" in their own eyes, but as culturally distinct from the Oklahoma middle class as they are from Cherokee Indians. Although their level of education is low and their dropout rate is high, they are slightly better educated than their Cherokee neighbors.

Folk Anglo-Saxons are quite poor, and the Cherokees are poorer still. Both populations work predominantly at unskilled jobs. Among both populations unemployment rates are astronomical. In short, both populations rank among the peoples Americans feel privileged to call "underprivileged." Only recently have the poverty and lack of education of these people been officially recognized, but already intense efforts are being made to help them to (in the current idiom) "participate in the mainstream of American life."

Such solutions to the problems of these folk as are being put into practice reflect great faith in education as a palliative. In addition to renewed state concern with school consolidation and administrative reform, new Federal programs are being introduced: Project Head Start, an attempt to imprint underprivileged children with the school mother-image; Neighborhood Youth Corps, which offer money and the promise of a student consumption level equal to the more privileged student body as an inducement to continuing education; and, Upward Bound for the survivors of high school. At the same time, other new vocabulary and another new complex of programs indicate that local planners see a relationship between nonparticipation and cultural differences. The former Cherokee Nation is coming to be identified as a part of a newly discovered culture area, "Ozarkia," for which a special web of legislation is being woven. The Bureau of Indian Affairs has been entrusted with setting up new adult education courses within Indian communities. The leading educational establishment within the state, the University of Oklahoma, has joined with socially conscious state politicians to form a powerful new organization, Oklahomans for Indian Opportunity (OIO).

The OIO program depends heavily on creating a better fit between Indian communities and local school systems by inviting selected members of Indian communities to attend "leadership training seminars" at the university, and by establishing "human relations centers" in Indian communities to promote programs of educational encouragement. Taken together, these programs reflect a pervasive concern with fitting people as individuals (and perhaps even as communities) into a school system. There are even some indications, such as a proposal by the OIO to teach educators and school administrators more about Indians, that in some instances the school system may be altered to fit people and their communities.

In eastern Oklahoma, we see the stereotype of the "education problem" in the United States: a "problem" population low in income, education, and social rank dealt with by an administrative elite attempting to solve problems by acquiring power and money with which to amplify and strengthen educational and social institutions.

We maintain that the problem is not in the fit of people to their schools and institutions, as has been suggested by so many modern academic critics of the American school system. It is true that if a community is facing a stable environment and simply wants to maintain its life style, there will of course be a perfect fit between school and community. However if a community facing a rapidly changing environment responds by wishing to train its children to live in a different and more advantageous way, then members of the community will deliberately create or utilize an educational system that does not fit themselves or their children. This was the case with the immigrant communities in many American cities in the 1900s, with Cherokee Indians who entered mission schools in the early 1800s, and possibly is true of some West African peoples today. Modern critics are convinced that the fit between school and community is a problem because so often they observe schools that do not "belong" to the communities they serve. It is the experience of the student for whom school is a daily symbolic reminder that he is an unwelcome alien in a foreign province that makes the question of "fit" seem important. It is not the fact that he does not fit the school that damages a student; it is the expectation that any "normal" student *ought* to fit, or be made to fit. So, the problem lies in who does the fitting and why.

The Ozark area of Oklahoma is of interest not so much because of the peculiar ethnicity of its population but because it is an area involved in catching up with a "culture lag." The social change that in more urbanized parts of the United States took place steadily since the early 1930s is now taking place in the isolated Ozarks, at a more accelerated pace. In eastern Oklahoma we are able to see the history of small communities and their school systems throughout the United States recapitulated as they were affected by the increased urbanization and centralization of power that betoken participation in the modern American social system. As the social system of this area has developed and become more akin to modern middle-class America, both the Cherokee and the folk Anglo-Saxons have become casualties—educationally and socially.

Increasingly, eastern Oklahoma is coming to be an integral part of the American social system; increasingly the Cherokees and folk Anglo-Saxons are becoming alienated from it. No matter how greatly the Cherokees and folk Anglo-Saxons differ in the ethnographic particular, it is their common role as "out of it" communities in the midst of an evolving and ceaselessly closing social system that is definitive of their problems. The relationship of these communities to the educational system that now confronts them—their position vis-à-vis the schools that now serve as the intermediary between individuals and "the system"—tells us explicitly how the United States is put together.

Administrators, educators, and a school of social scientists see such communities as aggregates of underprivileged individuals. Lacking, it seems, the ability to perceive a functioning community in the first place, they perceive the problems of such communities as caused by an unsatisfactory relationship between individuals and "Society." Given this perception of causality, a solution based upon giving more power to institutions (such as schools) on the assumption that deprived individuals can be encouraged to participate in them follows logically enough. In this paper we assert that this very set of perceptions, assumptions, and power relationships is the cause of the problem. When scholars and administrators can gather in Denver, Colorado, to discuss the "Indian problem" in eastern Oklahoma, *that* is an Indian problem. Human beings exist within systems of human relationships. Human communities exist within the broader reaches of these same systems of relationships. Their problems, as communities of people, are caused by the relationship of community and social system.

It takes no great sociological insight to see that this is the case. Even a very brief historical sketch of the relationship between Cherokees and their schools demonstrates that, when the Cherokees as an ongoing people realized that they needed education in order to deal with the conditions that confronted them, they gradually developed a means of education for themselves that, of course, being *of* the community fit the community. Whenever the relationship of the Cherokees to their environment was disrupted, and traumatic events left the Cherokees incapacitated, their school system—in the absence of conditions that demonstrated its utility—suffered precisely the problems (lack of fit and alienation from community) that now beset it and other contemporary American school systems.

CHEROKEES AND THEIR SCHOOLS

Throughout the entirety of their known history, the Cherokees have been a populous, classically "tribal," conservative, but astoundingly pragmatic people. During the past 400 years, the Cherokees have faced a continual procession of dramatic, complex, and traumatic occurrences. As a tribe they weathered these experiences and learned. They were never smashed to the earth and disintegrated, as were many tribes. When, like the mink, their foot was caught in a trap, they gnawed it off; when for their protection they needed sons with the knowledge and cunning of White men, they "farmed out" their own sons and let them scout the destiny of the tribe; and when these sons worked against their fathers and brothers, they cut them adrift, drawing the ranks of the tribe close against their influence and leaving the castoffs to marry Whites and become a part of the society that had so turned their heads.

The modern Cherokee community participates in a way of life that has been consistent in form and direction since before the coming of the White man. In the 1700s, Cherokees lived in small settlements, each consisting of a single group of kinsmen, clustered around larger "mother towns." Periodically, kinsmen from smaller settlements joined with relatives in the mother towns to enact together the sacred ceremonial events that assured the whole people of a healthy, prosperous, and satisfying existence. These meetings of the people at their seven major ceremonies were periods of mutual deliberation. Life in a household is no more rewarding than a mother-in-law will allow it to be, and no mother-in-law is satisfied with witless, routinized propitiation. A sensible man takes his mother-in-law problem to his father, where in the shade of a tree an old man can be listened to and even argued with. So it is with a people. Even in times of peace and security, it takes the resources of all to adjust the intricate mechanisms of a shared life. About 400 years later, transported by a death march from the Southeast over a "Trail of Tears" to Oklahoma and surrounded by a nation of intruders, this is the consistency of Cherokee life. In eastern Oklahoma, small groups of Cherokee kinsmen live in nearly sixty settlements. The aboriginal village council of "beloved men" has shed its formality and sharp delineation. Instead, after dark and every Sunday, the yards of "white-headed" men are crowded with the cars of neighbors bearing news and seeking advice. The ceremonies have moved under the roof of a country Cherokee Indian Baptist Church and, with the exception of a minority of "pagans," at the precise seasons of the ancient ceremonials, delegations from country settlements join to reckon with the grace of the people during the seven days of the Cherokee Indian Baptist Association Convocation. The Cherokee social unit is unchanged; its superordinate purpose—simply "to be"—persists.

But tribal people are, by definition, people who live in response to their environment and who, because environments are everchanging, change through time. Twentieth-century America is the twentieth-century Cherokee's environment, and, for sixty years, the Cherokee response to that environment has been inertia. Hence, the Cherokees are poor, uneducated, and alienated.

Cherokees are totally withdrawn from the school system of the state of Oklahoma. Their median educational level of 5.5 school years results from the fact that Cherokees, on the whole, drop out of school at the earliest possible moment. This, however, is not because Cherokees fail to appreciate the benefits of education. When this country was in its infancy, Cherokees mastered the art of civilization. They were once a universally literate people and once established for themselves the finest school system in the Western United States. Cherokees know more about the consequences of formal education than do we.

In the late eighteenth and early nineteenth centuries, the Cherokee tribe faced its greatest crisis. Pandemic disease, decades of warfare, and encroaching White colonists disrupted the Cherokee style of life. Entire towns were burned, and the eastern lands of the Cherokee nation were lost. Refugees lodged with distant kin. The day-to-day relationships of a man to his neighbors became now more challenge than comfort. Men who were entrusted with irreplaceable knowledge—of the past of the people, of curative medicine, of the sacraments that kept the people united and invulnerable—were dead before their apprentices had been trained. Anglo-Americans had become powerful and demanding, game was scarce, and the hunting grounds were gone. Cherokee husbandry was demonstrably inferior to that of the Whites, and no arable land was safe from seizure. The people, high tempered and smarting, could not restrain their young men from striking back at the Whites. When the irresponsible blow was struck—a frontiersman burned out and his wife carried off— the whole people were made to answer. Each Cherokee act of vengeance against Whites netted a war of destruction in reprisal. Each man's answer to the problems posed by a White nation to an ongoing tribe was prized, and the answers, couched as responses to individual difficulties, were many.

To the problem of an Indian tribe unable to answer to the Whites for the uncontrolled actions of its individual members, nor to contest the policy of the Whites, came the answer of a Cherokee Nation. Over a base of constituent small face-to-face communities, and through arrangements that ensured that a common consensus among them would determine the course of their national policy, the Cherokees built a "voluntary native state" with a constitution, code of laws, and bicameral legislature.

To the problem of the loss of traditional knowledge through the premature death of Cherokee specialists came Sequoyah's answer: the native invention of a Cherokee syllabary. In the three or four years following the perfection of the syllabary in 1821, the Cherokees became universally literate in their own language. A rash of innovation followed. Cherokees became printers, readers, letter writers, jurists, codifiers of law, newspaper editors, and biblical scholars—the printed word was woven into the texture of Cherokee life.

To the problem of White men who manipulated laws so as to sanction the expulsion of the Cherokee from their homeland, and interpreted with oratory and Scripture the morality of this expediency, came the answer of Cherokees educated to contest Whites on their own grounds. Equally, Cherokees imported White tutors into their own homes ıd sent their sons to the best schools in the United States. To gain education in the interest of preserving their tribal community, the Cherokees were willing for a while to tolerate the growth of a "cultured" elite. When the elite proved to be insufficiently subservient to the direction of the tribe, the Cherokees turned to the principle of universal education, in their own language and in their own schools.

The Cherokees, already a tribal state before their removal in 1839, established the autonomous Cherokee Nation in Indian Territory (which later became Oklahoma). The struggle to cope with the greed of the State of Georgia and an expansionist Federal government, the rapid and differential acculturation that had been undertaken to rise to these tasks, and the trauma of Removal, broke the consensus of a people, now of many opinions, about how to survive. The tribe formed into factions and was able to unite only as a coalition. In the West, the Cherokee Nation was established in 1839 and was controlled by "traditionalists" not only in electoral office but at home along the creeks and hollows of the Oklahoma Ozarks where, by the rumblings of mass armed nativistic reaction, the most isolated and deeply traditional of Cherokees "cracked the whip" on their own national leadership. By the 1850s, the Cherokees were inseparably both a technologically modern, educated, literate, nation-state and a functioning tribe, unified by person-to-person interaction and an unyielding tribal view. If to survive as a tribe one had to compete as a nation, this price could be accepted with dignity.

Investment in education was, for the Cherokees, what investment for national defense has become for present-day United States, and the Cherokees equaled us in lavishness and compulsiveness, building for themselves a school system that was known to be the finest west of the Mississippi. What was defended by education was, ultimately, the country kin settlement. With the tendency of tribal people to share the skills essential to survival, and still tasting the bitterness of being sold out by an elite of "treaty signers," the Cherokee community repeatedly tugged at its government in an effort to maintain a school system adapted to the demands of the local community. For the traditional Cherokees, the Civil War seemed to break suddenly. When the armies finally dispersed, virtually no house was left standing, no field unscorched. The Cherokees, as a consequence of being blind to perilous developments in their relationships to the world of English-speakers, had been spared extermination, but they had been grievously punished for their lack of attention to their environment. When the smoke cleared, the Cherokees began to force their government to hand over their schools, and when their schools were at their command, they poured in their children. In 1873, the Cherokees were on the threshold of this resolution. Chief William B. Ross told his Nation:

> If the public schools have not been attended with all the success that might have been wished or expected, no deliberate, candid, mind, it appears to me, can deny that they have been productive of great good and are *still* the means of imparting much knowledge to the children of our country. No one denies benefits derived from public schools by that portion of our people who have a knowledge of the English language. *But there are those who contend that the present system has been a failure so far as those are concerned who have not that knowledge.* [Thornton 1925, p. 36, italics ours]

That year the Cherokee-speaking community showed its muscle. Immediately, bilingual schoolteachers were assigned to Cherokee-speaking communities, textbooks were printed in the Sequoyah syllabary, and English was taught as a second language. Pupils became both learned and bilingual. Graduates of the neighborhood schools poured into the Cherokee Male and Female Seminaries that were by then among America's leading institutions of higher education. For the first time, sizable numbers of Cherokee children from the "traditional" faction ran the gamut of their national school system and emerged as young professionals in the service of their natal communities. As these men took their places on the floor of the National Council, behind country pulpits, or simply on their front porches, the Cherokees reached the zenith of their experience with education. For even in the 1890s when the first generation of educated traditionalists was taking its place within the Cherokee Nation, their faction—by then known as "Fullbloods"—became alienated from their own school system.

The rift between the traditionalist Ross party and the acculturated but unassimilated Treaty party in the Cherokee Nation grew into a complete falling-out between a "Fullblood" and a "Mixed-blood" faction. The majority "Fullbloods" held the "Mixed-bloods" responsible for their mutual disasters during the Removal and the Civil War. Slighted, mistrusted, possibly misunderstood or possibly understood only too well, the Mixed-bloods increasingly married White intruders in the Nation and became anxiously responsive to the growing and aggressive population of Boomers in Kansas, Sooners in the west of the Indian Territory, Railroad Boosters, and land promoters. By the late 1890s, the Mixed-bloods had become not only a majority, but were answerable to the expectations not of the tribal faction they had bested but of their aggressive White neighbors. Their last strategy of survival was to coerce their Cherokee

Nation into becoming more "American" than America. The only certain vehicle for the production of men who would be both Cherokee nationals and super-Americans was the Cherokee national school system. The Mixed-bloods did become superbly educated, but as early as the 1890s, the Fullbloods were confronted with a school system that was predicated on forcible acculturation. Gone from Cherokee government was the presumption that a Cherokee tribal community could survive. By intent, the school system no longer fit the Cherokee-speaking country settlements. Even then, the experience of attending a school intended to reshape a community was miserable. Angie Debo says (1941, p. 309) of the Creeks, who were in a similar predicament:

Perhaps it would have been wiser to conduct the day schools in Creek, for they were almost a complete failure in teaching English. The a-b-c method in vogue at the time was bad enough for the English-speaking children, but it was worse for the young Creeks. They learned to pronounce nonsense syllables like parrots, and to read rapidly in the First and Second Readers before they dropped out of school in disgust without knowing the meaning of a single word. Some of the teachers tried to work out a technique of their own by the use of objects, but they were under such strong pressure to show results in the glib reading of meaningless sentences that few were able to resist it. To make matters worse, none of the white teachers and few of the mixed-blood Creeks were able to speak the native language.

Nearly eighty years ago the Cherokees were alienated from the school system. In the interval the entire Mixed-blood faction assimilated into the general society, the Cherokee Nation was dissolved, and the State of Oklahoma was established in 1907 with stewardship of all formerly Cherokee institutions including the school system. When the Cherokee community lost the power to deal with its circumstances and thus the power to dictate the terms of its education, its participation in the schools ceased.

FOLK ANGLO-SAXONS AND THEIR SCHOOLS

Cherokees were coerced into the Indian Territory. The institutions they created there represent an attempt by them to make the best of an unfortunate situation. Folk Anglo-Saxons, by contrast, migrated into the Territory spontaneously and voluntarily. The institutions that they created reflect the free working out of the kind of community they most desired.

Indian territory was the last stop (short of California) for the original, individualistic, liberty-loving wanderers of the American frontier. The folk Anglo-Saxons who moved from Arkansas, Tennessee, and Kentucky at the turn of the century were drawn by the same selective process that caused Whites to populate the entire East of North America. They were the perennial expanders-of-frontiers. Life on the frontier, for some people, is rewarding. On the frontier, with its sparse population, nobody crowds in on a man. The North American environment is lush and rich. A man can live on fish and game, can create his environment to his own liking, can feel that he alone guides his own destiny, and can bear the responsibility for his own actions. But frontiers in this country have always been temporary. Increasing numbers of people crowd into newly opened territories, towns are planted, and commerce flourishes. A more complex division of labor is established, and institutions such as the church, the bank, and "the law" become powerful, and those who create for themselves a sedentary life that contributes to the growth and respectability of the community rank high in their favor. And the man who seeks to make life for himself and his family an individual creation, and for whom this total responsibility is the essence of manliness, feels emasculated, boxed in, and "out of it." For such men, the time to move has come. His place is one jump ahead of the Establishment. This kind of man, a seeker of the good life, strong-minded, a pirate, an authoritarian within his home, a *macho*, and often enough an outlaw, settled in the hills of eastern Oklahoma, wherever the Cherokees left a hollow unpopulated.

Folk Anglo-Saxons seldom came to Oklahoma as single men. Usually by the time they felt ready to pull up stakes, they had a wife and a healthy number of children. Often siblings moved together with their families. As immigrants frequently do, they often settled and sent for their kinfolk. As these Whites filled the hills of the Indian Nations they settled with their kinfolk around them in separate, small, kin-united communities. Even as they fled the Establishment they brought the seeds of the Establishment with them. Perhaps the deepest contrast between the folk Anglo-Saxon kin-based community and the Cherokee kin-based community is, among folk Anglo-Saxons, the irreparable tension between individual manly authority and the demands of community life. Folk Anglo-Saxons do not consider life complete without the minimum of community institutions. They concede that to deal with life, a man must learn more than his dad can teach him, for always the bankers, the lawyers, the womenfolk, and the supernatural loom before a man and his sons. They assert only the right to create their own institutions as they wish them, the schools included.

Folk Anglo-Saxons demand institutions accommodated to what they themselves are. They are livers. In Madison and Newtown counties of Arkansas, an environment precisely similar to the Oklahoma Ozarks, live the Anglo-Saxons who stayed behind. Their houses are sturdy, trim, ample, and rooted in the land. Their fields are meticulously cultivated, their gardens large, and orchards and flower gardens surround the houses. There are always several outbuildings and a large complement of domesticated animals. These farms are to provide an ample life, to load groaning tables with a variety of dishes, to pass on to one's sons. Church and schools, also, have an aura of permanency and elaboration. These are communities of builders. Pride in community here is pride in the things one is building and in the things that have already been built by people participating in the construction of a way of life. In the Oklahoma Ozarks, houses are seedy, farming is done with a lick and a promise, church services held in a parlor or in a madeover log cabin are as good as in a church house, and the same holds true in regard to schools. Community pride is pride in the quality of life that can be lived here, in the color and passion and freedom of it, and the kind of man that can be produced by it. Whereas the people of Jasper, Arkansas, feel gratified by an imposing courthouse, the people of Bunch, Oklahoma, take pride in a girl who "shows up fine" as Queen of the Strawberry Festival, or in a boy who outdoes the pros at the local rodeo, or even in a gutsy young burglar (who after all was only robbing town merchants) when he accomplishes a daring "human fly" escape from the county jail. What these people demand of communal institutions is an environment that allows for a maximum of passionate concern with others in an atmosphere of minimum coercion to participate. To submit to coercion is the end of manliness; to have the strength and concern to "carry" another man through hard times without putting him under obligation is the fruition of manliness. Thus, the folk Anglo-Saxon church is usually a Baptist or Holiness church, churches in which hierarchy is at a minimum, where preachers are of, and chosen by, the congregation, where a man can join his power with God's to heal his brother, where a man can shout praise when praise is due, but where the final responsibility is individual; a man must see the light himself and be saved by a revelation that is strictly an affair of honor between himself and his God. The political arena is the front porch of a crossroads store, not the county courthouse. No man is bound to participate in discussing the affairs of his community, but those with an axe to grind can count on an established place and a concerned audience.

The folk Anglo-Saxon school has traditionally been an institution outside the Establishment. The folk Anglo-Saxon sees his house as a citadel. Men say "As long as I'm under my own roof, I'll do as I please," and, to their sons, "As long as you're under my roof, you'll do what I say." The community, itself usually a cluster of related patriarchal families, is an extension of the home. The major institutions of the folk Anglo-Saxon community, the church, the school, and the store, are important—just by existing—as evidence of the completeness of life. They are each (and often interchangeably) places where the community can assemble for the pleasure of eating, playing, dancing, making music, and enjoying a demonstration that life is as it ought to be, or for serious discussion and decision-making that involves the community as a whole. The folk Anglo-Saxon community, embracing these institutions, is a self-contained social unit. As individuals, folk Anglo-Saxons are strongly "anti-Establishment." In the Cookson Hills, they produced and sheltered generations of Robin-

Hood-like outlaws who stole from the rich and gave to the poor. To them Pretty Boy Floyd is a folk hero. Their vote must be courted by promising to represent "the people, not just the big shots in the county seat." Bankers, "big shots," and the lawmen who represent them, are the enemy. Teachers, preachers, and storekeepers, with their relatively greater education and sophistication, are expected to be community resources, telling country folk what people in town have "up their sleeve" and acting as spokesmen for the interests of the rural community. There is, then, a clear boundary between the community with its institutions and "the system."

The schools that folk Anglo-Saxons built, rather than being the vehicle for entry into the Establishment, were the last line of defense against it. Folk Anglo-Saxon men consider schooling (and schoolteachers) "sissy" and essentially feminine. At the same time, they believe that a practical amount of reading, writing, and arithmetic are as necessary for personal protection as a "hogleg" pistol. They discourage any child from leaving school before he can read a newspaper, write a letter, and add a grocery bill. Beyond the attainment of these skills, unless a child seems interested in becoming an accepted professional within the community—such as a teacher or veterinarian—they consider education as an affectation.

According to folk Anglo-Saxons, the primary function of school is to impart useful defensive skills. The secondary function of the school is to socialize and even "civilize" children within the community. Placing socialization within the school resolves some of the tension between father and mother in the folk Anglo-Saxon family. Fathers encourage their sons to be a reflection (perhaps idealized) of themselves in their youth: wild, headstrong, reckless, and tough. They prefer their daughters to become polished ladies and, eventually, competent mothers, but if their girls are a little flashy and "high-stepping," they are not displeased. For children of both sexes, mothers are the refuge from the strong and often wrathful hand of the father. Mothers are the source of warmth and stability in the household. As such they cannot also be disciplinarians, nor dare they frustrate the wishes of their man. But mothers hope their children will surmount the very "evils" that the father encourages in them. They aspire toward gentle, docile children, free of the curse of wanderlust, who will stay rooted and sedentary. Between father and mother stands the school. The conflict is resolved by granting paternal authority to the school and insisting that it teach children "discipline" and make them "work hard." By demanding schools that discipline a child and work him "hard," folk Anglo-Saxons insist on the same opportunity they would give a child at home—a situation in which the child can demonstrate his own personal worth.

The folk Anglo-Saxon schools are part of the socialization system of a stable community. These schools support a sense of communal and personal worth within the community, and together with the students who pass through them to take their place within the community they are an essential part of the completeness of this communal life.

SCHOOL, COMMUNITY, AND SOCIAL SYSTEM
IN EASTERN OKLAHOMA

In the 1930s, the amount of education attained by the various populations of eastern Oklahoma differed only slightly from what it is today. Cherokees hardly went to school (the median number of school years completed by Cherokees was three), and had long since withdrawn from participation in the general society. Folk Anglo-Saxons stayed in school long enough to learn the 'three R's and then—even as they won independence from an authoritarian father and acceptance as an adult member of the family by knocking the old man on his ass—they quit. Children from small-town commercial families obtained enough education to enter and expand the family trade. Children who aspired to the professions finished school. The relation of school to the folk-life communities in the region was not ideal. Still, schools succeeded in imparting those skills that their constituent communities demanded. No one then concluded from contemporary statistics on educational attainment that eastern Oklahoma had an educational problem.

Today Oklahoma has a full-blown "educational problem," but the rough outlines of regional life are not that greatly changed, nor are new *skills* necessary for living there successfully. Now, as was true earlier, a prosperous merchant, secure in the middle class of a county seat, is as likely to have a fourth-grade education as a college degree. Over these decades, it is the requirements for status and social mobility that have most changed, and the newly formulated expectation that "education" will confer both. Completion of education is equated with arrival in the middle class. But, although many academic critics of our educational system overlook the point, this was no less true in 1930. What is new is the expectation that all youngsters *must* arrive in the middle class by completing their education, along with the new requirements for class mobility to which schools are tailored. Because schools are now exclusively producers of new entrants into the middle class, and because this is done by expanding the school's control over the student's environment, "school" acquires a new meaning even where the traditional formal relationship of school to community remains basically unchanged. These relationships, too, have changed, but the relationship of school to community is now far more changed by the fact that school itself has become something different than what it once was.

During the 1930s in eastern Oklahoma there was "the system"—which included a status ladder and differences in power and privilege—but, unlike the Cherokees and folk Anglo-Saxons today, no one was "out of it." Cherokees lived at a subsistence level with a "make-do" economy that combined petty farming and wage peonage. Folk Anglo-Saxons, living as rural farmers and stockmen, were the majority population, and from their ranks sprang prosperous town dwellers to take their place alongside the urbane "old settler" population of assimilated Cherokee Mixed-bloods. Town and country combined formed a self-sufficient social system, with people at each extreme of rank united by kinship. Countrymen, both as voters and producers, were securely in power, well able to reciprocate the favors they asked of their educated and sophisticated cousins in town.

Only this personal and reciprocal relationship between rich and poor was acceptable; beyond it countrymen resisted the expansion of power, repeatedly and forcefully. In 1917 Indians, Blacks, and Whites of eastern Oklahoma entered the Green Corn Rebellion as tenant farmers reacted against the abuses of tenancy and the military draft. In the following years the growing forces of Socialism and Populism in the state checked the power of the townsmen. During the 1930s, the shelter and protection that the countryfolk gave Pretty Boy Floyd made his career into a morality play that illustrated the vulnerability of bankers and big shots in the Establishment. Status was based upon wealth and family. To acknowledge country kin and conform to the behavior they dictated and appreciated was the only means to sanction and secure social position. Seemingly diverse routes of mobility were equally based on kinship. Often an extended family would "back" the youngest son and see to it that he was groomed for a "high-class" life. Alternatively, an extended group of males would pool their resources, marry their sisters to advantage, and, as a kin group, become mobile. (And elsewhere in the United States, entire immigrant communities became mobile.) Because there was rapid mobility by a variety of processes, although the mobility was dependent upon courting the power, kinship, and sanction of country folk, those who "made it" into the town middle class did not distinguish themselves, by their behavior, from the countryfolk. The country set the expectations of behavior for the entire social system. Only those few who were securely in the Establishment could afford the appearance of being "cityfied" or "dandy." Mobility was in no way contingent on behavior that was symbolic of allegiance to another class. Even today, the senatorial candidate with the deepest drawl and the best banjo picker in his entourage draws the vote.

In the 1930s, eastern Oklahoma schools reflected the communities they served. Policy was made by neighborhood school boards and adjusted to local conditions. Always school recessed in time to allow children to work through the peak agricultural season, whenever it fell during the year. School functioned outside of the Establishment. Teachers were specialized members of the local community, working where they were born and raised, and the school, lending its facilities to pie suppers, dances, and "socials," was a focus of community social life. Neither teachers nor administrators had extensive specialized training, nor did they conceive of themselves as professionals. Jobs within the school system were not channels of mobility. To the extent that school personnel sought mobility for their students, they, in league with parents and neighbors, sponsored and groomed selected pupils. To the community of which they were a part, they taught such skills as would enable its members to come to terms with the surrounding society.

In the years since 1930, eastern Oklahoma lost its integrity within the American social system. As an agrarian and rural state in an industrialized nation, its power and self-sufficiency were bled off. By the end of the 1930s, the American small farm economy stalled, and displaced farm hands were sucked into the industrial maw. The Oklahoma countryside became depopulated as the opportunistic and the disenfranchised moved by the thousands to cities on the Pacific coast. The local economy dissolved, kin groups fragmented, and countrymen became powerless and uninfluential. For lack of personnel and power, the political and social institutions that linked town to country evaporated, and with them, the customary channels of mobility. The widening gulf between town and country was accompanied by a backwash of urban immigrants into small towns, drawn by the opportunities for expanding service industries outside of the familiar grind of big cities. Rustic businessmen formed a community in interaction with urban newcomers adept at manipulating the system. At the same time Federal and state institutions, centralizing and expanding their control into rural areas, became "gate keepers" controlling the flow of cash into the local economy. Alienated from powerless country communities, the expanding population of townsmen came to depend upon members of the intrusive urban middle class to sanction their status. In a diffuse way, the opinion of urban Americans was empowered to dictate standards of behavior to eastern Oklahomans, for the only channel of mobility open was to join with the expanding generalized urban middle class on terms set by that class. Lacking any conception of the viability of rural community life, this new middle class sees as its mission the incorporation of Cherokees and folk Anglo-Saxons into the "mainstream of American life."

In a stagnant rural area, bereft of both farming and industrialization, with serious problems of unemployment and, because of migration, an underrepresentation of competent young adults, there is no ladder of occupations linking folklike country communities and the new middle class. Only those individuals who can make the behavioral adjustment to working in a service industry, dependent on the good will of an impersonal middle-class clientele, are assured mobility; and no sequence of occupations exists that allows Cherokees and folk Anglo-Saxons to experience the behavior that pleases middle-class consumers. As conditions for an impersonal but secure relationship, the middle-class demands an unspecified and mysterious personal transformation of Cherokees and folk Anglo-Saxons. The person that they are is unacceptable (what harried executive would purchase insurance from a salesman wearing cover-alls, rolling his own cigarettes, and speaking hayseed English?). Including Cherokees and folk Anglo-Saxons within the prospering class of the region demands the construction, from them, of acceptable persons. To the schools has been entrusted this act of creation.

As these changes occurred, the school system was taken over by the Establishment. School budgets were increasingly supplied by the state and Federal government, and control over schools was thereby centralized (compare Horton's essay in this volume). Power moved away from the local community school board and was bestowed on county superintendents who were responsive to state legislatures. Teachers' colleges and institutions of education grew in number and influence, and teachers became a corporate group with their own professional associations. Requirements for teachers were set by the state rather than by the country community. Administration was centralized in the interest of efficiency, and, as roads were improved and bus services offered, schools were consolidated—always over the protest of local people. The school system became an arm of the middle class, and teaching became a route into the middle class, and teachers, of necessity, were responsive to middle-class definitions.

In the absence of reciprocities that bind it to country communities, the Oklahoma middle class conceives of itself as "the world" and of its behavior as the American norm. Lacking the experience of the viability and vitality of Cherokee and folk Anglo-Saxon community life, members of the middle class see before them only low-ranked ethnic groups—individuals who for some reason have not "made it"—subsidized by middle-class productivity. In the absence of reciprocity, the power to coerce these peoples into entering the mainstream of middle-class life is seen as being entirely legitimate. Through the school system, the middle class dictates to the Cherokees and folk Anglo-Saxons the individual behaviors that they must adopt before they are admitted to the system. Since the middle class is an aggregate of individuated people who conceive of success as the result of individual goal-oriented self-improvement, it does not occur to them to provide opportunities whereby entire communities of people may improve their collective rank, nor do "deviant" communities of Cherokees and folk Anglo-Saxons have sufficient power to demand this concession. Thus, to all but mobile individuals, the system has closed.

In the Oklahoma school system, as it operates today, the expanding new middle class has taken over. Except in the deepest backwoods, middle-class students set the tone in the classroom. Thus, for both Cherokees and Anglo-Saxons, the middle class is an environment. Middle-class students, naturally, are unthreatened by this environment; it demands of them only that they "be." But, conspicuously demonstrated to the Cherokees and folk Anglo-Saxons by the successes of middle-class students and the awards given anyone who approximates their behavior, is the necessity of learning to become middle class. In this situation, Cherokees and folk Anglo-Saxons, both people with a strong sense of self-esteem, see only a reflection of the low-rank definition of their communities. Being men whose existence is embodied in a community, their experience of a school system, which, with newly implemented techniques for dealing with the "underprivi-leged" attempts to bring them up to an abstract standard of middle-class competence, denies their own communal concept of worthiness. As students—none of whom have internalized the middle-class conception of a perpetually improving self—do daily battle with this judgment of them, school becomes a discomfort disproportionate to any known reward it can offer. Significantly, the Cherokee dropout rate reaches its peak at the point at which students transfer from backwoods schools, where they are a majority, to consolidated high schools, where town middle-class students are the majority. Perhaps, then, since for these students the school is a middle-class environment, dropping out represents not failure but learning. Perhaps there is a lesson to be learned from the image these students have constructed of their environment. And perhaps the lesson that students are learning is that the middle-class-as-environment does not permit itself to be dealt with when a community strictly demands that its children be educated but not transformed.

AMERICAN SCHOOLS AND THE "OUT OF IT"

What has happened in eastern Oklahoma, an area where there has been a "cultural lag," is the start of what has happened elsewhere in America.

We hypothesize that in metropolitan ghettos as much as in rural hollows, schools have become something that must be dealt with by com-munities that are "out of it,"—i.e., nonparticipants in the power process and alienated from the ethos of middle- and upper-class North America. Many scholars have eloquently told us already that our schools are the colonial service of the middle class, that they do not fit the working-class and ethnic communities, and that programs designed to aid the disadvan-taged are a fiercely disintegrative experience for the "disadvantaged" youngster. What has produced this state of affairs? We suggest that the American social system, which in the 1930s included within it everybody from the working class to the aristocracy, has puffed into a middle-class monopoly. The new middle class, educated by its own school system to think that it *is* American life, has so expanded as to be itself "the system." There is, then, a double structure to America, for always what we have called "classes" have actually been ranked ethnic groups following one another through the experience of urbanization in an expanding, industrial society. Now, with a society that requires the expansion of producers and consumers of services instead of productive laborers, catering to the taste of an affluent middle class, the procession has halted. Groups retain their ranks, the Germans being higher than the Poles, and the Poles higher than the Puerto Ricans, but the real distinction is between those in the system and those out of it. No new enterprises will suck in the remaining communities of people in the way that the expansion of the garment industry set Jewish feet on the urban ladder, and the expansion of construction contracting broke in the Italians. In the 1930s, the United States reflected the slow process of urbanization-through-experience. The working class defined American mass media, leaving its mark on Fred Allen's "Alley," Broadway musical comedies, hearts-and-flowers greeting cards, and cinematic baseball biographies. Each of these reflected, as only the Maggie and Jiggs comic strip and a few Jewish monologists do now, the days when Americans could climb the class ladder and still retain their working-class behavior. Now, the middle class is the system and the system is closed.

Formerly schools faced a pool of immigrants, flowing from the springs of Europe, naturalizing them as entire colonies, allowing one ethnic group after another to climb from the ghettos and field hand's barracks, imparting technical skills with which workers could plunge into a productive economy and claw their way upward via social, political, and economic institutions that related muscular new communities to the expanding system. Now, schools face a stagnant pond of "deprived" individuals who were left behind in the rush, cut off, as are the Cherokees and folk Anglo-Saxons of Oklahoma, by the evaporation and centralization of local institutions. The odor of a man's sweat in a steel mill no longer counts; rather, individual aspirants must be deodorized to fill the slowly expanding niches in corporations and service industry "dealing with the public" where correct behavior, not productivity, is valued. *We know full well that it was the experience of participation in urban life, and not the schools, that transformed the behavior of those in the system. How, then, can we presume that schools can teach urban behavior to "out-of-it's" who do not experience participation in urban life?* We know, too, from our experience with American Indians as well as from our red-faced retraction of the "theory of the melting pot" how doggedly intact ethnic communities resist attempts at forced acculturation or assimilation. Yet heedlessly, without regard to the well-being of the community in which the student is rooted, our schools are directed to preparing students piecemeal for employment situations where each must pass the inspection of a middle-class "gate keeper." Can any theory of learning or social integration justify this arrangement to us, as intellectuals, and to the "out-of-it's" who experience it? Or is it possible that what these communities (to the extent that they are, in fact, communities) are learning from this enforced manner of dealing with the system-as-environment is a lesson in their own lack of power? And if, although powerless, they refuse to surrender their communities, even at the price of remaining "out-of-it," what will be their response? And ours?

Specifically, we should ask:

If schools do exist to naturalize individuals from "out-of-it" communities and socialize them into the middle class, and if this is a legitimate job for the school system, how successfully is it being done? What kind of "out-of-it" children make it through school? Under what conditions do the schools become a vehicle for entry into the system? How many children take over the self-definition presented them by the school system?

How resistant are individuals and communities to this kind of natural-ization? What happens to individuals and communities that reject the school system's definition of themselves? Is their resistance uniform, or do some learn new ways to deal with the middle class (by "having a hustle," as Malcolm X called it) while others are embittered?

What is the real learning that takes place in school? From what they have experienced, what lessons do "dropouts" bring back to "out-of-it" com-munities? And what is it individual "out-of-it's" learn that enables a few of them to "make it"?

Is it possible—and if so, how—for individuals and communities who are "out-of-it" to use the existing educational system for their own goals? Is it possible for "out-of-it" individuals and "out-of-it" communities to have education and a slice of the pie in terms of the kind of people they already are and the kind of community they already live in?

If the middle class is now the permanent environment of "out-of-it" communities, and if "out-of-it" communities (as have most American Indian tribes) prove unassimilable, under what circumstances can such communities have a viable relationship to their environment? What kind of learning will have to take place before this is possible? Who will dictate the terms of this learning?

POSTSCRIPT

In 1966, faith in American magic was strong. The "Elders" in Congress sanctioned a new priesthood called the Office of Economic Opportunity whose cult promoted a minor deity, education, to the first rank of dogma. Few Americans realized then that educational institutions would become altars thirsting for the hearts of millions of captives. Fewer still suspected that the captives might revolt. Yet on the peripheries of the cult there were skeptics who doubted the new god. This skeptical essay is a document from that period. It was completed in October 1966.

During the summer of 1966, the Carnegie Corporation Cross-Cultural Education Project of the University of Chicago, directed by Sol Tax, had been underway for three years. The project focused on experimental re-search in literacy among Cherokee-speaking Indians of eastern Oklahoma. That summer, Stanley Diamond asked Thomas and Wahrhaftig, who were then in the midst of the project's anthropological field work, to contribute an essay on American Indians to a general symposium on education and schools. He suggested a piece that would outline the "problem" of Ameri-can Indian education and suggest fresh directions for further research.

By then, our fieldwork had convinced us that two processes were operating in eastern Oklahoma. For one thing, our freshly collected statistics demonstrated that local Indians and Whites were not achieving the degree of education ordained as desirable by those who dictated the goals of the school system. In other words, the school system was failing to educate on its own terms. Moreover, communities of Cherokees and communities of folk Anglo-Saxons were unable to utilize schools and education to further their own ends. That is, the school system was failing to educate in terms of the ambitions of the communities it serves. Our research suggested that these two processes were causally connected, and we surmised that this might be the case wherever the school system confronts communities that are "out-of-it"—excluded from the levers of power and alienated from the ethos of the educational establishment.

At that time, we wanted to tell the high priests of education that the school system was in bad shape in eastern Oklahoma. We wanted to trace the development of the existing situation, suggest parallels elsewhere in America, and hypothesize that innovative educational techniques alone could not be a panacea where educational problems reflected more general difficulties of communities in a structural and experiential dilemma.

At the time of this writing it is February 1969. We have seen the Reformation" and "Counter Reformation" at Ocean Hill-Brownsville while the money changers attempt to hold on to the Temple at San Francisco State. Such a reaction follows from our analysis. If we have a smug "I-told-you-so" attitude, it is to us small consolation for the fact that once again American social science is caught flat-footed with no solid body of research completed that might illuminate this now heightened dilemma. We hope that the findings of the Carnegie Project, when published, will be of some small help in this regard. Still, we have the sinking feeling that the problem will have assumed new dimensions by that time. Are we to be forever caught in a communications gap between social science and a public frantically dealing with rapidly changing institutions? Are we, as they say in Oklahoma, "like the ol' cow's tail, always behind"?

REFERENCES

Cullum, Robert M.
    1953 The rural Cherokee household: a study of 479 households within the 14 school districts situated in the old Cherokee Nation. Muskogee: U.S. Bureau of Indian Affairs, mimeoed.
Debo, Angie
    1940 And still the waters run. Princeton: Princeton University Press.
    1941 The road to disappearance. Norman: University of Oklahoma Press.
    1951 The five civilized tribes of Oklahoma: report on social and economic conditions. Philadelphia: Indian Rights Association.
Dumont, Robert V., Jr.
    1969 Cherokee children and the teacher. Social Education 33, no. 1 (January): 70–72.

ROBERT K. THOMAS AND ALBERT L. WAHRHAFTIG   251

————, and Murray L. Wax
1969 Cherokee school society and the intercultural classroom. Human Organization 28, no. 3 (Fall):217–226.
Gearing, Fred O.
1961 Priests and warriors. American Anthropological Association Memoir No. 93. American Anthropologist 64, no. 5 (October), Part II.
Hall, Tom Aldis
1934 The socio-economic status of the Cherokee Indians. Unpublished M.A. thesis, University of Oklahoma.
Thomas, Robert K.
1954 The origin and development of the Redbird Smith Movement. Unpublished M.A. thesis, Department of Anthropology, University of Arizona.
Thornton, Sarah
1926 A history of the Cherokee school system. Unpublished M.A. thesis, University of Oklahoma.
Underwood, J. Ross
1966 An investigation of education opportunity for the Indians in northeastern Oklahoma. Unpublished Ph.D. dissertation, School of Education, University of Oklahoma.
Wahrhaftig, Albert L.
1966 Community and the caretakers. New University Thought 4, no. 4 (Winter 66/67):54–76.
1968 The tribal Cherokee population of eastern Oklahoma. Current Anthropology 9, no. 5 (December), Part II:510–518.
1969 Social and economic characteristics of the Cherokee population of eastern Oklahoma: report of a survey of four Cherokee settlements in the Cherokee Nation. Anthropological Records (microcard).
————, and Robert K. Thomas
1969 Renaissance and repression: the Oklahoma Cherokee. Trans-Action 6, no. 4 (February):42–48.
Wax, Murray L. et al.
1969 Indian education in eastern Oklahoma. (Final report, Bureau of Research, U.S. Office of Education, Contract No. OE–6–10–260; Bureau No. 5–0565–2– 12–1), Lawrence: University of Kansas, mimeoed.

18: *Learning in American Indian Children*[1]

COURTNEY B. CAZDEN
AND VERA P. JOHN

Indian children are taught to learn in two different ways. In school they learn "in the ways of the White Man," as Mrs. Wauneka, the Navajo educational leader, puts it. In their homes the Indian children learn in the ways of their people, in traditional cultural patterns that have remained durable even after 400 years of life among the White man.

This duality of Indian life with its impact upon children's learning styles should be the focus of serious study. Customary procedures of educational research, however, militate against a faithful recording of how, in fact, the Indian child does learn. Studies of these children are usually carried out in school, although we know that the school is still an extremely threatening place to most Indians. Timed tests are administered, although we know that time for the man who lives by nature is not the same as time for the urban man who lives by the clock. Children are tested in English, although for many Indian children living on reservations, their own language is the more logical medium through which to examine the level of their learning.

Of the many additional questions that can be raised, we mention two very important ones: Who should be present when Indian children are tested? (Fishler, in a study quoted in a later portion of this paper, reports how the young Indian child responds to parental encouragement in the testing situation. But parents are seldom present during tests.) How representative are the samples of Indian children on whom research data has been gathered? (Weather and road conditions on the reservations make access to many Indian families very difficult.)

Thus, when presenting research findings on Indian children, we are

[1] An earlier version of this paper was prepared for a conference on styles of learning among American Indian children held at Stanford University, August 1968, and published in the conference report (Ohannessian, 1969). For ideas and references the authors are grateful to: Glen Nimnicht of the Far Western Laboratory for Educational Research and Development, Jeanette Henry of the American Indian Historical Society, Robert Dumont of the National Indian Youth Council, Dell Hymes, Arthur Jensen, and Wick Miller.

forced to begin with a disclaimer. Because of important unresolved questions of research ideology and strategy, the reader is urged to be cautious in interpreting the review of research literature that follows.

The review is divided into five sections: (1) tests of learning prior to school entrance; (2) styles of learning; (3) conflicts in values; (4) patterns of socialization; and (5) a discussion of styles of learning, cultural values, and Indian education. At several points, we will also give examples of ways in which curricula and educational institutions could be designed to take advantage of the learning styles of Indian children rather than conflicting with them. Curriculum suggestions for other important goals —such as enhancing the child's pride in his native culture—are, however, outside the scope of this paper.[2]

TEST OF LEARNING PRIOR TO SCHOOL ENTRANCE

Glen Nimnicht of the Far Western Laboratory has stated that (personal communication, 1968) it was his impression that Indian children arrive at school without the general cognitive disadvantages of children living in urban slums. Available evidence supports this view. Scores on the Gesell Developmental Scales are available for Paiute children of Inyo County, California, who are the subjects of a longitudinal study conducted by the Child Development Clinic at the Children's Hospital in Los Angeles. This study is still in process and the following information is from a personal communication from the chief psychologist, Dr. Karol Fishler. Table 18–1 reports the scores for forty-four children in the first year. The Gesell scales are designed to yield an average score equal to the child's chronological age in months (12 for a 12-month old, and so on) and an average developmental quotient (DQ) of 100. Scores for subsequent years, as each group becomes one year older and a new group is added at the youngest age, are almost identical. The 1966 progress report concludes tentatively:

It appears that Indian children at age levels one, two, three and four show normal development comparable with other infants and normal children of same ages . . . All Indian children show consistently slowest gains in their language achievement at all age levels tested. . . . Most Indian children, in

2 These curriculum ideas came from the authors' work during the summers of 1968 and 1969 in programs for training kindergarten teachers run by the National Association for the Education of Young Children under contract with the Bureau of Indian Affairs. In 1969 John also taught a course in bilingual education at the Rough Rock Demonstration School. Participants in the course came from the entire staff of the school, and the curriculum materials developed by the Navajo aides show the possibilities for curriculum development by Indians themselves. Based on the immediate experience of the young Navajo child—native plants, traditional colors used in weaving, familiar animals to illustrate size concepts—these materials were striking in both conceptualization and production. For an excellent general bibliography on Indian education, see Berry (1969).

TABLE 18-1

*Summary of Gesell Developmental Testing on
Paiute Indian Children in Bishop, Inyo County
February–March 1964*

	N = 44			
	Group 1	Group 2	Group 3	Group 4
	N = 10	N = 17	N = 13	N = 4
Age in Months:	6–17	18–29	30–41	42 Plus
Developmental Variables and Levels in Months				
Motor	13.3	26.1	36.5	46.5
Adaptive	12.4	23.2	34.2	40.5
Language	11.1	21.2	31.2	39.0
Personal social	12.7	22.8	37.4	42.0
Mean Level:	12.37	23.32	34.82	42.0
Range DQ:	94–117	82–107	79–121	83–94
Mean DQ:	104.10	95.53	100.30	88.50
Sample Grand Mean DQ = 97.36				

(Fishler, personal communication, 1968)

their first three years of life, show excellent gains in their self-care involving self-feeding, toilet training and dressing . . . Behaviorally, Indian children, particularly those at these age levels, seem rather shy and cautious in social situations with strangers. However, for the most part, they seem well-disciplined and with parental encouragement even the youngest follow instruction and occasionally overcome their shyness. [Fishler, personal communication, 1968]

Spellman (1968) studied the shift from a preference for matching figures by color to matching them by form among Anglo, Black, and Caddo Indian children in an Oklahoma Head Start program and among similar children who were not in school. Other psychologists have found that children make this shift between four and seven years of age, and that the age when that shift occurs varies with indices of environmental opportunities such as social-class or minority-group status. Spellman presented the children with cards showing three pictures, a red circle, a red rectangle, and a blue rectangle, and asked them to "point to the two that look most alike." The children were tested either two or three times during the school year. Contrary to his expectations, Spellman found that the Indian children made a more rapid shift to form responses than the other two groups. His results are shown in Figure 1. He concludes tentatively that "probably the basic assumption that lower-class Indian children are more culturally deprived than lower-class Anglo children is not correct" (Spellman, 1968, p. 78).

Data on a larger sample of Indian children (tribes unspecified) were collected in the fall of 1965 as part of the Office of Education-sponsored study of educational opportunity (Coleman, 1966). Three tests were given to first-grade children: (a) a nonverbal classification test on which

FIGURE 18-1

*Mean Number of Form Responses as a Function
of Race and Group over Testings*

Spellman, 1968, p.69.

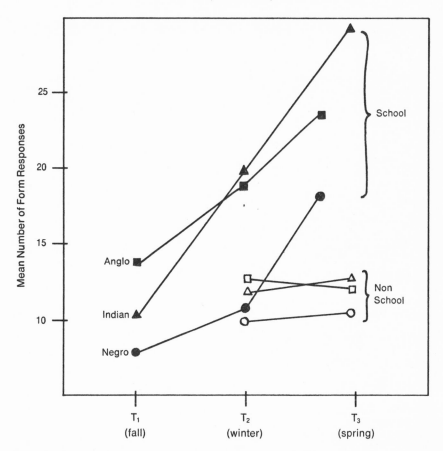

the child is asked to select one of four pictures that go with the first one, namely,

hat / horse dog cat man;

(b) a nonverbal association (or discrimination?) test on which the child is asked to select the one that is not like the others namely,

hi hi ki hi;

(c) a picture vocabulary test. Scores were converted to a scale on which the national median for all children is 50. Scores for Indian, Black, and majority White children in the first grade are given in Table 18–2.

Finally, Havighurst (1957) reviews studies of the intelligence of Indian

TABLE 18–2

Nationwide First-Grade Test Scores

	INDIAN	BLACK	WHITE
Nonverbal	53.0	43.4	54.1
Verbal	47.8	45.4	53.2

(Coleman, 1966, p. 20)

children before and after 1935 and concludes that all recent studies show that on nonverbal performance tests, Indian children have the same average scores and show the same range of performance between tribes and between communities within tribes as White children between and within communities.

Although these studies are important in supporting a general picture of normal nonverbal development at the time of entrance into the school, the use of standardized testing procedures raises questions about the meaning of particular tests to children from different ethnic groups, even from different tribes. Identical stimuli are not necessarily subjectively equivalent to different groups of children. (See Sears, 1961, for further discussion.) In some cases, the lowered verbal scores may be caused by premature bilingualism (further discussed later). But even for English-speaking Indians (such as the Paiutes), language remains an aspect of behavior burdened with cultural conflict. This conflict may be reflected both in parents' behavior in the setting for language learning within the family, and in the child's restricted verbal performance in the testing situation itself. See Pasamanick and Knoblock (1955) for comparable data on Black children.

STYLES OF LEARNING

Learning by Looking

Throughout the literature on Indian children, we find suggestions that their style of learning is more visual than verbal, more learning by looking than learning through language. Learning by looking may be reflected in several different performances: relative superiority on tests of visual abilities, skill in interpreting photographs, proficiency in spelling culturally developed forms of visual art that are tapped by the Draw-a-Man (DAM) test, and learning by imitation.

Visual abilities: Lombardi (1970) gave the Illinois Test of Psycholinguistic Abilities (1969 version) to eighty Papago children in the first and third grades in and around Tucson, Arizona. In comparison with the group on which the test was standardized, the Indian children generally received lower scores, but on one of the twelve subtests, they received significantly higher scores. The exception was a test of "visual sequential memory" in which the examiner arranges a set of small geometric shapes in a certain order, leaves them before the child for five seconds, and then mixes them up and asks the child to arrange them in the original order.

To our knowledge, the Lesser version of the Primary Mental Abilities Test (Stodolsky and Lesser, 1967) has not been given to Indian children. It would be interesting to know whether they would excel, as the Chinese children did, on the spatial ability subtest.

Interpreting photographs: While using photography as a research tool in anthropological research, Collier discovered that Navajos excelled at identifying and interpreting details in photographs of familiar scenes "as long as the visual circumstances were such that they were willing to discuss and explain the photographic content" (1967, p. 57). Some of the details were not even "visible" to Collier himself without a magnifying glass.

We are dealing with a phenomenon having nothing to do with modern acculturation—exposure to movies and weekly reading of *Life* magazine—but with the sensory perception of a preliterate culture in which a man must survive by astute visual analysis of the clues of his total ecology. Hosteen Greyhills [an informant] was applying to our photographs the same level of visual perception and fluency he would apply as he stepped out of his hogan to look around the horizon for his grazing horse. We surmised that people living close to nature have to be specialists in natural phenomena to survive . . . The Western observer in urban culture is usually a specialist in a single field. Outside this area, modern man tends to be visually illiterate. [Collier, 1967, p. 54]

Modern (urban) man also lives in an environment cluttered by nonfunctional visual stimuli such as neon lights and billboards that may encourage him to tune out parts of the visual field.

Spelling: Spelling is at least partly a matter of visual discrimination. Older Indian children continue to show relative superiority in the visual discrimination skill measured in the second of the three tests administered by Coleman (1966). In their survey of academic achievement of 13,000 Indian children in 11 states, Coombs et al. (1958) found that relative to their non-Indian schoolmates and neighbors, Indian children do poorest on reading vocabulary tests, but best in spelling. On the California Achievement Test, the pupil is asked to identify which one of four words is misspelled. Coombs et al. suggest that visual imagery and form perception are reflected here (1956, pp. 92–93).

Draw-a-Man Test: There is considerable evidence that Indian children from various tribes excel in the kind of ability tapped by the DAM test that is scored for accuracy in proportion and detail. In 1942–1943, as part of the Indian Education Research Project of the Committee on Human

Development of the University of Chicago, this test was given to 1,000 Hopi, Navajo, Papago, Sioux, Zia, and Zuni children. When converted to IQ's, the average score ranged from 117 for the Hopi children to 102 for the Sioux children (Havighurst, 1957). Havighurst, Gunther, and Pratt conclude:

> The children of Indian tribes which have kept close touch with the world of nature and with their indigenous cultures are specially stimulated to observe accurately, to organize their observations and express them aesthetically, and thus may be expected to do well on the DAM test. White children, and urban white children especially, may have much less chance to form concepts from firsthand observation, but must rely more upon books and words. [1946, p. 61]

Correlation between scores on the DAM test and the Grace Arthur general nonverbal intelligence scale was lower for Indian than for White children.

Dennis (1940, pp. 341–348) gave the same test to 152 Hopi children with similar results: IQ–108.3. In both studies the Hopi boys exceeded the Hopi girls, presumably because "graphic art is almost entirely a masculine activity in Hopi culture" (Dennis, 1940, p. 342).

Free Drawings: In the Havighurst study, free drawings from 90 Hopi children were also evaluated by an art teacher. In comparison with the drawing of 1,400 children in Cleveland, many of whom attended special art classes, the Hopi children go through the same developmental sequence toward realism and spatial representation but reach the fourth of five stages a year or two earlier, by age 12. After that time, the competing pressure of tribal conventions toward stylized Katchina forms takes precedence and shifts the Hopi development away from the Cleveland pattern (Havighurst and Neugarten, 1955, pp. 179–185).

Learning through imitation: Learning through imitation is reported in many ethnographic studies. It may be related to the previous kinds of learning by looking, or it may represent a different underlying process.

From his survey of ethnological literature, Pettitt (1946, pp. 40–58) agrees that the dominance of imitation is a commonly accepted characteristic of education in nonliterate societies. In contrasting nonliterate and literate societies, Pettitt suggests that "a greater proportion of the culture of a primitive society is within the direct reach of the sensory organs of the primitive child" (1946, p. 40), while in more complex societies adult activities are less understandable by observation alone, less appropriate for the active play needs of children, and therefore less directed by adults for instructional purposes. As a result, play at home and learning at school have perhaps inevitably become more separated. Within nonliterate societies, Pettitt found that "primitive play, where it reflected adult pursuits, was to a large extent directed practice rather than merely imitation" (1946, p. 44), and that such practice was encouraged —positively by praise, ceremonial recognition, and the reward of specific privileges, and negatively by ridicule.

Lee retells the autobiography of a Dakota Indian boy to show how learning by looking, by discovery from independent observation, is taught:

Chiyesa . . . points out how he was brought up to discover. He was being raised by his uncle and his grandfather. He tells how when he was about five or six he would leave at daybreak. He just went out . . . Nobody asked him what he was going to look for or to take his rubbers along. However, his uncle was there and all he said was "Look carefully at everything you see . . ." In the afternoon when he returned . . . his uncle would question him, saying "On which side of the tree did the bark grow the thickest?" The small boy had not been told to look at the tree or the bark but he had been told to look closely, and he had been taught to be alert—to look and listen fully—in order to answer any question he might be asked. [Lee, 1967, p. 58]

Rohner contrasts this style of learning with the demands of formal education: "Kwakiutl children typically learn by observation, manipulation and experimentation in their native setting, but they must learn by verbal instruction, reading, and writing in the classroom" (1965, pp. 334–335).

Such discontinuity is not inevitable. Instructional methods can be changed. The Indian child's visual abilities can be used as a foundation for learning in other areas. Mathematics can be learned through the manipulation of concrete materials such as Cuisenaire rods. Language development can be nourished by asking children to express in words those visual discriminations that have been previously well learned either out-of-school or in school. For example, a rodeo lotto game for Navajo children would require them to express in words distinctions already well learned in visual terms such as the sizes and sexes of animals and the positions of riders. Or, after two children each learn to do a particular jigsaw puzzle, they can work together—one child supplying the pieces, the other child asking for them one-by-one to put in his frame: "Give me the piece that fits under his neck"; "Give me the big, white one." Visual abilities can also be channeled into other forms of expression. For example, map-making and photography could be done in the classroom. See Stodolsky and Lesser (1967) for further discussion of goals and methods in matching instruction to children's abilities.

Learning through Language

Problems in learning a second language, either English or an Indian language, were discussed in the report of the preceding conference (Ohannessian, 1967) and will not be included here. Five other aspects of learning through language may be important in the education of Indian children: cognitive implications of the syntax or semantic structure of the child's native language; cognitive effects of various forms of bilingualism; developmental retardation in the child's native language; sociolinguistic interference between patterns and functions of communication at home and at school; and the art of story telling.

Language and cognition: The hypothesis that the structure of a person's native language influences the structure of his thought was first based on Whorf's analysis of American Indian languages. He suggested, for instance, that the concept of relativity in physics could be expressed (and therefore thought about) more easily in Hopi than in English (1941). Subsequent experimental studies with Indian subjects have shown that language differences do affect cognitive behavior in certain limited ways— such as the ease of recognizing colors (Lenneberg and Roberts, 1956) or the preference for matching by form rather than color (Carroll and Casagrande, 1958). And the relation of language to cognition continues to be a lively area of research and controversy. But the assumption implicit in some current educational programs, an assumption for which Whorf is certainly not responsible, that Standard English is somehow a preferred medium for abstract thought is, to our knowledge, wholly without support. See Labov (1970) for a powerful argument against this assumption (also the discussion by Hymes in this volume).

The study by Carroll and Casagrande (1958) is worth describing in more detail not only for its substantive findings but also for its thoughtfully planned research procedures with Indian children. In Navajo verbs of handling, the verb form must be selected according to the shape of the object of the verb. Because of this obligatory categorization of objects, it seemed reasonable that Navajo-speaking children would learn to discriminate form attributes of objects earlier than their English-speaking age-mates. Stimuli for an experiment to test this hypothesis consisted of ten sets of three objects: for example, a yellow stick and a blue rope, and then a yellow rope. The child was shown the first two and then asked which one was like the third. The subjects were 135 Navajo children from an Arizona reservation, 3–10 years old and 3 language groups: monolingual in Navajo or Navajo-predominant (59), balanced bilinguals (33), and English-predominant or English monolinguals (43).

The experiment was conducted in Navajo or, with appropriate modifications in the instructions, in English, as indicated . . . most of the testing was done in the children's homes—usually Navajo hogans of the traditional sort—and in the presence of parents, grandparents, siblings, and other interested and very curious onlookers. [Carroll and Casagrande, 1958, p. 28]

The hypothesis that the Navajo-dominant children would be more likely than the other Navajo children to select on the basis of form was borne out by the data. But a separate control group of forty-seven white middle-class children in Boston also tended to group the objects by form, presumably because of previous experience with formboard types of toys.

In the light of the already mentioned Spellman research reported, we should note that two interpretations of the Carroll and Casagrande results are now possible. One interpretation is based upon the structure of language that the study was designed to tap. The other interpretation is that for some as yet unexplained reason independent of language (since

Spellman's research was with Caddo children, not with Navajo), Indian children tend to show a preference for matching figures by form earlier than Anglo children, but that this tendency is diminished in children whose bilingualism indicates greater acculturation to Anglo life. In the Carroll and Casagrande study, effect of Navajo language structure and degree of acculturation were confounded.

Bilingualism: Stafford (1968) has studied the effects of compound versus coordinate bilingualism on the problem-solving abilities of 105 Navajo eighth graders in Ft. Defiance and Chinle, Arizona. Each subject was asked to determine which pattern of squares or triangles presented on a 2 feet × 2 feet screen was "correct." Four concepts to be learned varied from the simplest—"Push the button next to the square regardless of its location," to the hardest—"Push the button by the square when two figures are side-by-side on the screen; push the button by the triangle when the figures are diagonal on the screen." Subjects were divided into compound bilinguals who had learned both English and Navajo before starting school (41), and monolinguals in English (20). A sample of monolinguals in Navajo could not be tested. Directions were given in English. Performance was scored on the basis of a number of trials out of a possible one hundred needed by a child to reach a response of ten correct, and in the analysis of these data, IQ was used as a covariant. The results showed coordinate bilinguals did better than compound bilinguals; bilinguals who reported using only one language did better than those who used both; but, contrary to expectations, coordinate bilinguals were not inferior to monolinguals.

Although there is no evidence to support the assumption that one language is superior to another as a tool of cognition, if the Indian child has not had the chance to develop his mother tongue before he is taught English, he may find himself in the position of the compound bilinguals in Stafford's study who rely on both languages and show the poorest performance. The psychological effects of compound bilingualism may be particularly critical during the age period between five to seven years when the role of language in cognition is just being established. See White (1965) for a review of the developmental changes that take place during this critical period that coincides with the beginning of school.

Language development: We find no evidence on the status of language development of Indian children in their native language. Research here is sorely needed.

Sociolinguistic interference: Research is also needed on sources of sociolinguistic interference in the classroom. For example, a comment often made about Indian children is that they behave in ways we label as "shy": they withdraw from participation and seem especially reluctant to talk. Such behavior in the Anglo culture would invoke explanations of retarded language development or psychological problems in interpersonal relationships. Such behavior in Indian children may be explained by cultural influences on communicative competence. (See Hymes chapter in this volume.)[3]

There are cultural influences on what children have learned about the amount and kind of appropriate conversation. For example, Apaches consider too much talking as foolishness. In the Sunrise Dance, the Apache coming-of-age ceremony for girls, the young girl lies down and her grandmother places her hand on the girl's mouth to signify that she should not be a talkative woman.

There are also cultural influences on listening behavior. The child may attend in ways normal for his culture but misundertood by the teacher. Hall describes Navajo listening behavior, at least in the 1930s:

> Unlike middle-class whites, the direct open-faced look in the eyes was avoided by Navajos. In fact, Navajos froze up when looked at directly. Even when shaking hands they held one in the peripheral field of the eyes . . .
> By now some of my readers are undoubtedly thinking what it must have been like to be a small Navajo child in schools taught by whites where many teachers were frustrated by behavior they couldn't understand . . . The teacher would raise his voice, while looking directly at the child hanging his head. "What's the matter? Can't you talk? Don't you even know your own name?" [1969, p. 379]

Finally, there are cultural differences in preferred ways of learning. We have discussed the contrast between learning by looking and learning through language. Werner suggests a more general contrast between contemplation in Navajo learning and empiricism in Anglo learning:

> The Navajo approach . . . stresses the acquisition of competence as a prerequisite for performance. Navajos seem to be unprepared or ill at ease if pushed into early performance without sufficient thought or the acquisition of mental competence preceeding the actual physical activity . . . This philosophy of learning can be summed up in the following 'artificial' proverb: "If at first you don't think, and think again, don't bother trying."
> The Anglo approach stresses performance as a prerequisite for the acquisition of competence . . . The comprehension of the principles is perceived as a corollary and automatic by-product of the ability to perform. This philosophy of learning can be summed up in the well known proverb: "If at first you don't succeed, try, try again." [1968, pp. 1–2]

Werner finds support for this contrast from a contrastive analysis of the meaning of *thought, instruction,* and *learning* in Navajo and English, and from an analysis of Navajo legends.

Story telling: Despite the emphasis on learning by looking, the importance of story telling in primitive education should not be overlooked. Pettit (1946, pp. 151–160) provides extensive evidence that story telling was specifically directed to children—to supply reasons for rules in dramatic form, and to convey religious and social knowledge. Wherever such traditions survive, it cannot be claimed that children come to school

[3] See also the chapters by Dumont and Phillips in *The Functions of Language in the Classroom,* edited by Courtney B. Cazden, Vera P. John, and Dell Hymes (New York: Teachers College Press, in press).

with no experience in learning through language. Currently, the more than 100 Head Start programs administered by the Office of Navajo Economic Opportunity are using tribal elders as auxiliary personnel in the classrooms for telling traditional tales to the young children.

CONFLICT OF VALUES

Brophy and Aberle (1966) suggest three sources of conflicts in values: the Indians' concepts of time, their disposition to conform to nature rather than dominate it, and their social withdrawal in school. The same three sources of conflict appear in Zintz's contrasts between the values of the public school and the traditional Navajo and Pueblo cultures (1963, pp. 151 and 175). While these values are separable from learning narrowly conceived, they are so frequently suggested as explanations of the low school achievement of Indian children that each merits further discussion from additional sources.

Concepts of time: Differences in time orientation could affect school performance in at least four ways. First, attendance may be lowered, particularly where school bus schedules increase inflexibility (Adcock, 1968, p. 4). Second, in school, it may be more difficult to command children's attention according to teacher-designed schedules. Wolcott suggests that the "fooling around" behavior of Kwakiutl children that teachers interpret as "poor motivation and short attention span" is more of an unhurried view of the cosmos: pupils seem to pause to daydream, to draw, or to do anything except what the teacher has planned" (1967, p. 92).

Third, differences in time orientation probably adversely affect scores on any tests or testlike assignment that are timed. Havighurst and Hilkevitch (1944) report an experiment by Klineberg in which Yakima children worked more slowly but more accurately than White children on a nonverbal test. In their own research, Havighurst and Hilkevitch found that of the subtests of the Grace Arthur Point Performance Scale on which Indian children in the six tribes did as well as White children, two were timed tests. Similarly, the two nonverbal performance scales given to first graders in the Coleman (1966) Report were both timed. These three studies are not necessarily contradictory, however, for it may be the case that the Indian children would have been in an even stronger comparative position if the pressure for speed were removed. See Haggard (1954) for further analysis of the speed factor in intelligence tests, and see Fishman et al. (1964) for recommendations on testing minority-group children.

Fourth, time orientation may be related to willingness to plan ahead and delay gratification. According to Zintz, for the Navajo planning ahead "is considered 'bahazid,' i.e. dangerous. To talk about something too far in advance (a few days is all right; a year is too long) just is not done, not out loud anyway" (1963, p. 358).

Independent experimental evidence for these claims of a different cognitive or motivational component of time orientation is difficult to find. We located only two relevant studies. In "An Analysis of Time Perspective and Its Applicability to Cross-Cultural Comparisons," Roberts and Greene (1966) asked Navajo, Pueblo, Spanish-American, and Anglo-American ten- and sixteen-year-olds to tell stories about one "social" and one "religious" picture. The stories were scored for such dimensions of time orientation as temporal "location" of the main events, "extension" or duration of time in the story, and "movement" or number of changes in temporal location during the story. The stories were also rated for the presence and explicitness of any mention of specific temporal units.

Roberts and Greene found that more of the Indian stories contained no temporal movement (60 percent compared with only 33 percent for the Anglos); and they were more likely to extend over less than a one-hour period. Compared with the other groups, the Indian social stories were more likely to be written in the present, whereas their religious stories were more likely to be written in the past. The authors note that absence of the future may be related to inadequate command of English verb tenses. They report that a preference for the present and the past over the future was also found in Kluckhohn and Strodtbeck's (1961) study of Navajo and Zuni value orientations (perhaps also confounded with the subject's knowledge of English).

In his study of Stoney and Blackfoot eleven-year-old boys in Canada, Vernon included a "delay-of-gratification test" in which the boys were offered a small chocolate bar now or a double-size bar later. Of the Stoney boys 50 percent and of the Blackfoot boys 32 percent chose to wait, in contrast to 48–69 percent of the Eskimos and 75 percent of the English boys in a previous study. It is possible, even likely, that this test taps task- and situation-specific behavior rather than an enduring personality characteristic. Furthermore, experiments of this kind are open to question because of the differential availability in the child's home environment of the rewards used in the test situation.

Schools could be changed to adjust to differences in time orientation instead of fighting them or using them as justifications for poor academic performance. Adcock (1968) describes a successful summer program in which Crow children selected both their classes and the amount of time they wished to stay. See Steiner's (1968) description of an electronics factory without a time clock on the Yankton Sioux reservation in South Dakota.

Attitudes toward nature: According to Zintz, "the area of elementary science presents a segment of the school curriculum likely to be most in conflict with the child's out-of-school life, that is, with his set of cultural values" (1963, p. 297). He reports one study that found a strong inverse relationship "between the science achievement status of Indian children (Navajos and Pueblos in New Mexico) and the extent of their acceptance of certain unscientific societal beliefs" (Zintz, 1963, p. 298).

One could conclude from this study that preserving indigenous religion and learning modern science are incompatible. But Havighurst's (1957) findings in the domain of game rules suggest an alternative. In an isolated Navajo community twenty-four children were familiar with both the traditional Navajo games and White men's games such as baseball or marbles. When asked who made the rules and whether they could be changed, the children gave two separate answers.

Concerning the "white" games, they generally said that the rules were made by the coach, or the teacher, or some person in authority, and that these rules would be changed by agreement among the people playing the game. This kind of answer is given by white children. But when asked about rules of traditional Navajo games, the Navajo mountain youth said unanimously that the rules were first made by the "holy people," or by the "ancient ones," or by the "animals"—who in ancient days possessed human characteristics—and that no human could change the rules. [Havighurst, 1957, p. 108]

Borrowing terminology from the bilingualism area, we call this kind of compartmentalization a "coordinate belief system." One solution to some of the problems in Indian education may be to encourage the development of such coordinate systems in many areas of belief and behavior.

Social withdrawal: The social withdrawal of Indian children in school is frequently attributed to value conflicts over cooperation versus competition, aggression versus compliance, or anonymity versus self-assertion, depending upon the author and tribe being discussed. The following are examples of descriptions of particular tribes.

Kwakiutl

Forms of independence and aggression, for example, are rewarded in non-school activities but they are discouraged in the classroom . . . The child must learn a form of compliance behavior which is not expected out of school; competition with peers rather than sharing and cooperation is expected. [Rohner, 1965, p. 334]

In meeting their classroom assignments the pupils interpreted their tasks as a matter of group as well as of individual concern. This had one major advantage in that for many tasks pupils paired off and completed assignments in informal competitions . . . The motivating effect of their self-imposed competition was more than offset from the teacher's point of view by the tendency of pupils constantly to help each other. [Wolcott, 1967, p. 104]

Sioux

There are situations where rivalry holds full sway. Usually these involve contests between the folk of the community and some other group who are or can be regarded as outsiders. Thus the youthful Sioux are transfigured when they are matched with outsiders in basketball tournaments or dancing contests . . . Outside of school, if a young kinsman should get into trouble with "strangers" the child knows that he is supposed to stand by him. But within the school, if he does not know an answer, the teacher says he is not to help him. [Wax, Wax, and Dumont, 1964, pp. 54 and 82]

Thus, on the Pine Ridge reservation a majority of the young men arrive at adolescence valuing elan, bravery, generosity, and luck, and admiring outstanding talent in athletics, singing and dancing . . . (Yet) in order to graduate from high school, they are told that they must develop exactly opposite qualities to those they possess: a respect for humdrum diligence and routine, for "discipline" . . . and for government property. [Wax, 1967, p. 45]

Pueblos

The Indians of the Southwest, and especially the Pueblo tribes, are notably co-operative. Consequently, if a teacher in a government school, who has been accustomed to assume that children are competitive, tries to appeal to this kind of motivation by using spelling contests or by encouraging children to call attention to the mistakes of other children, the teacher may be perplexed to find that such teaching methods do not work very well. The Indian children may not parade their knowledge before others nor try to appear better than their peers. [Havighurst, 1957, p. 109]

In General

This expert [a psychiatrist speaking at a conference on Indian education] stated that the Indian youth were not competitive, that they were undisciplined at home. Nothing is further from the truth. The Indian is extremely competitive. He delights in being the best, the most, the brightest. But when an Indian child is turned off—first by his history, next by his economic conditions, and then by what is being taught in the schools—what else can you expect but that he will drop out if he finds the situation intolerable? [Costo, 1968, p. 8]

PATTERNS OF SOCIALIZATION

Other frequently mentioned sources of value conflicts are indigenous patterns of socialization.

The complaint voiced by many administrators at the site schools that Indian parents were unwilling or unable to discipline their children should be re-examined. As mentioned earlier, previous studies of Indian communities have consistently concluded that discipline is maintained through teasing rather than direct criticism or restraint . . . My experience with Indians during this project has repeatedly shown me that teasing is the dominant mode of reducing an individual's (in this case my own) sense of importance . . . If it is a fact, as our present data suggests, that teasing is the primary form of discipline within Indian groups, it follows that the school cannot expect parents to directly criticize their children in the principal's office or to lecture their children at home. Teasing is an indirect form of criticism and as such, it needs a regular and relaxed context to be effective." [Adcock, 1968, p. 24]

In their stress upon the distinctive nature of Sioux values and ethos, Bureau personnel are in company with many anthropological students of American Indians, including ourselves. Where we differ—both with the Bureau and with some of the preceding students of the Sioux—is in the exact characterization of this ethos and in the judgment which is rendered, accordingly, upon the possibilities of Sioux adjustment to the greater national society . . . it may be worthwhile to note some of the distortions that have crept both into anthropological writings and into the speech of some Bureau personnel. For example, it is said that Indian children are treated with such excessive permissiveness and indulgence that they are never subject to any discipline. Yet the same observers who assert this will comment on how well Indian children behave in a significant variety of social situations. [Wax, Wax, and Dumont 1964, p. 39]

According to Pettitt (1946, pp. 6–14) while "stress is put upon the family responsibility to see that a child turns out well" (p. 8), successful child rearing does take unique forms among Indian tribes. First, "it seems obvious that the chief inhibition to corporal punishment as a disciplinary measure derives from the fact that pain per se cannot be used as a fear-producing, coercive force in a social milieu which places a premium upon ability to stand pain and suffering without flinching" (Pettitt, 1946, p. 8). Second, there is a "universal tendency to refer discipline or the authority for it to some individual or agency outside the group, and the tendency to rely most practically on supernatural agencies as the ultimate reference" (Pettit, 1946, p. 14). Third, Pettit suggests that the widespread use of cradleboards, while not affecting motor development, may have the psychological effect of making Indian children especially amenable to early training. Fourth, there is the important role of ridicule or teasing as a means of social control. See Wax, Wax, and Dumont (1964, pp. 79–101) for a grim picture of how this behavior is transformed into picking on and bullying under certain school conditions.

STYLES OF LEARNING, CULTURAL VALUES, AND INDIAN EDUCATION

In this paper we have tried to present research that goes beyond the usual presentation of achievement data on Indian children. The question, "Are there culturally specific ways in which Indian children from various tribes approach structured tasks and discover the world around them?" is an important one. However, difficulties inherent in gathering valid and reliable information about Indian children cannot be mentioned often enough.

Consider a final example. In the Coleman study (1966) two expressions of pupil attitudes, "sense of control of environment," first, and "self-concept," second, were more strongly related to school achievement than any other measure of family background or school facilities. Percentages of twelfth-grade Indian, Black, and White pupils for these two attitudes are shown in Table 18–3.

TABLE 18–3
Percent of Twelfth-Grade Pupils Having Certain Attitudes

	INDIAN	BLACK	WHITE
Sense of Control of Environment			
Luck more important than work	11	11	4
When I try, something stops me	27	22	14
People like me don't have			
much of a chance	14	12	6
Self-Concept			
Believes self to be brighter			
than average	31	40	49
I just can't learn	44	27	39
I would do better if teacher			
didn't go so fast	26	21	24

(Coleman, 1966, p. 24)

On all six comparisons the Indian children are in the worst position. The young Indian's feeling of powerlessness exceeds that of his White and Black age-mate. But how accurate is this finding? One may question the sample. A substantial percentage of reservation Indians have quit school long before the twelfth grade, and those who live in the city are often difficult to identify. These results may then apply only to a special subset of Indian youth.

The interpretation of these findings also presents problems. Different groups may have different attitudes toward answering questions about themselves. Or, if we accept the data as presented, the articulation of lack of control over the environment may simply be a realistic report about life observed by the growing Indian child who sees his elders' powerlessness in the White society. And the widespread self-doubt among Indian youth—nearly half of whom agreed with the statement, "I just can't learn"—may be related to the severe alienation of teachers and students from each other depicted in the studies of the Waxes and their coworkers (1964).

Many social scientists concerned with learning styles and conflicts in values have been searching for possible barriers to the assimilation of Indians into the majority society. For example, the research reported by Brophy and Aberle (1966) was commissioned after a 1953 resolution was passed by an assimilation-oriented United States Congress. In dramatic contrast to this point of view, many young Indian intellectuals speak for a new tribalism. For instance, an unsigned editorial in the National Congress of American Indians' *Sentinel* 11, no. 2 (1966), stated in part:

Recent events seem to be preparing the ground for a new understanding and appreciation of Indian tribes in modern society. . . . Indians are standing up for their rights in the same manner as people all over the globe. There seems to be . . . a real desire by American Indians to learn what American society is and how one finds economic security in it. At the same time there is an ever increasing rejection of the social values of the "mainstream" and a return to Indian values.

There can be little doubt that technology has contributed the major impetus to this yearning for old ways. Technology has as a basis the creation of the inhuman human . . . (It) is inhuman in the sense that men now get little if any personal fulfillment from their toil . . . The foolishness of the present situation in Indian affairs is that too many people are trying to re-state old mass truisms such as "assimilation" without taking into account that in the present society for anyone of any race, creed, color, or religion to "assimilate" into the values of the mass of people whose lives are directed by technological considerations is to forfeit the chance to live constructively, beautifully and meaningfully . . . The tribe, we feel, must always receive primary consideration as it is the group within which people are allowed to express themselves and realize that they truly are people with definite values, ideas, hopes and goals and unless a society is allowed to express its goals, it cannot long endure. [Steiner, 1968, 299–300]

Depending upon the value orientation of the social scientist or educator, indigenous Indian styles of learning and cultural values will be seen as impediments to achievement in schools as they now are, or as guidelines to the establishment of schools better adapted to the cultural values of Indian children. In this area cultural conflict is great between observer and observed, teacher and pupils, and policymaker and target population. While it is potentially a very significant source of ideas for educational innovation, research designed and carried out by those raised in the culture will be essential to gathering the only kind of information on which meaningful recommendations for change can be based.

Our own belief is that educational research reflects underlying assumptions about the objectives of education. We join those who seek a kind of education that will provide a dual preparation for every Indian child in what we hope will be an increasingly pluralistic society. His education should equip the young Indian with the minimum skills necessary for urban society, if he chooses to participate in it. And it must do this without neglecting his growth within his traditional society, thus freeing him for the other choice of developing Indian life among Indians.

REFERENCES

Adcock, D.
　1968 Untitled paper on the schools in the National Indian Youth Council program, Berkeley, Cal.: Far West Laboratory for Educational Research and Development, May.

Allen, D. R. V.
1966,
1967 Two reports from Head Start. New York: Teachers College Record, Columbia University, pp. 443–447.
Berry, Brewton
1969 The education of American Indians: a review of the literature. U.S. Department of Health, Education and Welfare, Office of Education. Available from ERIC Document Reproduction Service, National Cash Register Co., Bethesda, Md. 20014.
Brophy, William A. and Aberle, Sophie D.
1966 The Indian: America's unfinished business. Norman, Okla.: University of Oklahoma Press.
Carroll, John B. and Casagrande, J. B.
1958 "The function of language classifications in behavior." *In* Readings in Social Psychology (3rd ed.). E. E. Maccoby, T. M. Newcomb, and E. L. Hartley, eds. New York: Holt, Rinehart and Winston, Inc., pp. 18–31.
Coleman, James S.
1966 Equality of educational opportunity. Washington, D.C.: U.S. Department of Health, Education and Welfare, Office of Education.
Collier, John, Jr.
1967 Visual anthropology: photography as a research method. New York: Holt, Rinehart & Winston, Inc.
Coombs, L. Madison et al.
1958 The Indian child goes to school. Washington, D.C.: U.S. Department of the Interior, Bureau of Indian Affairs.
Costo, Rupert
1968 Statement presented at Hearings of the U.S. Senate Subcommittee on Indian Education, San Francisco, January 4, 1968. San Francisco, American Indian Historical Society.
Dennis, Wayne
1940 The Hopi child. University of Virginia Institute for Research in the Social Sciences. Reissued as Science Editions paperback, New York: John Wiley and Sons, Inc., 1965.
Dumont, Robert V., Jr.
1967 The quality of Indian education and the search for tradition. Americans before Columbus. November, pp. 3–4.
Fishman, Joshua, Deutsch, M., Kogan, L., North, R. and Whiteman, M.
1964 Guidelines for testing minority group children. Journal of Social Issues 20: 129–145.
Haggard, Ernest A.
1954 Social status and intelligence: an experimental study of certain cultural determinants of measured intelligence. Genetic Psychology Monographs 49:141–186.
Hall, Edward T.
1969 Listening behavior: some cultural differences. Phi Delta Kappan 50:379–380.
Havighurst, Robert J.
1957 Education among American Indians: individual and cultural aspects. *In* American Indians and American life. G. E. Simpson and J. M. Yinger, eds. Annals of American Academy of Political and Social Science 311:105–115.
———, Gunther, M. K. and Pratt, I. E.
1946 Environment and the draw-a-man test: the performance of Indian children. Journal of Abnormal and Social Psychology 41:50–63.
———, and Hilkevitch, R. H.
1944 The intelligence of Indian children as measured by a performance scale. Journal of Abnormal and Social Psychology 39:419–433.
———, and Neugarten, B. L.
1954 American Indian and White children. Chicago: University of Chicago Press.
Kluckhohn, Florence, and Strodtbeck, F.
1961 Variations in value orientations. New York: Harper & Row, Publishers, Inc.
Labov, William
1970 The logic of non-standard English. *In* Georgetown Monograph Series on Lan-

guages and Linguistics, J. Alatis, ed. No. 22. Washington, D.C.: Georgetown University Press.

Lee, Dorothy D.
1967 A socio-anthropological view of independent learning. In The theory and nature of independent learning. G. T. Gleason, ed. Scranton, Pa.: International Textbook Co., pp. 51–63.

Lenneberg, Eric H. and Roberts, J. M.
1956 The language of experience: a study in methodology. Supplement to International Journal of American Linguistics 22, no. 13.

Lombardi, T. P.
1970 Psycholinguistic abilities of Papago Indian school children. Exceptional Children 36:485–493.

McKinley, Francis and Adcock, D.
n.d. Review of the research—formal Indian education. Berkeley, Calif.: Far West Laboratory for Educational Research and Development.

Ohannessian, Sirapi, ed.
1967 The study of the problems of teaching English to American Indians: report and recommendations. Washington, D.C.: Center for Applied Linguistics.
1969 Styles of learning among American Indians: an outline for research. Washington, D.C.: Center for Applied Linguistics.

Pasamanick, Benjamin and Knoblock, Hilda
1955 Early language behavior in Negro children and the testing of intelligence. Journal of Abnormal and Social Psychology. 50:401–402.

Pettitt, George A.
1946 Primitive education in North America. Berkeley, Calif.: University of California publications in American archaeology and ethnology. 43, whole no. 1.

Roberts, A. Hood and Greene, J. E.
1966 An analysis of time perspective and its applicability to cross-cultural comparisons. Final report to NSF grant no. 43 (May).

Rohner, Ronald P.
1965 Factors influencing the academic performance of Kwakiutl children in Canada. Comparative Educational Review 9:331–340.

Sears, Robert R.
1961 Transcultural variables and conceptual equivalence. In Studying personality cross-culturally. B. Kaplan, ed. New York: Harper & Row, Publishers, Inc.

Spellman, C. M.
1968 The shift from color to form preference in young children of different ethnic backgrounds. Austin, Texas: University of Texas Child Development Evaluation and Research Center.

Stafford, K. R.
1968 Problem solving as a function of language. Language and Speech. 11:104–112.

Steiner, Stan
1968 The new Indians. New York: Harper & Row, Publishers, Inc.

Stodolsky, Susan S. and Lesser, G.
1967 Learning patterns in the disadvantaged. Harvard Educational Review 37: 546–593.

Vernon, Philip E.
1966 Educational and intellectual development among Canadian Indians and Eskimos. Educational Review, Part I 18:79–91; 1966, Part II 18:186–195.

Wax, Rosalie H.
1967 The warrior dropouts. Trans-action, 4 (May):40–46.

Wax, Murray L., Rosalie H. and Dumont, R. V., Jr.
1964 Formal education in an American Indian community. Supplement to Social Problems 11, Whole no. 4.

Werner, Oswald and Begishe, K.
1968 Styles of learning: the evidence from Navajo. Paper prepared for conference on styles of learning in American Indian children, Stanford University (August).

White, Sheldon H.
1965 Evidence for a hierarchical arrangement of learning processes. Advances in child development and behavior 2:187–220.

Whorf, Benjamin Lee
    1941 The relation of habitual thought and behavior to language. Reprinted *in*
        Language, thought and reality: selected writings of Benjamin Lee Whorf, J. B.
        Carroll ed. Cambridge: The M.I.T. Press, 1956, pp. 134–159.
Wolcott, Harry F.
    1967 A Kwakiutl village and school. New York: Holt, Rinehart and Winston, Inc.
Zintz, Miles V.
    1963 Education across cultures. Dubuque, Iowa: Wm. C. Brown.

19: *Education of the Negro Child*[1]

JULES HENRY

The study of the education of the deprived child is now associated with the names of many workers.[2] All of these studies are of groups of children, and most of them rely upon test materials. Many emphasize the effect of language and usually stress the absence, in the life of the culturally deprived child, of a variety of cognitive experiences and material conditions not present in the life of other children. The conclusions all point toward the same direction—that the culturally deprived child begins his education with initial handicaps that make his failure almost a foregone conclusion. In spite of the evidence for the low probability of educational success of the deprived child, we know that some succeed, and it is necessary to find out why they do so that we can make more of them succeed. The only way to determine this is to study individual children. One of the best ways to do this is by a natural history method, in which research focuses not on groups but on particular children followed through their educational experience for a length of time manageable by the usual strategies of investigation.

This paper is a report on a very small pilot project in the natural history of the education of two Negro ghetto children from kindergarten through the first grade.[3]

OBJECTIVES

The purpose of this project is to study the natural history of the education of the poor Negro child. The natural history of the education of a child is a description of the learning experiences of a child in its

[1] Prepared during the author's tenure as Fellow at the Center for Advanced Study in the Behavioral Sciences, Stanford, California. The material on which this paper is based was collected by Gwendolyn Jones, as part of a study of the Pruitt-Igoe Project, a *de facto* segregated housing project in St. Louis, Missouri. Miss Jones is herself Black.

[2] A few references, directly relevant to this paper, are contained in the bibliography at the end. For an excellent review of the field, as well as massive bibliographic materials on deprivation and education, the reader is referred to *The Disadvantaged Child*, Joe L. Frost and Glenn R. Hawkes (eds.), Boston: Houghton Mifflin Company, 1966.

[3] Six children were then being studied.

natural habitat. The questions are: What is the habitat? What is a learning experience? Over how long a period is the history to be studied?

The child's habitat is his home, school, and the areas frequented by the child outside the home, together with the people in them.

For the purpose of this project *education* is defined as *all* the experiences of a child, because in all contacts with the external world the child may learn something. Under such a definition being beaten, hearing one's confused great-grandmother-caretaker be gulled by a sewing-machine sales-man—or watching her miscount a dozen and a half eggs—are just as much learning experiences as sitting through a reading lesson in school. It can be seen, especially, from the example of the confused great-grandmother, that in humans there are both positive and negative learnings; positive learning being learning congruent with dominant cultural conventions (including cognitive systems) and negative learning not congruent with such systems. It can be seen from these examples that "negative" is not synonymous with "aversive." One hypothesis of this study is that much more of learning is negative among the poor than among other classes.

The natural history of a single organism covers its life; but this study is limited to the child's learning experiences in kindergarten, in the first year in elementary school, and in his home peer-group during that period.

The rationale for a natural history of the education of any child is that by studying the *same* child over a wide range of his activities we can obtain a more complete idea of what helps *him* and what hinders *him* in learning. When the *same* child is studied for two years in the home, in kindergarten, in the first grade, and with peers, one obtains a better picture than when one studies him in only one of these situations. Furthermore, by following *specific* children over time, one obtains a more detailed and faithful picture of the vicissitudes of the educational experience of particular children than when one studies *groups* at a *single moment* in time, without reference to the question of the varieties of experience *over time* of each particular child. Thus in this study we aim at the significant detail of life experience of *particular* children rather than at global statistical formulations based upon *group* studies. We think that a study of the natural history of selected children will enable us to articulate, or, at least, to approximately articulate, the varieties of experience with one another. From the work of Deutsch, Riessman, Bruner, and others, we have been made aware of the probable relationship between milieu (home and peer) and school learning in culturally deprived children; we want to be able to specify that relationship in greater detail and with security.

Some factors in the home are as important to school performance as cognitive capabilities and reinforcements narrowly construed. We refer to factors generally called emotional. The cases of two poor Negro children, David Smith and Rachel Potter, cast light on the issue.

DAVID AND RACHEL

David and Rachel were described by the researcher as being outgoing and alert when they were first observed in kindergarten in 1964. Now both are in Mrs. Trask's first-grade class. Both children live in the same public housing project. Rachel's building has no bad odor; the halls in David's smell of urine. Rachel's family is stable "middle-class-like," David's is not.[4]

Rachel

Rachel is one of five children and lives with her father and mother. Her father, an unskilled worker, is a family man, but seems rather aloof from the children. Mrs. Potter was observed to be always deeply involved with them.

The Potters' apartment has four rooms: a combination living room and kitchen-dining area and three bedrooms. The apartment is always neat, and the furniture is so arranged as to make a clear distinction between living room and dining-kitchen areas. The front area presents the family "front" but the rear rooms are drab and bare. The children all have permanent bedroom assignments. Only members of the nuclear family live in the apartment.

Mrs. Potter seems affectionate with the children, although firm, and is always clear headed. She is active in a religious movement, and literature of the movement can be found throughout the house. The family has study periods devoted to the ideology of the movement.

The Potter children are highly competitive with one another but are obedient to maternal intervention, which is generally in the interest of maintaining proper conduct—"Give Pam a chance Rachel, it's not your turn." The children often play at school work, and television-watching seems to be subordinated to it.

David

David's household is held together by his illiterate fifty-nine-year-old great-grandmother Mrs. Thompson. At present the following persons seem to live there with some continuity: David and his four sisters; his violent (diagnosed) psychopathic but probably borderline psychotic, thirty-five-year-old great-uncle James, son of Mrs. Thompson; Mr. Thompson's fifteen-year-old "daughter" Josephine; and Thomas, a grandchild of Mrs. Thompson.[5] David's mother and father are separated, and neither lives in the apartment. Marilyn, the mother, characterized as "wild" by

[4] It is well known, of course, that ghetto Negroes are not a homogeneous class.

[5] The housing project has not been able to verify Mrs. Thompson's claim that Josephine is her daughter.

Mrs. Thompson, is an irregular resident of the home, as is Sandra, another daughter of Mrs. Thompson.

The apartment has the same physical layout as the Potters' but is always in a state of disarray, furniture being moved around frequently and no clear distinction being maintained between living room and kitchen-dining areas. The only person who has a fixed sleeping place is James.

Mrs. Thompson is almost entirely dependent upon public agencies. Marilyn (David's mother) receives ADC checks but none of it has been used to support the children.

Mrs. Thompson says she could not live without the children. Observation indicates she is well-disposed toward them but her contacts with them are rather impersonal. When speaking about them in their presence, she often belittles them and herself as well. She has had a stroke, her eyes are in poor condition, and she is quite confused but far from mentally ill. She is unable to discipline the children and has little authority or respect in the house. Mrs. Thompson's communication with the children is infrequent and is limited largely to commands and admonitions. David and his siblings interact competitively but most of their time at home is spent watching television. The children were never seen to do schoolwork at home. James is a punitive and threatening figure.

OBSERVATION IN RACHEL'S HOME

Both Mr. and Mrs. Potter are stabile figures in the lives of their children. Mrs. Potter has frequent, intimate, and affectionate contact with them. The father is absent from the house during his working hours and watches television in the evening. Mrs. Potter is a housewife and Mr. Potter is definitely a "family man." There is a very warm relationship between Mrs. Potter and her children, and she appears certain of her position as an authority and as a nurturant figure. Rachel spontaneously includes her mother in her play.

Rachel and several playmates are jumping rope.
R: "Mama, let me see you jump rope." Mrs. Potter smiled, said OK, and jumped rope.
(Rachel and several of her friends are playing school.) Mrs. Potter looked over at the kids, saw that Rachel was holding all the pencils. Mrs. Potter asked Rachel why she had all the pencils and Rachel replied that the other kids weren't supposed to be doing anything now. Mrs. Potter told her to give the children their pencils and Rachel repeated that they weren't supposed to be doing anything now. Her mother then told Rachel to give them their pencils. "Now—give Betty her pencil." Rachel sat pouting for a couple of seconds, and her mother said, "Give it to her!" and Rachel took one of the pencils and threw it to Betty who picked it up. Mrs. Potter told Betty to put

the pencil back down and for Rachel to give it to her. Betty did, and Rachel handed her the pencil. She then gave Alice and Jennie their pencils back. Rachel immediately turned her paper over and told the kids what to draw.

The kids were still playing school and Rachel now was just sitting and watching the other kids as they worked and Mrs. Potter said, "Look at Rachel. Rachel is lazy." And Rachel said, "I ain't. I ain't lazy either." And Mrs. Potter said, "You just have one thing to do and that's wipe off the table, and you didn't do that well today." And Rachel kind of grinned when she said this.

We continued watching the children and every once in a while Rachel would ask her mother something related to the work she (Rachel) was doing, or her mother would comment. At one point Rachel said, "I'm going to make six mice with cheese," and her mother said, "Mice with cheese. Show me how you draw that, Rachel." And Rachel began. When she finished she went to show her mother.

Rachel was telling the other kids that, "When I finish this you're going to have to draw it," and her mother said, "They're going to have to draw it, but you didn't draw that. Alice drew that." And Rachel said, "I know it, but I'm the teacher. They're supposed to do what I say."

These data show that there is a high level of verbal interchange between Rachel and her mother, that the mother intervenes constantly in Rachel's play and will participate in it if asked. Mrs. Potter's intervention is in the framework of positive learning: she teaches Rachel the right thing to do—not to be selfish, to give other children a chance (fair play), and not to try to run things. She intervenes in the interest of moral learning and justice. Her intervention is nonviolent, and she does not threaten Rachel with beating. There is an easy interchange between Rachel and her mother, and she brings her mother her work to look at as if she knows her mother will be interested.

OBSERVATION IN DAVID'S HOME

David's home is usually in a state of disarray, while Rachel's is always orderly. The different arrangement of furniture in the two apartments is illustrative. The furniture in David's house is usually covered with an assortment of articles; outstanding are the persistent piles of clothes that Mrs. Thompson is to iron:

The observer (R) asks: "Whose room is this? Who sleeps here?" Mrs. Thompson: "Room? Whose room? Oh well, I guess it's Josephine's room. I guess she's supposed to sleep here, but you never can tell. The kids just sleep all over. You never know who's going to sleep where. Sometimes I have a hard time finding a place for myself." R: "Oh, the kids don't have any special place they have to sleep?" Mrs. Thompson: "No, they just sleep anywhere they want."

We then watched television and there was very little comment during the program except for the kids laughing at some of the antics or jokes. When this program went off, "Petticoat Junction" came on and we watched it. During this program, David was sitting over on the bed also. Lila went over to where Mary was and tried to get her to move over so she could sit there too and Mary hit Lila saying, "Go away, move." The girls started hitting each other. Mrs. Thompson: "You all stop that. You all cut that out. Tillie, give me my switch, give me my belt over there." Both girls were crying by this time and Tillie looked in a drawer and came out with what seemed to be a plastic-covered extension cord, or a clothes line. It was looped several times over and she gave it to Mrs. Thompson who shook it at them saying, "You all hush up that noise, you just hush up that fuss," and she sat back down. Lila hit at Mary again.

Mrs. Thompson: "I told you about that," and she got up, and with both hands hit Lila on the ears several times, saying, "I told you to stop that." Lila started to cry and Mrs. Thompson said, "Go on in there and clear up them dishes." On the table, where apparently someone had been eating, were three plates with a lot of bones on them. They looked as if they may have been pig knuckles or pig-feet bones. Mrs. Thompson: "Go on in there and start them dishes." Lillie went also and after a few minutes David went too. R: "Where is Josephine tonight?" Mrs. Thompson: "Oh, I don't know. I don't know. I'll probably have to send these kids out to her again. I just don't know what I'm going to do with that girl."

It will certainly strike middle-class readers as strange that nobody should have a permanent sleeping place in this home; but when one considers that in this, as in many ghetto homes, the population of the household is in constant flux, and that each new person (in the sense of new arrival or of a former inhabitant returning) may require new adaptations, it makes sense not to insist upon rigid sleeping arrangements. Nevertheless, having a fixed space gives the child a certain advantage in learning over a child who is strange to such stability.

There is no play in David's home and verbal communication is low. The observer never saw any schoolwork being done in David's home, not even in play. Note also how quickly Mrs. Thompson moves from admonition to extreme violence. Readers not familiar with ghetto culture may not understand the significance of the plastic-covered extension cord: in some ghetto homes the cord is used to beat children, apparently because blows with the hand are so common that they lose effectiveness. At any rate, it is clear that Mrs. Thompson comes to feel very quickly that the situation is beyond simple scolding; that the situation is beyond her control unless she uses violence. As soon as the fighting ended and the children were ordered to clean up the kitchen, all verbal interchange ceased.

The answer to the question about Josephine is relevant to ghetto life: Josephine is fifteen years old and is probably already deep in the ghetto female sexual cycle.[6] Mrs. Thompson feels helpless about this and she objects to what Josephine is doing, even though she must know that such behavior is typical. Rejection of the ghetto female sex pattern in judgment, but accepting it eventually as a fact, is characteristic.

[6] See Lee Rainwater, "The Negro Family, Crucible of Identity," *Daedalus* (Winter 1966).

The next observation is of James and David. James—arrested by the police because of violence to one of his sisters and for having smashed Mrs. Thompson's furniture—has been diagnosed as a "psychopathic personality." The observation follows:

> James entered the room and said to Miss Jones, the researcher, "You David's teacher? You taking him somewhere?" And (Miss Jones continued) I said, "No, I'm not a teacher but I'm going to take him out today." Lillie (a sister) said, "Granma said he could go. She said he's supposed to go." James grabbed David, put his arms around him, and all of a sudden slapped him hard on the head. I guess I must have shown some obvious signs of shock, because James then rubbed David's head and said, "He knows I'm not mad at him. He knows the difference between my hitting him when I'm not mad and when I'm mad."[7] I gave a kind of half-hearted smile, nodded my head, and sat down. When we left, James was careful to pin up David's coat.

In the summer of 1965 David "took to running away," says Mrs. Thompson, "with a group of them little bad boys around here." Sometimes he wouldn't come home until two or three o'clock in the morning. People would report having seen him in a wide variety of places. Once he went all the way down to the river. At her wits' end, Mrs. Thompson got somebody to round up David's father, in the hope that he could stop the child from running away. Although David's father shows no interest in him, is not living with David's mother, and never appeared in the home, he did come in answer to this summons, and, Mrs. Thompson said, "When he brought David back he beat the living daylights out of him. He beat the boy hard for an hour; he just took off his belt and just wore him out."

When Miss Jones was still getting to know the family, she paid a visit one day, and David, whom she already knew quite well, was called into the room by Mrs. Thompson, but was quite shy in responding to Miss Jones:

> Mrs. Thompson sat down in the armchair by the window and asked me (Miss Jones) if I thought something was wrong with David, if maybe he couldn't learn. She said she tried and tried to get him to speak up and to say something but he just won't. She said she tried to get him in every program at school and then she corrected herself and said in all the programs at church. She said that there's going to be an Easter program and that there was a real good part in it and David was supposed to be in it but he won't say anything. He'll just get up there and mumble and you just can't understand him. She asked me again if I thought there was something wrong with him, that he couldn't learn. I told her I was sure there wasn't. I then asked her what church they attend and she said, "The People's Church." She said that "David just acts so dumb at times."

Mrs. Thompson belittles the other children, and herself. Thus David gets nothing at home that makes him feel intelligent. Observed in kindergarten with his peers at their desks, David is very talkative. When Miss

[7] I'm not at all sure that this very good King's English isn't Miss Jones's modification.

Jones brought him and Rachel to the university to visit me, he talked a blue streak, and coherently.

From the next excerpt of Miss Jones's observations, we obtain a good picture of Mrs. Thompson's confusion and the lack of respect for her by other adults who come to the house. The reader should recall that Mrs. Thompson is illiterate and cannot see well. Our project had been trying to have her go to an eye clinic for some time, but when I left St. Louis in June 1966, we had not yet succeeded, even though we were going to pay the fare and the cost of the glasses.

I (Miss Jones) entered the apartment and sitting on the right hand of the table was a white man. On the table was a new portable Singer sewing machine. Mrs. Thompson sat down and said that she just wasn't too well, that she had just gotten back from downtown (on a table and chair where the sofa had previously been were a lot of packages) and that that girl (her 15-year-old niece) had just talked her out of spending every penny in her pocketbook. She shook her head and said she just didn't know why she had done it, she just didn't know. I asked who she was referring to and she said that she was talking about that big girl that had been there when I was there before. She told me that she had said that she wasn't going to buy that girl anything for Easter because she had been disobeying her for about the past three weeks but somehow or other she had talked her downtown and just talked her out of all her money and buying her a new dress, pocketbook, shoes and just everything. She kept repeating that she just didn't know why she had done it. She then asked me if I thought maybe she was losing her mind and I said that these things happen to a lot of people. She shook her head again and repeated that she had said she wasn't going to buy that girl anything. She then said, "Someone must have sprinkled some [gooby] dust on her.". . .

The white man looked in his pocket for something or other and stood up and began talking to Mrs. Thompson about this new sewing machine on the table. I think they were continuing the conversation I had interrupted when I arrived. Mrs. Thompson told me that she would have to give him the $12 next week and that she guessed he'd take the new machine back and she'd keep her old machine until she had the money and the salesman then said it was supposed to be $20, that she had already given him $8 so she could keep the new machine and he'd just pick up the money next week. She said no, she guessed he'd better take the new machine on back until next week because you're supposed to have the $20. The salesman then explained that the $20 had already been paid to the company, that he had taken the $8 she had given him and put the other $12 in from his own pocket and given it to the company; so the $12 she would give him next week would be his, and the company had its money for the machine. . . .

The salesman went and brought in what was apparently Mrs. Thompson's old machine. He sat it down and Mrs. Thompson said, "You don't reckon I've got $50 in that, do you?" He said, "I beg your pardon." She said, "You don't reckon I've got $50 in that?" He asked if she meant that the machine wasn't worth $50, and she said, "I didn't think so but look in the drawer." She looked in the drawer and started taking some pins out. The salesman said that he had taken everything else out of the drawer and put it on the table back there. (I am unclear myself as to whether Mrs. Thompson was wondering if the machine was worth $50 or if she had $50 in the drawer of the machine.) . . .

Almost as soon as he had left the apartment, Mrs. Thompson's daughter

Sandra, a woman in her middle or early 30's who looked as if she were about 7 months pregnant, entered the room. She was wearing a red and white striped maternity top and Jamaica pants. She was wearing a wedding ring. Sandra picked a cloth bag off the table that had the Singer emblem on it and said, "What this go to? I could sure use this. I could use this." And Mrs. Thompson said, "Put that down, Sandra, that's to my machine." The girl said, "I could sure use this; aw, it's not important." The salesman then reentered the apartment and looked around and Mrs. Thompson said, "Sandra, get up and let the man have that seat." The girl said, "I'll get up when Sandra's ready to go." The man said, "Oh, that's all right," and he opened his attaché case on the floor and took some papers out of it. While he was doing this, Sandra looked at him and said, "You don't want this seat, do you?" And he said, "No." Mrs. Thompson said, "Give the man the chair." Sandra said, "I done ask if he wanted it and he said no." She was still holding the cloth bag and Mrs. Thompson asked the salesman, "Is that bag mine? Does that bag go to the machine? What's it for?" He said, "It's to cover the foot pedal with, to hold the foot pedal when you aren't using it." She said, "Put that down, Sandra, it's mine." And Sandra said, "You don't need this. It'll be on the floor more than anywhere else anyway."

Mrs. Thompson then told the salesman, "I don't know, maybe I should keep my old machine this week. I made two dresses already but I've got three more Easter dresses to make tonight." (On a pole lamp by the sofa two new dresses were hung. In all probability these are the dresses Mrs. Thompson has already completed.) The salesman said, "It's easy to use this machine. You'll be able to sew so much better with it." Mrs. Thompson then said, "But I don't know if I know how to work it and I got these three dresses to make. Maybe I should use my old machine to finish those dresses." The salesman said, "Here's the book and do you want me to show you how to use it again? I'll show you." Mrs. Thompson: "Not right now. I still think I ought to keep my old machine now, even if it is old. I've had it 20 years, let me see . . . yeah, been 20 years and I don't know if I can change now. It doesn't act right sometimes and it skips stitches at times but I know how to use it. I'm used to it." She then asked me, "Don't you think I'm too old to learn this new machine, these new things now?" And I said, "Oh I don't know about that." And Mrs. Thompson said, "I don't know, I'm too old to be getting into all of this debt. I'm paying $400 for that machine."

By this time Sandra had gone into the kitchen area and was putting something in a paper bag and she said, "Hmmp, this one's cracked," and laid an egg to one side. Mrs. Thompson: "Those are hard boiled eggs." Sandra: "No they ain't. I just took these out of the refrigerator." Mrs. Thompson: "Oh, how many eggs you taking, Sandra? I know you taking a dozen and a half. I know 12's in a dozen and a half a dozen would be about six more. You ain't fooling me; I know you taking more than a dozen." Sandra: (who in the meantime keeps putting eggs in the bag) "Aw mama, you don't know.". . . . Mrs. Thompson: "Sandra, don't take all of my eggs!" Sandra: (looking in the bag) "Aw, I'm just taking a dozen and one in case one of 'em breaks so I'll have an even dozen. I just took 14, maybe 16 or 18." Then she stops taking eggs and puts the bag to one side. The salesman has left the apartment again, I guess to go back to the car for something. Sandra then goes over to the piano and begins playing something. Mrs. Thompson: "Sandra, don't play the piano, it makes me nervous. I can't take it today." And Sandra keeps on playing and says, "Aw it's not long." Mrs. Thompson: "Sandra, don't play the piano, it's making me nervous I say." Sandra: (finishes what she was playing) "I don't know but one number anyway."

The following points should be stressed in connection with these observations: (1) Mrs. Thompson's general confusion and inability to make a decision and stick to it. (2) The ease with which adults, Black or White, push her around. (3) The chicanery of the White salesman, who insists on selling Mrs. Thompson a sewing machine when she obviously will not be able to run it and when she is obviously confused about costs, and about her ability to pay for it. (4) The lack of respect for her by members of her own family. Thus, David does not have before him models of adults who are honest or solicitous; the major adult influence in his life, his great-grandmother, does not provide him with any firm basis for making a decision. She can't even make clear to him how one counts—not even the difference between a dozen and a dozen and a half eggs. In sum, David's home environment lacks important dimensions that usually give firmness to life, including perception and cognition.

The following suggests a further source of confusion and even despair.

Mrs. Thompson began crying and said, "I just don't know, I'm at the end of my rope; all of the knots are being pulled and I've just nowhere to go now." She then said, "Excuse me." She went into the apartment and got a handkerchief and came back out and wiped her eyes and sat back down and said, "You see, that's one of the reasons I'm cleaning out all this junk now, so that when we move we won't have so much stuff to worry about." I then asked Mrs. Thompson where she was planning to move. She said, "I don't know, find someplace I guess, I don't know." I then asked her when were they going to move and Mrs. Thompson said, "When they throw us out of here, when they come and lock the door and set all our stuff outside, that's when we gon move cause we can't pay the rent and I don't see where any money is coming from so I just don't want to have all of this stuff setting out here when they lock us out of the house."

Mrs. Thompson was in constant trouble with the housing administration because she was falling behind in her rent payments; they threatened to sue her and to evict her, until they realized that she was a confused woman of exceedingly limited financial resources. Thus, at this point, David's problem is twofold: constant material insecurity, and constant confusion, and an adult figure who, on the one hand, never knows where the money is going to come from to pay the rent, and, on the other, does not know how to protect the money she does have, by limiting her expenditures.

In summary, one would have to say that the environment of David's home does not prepare him for the expectations of school.

RESULTS FROM KINDERGARTEN AND FIRST-GRADE ANALYSIS

It would seem, now, as if the stage were set for the conclusion that David's performance in school was miserable from the beginning and that "he never had a chance," considering his background. Our studies of the cases do not fit the stereotype. The following is a partial analysis of the data up to February 1966.

A. We coded observations of David and Rachel in kindergarten and the first grade as follows:

1. Shows leadership or helpfulness.
2. Neglects work or acts up.
3. Gives right answer to teacher's question.
4. Gives wrong answer to teacher's question.
5. Gives confused answer to teacher's question.

The results of the two children are as follows:

Percent of Type of Answers As Related to Total Answers

	KINDERGARTEN DAVID	RACHEL
Right answer	54	80
Wrong answer	20	19
Confused answer	26	1
Number of times showing leadership	8*	0
Number of times acting up	8*	0
	FIRST GRADE	
Right answer	70	55
Wrong answer	30	45
Number of times inattentive	2*	0
Thumbsucking in class	2*	0

* The last two items are not percentages but acts.

B. In February 1966 the children received identical report cards in the first grade. The teacher's comment on the two children follows:

(The researcher reports): Mrs. Trask told me that Rachel is a good student who usually thinks. She said the reason for Rachel's success in school appears to be more one of control and discipline than of capacity; with drive and push Rachel will be consistently good. David has it but he's not so controlled and he's getting into trouble in the school yard. He's becoming a behavior problem. He's very aggressive and is generally a little tough boy and won't study his words.

David is also beaten by James, who has created violent scenes in the household. David was recently whipped by the school principal for urinating on the playground, and he was also seen by the researcher to be struck by the teacher in kindergarten. On the positive side: Mrs. Trask, as contrasted with David's kindergarten teacher, is interested in him and plans so that he will perform at the best possible level in her class.

This brings us to the problem of the school.

THE CULTURE OF THE SCHOOL

Whether or not David and Rachel will or will not succeed in school is a function of the interplay between the culture of the school and the culture outside the school. The question is, What do we mean by "the culture of the school"? The answer to the general question is obtained by finding answers to the following subsidiary questions among others:

1. What are the values, perceptions, and attitudes of the people in the school? Since, whenever the child is in school, he is a member of the school culture, answers to the question apply to him just as well as to the school personnel. Thus, for example, we study the class position of pupils, teachers, and principals; their values, their perceptions of one another, their attitudes toward the school, and so on. We want to know the *general* value orientations of school personnel as well as the values they use in judging one another and their pupils; and we want to know the same about the pupils. We also want to know how the pupils perceive the teachers and vice versa, how the teachers perceive one another and the principal, and how he perceives them. We want to know what the attitudes of all the members of the school culture are toward the school itself.

2. What is the internal structure of the school? What is the hierarchy of power in each school? Who are the pace-setters, the cultural maximizers, the arbiters of value judgments? What are the roles of the teachers and the principal? How much freedom of choice is there for a teacher? What are the relative power positions of the newcomers and the old hands; the insiders and the outsiders (if any)? What in general are the lines of formal and informal communication and organization? Is it possible to evade the formal structure? Does it really exist? What is the relationship between types of structure and communication and accomplishing anything? What are the patterns of socialization of new teachers into the on-going "tradition" of the particular school? What are the patterns of recruitment into the school? What are the "quit" patterns? What processes determine turnover, advancement, and so on?

3. What are the formal and informal relationships between the educational bureaucracy and the factors listed in no. 2?

4. What is the relationship between the parents and the school system?

5. What goes on in the classroom? The format of the answer to this question is given in "A Cross-Cultural Outline of Education" (Henry 1960). Some illustrations from the kindergarten class of David and Rachel are appended.

The dynamic sum of the answers to questions 1–5 constitute the ethnography of the school; and from this one should be able to derive a general answer to the question, What is the culture of the (particular) school?

This should yield an answer to a question such as, Why did David's kindergarten teacher hit him? At the end of the study, the answer to the question should resemble the following: David's teacher hit him for the following reasons: (1) He acts up in a school that insists on strict order and discipline even in kindergarten (value of order). (2) The teacher is from the middle-class and devalues David because of his background. (3) The principal and teachers believe that the only thing that "makes an impression on kids" is a strong arm. (4) The school district is under pressure to "make a showing" and "it's kids like David who give us all a black eye." (5) The teacher's status (and pay increments) is related to the achievement records of her children. (6) The principal is a "no-nonsense" man who believes in keeping a tight rein on his "outfit." (7) The principal knows he is under scrutiny by the district superintendent whose ambition it is to make a showing with his plan for bettering the condition of the children in his district. (8) Since David has his own emotional problems that do not allow him to follow the rules, he is often inattentive and the like, and so arouses the teacher who, *under the conditions stated*, is likely to express her irritation with children by violence.*

MODEL

If we let O stand for the outcome of David's total educational experience at home, P for his peer-group experience, S for the influence of the school culture, and T for time, then

$$O = f(E + S + P)T$$

The fact that David's teacher struck him, or that he succeeds in the first grade, is a function of the influence of the school, and of his relationships with his peers and of his life at home—in the widest sense, of an emotional as well as a cognitive experience. Complex as each of its elements is, the model suggests the following hypotheses, among others: (a) That the outcome of the schooling depends upon a complex of factors; (b) that if one factor, let us say E, takes on a largely negative significance—negative learning exceeds positive—this might be overcome if certain factors in S were maximized—such as an improvement in teaching methods; (c) that if one factor is maximized—such as, for example, a great improvement in teaching methods—it might be canceled by a negative indication in another, as in the home or peer-group situation, for example. We have entered T as a *multiplier* with some hesitation, and with the reservation that T *is no more a simple multiplier than* $E+S+P$ *is a simple sum*. We have in mind the fact that the longer any process continues the

---

* This is merely a paradigm, not a conclusion.

greater effect it will have on the outcome. We add the time dimension also because the study is a life-historical one. Meanwhile, the presence of *T* suggests sampling *O* for particular children at particular times.

CONCLUSIONS AND POSITION

Obtaining an understanding of the educational vicissitudes of children will be expanded by passing from correlational analysis of groups to the study of individual children in their natural habitat; and it is not only the culturally deprived that will be helped in this way but all children. Our findings, miniscule though they may be at present, suggest the obvious: that the outcome of a child's experience with the formal educational system is the sum of several types of experience—home, school, and peer group. Any one factor taken alone cannot explain why some fail and others succeed. Plans for improving the education of children must be based, therefore, on an understanding of the relationship among the factors. While we cannot know what is going on in the life of *every* child, we have to assume that among deprived children there are those who always suffer a heavy burden of extracurricular environmental disability. Provision ought to be made for it in the school culture. Most obvious is the training of teachers to handle these children. Too often, among Black as well as among White teachers, the attitude toward the ghetto child is such as to make his life in school almost as harsh as his environment at home. The result is an accumulation of anxieties beyond the point where school learning is possible.

APPENDIX

OBSERVATIONS IN DAVID AND RACHEL'S KINDERGARTEN CLASS

Mrs. M.: "Michael, will you collect all the papers, please?" David said, "Mrs. B., can I help?" Mrs. B.: "He can do it by himself."

Mrs. B. left the room. . . . The noise level is 3. . . . David came up to me and asked, "You want me to keep them quiet?" I told him that I was not in charge and he returned to his seat. . . . The noise level is up to 4. . . . David yells, "Everybody be quiet! Be quiet!" The noise level drops to 3.

However, several months later he began to be inattentive in class, helping others with their work rather than doing his own, and getting into trouble with the teacher:

Everybody is at the weather dial paying attention except for David who is opposite me looking at a book. . . . Mrs. B.: "Who can tell us what the

weather is outside today? Raise your hands. David." David was running around
the book table at this point. He didn't say anything. . . . Mrs. B.: "Let's come
back to the piano, little people," and everybody was over to the piano except
David who is still running around the book table.

Mrs. B.: "Let's bow our heads," and the class began saying the prayer. However, David, George, Frederick, and Maurice were not paying attention.

To a considerable extent, school for David is now an institutionalized
version of the harsh, impersonal treatment he receives at home.

When I arrived in Mrs. B.'s class, the children were seated around the piano
and she was slapping some little boy (Benny) on the side of his head saying
in time to the slaps, "You will listen to me."

11:30. Mrs. B.: "We will all wash our hands at one time, children. Do not
wash your hands now, please."

11:31. "Children, what's wrong with your ears this morning? What did I
just say?"

She was referring to washing hands.

11:32. "Billie," and he says "Huh?"

Mrs. B.: "Come here . . . Where are you going?" Billie says, "In the bath-
room."

Mrs. B.: "For what?" Billie: "To wash my hands."

Mrs. B.: "What did I just say? Boy, if you don't sit down," and she paused,
"I'm going to spank you."

Mrs. B.: "David, I asked you to use your hand, not your mouth." She
whipped David rather hard with the pointer.

Mrs. B. returns and says, "Little people you are not to do anything with
these papers. Now I didn't tell you that. All little people who have put something on your paper, ball the paper up and put it in the trash can please."
About thirteen students do. . . . She reiterates about putting the paper in
the can and says, "You children are so hard-headed, why did you mark on
that paper? I didn't say anything about it. You didn't know what I wanted to
do with them." Some little girl balls her paper and Mrs. B. hits her on the
arm several times with the pointer and says, "Why did you mark on this
paper?" Then she says, "Lock your lips. All those who have to throw papers
away line up at the desk." When they do she gives them another piece of
paper and says, "You're going to have to get a spanking." However, she does
nothing to carry out her threat.

Mrs. B.: "Children, why did you draw lines? Why did you draw lines? I
asked you not to make lines. You little people don't listen. Those of you who
drew lines, put your papers in the waste can. You'll have to do your papers
over. You'll be behind the other children."

Mrs. B.: "Little people, stand behind your chairs, don't bother the crayon."
And the children still played with the crayon whereupon Mrs. B. went over to
Pam and David and hit them while she was saying in an angry voice, "Keep
your hands away from the crayon. You little people are hard-headed." She
really hit these kids this time.

Proper, correct behavior is very rarely rewarded and about the only time
Mrs. B. appeared aware of the child as a person, as an individual, was in
a punishment situation. Since Rachel was well behaved, did as she was
told, and never volunteered, we have no observations on her that parallel
those on David.

SELECTED REFERENCES

Ausubel, David P.
  1963 A teaching strategy for culturally deprived pupils: cognitive and motivational considerations. The School Review (Winter):454–463.
Bernstein, Basil
  1960 Language and social class. British Journal of Sociology, 11:271–275.
  1961 Social class and linguistic development: a theory of social learning. In Economy, Education and Society. A. H. Halsey, J. Floud, and C. A. Anderson, eds. New York: The Free Press.
  1962 Linguistic codes, hesitation phenomena and intelligence. Language and Speech. 5, no. 1.
Bruner, Jerome S.
  1960 The process of education. Cambridge, Mass.: Harvard University Press.
  1961 The cognitive consequences of early sensory deprivation. In Sensory deprivation, Philip Solomon, ed. Cambridge: Harvard University Press.
  1964 The course of cognitive growth. American Psychologist 19:1–15.
Crandall, Virginia.
  1964 Achievement behavior in young children. Young Children (November) 77–90.
Deutsch, Martin
  1963 Nursery education: the influence of social programming on early development. The Journal of Nursery Education (April):191–197.
  1964a Papers from the Arden House conference on pre-school enrichment. Merrill-Palmer Quarterly of Behavior and Development 10:207–208; 249–263.
  1964b The role of social class in language development and cognition. American Journal of Orthopsychiatry 25:78–88.
  1964c Some psychological aspects of language in the disadvantaged. Presented at the Boston University Development Conference on the Teaching of Disadvantaged Youth (ms).
  ——, with Alma Maliver, Bert Brown, and Estelle Cherry.
  1964d Communciation of information in the elementary school classroom. Cooperative Research Project No. 908. Institute for Developmental Studies, Department of Psychiatry, New York Medical College (ms).
Henry, Jules
  1955a Culture, education and communications theory. In Education and anthropology, George Spindler, ed. Stanford, Cal.: Stanford University Press.
  1955b Docility, or giving teacher what she wants. The Journal of Social Issues 11, no. 2.
  1957 Attitude organization in elementary school classrooms. American Journal of Orthopsychiatry 27, no. 1.
  1959 The problem of spontaneity, initiative and creativity in suburban classrooms. American Journal of Orthopsychiatry 29, no. 1.
  1960 A cross-cultural outline of education. Current Anthropology 1:267–305.
  1963 Golden rule days: American schoolrooms. In Culture against man. New York: Random House, Inc.
  1965a Death, fear and climax in nursery school play. In Concepts of development in early childhood education, Peter Neubauer, ed. Springfield, Ill.: Charles C Thomas.
  1965b White people's time, colored people's time. Trans-Action (March/April).
  1965c Hope, delusion and organization: some problems in the motivation of low achievers. In The low achiever in mathematics. Lauren G. Woodby, ed. U.S. Department of Health, Education, and Welfare. OE 29061. Bulletin 1965, no. 31.
  1966 The study of families by naturalistic observation. Psychiatric Research Report 30. American Psychiatric Association: 95–104.
John, Vera P.
  1963 The intellectual development of slum children. American Journal of Orthopsychiatry 33:813–822.

Olson, James L. and Larson, Richard G.
  1965 An experimental curriculum for culturally deprived kindergarten children. Educational Leadership (May):553–558.
Riessman, Frank
  1962 The culturally deprived child. New York: Harper & Row, Publishers, Inc.

PART III

*Tools for Further
Research in Anthropology
and Education*

20: *Comparative Research upon the Schools and Education: An Anthropological Outline*

MURRAY L. WAX

1. Given the large volume of literature dealing with education and the schools, what can anthropologists possibly contribute? I suggest that our approach (as demonstrated by the essays and bibliography in this volume) has the following distinctive qualities of being (1.1) comparative and historical, so that we would be moved to inquire as to the nature of the schools and the educational process in the various societies of the world, past and present, (1.2) contextual yet concrete, so that we would seek for the specific transactions of the schoolroom and the school, and yet interpret these within the larger context (or natural whole) that includes cultural traditions, social systems, and ecological environments, and (1.3) continually oriented toward serving as the literate spokesman and interpreter for those whose lack of power and of sophistication tends to deprive them of a voice in the councils of the educated and mighty.

2. Most outlines for research and discussion on the schools in the United States analyze them in terms of their social and educational components (cf. any textbook on educational sociology): thus, pupil, teacher, supervisor, board, curriculum and the extracurricular, and so on. Since those outlines and analyses are neither contextual nor concrete, I suggest that we begin comparatively and remind ourselves of the ranges of types of schools in relationship to their sociocultural contexts. Under no. 3 and no. 4, I shall give a rough list of schools and environments: (2.1) In relationship to its sociocultural context, is the school homogenetic or heterogenetic (Redfield and Singer 1954)? Is the school organized to convey a tradition that has its roots among the local population, or to convey a tradition that is culturally alien? At one pole we have the little school that is a creature of the (relatively) autonomous rural community (the little red school house of U.S. history), while, at the other pole, we have a Western-type university bearing its Great Tradition to a people only slightly or partially acculturated toward the Western models. (2.2) How total is the incorporation of (2.21) students and (2.22) educators into an

educational community that is an encompassing and isolated whole (cf. Goffman [1961: 1–124]) or "total institution" (Redfield [1960a: chapters 1 and 10] on little communities and natural wholes)? At one pole, we have the English "public school" of the past, or similar boarding schools, encompassing a constant body of pupils in close intimacy for many years, and at the other pole, we have an urban slum school whose pupil turnover may be 100 percent or more during the school year and whose teacher turnover may be similar, and whose organization is such as to inhibit the development of solidarity and intimacy. (2.3) Biologically speaking, at what population is the school directed (children, juveniles, adolescents, young adults, mature adults, male/female)? Nursery schools contrasted with postgraduate schools; schools for nurses contrasted with schools for commandos. (2.4) How homogeneous is the student body vis-à-vis the educational and supervisory staff: (2.41) Are they ethnically and culturally of common background? (2.42) Do they become socially unified in opposition to the school authority? (2.5) What is the organizational structure of the school system? At one pole we have the large bureaucratic system of the modern metropolis with its compulsory attendance and status *in loco parentis*, and at the other pole, the small cluster of disciples gathered about the charismatic teacher (the rabbi or guru). Relevant here are considerations of size, or organizational complexity; obligations to attend as students; modalities of cooperation, power, integration, and competition. (2.6) What are the avowed goals of the process of formal education? Is the school supposed to instruct in a particular and limited skill, or is it supposed to create (or recreate) a particular kind of man, and, if the latter, what kind of man: a religious disciple, a military officer, a political conspirator, a gentleman, a dedicated scholar, *et al.?*

3. This list of schools and their sociocultural environments is neither systematic nor exhaustive, but is intended to remind us of the great varieties that exist and have existed, and to suggest (or inquire) as to whether comparisons and contrasts might be promising. At the least, we might ask, whether or not we should encourage more research on these schools. The only order I have made in the listing is some grouping, e.g., I begin with the more "total" establishments for the young. For these schools early on the list, I have tried to suggest how they might be classified in relationship to the dimensions presented under no. 2. For reasons of space, I have listed schools serving adults under no. 4.

3.1 The preparatory academy offering an elite education for juveniles and adolescents from elite families, e.g., the English "public school" and the academies of New England, Switzerland, and France. Small, total, homogenetic in tradition, student bodies homogeneous as to social class and status (although perhaps not in ethnicity), oriented toward producing civic leaders and gentlemen.

3.2 The reformatory or "assimilation mill," e.g., the juvenile detention or correction home or "industrial school," or the boarding schools as formerly conducted by the U.S. Indian Service (LaFlesche 1963; Brown 1952). Involuntary enrollment by students, authoritarian coercion, heterogenetic in tradition, student body homogeneous in class (but rarely in culture, even in the Indian case), training for manual skills and for civic docility.

3.3 The mission-operated boarding school in a colonial or ex-colonial environment. In colonial times, it may have operated more like 3.2 but now has shifted toward 3.1. and may serve the children of the elite or just the outcasts.

3.4 The school for disciples—religious, political, small, total, voluntary, personally transformative, e.g., Hindu ashram, monastery, chasidic rabbi, conspiratorial cell.

3.5 The urban public school serving children of (3.51) an ethnically homogeneous and integrated community (Hargreaves 1967) or (3.52) an ethnically diverse and unintegrated community (Herndon 1968; Eddy 1967).

3.6 The suburban school serving children of an upper middle-class professional population.

3.7 The small school of rural United States and village Europe (e.g., Wylie 1964).

3.8 New public schools in "new nations" (e.g., Foster 1965).

4.1 Vocational and trade schools, e.g., business colleges, schools operated by the military, or by private corporations.

4.2 Night schools, study groups, educational programs operated by labor unions, political factions, religious and other voluntary associations.

4.3 The community colleges of modern United States.

4.4 The small colleges of a half-century ago serving the United States elite.

4.5 The college in the multiversity (Becker, Geer, Hughes, 1968).

4.6 Graduate schools of the modern university.

4.7 Professional schools (Hughes, 1961; Becker et al. 1961).

Comment: doubtless many schools have been slighted. Do we need headings for the village school of rural Islam, the Sunday School of rural United States, the school of the kibbutz, the schools that teach ballet, karate, diction, "charm," or foreign languages to urban Americans and their children? Do we need to investigate the school in the bilingual or multilingual environment?

5. To present such a listing of schools is implicitly to ask a series of research questions. At the least we are driven to ask whether we know as much as we should about each of these types of schools. Are our researches overly slanted toward 3.6 because our children attend them or toward 3.52 because they are in the news?

5.1 Relative to the accomplishment of various types of goals, which of the schools have proven most successful?

5.2 In particular were the elite schools of the past half-century—the Gymnasium, the preparatory academy, and the religiously affiliated small college —as successful as they now appear to have been in creating an educated class?

5.3 What is happening at the grass-roots educational level within the new nations?

5.4 What historical-comparative situations are most promising of illuminating the problems associated with (3.52) and "cultural deprivation"?

5.5 Are contemporary reformers properly or overly concerned with grasping the very young and subjecting them to intensive training (e.g., Head Start in the United States)? These programs are especially designed to affect the poor and powerless.

5.6 Should we encourage the philanthropic foundations of the United States to support a broad program of comparative and historical research on schools and education, or does it seem wiser to confine ourselves to the modern urban school?

5.7 Do we really need to know more about schools and education, or is the problem more that of organization and reform, practice and demonstration, utilizing the wisdom we already possess?

6. The school of the contemporary metropolis is a crucial area inviting research by social scientists and especially anthropologists, yet challenging our efforts to comprehend the complex actualities. In particular, the following circumstances thwart our comprehension and suggest the need for further and carefully planned team projects: (6.1) In critical lower-class areas, the turnover among pupils (and even educators) has become so great that the classroom is not a stable social entity and the school scarcely constitutes a community; hence, conventional anthropological techniques of research (e.g., the entrance as participant-observer of the ethnographer into the school community) fail to provide a stable basis for the investigation. (Nor are sociological techniques substantially superior, since they too have been based on stabile residential populations.) (6.2) The population of most metropolitan areas is remarkably hetereogeneous and only appears homogeneous because of the common intent and orientation of civic agencies. Peoples that are included are of diverse ethnic backgrounds, language dialects, religious persuasions, and participations; relationships to the greater economy; familial and kin structures, and abilities to cope with the exigencies of life. Hence the reports on the urban slums and lower classes tend, not so much to be in error, as to be limited each in its sample and therefore restricted in its findings to a specific subpopulation. (6.3) Given this heterogeneity and the middle-class orientation of most social and educational surveys, the survey instruments tend to measure how far these people deviate from middle-class norms (intelligence quotients, educational achievement, neurotic tendencies, dialects, income). Thus they emerge as being "culturally deprived," yet any anthropologist acquainted with the viability of the folk (or peasant) cultures from which they have sprung (and sometimes only recently migrated) tends to be dubious about the accuracy of these measures and has to wonder whether there has been a fair assessment of their cultures vis-à-vis the urban middle class. (6.4) The school system as a huge and complex system invites further study, including not only its educational orientation but its economic, political, and social relationships

to its urban environment. (6.5) Clearly, the school system seems to "fail" in its relationship to lower-class children. Yet, would its "success" be more tolerable (Friedenberg 1965)? And, as our eminent social critics have been asserting, are its "successes" in the suburban context more often *human* failures? (6.6) Given the power of the school to close its doors and prevent inspection and investigation by potential critics and adversaries, has contemporary research on schools been gutted because of an inability to gain access to the subject or a fear of publishing honestly what has been observed? (My own experience indicates that the decision to investigate a school system may trigger all manner of adverse reactions from a power elite and that these reactions can travel surprisingly far, quickly and emphatically. My recent experience parallels that of Hortense Powdermaker (1966) in the Deep South of the United States. I would expect that those who have studied urban schools have had problems that are different in quality. (See Wolcott's discussion of this issue in his essay in this volume.) If anthropologists are to become more involved in the study of schools, do they need some assistance from foundations (or elsewhere) so that classroom doors and school files will be opened to them and so they are not subjected to restrictive pressures by governmental funding agencies that are highly responsive to pressures from local agencies that feel endangered by outside investigators?

7. I have confined myself mainly to the sociocultural study of education and the schools. In so doing I have neglected issues of ecology and of physical anthropology. Offhand, let me comment that from my own observations, most public schools are unsatisfactory as aesthetic or physical environments (and are evidently designed by architects who have not tried to live within their own buildings). Likewise, I would argue that the actual daily programs of most schools are damaging to the best physical development of their pupils. The lack of mobility (or exercise), the poor diet, the foul air, and the excessive noise of the environment provide a poor basis for healthy growth.

Since schools are now being diffused about the world in a wave of proselytization—as if formal education were a secularized missionary activity from the developed to the less developed nations—and since schooling is being blessed by so many of the parties active in this process as if it were the ideal and neutral solution to the problems of poverty, economic underdevelopment, ill health, and international conflict, anthropologists with a social conscience had best re-examine the matter. At the time of this writing college students all over the world have been rioting and causing disturbances: Many of their grievances are real, and many of their goals are laudable. It is equally likely that a pattern of grievances and conflicts will soon become established at the lower levels of the system of formal education, so that what has recently been visible in

Brooklyn, U.S.A., will be duplicated elsewhere with corresponding changes in the (culturally defined) skin coloration of the actors, but similar patterns of class, caste, power, and status.

As anthropologists, we are wedded to the great tradition of scholarship, higher education, and science. Our prejudices thus make us advocates of the schools, insofar as they clothe themselves with the mantle of formal education; and we are inclined to accept without questioning the notion that "the function" of "the school" is "to educate the young." But (as Khleif argues in his essay in this volume) the actual institutional complex that is the school system of an urban industrial nation is an affair that had best be approached through such conceptual categories as bureaucracy, status, class, and power. There is a need for anthropologists to study the schools with a critical and comparative gaze.

REFERENCES

Becker, Howard S., Blanche Geer, and Everett C. Hughes
　1968 Making the grade: the academic side of college life. New York: John Wiley & Sons, Inc.
　——, et al.
　1961 Boys in white: student culture in medical school. Chicago: University of Chicago Press.
Brown, Estelle
　1952 Stubborn fool. Caldwell, Idaho: Caxton Printers.
Eddy, Elizabeth
　1967 Walk the white line: a profile of urban education. New York: Doubleday & Company, Inc., Anchor Books A570.
Foster, Philip
　1965 Education and social change in Ghana. Chicago: University of Chicago Press.
Friedenberg, Edgar Z.
　1965 Coming of age in America: growth and acquiescence. New York: Random House, Inc.
Goffman, Erving
　1961 Asylums. Garden City, New York: Doubleday & Company, Inc., Anchor Books A277.
Hargreaves, David H.
　1967 Social relations in a secondary school. London: Routledge and Kegan Paul, Ltd.
Herndon, James
　1968 The way it spozed to be. New York: Simon & Schuster, Inc.
Hughes, Everett Cherrington
　1961 Students' culture and perspectives: lectures on medical and general education. Lawrence, Kansas: University of Kansas School of Law.
LaFlesche, Francis
　1963 The middle five. Madison: University of Wisconsin Press. (original text written in 1900).
Powdermaker, Hortense
　1966 Stranger and friend: the way of an anthropologist. New York: W. W. Norton & Company, Inc.
Redfield, Robert
　1955 The educational experience. Pasadena, California: The Fund for Adult Education.
　1960a The little community. Chicago: University of Chicago Press, Phoenix Books P53 (first published 1956).

1960b Peasant society and culture. Chicago: University of Chicago Press, Phoenix Books P53.
———, and Milton B. Singer
1954 The cultural role of cities. Economic Development and Social Change 3:53:73.
Spindler, George D., ed.
1963 Education and culture: anthropological approaches. New York: Holt, Rinehart & Winston, Inc.
Wax, Murray L., Rosalie H. Wax, and Robert V. Dumont, Jr.
1964 Formal education in an American Indian Community. Monograph no. 1, The Society for the Study of Social Problems. (Issued as Supplement to Volume II, no. 4, of Social Problems.)
Wylie, Laurence
1964 Village in the Vaucluse (2d ed. rev.) New York: Harper & Row, Publishers, Inc., Colophon Books CN 24.

Epilogue

Although anthropologists have been studying, indeed reifying, culture for close to a century, they have rarely been concerned with education except as a category of culture and this, as we shall see, is a paradox. In the professional lexicon, "education" was usually divided into two aspects or phases—socialization on the one hand and formal schooling on the other. Socialization was characteristically defined as the rearing of children within an immediate circle of kin with specific attention to "values," and the process was almost always conceptualized in the language of Western theoretical psychodynamics. Even if such theories were ethnographically rebutted in detail, their assumptions were accepted in a relativized form. The focus on socialization, in short, created the sub-discipline of personality and culture, but cognitive processes, as the basis for learning theory, were overlooked. And formal schooling was almost entirely neglected for obvious reasons. In traditional societies formal schooling more often than not represented a colonial intrusion; the school was a nontraditional institution. Studying such schools would have converted ethnographic, structural-functional or, more generally, relativistic efforts into historical studies of social and cultural change, for which anthropology was, and remains, unprepared in fact and deficient in theory.

Anthropologists have, for example, rarely examined the curricula of schools in societies they conventionally study; nor have they been critical, despite their formalistic relativism, of colonial colleges or secondary schools that taught British, but not African, history; or the eighteenth-century romantic poets, but not Ewe literature; the humanities, but not "technical" subjects; and so on. Schooling, in short, was an instrument of conquest along with the missions, the trading companies, the administrators, and the soldiers. Therefore, "education" was discreetly overlooked, particularly in territories in which the anthropologist was the "guest" of a colonial government. In the United States, similar inhibitions existed with reference to the education of Blacks and Indians, but the agitation for modern schooling "as good as ours" was more readily engaged in, since it did not involve the anthropologist in the contradictions that bound him in more conventionally defined colonial situations; it was assumed that Blacks and Indians were no less, and no more, than economically deprived Americans. The point is that an anthropology sensitive to these issues would have had to examine its own origins and claims rather more honestly than has been the case.

Conversely, in traditional or primitive societies wherein formal schooling does not exist, the actual process of learning was rarely, if ever, subject to careful and informed scrutiny. Learning in such societies is embedded in socialization. That is, the learning of skills and attitudes has not been functionally rationalized in segregated institutions; it takes place in a network of personal relations based on the paradigm of kinship. There are no socially discrete and discontinuous, hierarchically structured, impersonally administered learning groups; and there are no subtly engineered examination systems creating and perpetuating an "educational elite." Formal schools in primitive societies would be as strange and as repugnant as jails. Primitive learning, on the contrary, is an instrumental-cognitive-affective enterprise, which has the effect of integrating the person with his culture and preparing him—a process that never ends—for the journey from childhood to maturity and death, confirmed, in turn, by the periodic crisis rites which can also be interpreted as learning experiences.

It follows that the learning group is never confined to a mechanical collection of peers. Older siblings may instruct the younger while caring for them, thus combining nurturing and "teaching" functions, in itself an educational experience of no mean dimension. Special categories of relatives—not only natural parents, but mother's or father's brothers or sisters, grandparents, age-mates (who are assimilated to kin), among others—teach while interacting. Sometimes a particular class of persons has a special educational function relative to a given child. Learning is not an academic but a dialectic process—in its union of thought and action, person and mentor, instrument and affect. Instrumental skills are, for example, taught (we still don't know precisely how), but the world is not thereby objectified; abstract-deductive thinking is not a dominant mode. The world is, rather, incorporated into the structure of kin. The mentorial relationship is never reduced to the functionally rational; the learning group is flexible and, save for rare instances, is indistinguishable from the natural associations that define the society at large. That is, everyone is at once a teacher and a pupil in a variety of contexts.

There can be no "failures" in the course of the primitive learning experience, only the expression of differential talents reared on a base of commonly taught and practiced skills. Moreover, this develops, one should note, in the absence of writing, the initial exploitative context of which has been remarked on by Lévi-Strauss, Paul Radin and others. As anthropologists know well, the absence of writing does not imply cognitive impoverishment. The average person in a nonliterate society learns a wide range of attitudes and instrumental skills, including verbal skills, to which we may, perhaps, subsume memory; the result is a personally mastered ensemble of functions, rich in symbolic content, that seems especially impressive in contrast with the specialized worker, clerk, or executive in modern society. The latter do not command their cultural inventory; each in his own way has become an object in the processes of production and communication.

Anthropologists, then, have hardly studied education, that is, learning, in primitive societies, and have largely ignored the critical comparative implications of such a focus; with rare exceptions, they have assumed that learning occurs pretty much the way it does in our own society, although differing in cultural detail. By separating learning from socialization, which reflects the contemporary, civilized situation, they have been led also to overdetermine their work in the direction of personality and culture studies; the latter reflects the categories of our culture with particular reference to clinical or pathological nosologies.

But there is one issue, closer to home, that such studies seem to have missed, namely, that the division between the cognitive, affective and instrumental factors in the growth and behavior of the person may be a primary source of contemporary psychopathology. The segregation of these human functions from each other is, itself, a function of the shrinking circumference of direct personal ties both within and between the generations in our society. Correlatively, as the area of socialization diminishes, the area devoted to increasingly specialized education of an impersonal character increases. *We may, therefore, be nurturing a fundamental paradox, namely, that inadequately socialized persons are and will be drafted by modern society for increasingly narrow and technical training.* This is not merely a split between the so-called "two cultures" but represents a fundamental division at the very heart of our society involving all of us—parents and children, teachers and pupils, workers and managers, scientists and artists, engineers and housewives.

In consequence, and this is the surprising but utterly logical result, anthropologists have failed to approach learning—education—if you will, as synonymous with culture. Culture, they say, is socially transmitted or learned behavior; that is, culture *is* education in every sense of the term. But the process of transmission, the very heart of cultural dynamics, and, therefore, the basis for a critical examination of our own society, has been neglected. I am reminded of the response of a distinguished anthropologist, a professor emeritus, to the suggestion that he seriously consider undertaking a study of the university with which he had been associated for nearly two generations. He responded that he knew nothing about education and very little about his university.

However, when Clark Wissler suggests (in 1923!) that education is America's magic, he points toward a deeply critical examination of the uses of education as does Leslie White, who contends, following Durkheim, that education can do no more than reflect society. Although the opinions in each case are far from dialectical in intent—that is, Wissler locks education within a relativistically conceived system on the one hand and White within a technologically determined society on the other —they nonetheless share a broad cultural dimension.

This dimension has largely been lacking in studies of schools and of education generally, undertaken by social scientists, including anthropologists. The school as an institution and, by extension, the educational system in its present outline is accepted as vital and necessary. It may need improvement, let us say, in curricula, student-teacher interaction, and parent-teacher relationships; or it may require more attention to, and space for, the economically and culturally disadvantaged. The rehabilitation and redesigning of physical plants, and the creating of a more "permissive" atmosphere may be in order, and so on. But strangely enough, there is little or no historical and critical perspective on institutionalized schooling as such. The anthropologist, despite his work in primitive and traditional societies, seems to have uncritically accepted the assumptions of his own society about the inevitability and desirability of such schooling. He is, after all, an academic, even if less conventionally so than other scientists and educators. It is sobering, to say the least, that not a single major educational innovator directly responsive to the educational, which is, by definition, the cultural crisis of our time, has been an anthropologist. And it is perhaps here that the professional relativism of the anthropologist reduces him to the role of institutional tinkering, as opposed to a revolutionary look at a situation that is rooted in the very heart of our society. For the fact is that what we colloquially call mass education is a failure. And more mass education will not make it a success. What is needed is a qualitative, not a quantitative change.

The idea of mass education has its origins in the eighteenth century, the Euro-American Enlightenment, in the positivistic notions of those who believed that scientific progress and human perfectability were inevitably linked (not, however, in Rousseau, whose *Émile*[1] is the very antithesis of the idea). But the actual establishment of mass, that is universal, compulsory education, with increasing age limits and accelerated state support, is an achievement of nineteenth-century industrial capitalism. The United States was the laboratory of this enormous experiment. Schools served to "process" immigrant populations, standardizing values, teaching idioms, and opening the channels for upward mobility. Indeed, one can make a good case that American culture was created in the schools. Mass education in America cannot be understood apart from the dynamics of class. However, upward mobility does not necessarily correlate with either academic achievement or specific training but with the various levels of certification as phases of the educational process from grammar school through the graduate university.

Nor do the most powerful figures in society apply what they *manifestly*

[1] After reading, or, at least, hearing about the publication of *Émile*, the Parliament of Paris issued a warrant for Rousseau's arrest.

learned at school. How many bankers or real estate operators had (or have) degrees in business? How many politicians have studied political science, and so on? Even if this disjunction between training and vocation did not exist, which is not to imply that narrowly conceived vocational training is a societal good, it is clear that the fluctuations in the business cycle would have had the same effect by recirculating individuals through the system in search of subsistence. A recent instance is in the collapse in the market for theoretical physicists and graduate electronic engineers

But the major point remains—mass education in the United States continues to serve as a general admission ticket to the merry-go-round of social mobility. And it is this general condition which permits us to assimilate our educational system with a modern version of, as opposed to primitive, magic, since it certifies persons without qualifying them, or better, it qualifies them for social position and economic reward without effectively teaching them the subject matter of their presumed interests. Actually, the time-honored *manifest* functions of formal education—the "training of the mind," "self-examination," the acquiring of specific skills—are actually honored in the breach, for the *latent* function of mass education, particularly in the United States, has been to train the person in the arts of social opportunism, based on the manipulation of persons rather than the command of things. Formal education, becomes, in short, the affirmation and confirmation of middle-class values and occupations. This was accomplished for the most part *latently*. The very atmosphere of the classroom in which students are objectified, the narrowly defined emphasis on competitive performance, the grade as the ticket to success, the methodological specialization and trained incompetence of teachers, these and other familiar factors, convert the culture of the classroom into the medium that transmits the message of the culture at large. And this message becomes all the more emphatic with the increasing attrition of the family as the basic mediator between the person and society. Socialization towards objectification encounters a minimum of resistance. At the same time, the rewards that the school system promises—as a temporary surrogate of the society at large, along with the mystification involved in judgments made about promising, as opposed to unpromising, students—have the effect of rendering students of all ages malleable to received social authority. The failures are encouraged to define themselves as failures. The classroom reenacts the culture, in both its conscious and unconscious dimensions.

It is, of course, no wonder that the youth rebellions were initially confined to schools, not merely because schools confined and defined the young, but because they symbolized the irrelevant and invidious aspects of social authority at large. Many among the young, in dropping out, in passive or active rebellion, have come to realize that formal schooling, *education*, represents culture in process. Therefore, any cultural protest must inevitably involve the schools, particularly in the United States, where schools are ubiquitous and are, moreover, the only consequential brokers between society and the growing person.

Nineteenth-, and with insignificant exceptions, twentieth-century mass schooling, then, was far removed from the experimental anticipations of the eighteenth century. Schooling became an aspect of industrial bureaucratic capitalism and collectivism. The assembly line, the core of the factory system, including its recent automated and cybernetic elaborations, became the paradigm for the educational process, in startling contrast to the personal learning context in traditional and primitive societies. That is to say, the curricula are fragmented and specialized, thought is divorced from action, the reflexive job defines creative work in the world, the instrumental and the affective are divided while an all-embracing cultural discontinuity is preserved between the *pretensions* of the school and society. And this *pretended* discontinuity, then, becomes the rationalization for the kind of academic who insists that the school is a special province in which a superior species of cognition is supposed to take place, unimpeded by the demands or conflicts of society. The humanities, the sciences, including the social sciences, share that mystique of the school as embedded in society but somehow removed from, or above, society, Obviously that is the classic definition of a privileged, an immune position, and it is the opposite of the effort to generate an educational system which can serve significantly in the process of cultural change, in the effort to humanize our society.

If we are to put ourselves in the perspective of a nonliterate society, the middle-class, bureaucratically structured and supported schools, that is, mass education, necessarily restricts the creative energies that exist among the population at large. Industrial workers almost by definition rarely attain more than a high-school diploma which, in the United States, is a mark of personal and social inferiority. It is assumed that what workers need to learn they can learn on the job through apprenticeship or in special training programs that omit the executive and creative possibilities of the work being rationalized. On the other hand, technical schools as such, except on the highest levels, are also considered inferior. Socially, they lead nowhere, although they may insure earning a living. On the highest levels, in the graduate engineering and scientific faculties, there is a constant tendency toward the teaching and exercise of pure theory divorced from application and pragmatic considerations. Here again the conflict between idea and action cripples both the scientist and the worker and renders each more malleable to the reified demands of the industrial system as it is defined by the manager and the politician.

Obviously, then, any critical and cultural interpretation of the crisis in education must reach to the root of our society. We are obliged to examine our notions of science, our concept of the person, the definition of mass education, the deterioration of informal learning, and so on. This can only occur in a comparative and historical context. Correlatively, we also have the obligation to understand and reveal the exploitative functions of our educational system, as we have exported it to underdeveloped, that is, ex-colonial areas. Some anthropologists may even dare to suggest alternatives to the bureaucratic apparatus of formal schooling in emerging societies, not to speak of our own, if anyone still cares to listen. If the foregoing essays help move anthropology in that direction, they will have accomplished a great deal.

A World Bibliography of Anthropology and Education, with Annotations.[1]

HARRY M. LINDQUIST

CONTENTS

[1] At the present time it has not been possible to include detailed bibliographic coverage of Latin America. In part, this omission reflects the limitations on my own time and resources and, in part, the limitations on the size of this volume. While such limitations are regrettable, it is better, at this time, to print a bibliography covering much of the world than to delay the entire enterprise for the sake of a completeness that can never be achieved, given the continual growth of the field. Some references to the Latin American literatures will be found in the items listed in the initial "General" section which opens the bibliography.

ABBREVIATIONS USED

app.; apps.	appendix; appendices
asst.	assisted
biblio.	bibliography
biblio. foot.	bibliographical footnotes
biblio. ref.	bibliographical references
diagrs.	diagrams
econ.	economic
ed.	editor
esp.	especially
figs.	figures
fold.	foldout
gloss.	glossary

H.M.S.O.	His (Her) Majesty's Stationery Office
illus.	illustrated
inc.	includes
indus.	industrial
intro.	introduction
M.S.U.	Michigan State University
p.; pp.	page; pages
ref.	references
sect.	section
trans.	translated by
univ.	university
USGPO	United States Government Printing Office

FOREWORD

Many correspondents and colleagues have aided me in preparation of this bibliography. One person, in particular, should be singled out: Murray Wax. I owe him a special debt of gratitude for his assistance and support during the eighteen months spent on this project.

A Guide to the Bibliography

HARRY M. LINDQUIST

INTRODUCTION

"Anthropology and Education" has just recently come to be a field of organized effort and inquiry. Until 1970, when the Council on Anthropology and Education formally organized itself and began the publication of a *Newsletter*, there were neither professional associations coordinating activities in the field nor periodicals acting as media for its findings. In consequence of the developing interest in the field, there is now a genuine need for a bibliography that brings together relevant materials from all over the world, but at the same time it has been difficult for the bibliographer to be properly inclusive of all relevant materials and exclusive of all that are nonrelevant. I have consulted a wide variety of sources, particularly journals and books in anthropology, sociology, and related sciences with an interest in the study of education; beyond this, I have engaged in much personal correspondence with anthropologists and educators all over the world.

Since the field is so new, any technique of organizing its materials must be more or less arbitrary, and I have chosen the simplest, of listing by geographic region and national boundary. In addition, there is one "general" section. This system has a major drawback, inasmuch as it conceals from the user the themes and subthemes that recur throughout the literature, and in this essay I have tried to compensate for the deficiency by noting some of these themes.

Before proceeding to that discussion, I should indicate the bases by which I have excluded from this bibliography items that might otherwise have been considered pertinent. For the resources devoted to education are great, and the interest in educational matters has been intense, such that the consequence has been the producing of a steady and ever increasing stream of materials—so vast, as quite to overwhelm the interested scholar. First, I have excluded all materials that are neither of current interest nor related to current questions. Also excluded are the official reports of national or international agencies, except for such reports that represent more than a compilation of official facts (or expectations). I have also excluded the superficial type of comparative literature that compares the pedagogical structures of various countries without subjecting the data to a critical or interpretive analysis. On the positive side, I have tried—to the extent possible with maintaining a manageable bibliography—to include the writings of indigenous scholars, provided that they are able to view their own societies and cultures with critical vision. And, generally, I have stressed the comparative literatures, whether produced by anthropologists, sociologists, or educational researchers of whatever disciplinary affiliation.

Since there is no autonomous field of anthropology and education at the present time, it is difficult to establish with any degree of definiteness what constitutes the base works in the field. I have, therefore, depended to a large degree on selecting the books and articles that are constantly referred to by people writing on topics relevant to anthropology and education.

Both anthropology and comparative education have experienced some fundamental changes in the recent past. In anthropology, field researchers have found themselves increasingly drawn toward urban populations or populations fundamentally influenced by urban areas. One effect of this increasing urbanization is an accompanying condition of a greater emphasis of education. As relatively isolated populations with little or only tangential contacts with urban areas have given way to the present generation of indigenous peoples whose sons and daughters look to the city and education as a means of mobility within an urban climate, anthropologists have started to regard educational institutions as focuses of research. The field of comparative education has, in the last decade, become less and less centered about Europe and North America. More and more articles on the educational problems and related social difficulties of Asian, African, and Latin American countries are finding their way into the comparative education journals. Finally, within education itself, as the base of the educated, and therefore the scope of the educational endeavor have both enormously increased, educational critics have also grown more numerous.

THEMES

A review of the literature relating to anthropology and education brings the reader constantly to recurring themes. We shall look at these themes individually. Neither this list of themes nor the materials cited should be considered to be exhaustive. At the same time, a review of the literature brings a reader time and time again to a consideration of one of several of the following themes: elitism, problems of minority education, the nature of educational planning, the split between urban and rural areas, the imbalance between local and national loyalties, and unemployment or underemployment of the educated.

ELITISM

Discussions of elites usually take one of the following paths: the failure of colonial regimes to establish educational institutions appropriate to developing areas; the failure of the government bureaucracies, which in many developing areas are the principal source of employment for educated persons, to serve the people over whom they exercise power; the attitudes and institutions that perpetuate a vocational preference for entering the relatively unproductive class of white-collar state employees; the relative capacities of various social and economic systems to reform educational systems in order to bring national needs and personal aspirations into greater congruence; and, finally, specific studies of the characteristics of individual national elites.

Studies conducted in the former British and French colonies, particularly in Africa, provide an excellent historical basis for any student of postindependence school systems in those areas (Africa, General: Africa Education Commission; Hailey and Baron; Carnegie Corporation Report; C. W. M. Cox; L. J. Lewis). One general trend, as time passed, was an increasing concern for the problems of mass education with discussions being centered on the general problems rather than on specific solutions. A perusal of studies such as those cited also provides a perspective on two other trends: the gradual development of a highly politicized indigenous elite and a correspondingly increasing degree of awareness of the colonial regimes that the provision of modern education, even to a select minority, raised many more problems than had been imagined.

In postindependence Africa, a major problem continues to be how to find a balance between the rising aspirations encouraged by the increasingly wide base of education and the persistent problems of slow economic development. Criticisms of the present situation often center on the incapacity or disinclination of educated people to obtain training relevant to national needs. Such criticisms frequently begin with a review of the type of education initiated under colonial administrations.

René Dumont, for example, has provided an especially incisive discussion of the failure of the French to establish vocational education facilities. He, in fact, regards the establishment of European-style education as an attempt to perpetuate colonial power through the new, indigenous elite (Africa, General).

The Nigerian elite, emerging from the British-established schools, has been especially well studied (Africa, Nigeria: J. F. Ade Ajayi; J. E. Goldthorpe; Hugh H. and Mabel M. Smythe). Those studies emphasize the divisive role of Western education, regional and tribal differences in motivation toward the acceptance of Western education, and the persisting conflicts confronting Nigerian society where an elite has been largely drawn from only one group in a religiously and tribally pluralistic nation-state. Whereas there are broad similarities between the British and French colonial policies in education, important differences of direction have affected the postcolonial period of development. Brian Weinstein (Africa, General) has pointed out that a practical application of knowledge has been much more emphasized by the British than by the French in the bureaucratic training provided to their former colonies.

An important issue in the analysis of the character of elites is the appropriateness of Western-modeled education in non-Western areas. Lord Ashby, for example, has treated extensively the problem of what he terms the "no-man's land" of the African university graduate. Such a person must somehow resolve the conflicts between the ideal value system that he has received through his education, the social and economic conditions from which he came, and the political and other demands of his native society, which, because of the disproportionate national investment in his higher education, regards him as a national resource. Ashby feels, furthermore, that the universities themselves present a fundamental, institutional problem in that their models, Western universities, have tended to be defenders of the status quo rather than agents of change (Africa, General).

In the same vein, two of the most anthropologically perceptive critics of Western educational models at the secondary-school level are Rémi Clignet and Philip Foster (Africa, Ghana; Ivory Coast) who have provided data and insight on the great personal, regional, and continental problems of any educational structure in a developing area that permits only a very few even to reach the level of high school graduate when even a modestly expanding base of literacy and the increasing presence of mass media result in deep cleavages between their aspirations and the actual chances of their being only partially, much less fully, realized.

Conflicts in the models of what constitutes an appropriate elite are not limited to non-Western, unindustrialized societies. Much of Spanish educational tradition is antiscientific and humanist. As the desire for modernization and industrialization increases at both the top and lower levels of Spanish society, conflicts between the traditional elite and the technocratic personnel required to achieve the new goals rise in incidence and tension (Europe, Spain: Juan Estarellas).

The question of whether there should be an elite based on education is not frequently raised with any degree of serious social action with one outstanding exception, the People's Republic of China. There are powerful elements in the Chinese government and society that favor an elite based on life experiences (the "red" expert) who would hold the ultimate veto power over the behavior and policy directions of the more highly educated class in schools, enterprises, and government (Asia, China: Baum and Teiwes).

Finally, in Western Europe, many of the recent reform efforts in education have centered on the question of how to break the upper and upper middle-class dominance of higher education

Recent studies, particularly in Europe, have concentrated on drawing out specific data that will illustrate the relationships between social class and educational opportunity (Europe, Belgium: Sylvain de Coster and Georges van der Elst; Germany: Hansgert Peisert, Harry Schwarzweller; Sweden: Gosta Carlsson and Bengt Gesser; USSR: Murray Yanowitch and Norton Dodge). Direct relationships are increasingly seen between the social class, status, occupations, and aspirations of European parents and the aspirations and achievement levels of their children. Sociological studies in the Soviet Union indicate that the problem of the relationship between social class origin and achievement in education is not limited to the capitalist West. Educational institutions, popularly regarded as the primary means of social advancement, are often, in sociological analysis, found to be a means for preserving social status and class.

PROBLEMS OF MINORITY EDUCATION

Critics of American education and American society often write and speak as though the United States were the only society confronting basic conflicts between its majorities and minorities. Even a brief perusal of the relevant literature in anthropology and education belies such an attitude. Nowhere are the conflicts involving minorities more vivid and sharp than in the questions of educational model and educational opportunity, since, as economic development becomes more widespread, access to opportunities to gain technical and technological expertise is open only through education. Young people, furthermore, are widely attracted to the egalitarian ideas present in the humanist writers of the West.

The minority problem is so widespread that I can cite only a few examples of the literature. In the bibliography I have made an effort to include substantive rather than moral comment on minority education. As nationalism has grown in the developing areas, there has been an understandable inclination of the newly formed governments to attempt to reserve economic and educational opportunities for their own citizens. At the same time, such policies have often tended to discriminate against nonnational, economically powerful elites. The treatment of the Asian minority in Eastern Africa, which has been rejected both by the indigenous East African regimes and often denied entry to the United Kingdom, provides a case study of the disenfranchisement of the economic and educational elite during postcolonial transition period (Africa, Asian minority: P. M. Rattansi and M. Abdulla). The other side of the coin is the maintenance of an elite through the suppression of the educational and social opportunities of the majority. Kuper has provided an arresting analysis of the Black man caught in the middle between the White elite and the vast majority of his educationally and socially disenfranchised people;

Kuper presents the dilemma of the educated African in South Africa who, in a sense, acts as a buffer between the Whites and the Blacks (Africa, South Africa).

In multilingual societies and nations, conflicts in education often center on which language or languages are dominant in the school system. This problem ranges from the relatively simple, as in Belgium (Europe, Belgium: Vernon Mallinson), and Wales (Europe, U.K.: W. R. Jones; Wales University College) to the vast, complex problems of a subcontinent nation such as India where the *lingua franca* of the intellectual is a foreign language (English) and multitudinous language families and dialects exist among the people as a whole.

Problems of minority education have been most visible in Europe and North America (e.g. see the essays in this volume by Henry, Leacock, Cazden-and-John, Thomas-and-Wahrhaftig). A crucial propaganda point between the capitalist and communist systems has been the relative beneficent treatment of minorities in the respective social systems. A review of the literature shows that the treatment of minorities in both of the social systems has been a "mixed bag." In the Soviet Union, for example, Harry Lipset has demonstrated that the treatment of minorities has not been consistent. In some cases, for example the Moslem populations, the Soviet government has been a great improvement over the Czarist regime. On the other hand, treatment of such minorities as the Jews has not been significantly improved (Europe, USSR: Harry Lipset).

In North America, both Canada and the United States have dealt, with varying degree of success, with the problems of educating their aboriginal minorities. (North America, Canada: A. Richard King; 1967: North America, United States: Murray Wax *et al.*; Rosalie Wax.) Whereas the failure of the urban-based middle-class model of education among American Indians in both Canada and the United States has long been apparent, the factors involved in this failure, insensitivity to peer-group relationships, lack of desire to make educational methods and goals meaningful to the students, and the implicit demand that the educated Indian reject his home community are only now being clearly elucidated (see the essays in this volume by Wax-and-Wax, Thomas-and-Wahrhaftig).

Both Canada and the United States are confronted with an entire array of cultural, social, linguistic, and racial problems in their school systems. Canada, on the one hand, has long tolerated schools that are ethnic in nature and that use, at least in part, the language of the ethnic minority represented in the school (North America, Canada: A. J. C. King, T. Krukowski). The United States, on the other hand, in the twentieth century has used the schools to implement a monolingual, unicultural policy. Despite the different directions and structures of the two national school systems, both societies face regional, racial, and cultural conflicts in their respective school systems.

THE NATURE OF EDUCATIONAL PLANNING

Educational literature contains no lack whatsoever of extensive planning material. The degree of realism in such planning is, however, open to many serious and fundamental questions. Several factors enter into the situation. First, few governments have such total control over their people that they are able to order individual preferences into a mold of national priorities. To find an example of a government of this type, we must turn to totalitarian regimes such as the Peoples' Republic of China. Second, among the intellectuals of the developing countries there is frequent conflict between realistic national priorities on rural development and the urban-oriented ideals of the type of broad humanist education found in European-modeled universities (Africa, General: Wilton S. Dillon; Guy Hunter). Third, given the increasing economic, political, and social interdependence among the developed and developing societies of the world, planners usually speak in terms of sending the most gifted and talented young people abroad to continue their studies and improve their skills so that upon their return they can devote what they have learned to the improvement of their native society. Such planning often ignores the infrequency of return of those students who go abroad—particularly to the United States—to study. A fourth factor is the sheer incapacity of present techniques of planning specifically and realistically to indicate the educational needs of the societies in which planners devise long-range courses of action.

NATIONAL VERSUS LOCAL LOYALTIES

Penelope Roach has offered a brief overview of this problem in Africa (Africa, General). An interesting comparative study of Kenya and Tanzania has been made by David Koff and George Von der Muhll (Africa, East Africa). The other side of the coin of the creation of a modern nation-state is the use of educational systems to preserve ethnic advantages. An extensive debate with regard to Ghana has recently developed in the literature with some, as for example, Philip Foster, feeling that ethnicity and regionalism are declining as criteria for access to schools and others, such as Herd and Johnson, feeling the opposite (Africa, Ghana: Philip J. Foster). The recent problems in Nigeria where one tribal group, the Ibo, had great economic, social, and educational status in a multitribal society, provide a case in point (Africa, Nigeria: John Hanson, Alan Peshkin, Hans N. Weiler). Problems of ethnicity and the interference of ethnic loyalties with broader national loyalties are not limited to the developing world. In Canada, for example, both region and language exercise powerful influences on local loyalties versus national loyalty (North America, Canada: John Cheal, A. J. C. King, Robert Lawson, M. R. Lupul). In the United States, especially with regard to the Black, Mexican-American, and Indian populations, serious criticisms of educational institutions as deculturalizing agents have been made. (Also, in this volume, note how the issue of national loyalty appears in the essays by Safa and Green.)

RURAL-URBAN SPLIT

An aspect of the question of acculturation is the increasing distance between rural parents and urban-oriented youth. This problem is, of course, most acute in those areas in which the majority of the people in the society live outside the cities, in rural areas (as in the case of Haiti, discussed in the essay by Safa in this volume). The general problem is augmented by the fact that school leavers are often unemployed so that their failure to fulfill roles suggested in their educations has added to the problem a general state of idleness and frustration (Africa, General: Rémi Clignet). Early school leavers who are unemployed become, in a sense, marginal men in their own societies (Africa, General: Albert J. McQueen). As the educational base grows and urbanization becomes more extensive, the problems of alienation, marginality,' and uncertain biculturality will persist (Africa, Bibliography: Ruth P. Simms).

UNEMPLOYMENT

Unemployment of those people who are literate but not fully enough educated to qualify for white-collar positions is growing rather than declining in the developing areas. In Ghana, for example, while the base of students represented in Ghanian universities increasingly widens, the gap between expectations, middle-school leavers and their actual economic and social progress is also growing more acute (Africa, Ghana: Margaret Peil). This general social problem in Africa is accompanied by consequent social and political problems (Africa, Unemployment: Archibald Callaway). The problem, once again, is not limited to the developing world. In England, for example, school leavers (who are often called dropouts in the United States) face similar problems of what to do with themselves (Europe, United Kingdom: Michael Carter, Thelma Veness). In the United States, the whole question of what constitutes a "dropout" has been seriously raised by both social and educational commentators (North America, United States: Rosalie Wax).

These topics suggest the scope of problems relevant to anthropology and education that have been alluded to, covered in some detail, and often despairingly cited in the literature. Not all of the citations represent work done by anthropologists. The citations are, however, representative samples of those problems that anthropologists interested in education are now facing and will increasingly confront in their future research.

GENERAL

Adams, Don and Robert M. Bjork
  1969 Education in developing areas. New York: David McKay Company, Inc., xiv + 161 pp., index tables.
        The authors examine the relationship between education and development in the Western world and Japan, Middle Africa, South Asia, Latin America.
Anderson, Robert H.
  1966 Teaching in a world of change. New York: Harcourt, Brace Jovanovich. Foreword by Paul Woodring. xi + 180 pp., index.
        A discussion of the relationships between teaching methods, internal school organization, and social change. Special focus on teaching innovations.
Armytage, W. H. G.
  1965 The rise of the technocrats a social history. London: Routledge and Kegan Paul, Ltd. vii + 448 pp., biblio. in notes, index.
        A wide-ranging discussion of the shift in education and society to respect for technicians and the implications of that shift.
Ashby, Eric and Mary Anderson
  1966 Universities: British, Indian, African: a study in the ecology of higher education. Cambridge: Harvard University Press. xiii + 558 pp., biblio., ref.
        A critical review of the background, past, and future functions of universities in the third world, which are based on British models.
Beeby, C. E.
  1966 The quality of education in developing countries. Cambridge: Harvard University Press. Foreword by Adam Curle. x + 139 pp., index.
        General discussion of educational strategies and stages.
Bereday, George
  1967 Reflections on comparative methodology in education, 1964–1966. Comparative Education 3, no. 3:169–187.
        Excellent bibliography.
  1969 Essays on world education: the crisis of supply and demand. New York: Oxford University Press. xiii + 359 pp.
        Essays are based on the International Conference on the World Crisis in Education, Williamsburg, Va. 1967
Blaug, Mark
  1964 A selected annotated bibliography in the economics of education. London: Institute of Education, University of Londor. viii + 106 pp.

Brameld, Theodore

1957 Cultural foundations of education an interdisciplinary exploration. Foreword by Clyde Kluckhohn. New York: Harper & Row Publishers, Inc. xiii + 330 pp., app., biblio. ref., index.

Theoretical treatment of education in a cultural and social context. Appendix concentrates on Ernst Cassirer.

1965 The use of explosive ideas in education, culture, class, and evolution. Pittsburgh: University of Pittsburgh Press. x + 248 pp., index.

An attempt to relate three basic social scientific concepts (culture, class, and evolution) to educational philosophy.

Brembeck, Cole S.

1966 Social foundations of education, a cross-cultural approach. New York: John Wiley & Sons, Inc. xiv + 540 pp., index.

The author examines social aspects of teaching and learning; the student and his family and group; social class and learning; groups within and influencing the schools; teachers; social problems and education.

————, and John W. Hanson, eds.

1966 Education and the development of nations. New York: Holt, Rinehart & Winston, Inc. xiv + 529 pp., app. (biblio.), index.

A collection of essays on education and development, ethics, economic development, cultural-scientific development, planning, and other related topics. A wide range of theoretical topics and specific studies is included.

Brickman, William, ed.

1956 Comparative education a symposium. New York: Payne Educational Sociology Foundation, Inc. 47 pp.

A reprint of The Journal of Educational Sociology 30, no. 3. A review of the comparative education field.

1960 A historical introduction to comparative education. Comparative Education Review 3:6–13.

1964 John Dewey's impressions of Soviet Russia and the revolutionary world. Mexico-China-Turkey, 1929. New York: Teachers College, Columbia University. 178 pp., biblio.

1964 Works of historical interest in comparative education. Comparative Education Review 7:324–326.

1966 Prehistory of comparative education to the end of the eighteenth century. Comparative Education Review 10, no. 1:30–47.

Burch, William

1967 Cross-cultural dialogues: some trained incapacities of educators and some opportunities. New Zealand Journal of Education Studies 2:113–124.

Burger, Henry

1968 Ethno-pedagogy: a manual in cultural sensitivity, with techniques for improving cross-cultural teaching by fitting ethnic patterns. Albuquerque, N.M.: Southwestern Cooperative Educational Laboratory. xxiii + 318 pp.

The author draws on his experience with American Indians in the

Southwest to provide suggestions for models of learning and teaching in a cross-cultural setting. He especially emphasizes the role of the teacher as a bicultural agent in relating his culture and that of the students.

Bühl, Walter
  1968 *Gesellschaftswandel und Schulsystem in modernen Industriestaat*. International Review of Education 14:277–299.

Butts, R. Freeman
  1967 Civilization as a historical process: meeting ground for comparative and international education. Comparative Education 3, no. 3:155–168.
      Discussion of relationships of study of education to archeology, anthropology, economics, history, political science, and sociology.

Coleman, James Samuel
  1965 Adolescents and schools. New York: Basic Books, Inc. xi + 121 pp., illus.
—————, et al.
  1963 The adolescent society: the social life of the teen-ager and its impact on education. New York: The Free Press. 368 pp., biblio. foot., illus.

Coleman, James Smoot
  1965 Education and political development. Princeton: Princeton University Press. xii + 620 pp.

Comparative Education Program
  1964 Comparative education: key-word in context. Ann Arbor: University of Michigan Press. Index, biblio.

Coombs, Philip
  1968 The world educational crisis: a systems analysis. New York: Oxford University Press. x + 241 pp., biblio. ref., illus.
      Educational responses to changing demands are discussed.

Council on Anthropology and Education
  1970 Newsletter. John Singleton, Ed. Pittsburgh: IDEP, University of Pittsburgh.

Cramer, John and George Browne
  1956 Contemporary education: a comparative study of national systems. New York: Harcourt Brace Jovanovich. xvi + 637 pp., biblio., diagrs., maps.
      U.S., Australia, China (Peking), Canada, England, Wales, France, USSR, West Germany, Japan, and India are discussed. A 2d. edition was issued in 1965.

Curle, Adam
  1963 Educational strategy for developing societies; a study of educational and social factors in relation to economic growth. London: Tavistock Publications, Ltd. xi + 180 pp., biblio., index.
      Discusses education as a tool to overcome "traditional inertia" and elites that impede development. Limitations of education as a tool are described. Agricultural and vocational education stressed.

De Landsheere, Gilbert
  1966 *Anthropologie culturelle et éducation comparée*. International Review of Education 12:61–72.

Diamond, Stanley, et al.
1966 Culture of schools. Report to the U.S. Office of Education, 4 vols. Includes international bibliography of books and periodicals of 5,000 + entries (1,000 + annotations). Bibliography available on microfilm from Library of Congress (Original on McBee KeySort cards), also available via ERIC system of U.S. Office of Education.

Dreeben, Robert
1967 The contribution of schooling to the learning of norms. Harvard Educational Review 37, no. 2:211–237.
The author related learning of norms of independence, achievement, universalism, and specificity to schooling.

Eisenstadt, Shmuel N.
1956 From generation to generation; age groups and social structure. New York: The Free Press. 357 pp., biblio. in notes, index.
Pp. 163–185 are especially useful.

Emmerson, Donald K., ed.
1968 Students and politics in developing nations. New York: Frederick A. Praeger, Inc. viii + 444 pp., biblio. in notes, index, tables.
Articles on Algeria, Congo, Ghana, South Africa, China, Indonesia, South Vietnam, Brazil, Chile, Cuba, and Venezuela are included.

Fishman, Joshua, Charles Ferguson, and Jyotirinda Das Gupta, eds.
1968 Language problems of developing nations. New York: John Wiley & Sons, Inc. xv + 521 pp.

Fraser, Stewart
1964 Jullien's plan for comparative education, 1816–1817. New York: Bureau of Publications, Teachers College, Columbia University.
———, ed.
1965 Government policy and international education: a symposium held at the International Center, George Peabody College for Teachers, Nashville, Tennessee, October 22–24, 1964. New York: John Wiley & Sons, Inc. xix + 373 pp., biblio.
A broad historical, political, and sociological review of the development of international education programs and their present status in a number of countries and political systems.
———, and William Brickman
1968 A history of international and comparative education: nineteenth-century documents. Glenview, Ill.: Scott, Foresman & Co. 495 pp., biblio.
Nineteenth-century documents and commentaries relating to U.S. and European education written primarily by Americans on European education and Europeans on American education.

Gusfield, Joseph
1966 Educational institutions in the process of economic and national development. Journal of Asian and African Studies 1:129–146.

Gottlieb, David, Jon Reeves, and Warren D. Tenhouten
1966 The emergence of youth societies: a cross-cultural approach. New York: The Free Press. xii + 416 pp.
Discussion of a model for adolescent behavior. Excellent and extensive bibliography by region and country.

Gruber, Frederick C., ed.
   1961 Anthropology and education. Philadelphia: University of Pennsylvania
        Press. 123 pp., biblio.
             The 1960 Martin G. Brumbaugh lectures in Education at the Uni-
        versity of Pennsylvania. Lectures by Anthony F. C. Wallace (Schools
        in revolutionary and conservative societies), Dell H. Hymes (Func-
        tions of speech: an evolutionary approach), Ward H. Goodenough
        (Education and identity), and Dorothy Lee (Autonomous motiva-
        tion) are reprinted.
Halsey, A. H., Jean Floud, and C. Arnold Anderson
   1961 Education, economy, and society: a reader in the sociology of educa-
        tion. New York: The Free Press. ix + 625 pp., biblio. in notes, index,
        tables.
             Selections on economic change, mobility, selection for education,
        social factor and education achievement, changes in schools' and uni-
        versities' functions, and roles of teacher.
Harbison, Frederick and Charles Myers, eds.
   1965 Manpower and education: country studies in economic development.
        xiii + 343 pp., tables.
             Articles on Argentina, Peru, Chile, Puerto Rico, Iran, Indonesia,
        China, Senegal, Guinea, Ivory Coast, Nyasaland, Uganda, East Africa,
        and Southeast Asia.
Havighurst, Robert J.
   1966 Education in metropolitan areas. Boston: Allyn & Bacon, Inc. xi +
        260 pp., app., biblio., index, tables.
             An examination of the development of metropolitan centers, educa-
        tional responses, and present conflicts.
———, ed.
   1968 Comparative perspectives on education. Boston: Little, Brown & Com-
        pany. xvi + 285 pp., index.
             Selections on the Hopi Indians, France, USSR, Japan, Brazil, China,
        Ghana, Tudor England, South Africa, New Zealand, the Sudan, and
        the Netherlands.
Heintz, Peter
   1967 Education as an instrument of social integration in underdeveloped
        societies. International Social Science Journal 19:378–386.
Herriott, Robert and Benjamin Hodgkins
   1969 Social context and the school: an open-system analysis of social and
        educational change. Rural Sociology 34, no. 2:149–166.
             An attempt to relate educational effectiveness with region, social
        class, and metropolitan environment. The article states that, in the
        long run, only changes in social organization will be effective in chang-
        ing schools serving poor populations. Enriched education programs
        have only short-run effects, and schools can act as an agent of change
        only when the social organization permits.
Hodkinson, Harold
   1962 Education in social and cultural perspectives. Englewood Cliffs: Pren-
        tice-Hall, Inc. ix + 243 pp., index.

Discussion of education and stratification, mobility, cultural lag, social change, motivation, learning theories, and social context.

Holmes, Brian, ed.

1967 Educational policy and the mission schools case studies from the British Empire. Preface by J. A. Lauwerys. New York: Humanities Press. xv + 352 pp., index.

Articles on the Bahamas, Ceylon, Kerala (Syrian Christians), Kashmir, Egypt, Cyprus, and Eastern Nigeria.

Holmes, Brian, and S. B. Robinson

1963 Relevant data on comparative education. Hamburg: UNESCO, Institute for Education. 143 pp.

A report of the Hamburg Institute for Education Conference (March 11–16, 1963). An extensive bibliography.

Holmes, Brian

1965a Problems in education: a comparative approach. New York: Humanities Press. x + 326 pp., biblio., biblio. foot.

England, Japan, U.S., and USSR are discussed.

1965b Rational constructs in comparative education. International Review of Education 11:466–478.

Husén, Torsten

1967 International study of achievement in mathematics. I. Stockholm: Almquist & Wiksell/Gebers Förlag AB. 304 pp., apps., index, tables.

A report of the International Project for the Evaluation of Educational Achievement, including Australia, Belgium, England, West Germany, Finland, France, Israel, Japan, Netherlands, Scotland, Sweden, U.S. Forthright description of great difficulties in controlling variables in comparative studies of education.

Kazamias, Andreas and Bryon G. Massialas

1965 Tradition and change in education: a comparative study. Foreword by Hobert W. Burns. 182 pp., index.

A discussion of comparative education, premodern models, contemporary European and American models, models in developing areas, relationships between the polity and education, and the democratization of education.

King, Edmund J.

1968 Comparative studies and educational decision. London: Methuen & Co., Ltd. vii + 182 pp. biblio., fig., index.

An examination of the nature of comparative education and its usefulness.

International Review of Education

1968 Special issue of this journal devoted to teacher training reform. xiv, no. 4.

Articles on the U.S. (Morris Cogan), England (William Taylor), Belgium (Jean Burion), and Sweden and the general teacher training problems (Sixten Marklund). Communications on Israel, West Germany, France, and Japan. In addition, there are eleven book reviews on this general subject.

Lasswell, Harold and Daniel Lerner, eds.

1965 World revolutionary elites: studies in coercive ideological movements.

Cambridge: The M.I.T. Press. xi + 478 pp., index, tables.

Articles on the ruling elites of the USSR, Fascist Italy, Nazi Germany, Nationalist China, and Communist China describe the various factors, including education, in the backgrounds of the elites.

Lewis, W. Arthur
1962 Education and economic development. Social and Economic Studies, X, no. 2:94–101. Jamaica: Institute of Social and Economic Research, University College of the West Indies.

A review of the problems of the high cost of education in poor countries, the dissatisfaction of primary school leavers, lack of adult education, and undervaluation of technical education.

Lindquist, Harry M., ed.
1970 Education: readings in the processes of cultural transmission. Boston: Houghton Mifflin Company Inc. 249 pp., biblio.

Concentration on the United States, Africa, Asia, and Europe.

Noah, Harold and Max Eckstein
1969 Toward a science of comparative education. New York: Crowell Collier and Macmillan, Inc. xv + 222 pp., app., biblio., index, tables.

A discussion of the theoretical and methodological aspects of comparative education.

Parsons, Talcott
1959 The school class as a social system. Harvard Education Review XXIX, no. 4:297–318.

Peaslee, Alexander
1967 Primary school enrollments and economic growth. Comparative Education Review XI, no. 1:57–67.

Discussion of relationships between having more than 10 percent of population in primary school in 1920 and the degree of economic development in 1958. Direct relationship described.

Roberts, K.
1968 The organization of education and the ambitions of school-leavers: a comparative review. Comparative Education 4, no. 2:87–96.

Discussion of the merits and deficiencies of selective and nonselective school systems. The comparison is primarily between the U.S. and U.K. Final occupational satisfaction is about the same in both societies.

Rosenthal, Robert and Lenore Jacobson
1968 Pygmalion in the classroom: teacher expectation and pupils' intellectual development. New York: Holt, Rinehart and Winston, Inc. xi + 240 pp., app., index, ref., tables.

A careful review of the data available to show a direct relationship between teacher expectation and student achievement.

Shields, James J., Jr.
1967 Education in community developments, its function in technical assistance. New York: Frederick A. Praeger, Inc. vii + 127 pp., biblio.

An analysis of data from AID projects.

Spolton, Lewis
1967 The upper secondary school: a comparative survey. New York: Pergamon Press. viii + 291 pp.

Springer, George P.
  1968 Universities in flux. Comparative Education Review, XII, no. 1:28–38.
       A discussion of various "models" of university education: U.S., non-communist Europe, Latin America. Discusses thirteen aspects of European education at the university level. Author feels Eastern European universities have more of a social-class balance than Western European universities. Five features of American universities discussed. Finally, university reforms in Europe, especially West Germany, are discussed.
Stenhouse, Lawrence
  1967 Culture and education. London: Thomas Nelson. viii + 156 pp., biblio.
       An examination of secondary education as a transmitter of culture.
Thut, I. N. and Don Adams
  1964 Educational patterns in contemporary societies. New York: McGraw-Hill, Inc. xii + 494 pp., biblio in ref., fig., index, tables.
       The authors examine educational patterns of Europe in the twentieth century: Spain, Germany, France, England, USSR, China, Japan, Latin America, India, and Middle Africa.
Warren, Richard L.
  1968 Some determinants of the teacher's role in influencing educational aspirations: a cross-cultural perspective. Sociology of Education 41: 291–304.
Weinberg, Ian
  1968 Some methodological and field problems of social research in elite secondary schools. Sociology of Education, 41, no. 2:141–155.
       Article concentrates on general problems of examining elites, special position of headmasters in elite schools, and study of students boarded in schools.
Worsley, Peter
  1964 The third world. Chicago: The University of Chicago Press. x + 317 pp., biblio., index, notes, tables.
       A general discussion of the needs and status of the non-Communist unindustrialized nations and society. Discussion of elitism is especially relevant.

AFRICA

Anonymous
  1966 Research services in East Africa. Compiled for the East African Academy. Nairobi: East African Publishing House.
Adino, Assoi
  1963 *Histoire des peuples noirs.* Abidjan: *Centre d'Edition et de Diffusion Africaines.* 192 pp., illus., maps. Revised, corrected, augmented by André Clérci.
       A textbook on African history written for and by Africans.

Africa Education Commission
   1922 Education in Africa; a study of west, south, and equatorial Africa by
        the African education commission, under the auspices of the Phelps-
        Stokes fund and foreign mission societies of North America and
        Europe. Report prepared by Thomas Jesse Jones, chairman of the
        commission. xxviii + 323 pp., illus. (maps) plates.
            A basic document for understanding the background of British plan-
        ning for education in Africa during the early twentieth-century colonial
        period.
   1924 Education in East Africa; a study of east, central, and south Africa by
        the second African education commission under the auspices of the
        Phelps-Stokes fund, in cooperation with the international education
        board; report prepared by Thomas Jesse Jones, chairman of the com-
        mission. New York: Phelps-Stokes fund. xxviii + 416 pp., biblio.,
        illus., map.
            Basic document in British colonial educational planning.
Africa Today
   1967 Special issue: Education in African development. 14, no. 2.
            Ethiopia, Southern Rhodesia, Sudan, South Africa, Malawi, West
        Cameroon, Tunisia, Nigeria, and general problems are briefly reviewed.
African Bibliographic Center, Inc.
        A current bibliography on African affairs. Bimonthly. P.O. Box 13096,
        Washington, D.C., 20009.
Ashby, Eric
   1964 African universities and Western tradition. The Godkin lectures at
        Harvard University. Cambridge: Harvard University Press. vi + 113
        pp., index, ref.
            Author has perceptive discussion of coming to terms with European
        traditions in Africa. He discusses European models, West African
        universities, the university and African nationalism, and the future.
        Discusses the "no man's land" of the African university graduate.
        "References" section offers excellent guide to early British reports on
        official plans for African education.
   ———— and Mary Anderson
   1966 Universities: British, Indian, African. a study in the ecology of higher
        education. Cambridge: Harvard University Press. xiii + 558 pp.,
        biblio., ref.
            A basic work in this area.
            A critical review of the background, past, and future functions of
        universities in the third world, which are based on British models.
Azevedo, Avila de
   1958 *Política de Ensino em África.* Preface by Silva Rego. *Lisbon: Minis-
        tério do Ultramar, Junta de Investigações do Ultramar, Centro de
        Estudos Políticos e Sociais. Estudos de Ciências Políticas e Sociais 13.*
        198 pp., apps., biblio., map, tables.
            A comparative review of colonial school systems in Africa, from the
        Portuguese point of view.
Beaver, R. Pierce
   1966 Christianity and African education; the papers of a conference at the

University of Chicago. Grand Rapids, Mich.: Eerdmans. 223 pp. +
biblio. foot.

Beeby, C. E.
1966 The quality of education in developing countries. Cambridge: Harvard
University Press. 139 pp., biblio. foot.
Emphasis on primary school education.

Brembeck, Cole Speicher and John P. Keith
1962(?) Education in emerging Africa; a select and annotated bibliography.
(Michigan State University education in Africa series 1). 153 pp.

Brokensha, David
1966 Applied anthropology in English-speaking Africa. Lexington, Kentucky: The Society for Applied Anthropology. 31 pp., biblio.
Description of studies, personnel, and resources in applied anthropology by region. pp. 11–12 and 21 (biblio.) are especially relevant.

Burns, Donald G.
1965 African education: an introductory survey of education in Commonwealth countries. London: Oxford University Press. vi + 215 pp.,
index, tables.
Discusses social-cultural bases of education in African societies;
primary school education; secondary education; technical, literacy, and
vocational educational efforts; teacher training; and present and future
needs.

Busia, Kofi Abrefa
1964 Purposeful education for Africa. The Hague: Mouton. 107 pp., biblio.
foot.

Carnegie Corporation
1936 Village education in Africa. Report of the interterritorial 'Jeanes' Conference, Salisbury, Southern Rhodesia, May 27–June 6, 1935. Lovedale, Cape: Lovedale Press.
A basic document in the development of education in colonial
Africa.

Catholic International Education Office
1966 Catholic education in the service of Africa, Pan-African Catholic education conference, August 16–23, 1965. Brussels: CIEO, Regional
Secretariat for Africa and Madagascar. 532 pp., biblios.

Clignet, Rémi
1964 *Education et aspirations professionelles. Tiers Monde* V, no. 17:61–82.
Great preference for employment in cities.

Collison, Robert L., comp.
1967 The SCOLMA directory of libraries and special collections on Africa.
2d ed. Hamden, Conn.: Archon Books. (4) 92 pp.
A guide to British-African collections.

Commission for Technical Cooperation in Africa South of the Sahara
1954 Education; inter-African and regional conferences: Tananarive (1954);
Accra (1950); Nairobi (1951). Tananarive. 40 pp., fold., tables.
Brief description of educational needs.

Couch, Margaret
1962 Education in Africa: a select comp. bibliography. London: Institute

of Education, University of London. (Education libraries bulletin, supplement no. 5, 9).

Cox, C. W. M.
   1943 Mass education in African society. London: H.M.S.O. 63 pp., diagr., illus. (Great Britain Colonial Office, Colonial no. 186).

Curle, Adam
   1963 Educational strategy for developing societies; a study of educational and social factors in relation to economic growth. London: Tavistock Publications. xi + 180 pp., biblio., tables.

Dakin, Julian, Brian Tiffen, and H. G. Widdowson
   1964 Some problems of inter-communication. The Journal of Modern African Studies 2, no. 3:395–403.

Dillon, Wilton S.
   1963 Universities and nation-building in Africa. The Journal of Modern African Studies 1, no. 1:75–89.
       The author, at that time Director of Research for the Phelps-Stokes Fund, makes general social scientific suggestions for approaches to doing fieldwork research on universities in the fabric of African nation-building. He emphasizes the potential value of community participation in planning and developing universities with African social realities in mind and the fact that such participation can be studied by social scientists interested in testing the truism that participation in planning change reduces resistance to that change.

Dione, Djibril
   1955 Conférences pédagogiques 1954–1955. Education Africaine, nouvelle série, no. 30.
       A discussion of conferences on education in a critical transition period.

Dinstel, Marion, comp.
   1966 List of French doctoral dissertations on Africa, 1884–1961. Boston University Libraries. Indexes by Mary Dorrah Herrick. Boston: G. K. Hall & Company. 336 pp.

Duignan, Peter, comp.
   1967 Handbook of American resources for African studies. Stanford, Cal.: Hoover Institution on War, Revolution and Peace. xvii + 218 pp.

Dumont, René
   1966 False start in Africa. Trans. by Phyllis Nauts Ott. Intro. by Thomas Balogh. Additional chapter by John Hatch. New York: Frederick A. Praeger, Inc. 320 pp., apps., biblio.
       Especially relevant are pp. 88–97, 195–210. Criticism of elitist education, which the author sees as, in part, a colonialist attempt to maintain power in Africa. Recommends specific, vocational, nonelitist training. General views are especially relevant to former French areas in Africa.

   1962 L'Afrique noire est mal partie. Paris, Edition du Seuil.

Fanon, Frantz
   1961 Les damnés de la terre. Paris: Francois Maspéro Cahiers libres nos. 27–28. English ed. Constance Farrington, trans. The wretched of the earth, 1963.
       A controversial description of the effects of colonialism.

Fox, Frederic
  1962 14 Africans vs. one American. New York: Crowell Collier & Macmillan, Inc. xix + 171 pp.
    Comments from students attending the Africa Writing School at Kitwe, Northern Rhodesia. The students are from Tanganyika, Basutoland, Ghana, Nigeria, Northern Rhodesia, Nyasaland, Liberia, Kenya. Interesting for views of urban, middle-class, fairly well-educated Africans. Class was designed to train writers, editors, and journalists.
Godfrey, E. M.
  1966 The economics of an African university. The Journal of Modern African Studies 4, no. 4:435–455.
Greenough, Richard
  1966 African prospect: progress in education. Paris: UNESCO. 111 pp.
Hailey, William and M. H. Baron
  1945 [1938] An African survey: a study of problems arising in Africa south of the Sahara. London: Oxford University Press. 2d ed. xxviii + 1837 pp., maps.
    A classic British study during the colonial period.
Hama, Boubou
  1968 *Essai d'analyse de l'éducation africaine*. Paris: *Présence Africaine*. 395 pp., plates.
Hanson, John W. and Geoffrey W. Gibson
  1968 African education and development since 1960: a select and annotated bibliography. East Lansing: Michigan State University, Institute for International Studies in Education and African Studies Center. 327 pp.
Harbison, Frederick and Charles A. Meyers
  1964 Education, manpower, and economic growth; strategies of human resource development. New York: McGraw-Hill, Inc. xiii + 229 pp. diagrs., tables.
    A joint project of the Indus. Relations Sect., Princeton University, and the Indus. Relations Sect., M.I.T., as part of the Interuniv. Study of Labor Problems in Economic Development.
Harvard University Library
  1965 Widener Library shelflist number 2: Africa. Cambridge: Harvard University Press. 3 vols. 302 pp., 204 pp., 196 pp.
Henderson, John P. and Margaret Y. Henderson
  1967 The African image of higher education in America. International Educational and Cultural Exchange: 45–56.
Hevi, Emmanuel J.
  1963 An African student in China. New York: Frederick A. Praeger, Inc., 220 pp., apps.
    A highly critical but interesting account of student life in China and Chinese attitudes toward Africa.
Hodgkin, Thomas
  1967 African universities and the state: another view. Comparative Education, 13 no. 2:107–114.
    African universities have European models that defend the status quo.

Conflict between autonomous choice of profession and national needs is inevitable.

Hoover Institute
1967 U.S. and Canadian publications on Africa in 1965. Bibliographical series XXXIV. Stanford: Stanford University Press.

Hunter, Guy
1967a Education in the new Africa. African Affairs 66, no. 263:127–139.
Author stresses the following points:
More than 90% Africans "self-employed at low productivity."
Agricultural reform is basic.
Primary school leavers have very few options; very few can continue education.
Primary emphasis must be on agriculture.
Some kind of postprimary training is required to prevent huge waste of investment in primary education.
Rural evening institutes are essential.
Africa retains an advantage over India and Latin America: much less landlordism, little usurer power in rural areas.
1967b The best of both worlds? A challenge on development policies in Africa. Foreword by Philip Mason and William Clark. London: Oxford University Press. Published for the Institute of Race Relations, London. vii + 132 pp.
Chapter V (Education, pp. 96–117) is relevant. Author argues for high standards in the universities, secondary education directed toward practical matters, economic allocation toward rural employment rather than primary school expansion, and development of parttime adult education.

I.E.D.E.S.
1964 *Problèmes de planification de l'éducation. (Institut d'étude du developpement économique et social.)* Paris: *Presses Universitaires de France.* 167 pp., diagrs., tables.
Concentrates on Black African education.

Jahn, Janheinz
1965 Bibliography of neo-African literature from Africa, America, and the Caribbean. New York: Frederick A. Praeger, Inc. 359 pp., map.

Jahoda, Gustav
1968 Some research problems in African education. The Journal of Social Issues XXIV, no. 2:161–178.
Presentation of research problems from a social psychological viewpoint: early development rate in African children, disease and nutritional factors in development of children's capacities in school, social-economic factors in school performance, and factors in great dropout rates.

Kellaway, George P.
1967 Education for living. Cambridge: Cambridge University Press. 151 pp., app., index.
A general discussion of education of children with brief reference to West Africa where the author has taught.

Kitchen, Helen, ed.
1962 The educated African: a country-by-country survey of educational de-
velopment in Africa. New York: Frederick A. Praeger, Inc. Survey includes North: Algeria, Morocco, Tunisia, Libya, Sudan; East: Somali
Republic, French Somaliland, Ethiopia, Kenya, Tanganyika, Uganda,
Zanzibar; Central: The Congo Republic (Léopoldville), Ruanda-
Urundi, Rhodesia Federation, and Nyasaland; South: Malagasy Re-
public, South Africa, Basutoland, Bechuanaland, Swaziland, South-
West Africa; Spanish Africa; West: Bamgia, Ghana, Liberia, Nigeria,
Sierra Leone; Equatorial: Central African Republic, Chad, Republic
of the Congo (Brazzaville), Gabon; West (French-speaking): Senegal,
The Ivory Coast, Dahomey, Niger, Upper Volta, Mali, Mauritania,
Togo, Cameroon, Guinea.
Lewis, L. J.
1962a Phelps-Stokes reports on education in Africa. Abridged, with an Introduction by L. J. Lewis. London: Oxford University Press. 213 pp.
Selections from two classic studies of African education: Education in Africa (1922) and Education in East Africa (1924). Includes
selections on Africa and education, adaptations of education, organization and supervision, mass education and native leadership education, cooperation for African education, and female education. Of
special interest is the persistence of problems isolated by the Commission.
1962b Education and political independence in Africa and other essays.
Edinburgh: Thomas Nelson. 128 pp., tables.
Lindfors, Bernth
1968 Additions and corrections to Janheinz Jahn's bibliography of neo-
African literature (1965). African Studies Bulletin 11, no. 2:129–148.
Lystad, Robert A., ed.
1965 The African world: a survey of social research. New York: Frederick
A. Praeger, Inc. 575 pp., biblio.
Mannoni, Dominique O.
1965 Prospero and Caliban: the psychology of colonialization. Trans. by
Pamela Powesland; Foreword by Philip Mason. London: Methuen &
Co., Ltd., 218 pp., biblio., index.
A translation of *Psychologie de la colonisation*. (Paris, 1950: *Edi-
tions du Seuil.*) A general work with a focus on Madagascar (Malagasy).
Important for understanding some of the psychological problems in
contemporary education in the third world where nonindigenous,
European models remain powerful.
Matthews, Daniel, ed.
1967 African affairs for the general reader: a selected and introductory
bibliographical guide, 1960–1967. Compiled by the African Bibliographic Center for the Council of the African-American Institute
(866 U.N. Plaza, New York, New York 10017). 210 pp.
McQueen, Albert J.
1968 Education and marginality of African youth. The Journal of Social
Issues XXIV, no. 2:179–197

An extensive examination of the growing school-leaver problem. Theoretical approaches to roles that school leavers will play are described.

Moumouni, Abdou
   1968 Education in Africa. Trans. by Phyllis Nauts Ott. Preface by L. J. Lewis. London: Andre Deutsch, Ltd. 320 pp., app., biblio., index.
Murray, A. Victor
   1929 The school in the bush: a critical study of the theory and practice of native education in Africa. London: Longmans, Green and Co. xx + 413 pp. illus. (incl. plans), plates, fold. map.
       [1967 ed. by Barnes & Noble, Inc.]
       Reprint of a pioneer study.
Ponomarev, Dmitrii Konstantinovich
   1963 *Prosveshchenie v kolonial'noy Tropicheskoy Afrike, 1945–1960.* Moscow. 214 pp., biblio.
       A critical study of education in tropical, colonial Africa during the late colonial period.
Rado, E. R.
   1966 Manpower, education, and economic growth. The Journal of Modern African Studies 4, no. 1:83–93.
       Basing his discussion on two recent books by F. Harbison on manpower development and education with particular reference to developing areas, the author criticizes the approach on two grounds: manpower planning's concentration on skilled rather than semiskilled personnel, the former undersupplied and the latter oversupplied; and, failure to take into account the amount of educational costs.
Rattansi, P. M. and M. Abdulla
   1965 An educational survey *In* Portrait of a minority, Dharam P. Ghai (ed.). Nairobi: Oxford University Press:113–128.
       A description of education for Asians in Tanganyika, Kenya, and Uganda through the early 1960s. Asian Indians are the principal focus. Problems of integration and Asian achievement in an African, nationalistic context are underscored.
Rimmington, Gerald T.
   1965 The development of universities in Africa. Comparative Education 1, no. 2:105–112.
Rivkin, Arnold
   1963 Cambridge conference on some aspects of development. Queen's College, Cambridge, September 22–October 5, 1963. The Journal of Modern African Studies 1, no. 4:542–544.
       Four problems are considered primary: the cost of education; the political necessity of universal primary education; unemployed, urban primary school-leavers; and the lack of secondary, vocational, and collegiate institutions.
Roach, Penelope
   1967 Political socialization in the new nations of Africa. Intro. by David G. Scanlon and L. Gray Cowan. New York: Center for Education in Africa, Teachers College Press, Columbia University. ix + 31 pp., biblio

A review of the general problems with special reference to theory in studying African education and political socialization.

Rosen, Seymour M.

1963 Soviet training programs for Africa. Washington, D.C.: U.S. Department of Health, Education and Welfare, Office of Education. 13 pp., table.

Sasnett, Martena and Inez Sepmeyer

1966 Educational systems of Africa; interpretations for use in the evaluation of academic credentials. Berkeley and Los Angeles: University of California Press. xliv + 1550 pp., biblio., maps.

Includes primary, secondary, vocational, technical, teacher training, and higher education systems of forty-four countries.

Scanlon, David G., ed.

1967 Church, state, and education in Africa. New York: Teachers College Press. 313 pp.

Stabler, Ernest

1968 Pressures and constraints in planning African education. Comparative Education Review XII, no. 3:350–356. Reviews nine UNESCO studies on Uganda, Nigeria, Tanzania, Ivory Coast, and Senegal. General conclusions: universal primary education, a colonial rebellion goal, has had to be deferred in view of costs; higher education has expatriate and therefore expensive staffs; primary education is changing to meet African needs but secondary schools, severely pressed by numbers, have changed little and lack indigenous teachers; the greatest problem lies in what to do with primary school leavers, the great majority of whom cannot go on to secondary schools or obtain jobs. Primary school education must therefore concentrate on skills to develop the underskilled agriculture of Africa.

Standing Conference on Library Materials on Africa

1964 Theses on Africa, accepted by universities in the United Kingdom and Ireland. Cambridge: W. Heffer. x + 74 pp.

Sutton, Francis X.

1961 Education in changing Africa. *In* Cowan et al. (1965). Raises the question of whether on-the-job training may, in many cases, be more effective than practical education.

UNESCO

1963 Conference on the development of higher education in Africa, Tananarive, 1962. The development of higher education in Africa, report of the Conference . . . September 3–12, 1962. Paris: UNESCO. 339 pp., diagrs., tables.

Important for understanding formal plans and official views of deficiencies in African education.

Weinstein, Brian

1966 Training administrators in Africa: some comparisons between ENA's and IPA's. Journal of Modern African Studies 4, no. 2:244–250. Comparative analysis of *Ecoles nationales d'administration* and Institutes of Public Administration. The *Ecoles* are staffed by the French, exclusively oriented toward French models, theoretical in orientation, and generally train civil servants with a common tradition over all

former French Africa. The Institutes (British) are more locally oriented, more internationally staffed, and have a more technical and
vocational curriculum. Both emphasize memorization.

Worsley, Peter
1964 The third world: Chicago: University of Chicago Press. x + 317 pp.,
biblio.

ANGOLA

Samuels, Michael
1967 The new look in Angolan education. Africa Report, 12, no. 8:63–66.
A brief look at recent changes in the education policies of the Portu-
guese colony.

CAMEROON

Vernon-Jackson, Hugh O. H.
1967 Language, schools and government in Cameroon. New York: Teachers
College Press, Columbia University. 31 pp.

CONGO AREA

Ching, James C.
1968 Public education trends in the Democratic Republic of the Congo:
1960–1967. Comparative Education Review XII, no. 3:323–337.
Formidable problems in facilities, staffing, and administration are
described.

Fukiau, André
n.d. *Twaduswa ye Twadisa* (to be taught and to teach). Republic of the
Congo (Brazzaville): Mondouli, B.P. 11, Académie Congolaise. 17
pp. (mimeo.)
Traditional concepts of education examined.

George, Betty Grace
1966 Educational developments in the Congo (Léopoldville). Washington,
D.C.: U.S. Department of Health, Education, and Welfare, Office of
Education. x + 196 pp., illus., map.

Georis, Pol and Baudouin Agbiano
1965 *Evolution de l'enseignement en République Démocratique du Congo
depuis l'Indépendence.* Brussels: CEMUBAC. 166 pp.
The authors place education in the Congo in the context of the
Belgian heritage, present political division of the country, and future
prospects.

Golan, Tamar
1968 Educating the bureaucracy in a new polity: a case study of *l'Ecole
Nationale de Droit et d'Administration,* Kinasha, Congo. Introduction
by James T. Harris, Jr. New York: Teachers College Press, Teachers
College, Columbia University. Center for Education in Africa, Institute of International Studies. xv + 78 pp., app., biblio.
A discussion of attempts to relate training of bureaucrats to serving

in areas of need and thus breaking the elitist cycle. A critical review of the present situation and requisite changes.

Heerma Van Voss, H. O.
1966 Secondary education in the Democratic Republic of Congo. Teacher Education 7:99–112.

CUBA AND AFRICA

Clairmonte, Frederick F.
1964 Cuba and Africa. The Journal of Modern African Studies 2, no. 3: 419–430.
  The article, in part, discusses Cuban attempts to reform education and shift emphasis to technological education.

DAHOMEY

Tardits, Claude
  Réflexions sur le problème de la scolarisation des filles au Dahomey. *Cahiers d'études africaines* III (2me cahier, no. 10):266–281.

EAST AFRICA

Beck, Ann
1966 Colonial policy and education in British East Africa. Journal of British Studies 5:115–138.
Carter, J. Roger
1966 The legal framework of educational planning and administration in East Africa. Paris: UNESCO, International Institute for Educational Planning. 33 pp.
Castle, Edgar B.
1966 Growing up in East Africa. Nairobi: Oxford University Press. xii + 272 pp., biblio., index.
  The author concentrates on education.
Hunter, Guy
1963 Education for a developing region: a study in East Africa. London: George Allen and Unwin Ltd. xvi + 119 pp., apps., index.
  A publication under the auspices of P.E.P. (Political and Economic Planning) and The Institute of Race Relations. A study of the historical background and primary policy issues. Focus is on Kenya, Tanganyika, and Uganda.
Koff, David and George Von Der Muhll
1967 Political socialization in Kenya and Tanzania—a comparative analysis. The Journal of Modern African Studies 5, no. 1:13–51.
  Authors point to great divergences in responses of primary and secondary students, with cross-national similarities at the same levels.
Molnos, Angek
1965 *Die sozialwissenschaftliche Erforschung Ostafrikas* 1954–1963 (Kenya, Tanganyika, Sansibar, Uganda.) Berlin: Springer-Verlag. xv + 304 pp., app., map.

Niane, Djibril Tamsir
  1960 *Histoire de l'Afrique occidentale.* Guinea: Ministry of National Educa-
       tion.
Raum, O. F.
  1967 Chaga childhood. a description of indigenous education in an East
       African tribe. Oxford: Oxford University Press. 422 pp.
Shields, J. J.
  1962 A selected bibliography on education in East Africa 1941–1961.
       Kampala, Uganda: Makerere University College. 39 pp.
West Virginia University Library
  1967 Periodicals in East African libraries. a union list. Morgantown: West
       Virginia University.

EGYPT (U.A.R.)

Samaan, Sadek H.
  1955 Value reconstruction and Egyptian education: a projection of a cul-
       tural and philosophical foundation with reference to secondary schools.
       New York: Bureau of Publications. Teachers College, Columbia Uni-
       versity. xi + 157 pp., biblio.
            Especially useful for a critical look at secondary schools. Bibliog-
       raphies in English and Arabic are thorough.

FRENCH AFRICA

Bolibaugh, Jerry B. and Paul R. Hanna
  1964 Education as an instrument of national policy in selected newly de-
       veloping nations; phase 2: French educational strategies for sub-
       Saharan Africa: their intent, derivation, and development. Stanford:
       Comparative Education Center, Stanford University.

GHANA

Anonymous
  1967 A bibliography of Ghana: 1958–1964. Africa Studies Bulletin X,
       no. 2:35–79.
Birmingham, Walter B., I. Neustadt, E. N. Omaboe, eds.
  1966 A study of contemporary Ghana. some aspects of social structure.
       Evanston, Ill.: Northwestern University Press. 271 pp.
            Education is one of the topics examined.
Brokensha, David
  1966 Social change at Larteh, Ghana. London: Oxford University Press.
       xx + 294 pp., biblio., gloss., illus., maps, tables.
            Chapter XI (The schools, pp. 236–263) is particularly relevant.
       The author describes the position of missionary schools both his-
       torically and in contemporary terms. Importance of education in de-
       veloping nationalism, local status of the educated, sources of local
       pride in products of Larteh schools, economic significance of the
       schools and their personnel, effects of tribal loyalties on the schools,

and application of Margaret Read's developmental framework to Larteh schools are discussed. Brokensha challenges assumption of Africans being passively affected by foreign educational models.

Clignet, Rémi and Philip Foster
  1964 Potential elites in Ghana and the Ivory Coast: a preliminary comparison. American Journal of Sociology LXXX, no. 3:349–362.
    The authors present the similarities and differences in educational and related influences on leadership in the two nations.

Du Sautoy, Peter
  1958 Community development in Ghana. London: Oxford University Press. ix + 209 pp., illus., plates.

Foster, Philip J.
  1962 Ethnicity and the schools in Ghana. Comparative Education Review 6, no. 2:127–135.
    A review of regional and ethnic differences in access to schools.
  1968 Comments on Hurd and Johnson, education and social mobility in Ghana. Sociology of Education 41:111–121.
    Relevant discussion of relative openness of mobility in Ghana.

Kaye, Barrington
  1962 Bringing up children in Ghana. an impressionistic survey. London: George Allen & Unwin, Ltd. 244 pp., biblio., index, illus., map.
    Chapter 19 (Schooling, pp. 180–189) is particularly relevant. Schooling is described in the context of kinship relationships, materialistic expectations of students' families, increasing tendencies to send girls as well as boys to school, the change in students' attitudes from fear of teachers to respect for them, peer-group relations, and sexual behavior. Biblio. I (213–216) has a list of child training studies written by African students.

Peil, Margaret
  1963 Ghanian university students: the broadening base. British Journal of Sociology XVI, no. 1:19–28.
    Examination of recent changes in the social and economic background of the student body.
  1966 Middle school leavers: occupational aspirations and prospects. Ghana Journal of Sociology 2:7–16.
    An examination of expectations and actual prospects of youth in Ghana who will not continue to higher education.

Selormey, Francis
  1967 The narrow path. London: William Heinemann Ltd. African Writers Series no. 27. 184 pp. A Ghanian novel dealing, in part, with education.

IVORY COAST

Cerych, L.
  1967 *L'Aide extérieure et la planification de l'éducation en Côte-d'Ivoire.* (African Research Monographs No. 12.) Paris: UNESCO, International Institute for Educational Planning. 49 pp.

A description of the relationships between foreign aid and the development of Ivory Coast educational planning.

Clignet, Rémi and Philip Foster

1964 Potential elites in Ghana and the Ivory Coast: a preliminary comparison. American Journal of Sociology LXXX, no. 3:349–362.

1966a The fortunate few: a study of secondary schools and students in the Ivory Coast. Evanston, Ill.: Northwestern University Press. xv + 242 pp., apps., figs., index, tables.

A careful and relevant comparison of the background, aspirations, realistic chances, and national priorities of Ghana and the Ivory Coast. Discussion is placed in a broader African and developing area context.

1966b *La préeminence de l'enseignement classique en Côte-d'Ivoire: un exemple d'assimilation. Revue Française de Sociologie* 7:32–47.

Discussion of uses of French models in Ivory Coast education.

Farine, Avigdor

1968 *Les couts de l'enseignement en Côte-d'Ivoire. L'Actualité Economique* 44:219–239.

Sigel, Efrem

1967 Ivory Coast education: brake or spur? Africa Report 12, no. 1:48–51.

The author, a former peace corpsman in the Ivory Coast, feels that education is dominated by Europeans and not geared to local needs. Ivory Coast shares common African problems: expensiveness of education, a wide primary base and a narrow secondary tip to the triangle, high dropout rate, and undervaluation of technical education, a French-type system, youth unemployment, and student orientation toward white-collar positions.

KENYA

Anderson, John

1968 Primary school-leavers in progressive rural areas in Kenya. Teacher Education 8:201–214.

Gorman, T. P.

1968 Bilingualism in the educational system of Kenya. Comparative Education 4, no. 3:213–221. Discussion of the educational approaches to the need for English, Swahili (Kiunguja dialect), and other vernaculars in Kenyan education.

Kenyatta, Jomo

1938 Facing Mount Kenya, the tribal life of the Gikuyu. Intro. by Bronislaw Malinowski. London: Secker and Warburg, Ltd. New York: Vintage, 1962.

Mboya, Tom

1963 Freedom and after. Boston: Little, Brown and Company, 288 pp., illus.

Significant for discussion of the late leader's uses of Western education in an African context.

Sheffield, J. R.

1966 Conference on education, employment, and rural development, Kericho, Kenya, September 25–October 1, 1966. Journal of Modern African Studies 4, no. 3:371–375.

Urch, George E. F.
1968 The Africanization of the curriculum in Kenya. University of Michigan Comparative Education Dissertation Series No. 12. Ann Arbor: Malloy Lithographing Inc. iii + 273 pp.

Webster, John B., comp.
1967 A bibliography on Kenya. Syracuse, N.Y.: Syracuse University, Program of Eastern African Studies. 461 pp.

Weeks, Sheldon
1967 Divergence in educational development: the case of Kenya and Uganda. New York: Center for Education in Africa, Teachers College Press. ix + 36 pp.

LESOTHO

Turner, John
1968 Continuity and integration in in-service teacher education in Lesotho. Teacher Education 8:215–229.

LIBERIA

Gay, John and Michael Cole
1967 The new mathematics and an old culture: a study of learning among the Kpelle of Liberia. New York: Holt, Rinehart and Winston, Inc. x + 100 pp.

Smith, Robert
1966 Adult education in Liberia. International Review of Education 12: 202–211.

MADAGASCAR

De Nucé, M. S., and J. Ratsimandrava, eds.
1966 *Bibliographie annuelle de Madagascar, 1964.* Tananarive: Université de Madagascar, *Bibliothèque Universitaire.* 262 pp.

MALAWI

Kayira, Legson
1966 I will try. London: Longmans, Green and Co., Ltd. 243 pp., map.
     The epic of a young man from Malawi and his education.

Paulston, Rolland G.
1967 *Problemas de Tradición y cambios en la educación superior de Marruocos. Educación Universitaria Comparada* 4:1–16.

Read, Margaret
1968 Children of their fathers: growing up among the Ngoni of Malawi. New York: Holt, Rinehart and Winston, Inc. xi + 97 pp., biblio., figs., glossary, illus., maps. 2d rev. ed.

Rimmington, Gerald T.
  1966 Education for independence. a study of changing educational adminis-
       tration in Malawi. Comparative Education 2:217–223.

NIGERIA

Achebe, Chinua
  1966 A man of the people. New York: Doubleday & Company, Inc., 141 pp.
            A novel by a leading Nigerian writer on personal and structural
       ironies in some aspects of modern African education.
Adetoro, J. E.
  1966 Universal primary education and the teacher supply problem in Ni-
       geria. Comparative Education 2:209–216.
Ajayi, J. F. Ade
  1965 Christian missions in Nigeria 1841–1891: the making of a new élite.
       Intro. by K. Onwuka Dike. Evanston, Ill.: Northwestern University
       Press. xvi + 317 pp., app., biblio., illus., index, maps.
            Many references to education and schools.
Ayandele, Emmanuel A.
  1966 The missionary impact on modern Nigeria 1842–1914: a political and
       social analysis. Intro. by K. Onwuka Dike. London: Longmans, Green
       and Co., Ltd. xx + 393 pp., biblio., illus., index, maps.
            Chapter 9 (The mission and education, pp. 282–304) is particu-
       larly relevant.
Bittinger, Desmond Wright
  1941 An educational experiment in northern Nigeria in its cultural setting.
       Philadelphia: University of Pennsylvania Press. xvi + 343 pp., biblio.,
       index.
            An early and relevant attempt to combine anthropology and educa-
       tion in the study of a sample of native education in Africa.
Calcott, D.
  1968 Some trends and problems of education in Western Nigeria, 1955–
       1966: part II. West African Journal of Education 12, no. 1:11–17.
  1968 Part III. West African Journal of Education 12, no. 2:106–109, 112–
       116
Callaway, A. and A. Musone
  1968 Financing of education in Nigeria. (African research monographs, no.
       15.) Paris: UNESCO, International Institute for Educational Plan-
       ning. 150 pp.
Diamond, Stanley
  1967 Nigeria: model of a colonial failure. New York: American Committee
       on Africa. vii + 88 pp.
            Curious but interesting collection of Diamond's analyses and re-
       joinders by Nigerian figures. The book is relevant since education is a
       major component in any appraisal of the colonial enterprise in Nigeria.
Dipeolu, J. O.
  1967 Bibliographical sources for Nigerian studies. Evanston, Ill.: North-
       western University Press. 26 pp.
            Pp. 13–14 are especially useful.

Fuchs, Estelle
1964 The compatibility of western education with Ibo culture: an examination of the complex dynamics involved in the successful diffusion of literacy and schooling to the Ibo of Eastern Nigeria. New York: Columbia University Ph.D. Thesis. iv + 239 pp., biblio., maps, tables.

Goldthorpe, J. E.
1965 An African elite: Makerere College students 1922–1960. Foreword by Julius Nyerere. Nairobi: Oxford University Press for the East African Institute of Social Research. ix + 109 pp., apps., biblio., illus., index.
Focus: students from Kenya, Tanganyika, and Uganda. Reviews education in East Africa, Makerere student social origins, adjustment problems of students, and eventual employment.

Graham, Sonia
1966 Government and mission education in northern Nigeria 1900–1919 with special reference to the work of Hanns Vischer. Introduction by A. H. M. Kirk-Greene. Ibadan: Ibadan University Press. xxvii + 192 pp., apps., biblio., maps, index.
A historical study with special reference to the first Director of Education in northern Nigeria (H. Vischer).

Hanson, John W.
1968 Education, Nsukka: a study in institution building among the modern Ibo. With field assistance from Magnus Adiele, Pius Igboko, and Charles Okpala. East Lansing, Mich.: African Studies Center and the Institute for International Studies in Education, Michigan State University. 410 pp., app., biblio. in notes, diags., notes, tables.
A case study of institution building, specifically the College of Education, Nsukka. Focus is on leadership functions and the environment in which leadership is exercised. Leadership is especially placed in the Ibo context in which the institution was developed.

Harbison, Frederick
1960 High-level manpower for Nigeria's future. *In* Education and nation building in Africa, L. Gray Cowan, et al., eds. New York: Praeger. (1965). Capital and high-level manpower are greatly needed. Nigeria is predominantly agricultural but has great economic potential. Intermediate education is critical and requires expansion. Secondary-technology education is understressed. Regional and federal planning needs are discussed. Needs for nongraduate technicians are discussed.

Ikejiani, Okechukwu, ed.
1965 Education in Nigeria. New York: Frederick A. Praeger, Inc. xix + 234 pp.

Levine, Robert A. et al.
1966 Dreams and deeds: achievement motivation in Nigeria. Chicago: University of Chicago Press. 123 pp., biblio. foot.

Lewis, Leonard John
1965 Society, schools, and progress in Nigeria. Elmsford, New York: Pergamon Press, Inc. xii + 159 pp., biblio.

Moffet, J. B.
1968 The primary schools of Lagos, Nigeria. West African Journal of Education 12:29–33.

Muchenhirn, Erma F.
    Secondary education and girls in Western Nigeria. University of
    Michigan comparative education dissertation series, no. 9. Ann Arbor:
    Malloy Lithoprinting, Inc. 333 pp.

Nduka, Otonti
    1964 Western education and the Nigerian cultural background. Ibadan:
    Oxford University Press. viii + 168 pp., biblio.

O'Connell, James
    1963 Education, economics, and politics. West African Journal of Educa-
    tion VII, no. 2:64–66.

Peshkin, Alan
    1967 Education and national integration in Nigeria. The Journal of Mod-
    ern African Studies 5, no. 3:323–334.
        A discussion of the factors absent in Nigerian education that are
    essential to the development of nationalism.

Poole, H. E.
    1968 The effect of urbanization upon scientific concept attainment among
    Hausa children of northern Nigeria. The British Journal of Educa-
    tional Psychology 38, no. 1:57–63.
        An example of social psychological approaches to learning measures
    in developing areas.

Raphaeli, Nimrod
    1966 Education and political development in Southern Nigeria. *Civilisations*
    16:67–77.

Smythe, Hugh H. and Mabel M. Smythe
    1960 The new Nigerian elite. Stanford, Cal.: Stanford University Press.
    ix + 196 pp., biblio. in notes, index.
        Study based upon interviews with 156 members of the elite. Role
    of education in creation of elite is discussed throughout. Conflicts
    between class, tribal, and national loyalties are discussed.

Stabler, Ernest
    1968 Pressures and constraints in planning African education. Comparative
    Education Review XII, no. 3:350–356.

Stolper, Wolfgang
    1966 Planning without facts: lessons in resource allocation from Nigeria's
    development. with an input-output analysis of the Nigerian economy,
    1959–1960 by Nicholas G. Carter. Foreword by Chief S. O. Adebo.
    Cambridge: Harvard University Press. xx + 348 pp., app., biblio. in
    notes, index, tables.
        Occasional references to educational policy.

Thornley, J. F.
    1966 The planning of primary education in Northern Nigeria. (African re-
    search monographs no. 2) Paris: UNESCO, International Institute
    for Education Planning. 41 pp.
    1967 The integration of external assistance with educational planning in
    Nigeria. (Africa research monographs, no. 14). Paris: UNESCO, In-
    ternational Institute for Educational Planning. 78 pp.

Weiler, Hans N., ed.
    1964 Education and politics in Nigeria. (*Erziehung und Politik in Nigeria.*)

Freiburg im Breisgau: Rombach. (*Freiburger Studien zu Politik und Soziologie.*) 294 pp., biblio.

NYASALAND

Anonymous
1927 Nyasaland Protectorate: report of the native education conference held at Zomba. Zomba.
An early document dealing with potential problems in education of native peoples.

NORTHERN RHODESIA (SEE ALSO ZAMBIA)

Irvine, S. H.
1961 African education in northern Rhodesia—the first forty years. Teacher Education 2:36–50.

SOUTHERN RHODESIA

Kee, A. Alistair
1968 Underdevelopment—and how to maintain it. Rhodesia: Teachers College Record 69:321–329.
Mcharg, J.
1962 Influences contributing to the education and culture of the native people in southern Rhodesia from 1900 to 1961. Duke University: D.Ed. thesis. x + 158 pp., biblio., illus., maps.
Parker, Franklin
1960 African development and education in southern Rhodesia. Intro. by E. I. F. Williams. Columbus: Ohio State University Press. International education monographs. xiii + 165 pp., app., biblio. in notes, index.
A historical review and analysis of conditions, particularly of African education, of the late 1950s.

SENEGAL

Fougeyrollas, P., F. Sow, and F. Valladon
1967 *L'Education des adultes au Sénégal.* African research monographs no. 11. Paris: UNESCO, International Institute for Educational Planning. 46 pp.
Guillaumont, P., D. Garbe, and P. Verdun
1967 *Les Dépenses d'enseignement au Sénégal.* African research monographs no. 5. Paris: UNESCO, International Institute of Educational Planning. 51 pp.

SIERRA LEONE

Summer, D. L.
1963 Education in Sierra Leone. xi + 475 pp., map.

SOUTH AFRICA

Anonymous
  1957 The open universities in South Africa. Johannesburg: Witwatersrand
       University Press. 47 pp.
  1966 Education and the South African economy. The 1961 Education Panel
       second report. Johannesburg: Witwatersrand University Press. 152 pp.
Auerbach, F. E.
  1965 The power of prejudice in South African education. Cape Town: A. A.
       Balkema. xiii + 144 pp.
Behr, Abraham L. and R. G. Macmillan
  1966 Education in South Africa. Pretoria: J. L. Van Schaik. 386 pp.,
       biblio., illus.
Birley, Robert
  1968 African education in South Africa. African Affairs 67:152–158.
Carstens, W. Peter
  1966 The social structure of a Cape coloured reserve: a study of racial inte-
       gration and segregation in South Africa. Cape Town: Oxford Univer-
       sity Press. xiii + 264 pp., app., biblio., illus., maps.
          Schools are discussed (pp. 165–169; 219–224) in the context of the
       social structure of the reserve.
Hey, Peter D.
  1961a The rural Zulu teacher in Natal. Comparative Education Review 5,
       no. 1:54–58.
          General problems discussed are intercultural status of teachers and
       alienating role of teachers in relations between parents and children.
  1961b African aspirations for education in rural Natal. Comparative Educa-
       tion Review 5, no. 2:112–117.
          Focus: the Bidla tribe living in Pholela District. Based on inter-
       views, the author reviews aspirations and fears in young Africans con-
       cerning education. He stresses the unreality of the aspirations, wastage
       in education, and disruptive influence of education based on Western
       standards in relations between parents and educated children.
Kuper, Leo
  1965 An African bourgeoisie: race, class, and politics in South Africa. New
       Haven: Yale University Press. xviii + 452 pp., apps., biblio., illus.
          Pp. 143–257 are especially relevant.
Marais, J. M.
  1957 European education in South Africa, 1946–1955; a select bibliography.
       Cape Town: University of Cape Town School of Librarianship. biblio-
       graphical series. iv + 39 pp.
Munroe, David
  1966 Language and education in South Africa. McGill Journal of Education
       1:139–144.
          Study of relationships between apartheid, refusal to train Africans,
       and lack of skilled technicians.
Read, Margaret
  1960 Children of their fathers: growing up among the Ngoni of Nyasaland.
       New Haven: Yale University Press. 176 pp., apps., biblio., illus.

Chapter IX (Some educational reflections, pp. 166–172) is particularly useful.

Reader, D. H.
1966 Zulu tribe in transition. New York: Humanities Press. (Manchester: Manchester University Press.) x + 363 pp., app., biblio., glossary, illus., index, maps.

A study of change, especially in political, juridical, kinship, and economic relationships. Important for background to studying changes induced by education.

Rose, Brian
1965 Educational policy and problems in the former High Commission Territories of Africa. Comparative Education 1, no. 2:113–118.

SUB-SAHARAN AREA

Bolibaugh, Jerry Bevoly
1964 French educational strategies for Sub-Saharan Africa: their intent, derivation, and development. Stanford, Cal.: Comparative Education Center; School of Education, Stanford University. 112 pp., biblio.

A more extensive treatment of this topic is available in the author's thesis. vi + 297 pp., biblio. (Stanford; Ann Arbor: University Microfilms, Inc.)

Drake, Howard
1942 A bibliography of African education south of the Sahara. Aberdeen: The University Press. 97 pp. (Aberdeen University Anthropological Museum publication no. 2.)

South African Public Library
1961 A bibliography of African bibliographies concerning territories south of the Sahara. 4th ed. rev. to Nov. 1960. Cape Town. 79 pp. (Grey bibliographies, no. 7.)

SUDAN

Griffiths, Vincent L.
1953 An experiment in education; an account of the attempts to improve the lower stages of boys' education in the Moslem Anglo-Egyptian Sudan, 1930–1950. New York and London: Longmans, Green & Co., Ltd. 160 pp.

Sanderson, Lilian
1968 The development of girls' education in the northern Sudan, 1898–1960. Paedagogica Historica 8:120–152.

TANGANYIKA (SEE ALSO TANZANIA)

Cameron, John
1967 The integration of education in Tanganyika. Comparative Education Review 11, no. 1:38–56.

Smith, Anthony
1965 British colonial education policy—Tanganyika: a variation on the theme. *Paedagogica Historica* 2:435–454.

TANZANIA

Dodd, William
1968 Centralization in education in mainland Tanzania. Comparative Education Review 12, no. 3:268–280.
   Plans for ending religious and racial separation in schools are described.
Heijnen, Johannes Daniel
1968 Development and education in the Mwanza district (Tanzania): a case study of migration and peasant farming. Rotterdam: Bronder-Offset. 171 pp.
Hunter, Guy
1966 Manpower, employment and education in the rural economy of Tanzania. African research monographs no. 9. Paris: UNESCO, International Institute for Educational Planning. 40 pp., biblio. foot., tables.
King, Jane
1967 Planning non-formal education in Tanzania. African research monographs no. 16. Paris: UNESCO, International Institute for Educational Planning. 40 pp.
Knight, J. B.
1966 The cost and financing of educational development in Tanzania. African research monographs no. 4. Paris: UNESCO, International Institute for Educational Planning. 80 pp.
Koff, David and George Von Der Muhll
1967 Political socialization in Kenya and Tanzania—a comparative analysis. Journal of Modern African Studies 5:13–51.
Levitt, Leonard
1967 An African season. New York: Simon and Schuster. 223 pp.
   An account by a U.S. Peace Corps volunteer.
Mwingira, A. C. and Simon Pratt
1967 The process of educational planning in Tanzania. Africa research monographs no. 10. Paris: UNESCO, International Institute for Educational Planning. 102 pp.
Nyerere, Julius
1967 Education for self-reliance. Africa Report 12, no. 6:72–79.
   A critical look at Tanzanian educational foundations and future needs by the president of the country.
Resnick, Idrian N.
1967 Manpower development in Tanzania. The Journal of Modern African Studies 5, no. 1:107–123.
Skorov, George
1967 Integration of educational and economic planning in Tanzania. African research monographs no. 6. Paris: UNESCO, International Institute for Educational Planning. 78 pp.

Swantz, Lloyd W.
  1965 Church, mission, and state relations in pre and post independent Tanzania (1955–1964). East Africa in the modern world. Syracuse: Syracuse University. 50 pp., illus.

TROPICAL AFRICA

Anonymous
  1953 African education: a study of educational policy and practice in British tropical Africa. Oxford: Oxford University Press (for the Muffield Foundation and the Colonial Office). xii + 187 pp., tables.
Lloyd, P. C., ed.
  1966 The new elites of tropical Africa. London: Oxford University Press. 390 pp.
Lugard, F. O.
  1925 Education in tropical Africa. Edinburgh Review 242:1–19.
Mayhew, A.
  1933 A comparative survey of educational aims and methods in British India and British Tropical Africa. Africa 6:172–186.
Spencer, John, ed.
  1963 Leverhulme conference on universities and the language problems of tropical Africa. Ibadan, Nigeria, 1961–1962. Language in Africa, paper 1. Cambridge: Cambridge University Press. vii + 167 pp., biblio. foot.

UGANDA

Chesswas, J. D.
  1966 Educational planning and development in Uganda. African research monographs no. 1. Paris: UNESCO, International Institute for Educational Planning. 97 pp.
Fox, Lorene K., ed.
  1967 East African childhood: three versions. Written by Joseph A. Lijembe, Anna Apoko, and J. Mutuku Nzioki. London and New York: Oxford University Press. 139 pp., gloss., illus.
Scanlon, David G.
  1965 Education in Uganda. Washington, D.C.: USDHEW, Office of Education. vi + 115 pp., biblio. foot.
Stabler, Ernest
  1968 Pressures and constraints in planning African education. Comparative Education Review XII, no. 3:350–356.
Weeks, Sheldon G.
  1967a Divergence in educational development: the case of Kenya and Uganda. New York: Center for Education in Africa; Teachers College Press. ix + 36 pp.
  1967b Are hostels necessary: a study of senior secondary school pupils in greater Kampala. Journal of Developing Areas 1:357–374.
  1968 An African school: a sociological case study of a day secondary school in Uganda. Cambridge: Harvard University thesis.

Williams, Peter
  1966 Aid in Uganda—education. London: The Overseas Development In-
      stitute, Ltd. 151 pp.

WEST AFRICA

Banjo, S. A.
  1956 A West African teacher's handbook. London: University of London
      Press. 224 pp., illus.
Brown, Godfrey N.
  1964 British educational policy in west and central Africa. The Journal of
      Modern African Studies 2, no. 3:365–377.
Clignet, Rémi
  1967 Ethnicity, social differentiation, and secondary schooling in West
      Africa. *Cahiers d'Etudes Africaines*; 7:360–378.
  1968 The legacy of assimilation in West African educational systems: its
      meaning and ambiguities. Comparative Education Review XII, no. 1:
      57–67.
          Looks primarily at Ghana and the Ivory Coast. Recommends
      great caution in the use of the term, "assimilation."
Dowuona, M. and J. T. Saunders, eds.
  1962 International seminar on inter-university cooperation in West Africa,
      Freetown, Sierra Leone, 1961. The West African intellectual commu-
      nity; papers and discussions. Ibadan, Nigeria: (published for the Con-
      gress for Cultural Freedom by Ibadan University Press). 356 pp.
Hilliard, Frederick H.
  1957 A short history of education in British West Africa. Camden, N.J.:
      Thomas Nelson & Sons. 186 pp., illus.
Kellaway, George P.
  1967 Education for living. Cambridge: Cambridge University Press. 151
      pp., index, app.
          A general discussion of education of children with brief reference to
      West Africa where the author has taught.
Kuper, Hilda, ed.
  1965 Urbanization and migration in West Africa. Berkeley and Los Angeles:
      University of California Press. Published under the auspices of the
      African Studies Center, UCLA. viii + 227 pp., biblio., foot. with
      biblio. ref., index, maps.
          Articles by Horace M. Miner (Urban influences on the rural Hausa)
      and Michael Banton (Social alignment and identity in a West African
      city) are especially relevant: pp. 110–130; 131–147.
Little, Kenneth Lindsay
  1965 West African urbanization. a study of voluntary associations in social
      change. Cambridge: Cambridge University Press. vii + 179 pp., biblio.
Pauvert, Jean Claude
  1962 *Afrique noire: Tendances actuelles de l'éducation des adultes dans les
      états Africans d'expression française: L'Amenagement du lac Faguibine*
      (Republique du Mali). Paris: Presses Universitaires de France. 78 pp.

Wilson, John
1963 Education and changing west African culture. New York: Columbia University Press. x + 113 pp., biblio. foot., table.

ZAMBIA (SEE ALSO NORTHERN RHODESIA)

Anonymous
1966 A complete list of the publications of the former Rhodes-Livingstone Institute. Lusaka: Institute for Social Research, University of Zambia.
Coombe, Trevor
1967 The origins of secondary education in Zambia. (I) African Social Research 3:173–205.
A review of the 1930s.
Coombe, Trevor
1967 The origins of secondary education in Zambia (II) African Social Research 4:283–315.
A description of the decision to introduce secondary education.

ASIA

GENERAL

Kublin, Kyman, comp.
1964 Education in Asian countries: an introductory reading and buying guide for undergraduate colleges and libraries. New York: The University of the State of New York, Office of Foreign Area Studies. iv + 46 pp.
Muhammad Shamsul
1965 Education and development strategy in south and southeast Asia. Honolulu: East-West Center Press. x + 286 pp., apps., biblio. in notes, illus., index, maps.
A general review of concepts of development, economic value of educational philosophies, goals, implementations, and problems in South and Southeast Asia.

CEYLON

Jayaweera, Swarna
1968 Religious organizations and the state in Ceylonese education. Comparative Education Review 12, no. 2:159–170.

CHINA

Baum, Richard and Frederick C. Teiwes
1968 Ssu-ch'ing: the socialist education movement of 1962–1966. Berkeley: University of California Center for Chinese Studies. 128 pp., apps., biblio. foot.

Baum, Richard
    1966 Revolution and reaction in the Chinese countryside: the socialist edu-
        cation movement in cultural revolutionary perspective. The China
        Quarterly 38:92–119.
Biggerstaff, Knight
    1961 The earliest modern government schools in China. Ithaca: Cornell
        University Press. xi + 276 pp., biblio., gloss., index.
            A study of mid- to late nineteenth-century Chinese official attempts
        to establish schools that offered "Western learning." This book is of
        particular interest for students of the models of Western education
        used by the Chinese.
Chen, Theodore
    1966 Education in Communist China: aims, trends, and problems. *In* Con-
        temporary China, Ruth Adams, ed., New York: Pantheon Books, Inc.
        pp. 257–280.
Chi, Tung-Wei
    1956 Education for the proletariat in communist China. Hong Kong: Union
        Research Institute. 73 pp.
Chow, Tse-Tsung
    1960 The May Fourth movement: intellectual revolution in modern China.
        Cambridge: Harvard University Press. xi + 486 pp., apps., biblio. in
        notes, chronology, index.
            A basic study for understanding the forces involved in establishing
        the foundations of modern Chinese education.
Doolin, Dennis, ed.
    1964 Communist China; the politics of student opposition. Stanford, Cal.:
        The Hoover Institution on War, Revolution, and Peace. 70 pp.
Fraser, Stewart, ed.
    1965 Chinese Communist education; records of the first decade. Nashville:
        Vanderbilt University Press. xvi + 542 pp., biblio., index.
            A wide selection of essays on education by Chinese in the People's
        Republic.
Goldman, René
    1962 The rectification campaign at Peking University. May–June 1957. The
        China Quarterly 12:138–153.
            An analysis of party policy at a major university after the 100 flowers
        failure.
Hsu, Immanuel C. Y.
    1966 The reorganization of higher education in Communist China, 1949–
        1961. *In* China under Mao. Roderick MacFarquhar, ed. Cambridge:
        The M.I.T. Press, pp. 271–303.
            Politics takes command.
Hu, Ch'ang-Tu, ed.
    1962 Chinese education under communism. Preface by L. A. Cremin. New
        York: Bureau of Publications, Teachers College, Columbia University.
        viii + 157 pp., illus.
            A review essay by Hu and selections from Mao Tse-tung, Kuo
        Mo-Jo, Lu Ting-yi, and Yang Hsiu-Feng.

Lindsay, Michael
1950 Notes on educational problems in Communist China, 1941–1947. With supplements on developments in 1948 and 1949 by Marion Menzies, William Paget, and Sib. Thomas. New York: Institute of Pacific Relations.
A review of the practical and theoretical struggle in education in those areas under Communist control.
Munro, Donald J.
1967 Maxims and realities in China's educational policy; the half-work half-study model. Asian Survey 7:254–272.
Oldham, C. H. G.
1966 Science and education in China. *In* Contemporary China, Ruth Adams, ed. New York: Pantheon Books, Inc., pp. 281–317.
Orleans, Leo A.
1961 Professional manpower and education in Communist China. Foreword by Alan T. Waterman. Washington, D.C.: U.S. Government Printing Office (National Science Foundation). xii + 260 pp., apps., tables.
A critical review of Communist China's educational structure and goals. Appendixes provide much detail on structure in the late 1950s.
Peake, Cyrus
1932 Nationalism and education in modern China. New York: Columbia University Press. xiv + 240 pp., biblio.
A summary of primary, middle-school, and mass-education textbooks, 1905–1929.
Ryan, William L. and Sam Summerlin
1968 The China cloud, America's tragic blunder and China's rise to nuclear power. Boston: Little, Brown and Company. 309 pp., app., index.
A description of the role of U.S. trained Chinese scientists in Chinese nuclear development.
Tsang, Chiu-Sam
1967a Nationalism in school education in China. 2d ed. Preface by George S. Counts. Hong Kong: Progressive Education Publishers. v + 247 pp., biblio.
1967b The Red Guards and the great proletarian cultural revolution. Comparative Education 3, no. 3:195–205.
Yang, Allency H. Y.
1965 Red and expert: Communist China's educational strategies of manpower development. 270 pp. Ph.D. dissertation. Berkeley, University of California.
Yung, Wing
1909 My life in China and America. New York: Holt, Rinehart and Winston, Inc. vi + 286 pp.
Autobiography of the first Chinese college student in the United States.

INDIA

Dakin, Julian, Brian Tiffen, and H. G. Widdowson
1968 Language in education: the problem in Commonwealth Africa and

the Indo-Pakistan sub-continent. London: Oxford University Press. xi + 177 pp., gloss.

Gore, M. S., I. P. Desai, and Juma Chitnis, eds.
   1967 Papers on the sociology of education in India. New Delhi: National Council of Educational Research and Training. Coordinating Committee for Studies in the Sociology of Education in India. xx + 363 pp.

Greaves, Monica Alice
   1967 Education in British India, 1698–1947; a bibliography and guide to the sources of information in London. xx + 182 pp., maps.

Laska, John A.
   1968 Planning and educational development in India. Foreword by R. Freeman Butts. New York: Teachers College Press, Columbia University. xi + 129 pp., biblio., sources, tables.
      A review of Indian educational structure and educational requirements, goals, and plan implementations.

Mathur, S. S.
   1966 A sociological approach to Indian education. Agra: Vinod Pustak Mandir. ii + i + 342 pp., biblio. foot.

Ramanathan, Gopalakrishnan
   1965 Educational planning and national integration. London: Asia Publishing House. xi + 252 pp.
      A review of history of Indian education, the language question, employment problems, primary-secondary-university education, educational content and, educational administration.

Richey, J. A.
   1965 Selections from educational records: part II, 1940–1959. (1922) Calcutta: Superintendent Government Printing, India. Reprint: Delhi: published for the National Archives by the Manager of Publications, Government of India. xv + 504 pp., apps., biblio., illus., index, tables.
      An example of a series of background documents now being reprinted. See Sharp (1965).

Rosner, Victor
   1968 The impact of modern forces on the Oraons of Samtoli. Anthropos 63:177–186, esp. 179–181.

Sharp, H.
   1965 Selections from educational records: part I, 1781–1839. Calcutta: (1920) Superintendent Government Printing, India. Reprint: Delhi: published for the National Archives by the Manager of Publications, Government of India. xii + 255 pp., apps., biblio., illus., index, tables.

Useem, John and Ruth Hill Useem
   1955 The Western educated man in India. A study of his social roles and influence. Preface by Paul J. Braisted. New York: Holt, Rinehart & Winston, Inc. xiii + 237 pp.

INDONESIA

Hutasoit, Marnixius
   1961 Problems and potentials of Indonesian Education. Berkeley: University of California Press. 22 pp., map.

JAPAN

Abegglcn, James
 1958 The Japanese factory. New York: The Free Press. 142 pp.
  Provides background for understanding relationships between Japanese factory development and worker education.
Anderson, Ronald
 1959 Japan—three epochs of modern education. Washington, D.C.: U.S. Department of Health, Education, and Welfare, Office of Education. Bulletin 1959, no. 11. xii + 219 pp., biblio., illus.
Dore, Ronald P.
 1965a Education in Tokugawa Japan. Berkeley: University of California Press. xi + 346 pp., illus., map.
  Basic book for understanding background of modern educational development in Japan.
 1965b City life in Japan: a study of a Tokyo ward. Berkeley: University of California Press. viii + 472 pp., apps., biblio. in notes, illus., index. Chapter 14 is relevant.
Embree, John F.
 1964 Suye Mura, a Japanese village. Introduction by Richard Beardsley. Chicago: The University of Chicago Press. (Phoenix Ed.). xxxi + 354 pp., apps., biblio., illus., index. Chapter VI is relevant.
General Headquarters, Supreme Commander for the Allied Powers, Civil Information and Education Section, Education Division
 1948 Education in the new Japan. 2 vols.
  Basic documents on U.S. intentions in reforming Japanese education.
 1952 Post-war developments in Japanese education. 2 vols.
  A review of the successes and failures of U.S. effort in reforming Japanese education.
Kobayashi, Tetsuja
 1965 Tokugawa education as a foundation of modern education in Japan. Comparative Education Review 9:288–302.
Passin, Herbert
 1965a Society and education in Japan. New York: Bureau of Publications, Columbia University. xvii + 347 pp., illus.
 1965b Japanese education: guide to a bibliography in the English language. Comparative Education Review 9:81–101.
Singleton, John
 1967a Nichū: a Japanese school. New York: Holt, Rinehart & Winston, Inc. xii + 125 pp., illus.
 1967b Urban-rural comparisons in Japanese education. International Review of Education 13:470–482.
Vera, José Maria De
 1967 Educational television in Japan. Tokyo: Sophia University. (Monumenta Nipponica monographs no. 28) 140 pp.

NEPAL

Hillary, Sir Edmund
 1968 Schoolhouse in the clouds. Harmondsworth: Penguin Books, Ltd. 192 pp., illus.
Pandey, Sardar Rudra Raj, Kaisher Bahadur, and Hugh B. Wood, eds.
 1955 Education in Nepal. Report of the national educational planning commission. Kathmandu: Bureau of Publications, College of Education. 259 pp., diagrs., illus., map, tables.
Wood, Hugh B.
 1958 Education in Nepal. Seattle: Cascade Pacific Books. 84 pp., illus.
 1965 Mobile normal schools in Nepal. Comparative Education 1, no. 2: 119–124.
Wood, Hugh B. and Bruno Knall
 1962 Educational planning in Nepal and its economic implications. Draft report of the UNESCO mission to Nepal, Kathmandu, January–May, 1962. Paris: UNESCO. xxxvii + 143 pp., illus.

PAKISTAN

Curle, Adam
 1966 Planning for education in Pakistan: a personal case study. Foreword by Philip H. Coombs. Cambridge: Harvard University Press. xxii + 208 pp., diagrs., index, maps, notes, tables.
  Especially relevant are Curle's comments on the role of an adviser to an educational system in a developing nation.
Huo, Mohammed Nooruc
 1967 An application of the United States techniques and practices by the secondary schools in East Pakistan to achieve some of the Social Studies objectives common to both cultures. 235 pp. Ed.D. dissertation, Colorado State College.
Schuler, Edgar A. and Raghu Singh, eds.
 1965 The Pakistan academies for rural development; Comila and Peshawar, 1969–1964. East Lansing, Michigan: The Asian Studies Center, MSU. ix + 116 pp.

PHILIPPINES

Morales, Alfredo
 1967 The concept of culture applied to educational change in the Philippines. Education Quarterly 14, no. 4:13–39.

THAILAND

Thawisomboon, Sanit et al.
 1965 Education in Thailand and Vietnam; selected paragraphs from writings on education, by Sanit Thawisomboon and others. Honolulu: East West Center. 66 pp.

Wyatt, David Kent
  1966 An application of the United States techniques and practices by the
    secondary schools in East Pakistan to achieve some of the social studies
    objectives common to both cultures. 235 pp. Ed.D. dissertation, Colo-
    rado State College.

VIETNAM

Vu-Tam-Ich
  1959 A historical survey of educational developments in Vietnam. Lexing-
    ton: University of Kentucky. 143 pp., biblio., illus.
      A review of education during traditional, colonial, and independence
    periods in Vietnam.

WESTERN COLONIES—HONG KONG

Rowe, Elizabeth, et al.
  1966 Failure in school; aspects of the problem in Hong Kong. (Hong Kong)
    London: Oxford University Press. xvii + 167 pp., diagrs., plan, tables.

EUROPE

GENERAL

Anonymous
  1965 Paedagogica Europaea 1965; the European yearbook of educational
    research. Amsterdam and Brussels: Elsevier. (U.S.: New York: Ameri-
    can Elsevier Pub. Co.)
      An annual review in English, French, or German.
Apanasewicz, Nellie and Seymour Rosen
  1966 Eastern European education: a bibliography of English-language ma-
    terials. Washington, D.C.: U.S. Department of Health, Education
    and Welfare, Office of Education. vi + 35 pp.
Cros, Louis
  1963 The "explosion" in the schools. Paris: Seupen. 186 pp., biblio. foot.,
    illus.
      European academic situation since 1945 is described.
Dunlop, F.
  1966 Europe's guests: students and trainees. A survey of the welfare of
    foreign students and trainees in Europe. Strasbourg: Council for Cul-
    tural Cooperation of the Council of Europe. 187 pp., tables.
Halsall, Elizabeth
  1966 Intelligence, school and social context: some European comparisons.
    Comparative Education 2:181–196.
Little, Alan and Denis Kallen
  1968 Western European secondary school systems and higher education: a
    warning for comparative education. Comparative Education 4, no. 2:
    135–153.

AUSTRIA

Lister, Ian
   1967 The Austrian *"Oberstufe"* and the English sixth form, and some con-
         sequences for university studies. Comparative Education 3, no. 3:
         207–217.
Papanek, Ernst
   1962 The Austrian school reform, its bases, principles and development—
         the twenty years between the two world wars. Foreword by Hans
         Mandl. Intro. by William H. Kilpatrick. New York: Frederick Fell,
         Inc. xiv + 130 pp., biblio. in notes.
         A brief review of Austrian education 1848–1918 and an in-depth
         analysis of reform efforts between the collapse of the Hapsburg Empire
         and the initial stages of fascist rule.

BELGIUM

Coster, Sylvain De and Georges Van Der Elst
   1954 *Mobilité sociale et enseignement.* Brussels: *Editions de la Libraire
         Encyclopédique.* 164 pp.
         A study of the relationships between educational achievement and
         mobility.
Coulon, Marion
   1967 *Tendances et développements récents dans l'education primaire et sec-
         ondaire en Belgique.* International Review of Education 13:285–298.
         A review of current developments in primary and secondary Belgian
         education.
Deprez, Marcel
   1966 *L'Education permanente en Belgique d'expression Française.* Interna-
         tional Review of Education 12:159–175.
         A review of French-language education in Belgium.
Mallinson, Vernon
   1963 Power and politics in Belgian education, 1815–1961. London: William
         Heinemann Ltd. xi + 253 pp., apps., biblio., index.
         A review of political, religious, colonial, and economic factors.

BULGARIA

Apanasewicz, Nellie and Seymour Rosen
   1965 Education in Bulgaria. Washington, D.C.: U.S. Department of Health,
         Education and Welfare, Office of Education. iii + 27 pp., biblio., illus.
Georgeoff, Peter John
   1967 Higher education in Bulgaria. Educational Forum 31:455–464.
   1968 The social education of Bulgarian youth. Minneapolis: University of
         Minnesota Press. x + 329 pp., apps., biblio., index, notes.
         A detailed review of the nature of social education in elementary
         schools, the materials used, the teachers, and its place in organizations

such as the Pioneers and Komsomol. Especially valuable are the extensive appendixes containing relevant statistics and translations.

CZECHOSLOVAKIA

Apanasewicz, Nellie and Seymour Rosen
  1963 Education in Czechoslovakia. Washington, D.C.: U.S. Department of Health, Education and Welfare, Office of Education. iii + 40 pp., biblio.
Dixon, R. T.
  1967 Differentiated education in Czechoslovakia. Comparative Education 4, no. 1:3–8.
Maran, Stanislav
  1968 *Die gegenwärtige Entwicklung der tschechoslowkischen allgemein-bildenden Mittelschule. Vergleichende Pädagogik* 4:3–24.
    A discussion of the present development of Czechoslovak middle schools.

DENMARK

Brickman, William
  1967 Denmark's educational system and problems. Washington, D.C.: U.S. Department of Health, Education and Welfare, Office of Education. vi + 46 pp., biblio.
Thomsen, Ole
  1967 Some aspects of education in Denmark. Foreword by Bora Laskin. Toronto: Toronto University Press. Published for the Ontario Institute for Studies in Education. xii + 105 pp., biblio. foot.
    A series of lectures on secondary, technical, postsecondary, and adult education.

FINLAND

Kyöstiö, O. K.
  1961 Contemporary Finnish school legislation. Comparative Education Review 5, no. 2:130–135.
    The author analyzes principal problems in the education framework of Finland: the ways schools are separated, overbureaucratization of schools, outdated teacher-training methods, and lack of pressure to correct well-known deficiencies.
Leskinen, Heikki
  1968 The provincial folk school in Finland. Indiana University monograph, series in adult education, no. 3. Bloomington: Bureau of Studies in Adult Education, University of Indiana. 72 pp.
Owen, John
  1969 Teaching and learning in Finland. The Educational Forum XXXIII, no. 4:427–432.
    General review of Finnish national education.

FRANCE

Anonymous
  1965 La Réforme de l'enseignement. Revue des travaux de l'Académie des Sciences Morales & Politiques. 1er semestre: 1–52.
Artz, Frederick
  1966 The development of technical education in France, 1500–1850. Cleveland: Society for the History of Technology. x + 247 pp., biblio. foot.
Capelle, Jean
  1967 Tomorrow's education, the French experience. Foreword by Louis Armand. W. D. Halls (trans., ed., intro., notes). Elmsford, N.Y.: Pergamon Press, Inc. xvi + 229 pp., illus., index, tables.
       A review of 1960–1970 basic educational data; an analysis of educational forms, functions and personnel; and a commentary on higher education.
Clark, James
  1967 Teachers and politics in France: a pressure group study of the Fédération de l'Education Nationale. Syracuse: Syracuse University Press. xv + 197 pp., biblio.
Fraser, W. R.
  1963 Education and society in modern France. New York: Humanities Press, Inc. ix + 140 pp., biblio., illus.
Halls, W. D.
  1964 Educational planning in an industrial society: the French experience. Comparative Education 1, no. 1:19–28.
  1965 Society, schools and progress in France. Elmsford, N.Y.: Pergamon Press, Inc. xxii + 194 pp., biblio., biblio. foot.
Isambert-Jamati, Viviane
  1966 La Rigidité d'une institution: structure scolaire et systèmes de valeurs. Revue Française de Sociologie 7:306–324.
Male, George
  1963 Education in France. Washington, D.C.: U.S. Department of Health, Education and Welfare, Office of Education. viii + 205 pp., biblio., map, tables.
Rothera, Harold
  1968 The "new baccalauréat" in its context. Comparative Education 4, no. 3:183–197.
Schneider, Christian
  1963 Die Neue Erziehung und das Schulwesen in Frankreich; unter besonderer Berücksichtigung der Schulreformversuche von 1930 bis 1959. Heidelberg: Quelle & Meyer. 166 pp., biblio.
Talbott, John E.
  1969 The politics of educational reform in France, 1918–1940. Princeton: Princeton University Press. x + 283 pp., biblio., index.
       A study of attempts during the period between the two world wars to democratize the French educational system. The conclusion is an especially incisive overview of the conflicting motivations in efforts at reform.

Titmus, Colin
  1967 Adult education in France. Elmsford, N.Y.: Pergamon Press, Inc.
       xii + 201 pp., biblio.
Vignery, Robert J.
  1965 The French Revolution and the schools: educational policies of the
       mountain 1792–1794. Madison: The State Historical Society of
       Wisconsin for the Department of History, University of Wisconsin, xi
       + 208 pp., biblio., index, notes.
       This study includes examination of the National Convention influ-
       ence, the Condorcet plan, the Lepetier plan, the Second Romme plan,
       the Bouquier plan, and the sources of Jacobin educational thought.
Wylie, Laurence
  1957 Village in the Vaucluse. Cambridge: Harvard University Press. xviii +
       345 pp., illus., index.
       Pp. 55–76 are especially useful.

GERMANY

Arndt, Edward
  1966 An administrative history of the educational system of the German
       Democratic Republic from 1945–1964. Washington, D.C.: The Ameri-
       can University, Ed.D. dissertation. 352 pp.
       Relationship between USSR model, party control, and economic
       requirements are discussed.
Arsenjew, A. M.
  1967 *Hauptrichtungen bei der Verbesserung des Bildungsinhaltes in der
       Mittelschule. Vergleichende Pädagogik* 3:363–376.
       A discussion of the trends in middle-school reform.
Assmann, Ingeborg
  1967 West German education in transition. Los Angeles: University of
       Southern California. 293 pp.
       Author recommends modification and financial aid to increase access
       of all classes to higher education.
Edelstein, Wolfgang, Fritz Sang, and Werner Stegelmann
  1968 *Unterrichtsstoffe und ihre Verwendung in der BRD (Teil I): Eine
       empirische Untersuchung.* Berlin: Institut für Bildungs-forschung in
       der Max-Planck-Gesellschaft. xi + 319 pp.
       An empirical study of the uses of what is taught in schools.
Hilker, Franz
  1963 *Die Schulen in Deutschland* (Bundesrepublik und West-Berlin).
       Herausgeber, Hochschule für Internationale Pädagogische Forschung.
       Bad Nauheim: Christian-Verlag. 118 pp., biblio., diagr.
Huddleston, John
  1968 Trade union education in the Federal Republic of Germany. Interna-
       tional Review of Education 14:24–42.
Huebener, Theodore
  1962 The schools of West Germany. A study of German elementary and
       secondary schools. Foreword by George N. Shuster. New York: New
       York University Press. xii + 181 pp., biblio., gloss., index.

A brief history of German educational structure and a formal look at contemporary educational structure, personnel, curriculum, teaching methods, and attempts at reform.

Lawson, Robert F.
   1963 Reform of the West German school system, 1945–1962. Ann Arbor: University of Michigan. Ph.D. dissertation. 297 pp.
   The author does not see Occupation reforms producing major changes in German educational assumptions and structure.

Lynch, James
   1967 A problem of status—teacher training in West Germany. Comparative Education 3, no. 3:219–224.

Musgrave, Peter
   1967 Technical change, the labour force and education; a study of the British and German iron and steel industries, 1860–1964. Elmsford, N.Y.: Pergamon Press, Inc. viii + 286 pp., biblio.

Peisert, Hansgert
   1967 *Soziale Lage und Bildungschancen in Deutschland.* Munich: R. Piper. 206 pp.
   A study of the relationships between students' social status and their opportunities for education.

Picht, Georg
   1964 *Die deutsche Bildungs Katastrophe: Analyse und Dokumentation.* Olten: Walter-Verlag. 247 pp., biblio. ref.
   A critical study of German education.

Schwarzweller, Harry
   1967 Educational aspirations and life chances of German young people. Comparative Education 4, no. 1:35–49.

Stahl, Walter, ed.
   1961 Education for democracy in West Germany; achievements, shortcomings, prospects. New York: Frederick A. Praeger, Inc. xi + 356 pp., biblio., diagrs., illus.

Tietgens, Hans
   1966 *Wandlungen der Erwachsenenbildung in der Bundesrepublik Deutschland.* International Review of Education 12:144–158.
   A study of differences and changes in youth's experiences in growing up in Germany from previous times.

Van De Graaff, John
   1967 West Germany's *Abitur* quota and school reform. Comparative Education Review 11, no. 1:75–86.
   A critical review of attempts to enlarge educational opportunity within the three track system. Primary focus: gymnasium.

Warren, Richard
   1967 Education in Rebhausen: a German village. New York: Holt, Rinehart & Winston, Inc. xi + 114 pp., biblio., illus., map.

GREECE

Anonymous
  1965 Country reports: Greece. Paris: Organization for Economic Coopera-
       tion and Development. 195 pp., illus.

HUNGARY

Bencédy, József
  1967 *Tendances et développements récents dans l'éducation primaire et sec-
       ondaire en Hongrie.* International Review of Education 13:332–344.
       A review of recent trends and developments in Hungarian primary
       and secondary education.
Deubler, Hans
  1968 *Die Entwicklung der allgemeinbildenden Mittelschule in der Volks-
       republik Ungarn. Vergleichende Pädagogik* 4:43–61.
       A description of the development of general middle-school educa-
       tion in Hungary.
Hencz, Aurél
  1962 *A müvelödési intézmények és a müvelödésigazgátas Fejlödése,* 1945–
       1961. Budapest: Közgazdaság: és Jogi Könyvkiadó. 515 pp., biblio.

ICELAND

Josephson, Braji Straumfjord
  1968 Education in Iceland: its rise and growth with respect to social, politi-
       cal, and economic determinants. Ed.D. dissertation. Nashville: George
       Peabody College for Teachers.

IRELAND (EIRE)

Auchmuty, James
  1937 Irish education—a historical survey. Dublin: Allen Figgis & Co., Ltd.
       vi + 162 pp., biblio.
       A classic study.
Duffy, Patrick
  n.d. The lay teacher. Dublin: C. J. Fallon, Ltd. xx + 155 pp.
Mcelligott, T. J.
  1966 Education in Ireland. Dublin: Institute of Public Administration.
       viii + 201 pp., biblio.
       A historical study.
Peck, Bryan
  1966 Irish education and European integration. Comparative Education 2:
       197–207.
  1967 Protestant schools in the Republic of Ireland. International Review of
       Education 13:212–225.

ITALY

Anello, Michael
  1961 A critical analysis of the response of an educational system to increasing industrialization and technological change: technical-vocational education in Italy. Ithaca: Cornell University, Ph.D. dissertation. 169 pp.
    Reasons for general failure of technical-vocational education in Italy are discussed.
Berlin, Giovanni Maria, ed.
  1964 *Scuola e società in Italia, con contributi di Achille Ardigò e Luigi Meschieri.* Bari: Laterza. 230 pp., biblio. foot.
Scarangello, Anthony
  1962 Church and state in Italian education. Comparative Education Review 5, no. 3:199–207.
    Historical review of church-state relations with reference to schools in Italy. Present situation with Roman Catholic hegemony in compulsory religious education and state hegemony in secular education.
  1964 Progress and trends in Italian education. Washington, D.C.: U.S. Department of Health, Education, and Welfare, Office of Education. vi + 35 pp., tables.
  1966 Church and state in Italian education. New York: Columbia University, Ph.D. dissertation. 324 pp.
    Author defends religious instruction in schools as part of European tradition. Period 1859 to 1960's covered.

NETHERLANDS

Weeren, Donald
  1967 Historical and contemporary aspects of inter-religious relations in Dutch education and society. Ph.D. dissertation. Teachers College, Columbia University.

NORWAY

Huus, Helen
  1960 The education of children and youth in Norway. Foreword by Olav Hove. Preface by William H. E. Johnson. Pittsburgh: University of Pittsburgh Press. xxiii + 247 pp., apps., biblio., index, tables.
    A review of educational organization, education at the preschool, elementary, secondary, teacher education and postelementary but non-secondary levels; teacher education.
Jonassen, Christen
  1968 Community conflict in school district reorganization: a cross-cultural study. Oslo: Universitetsforlaget. 132 pp.
Norsk Laererskolelag
  1965 *Norsk laererutdanning: reform og forsøk.* Redaksjon: Einer Ness, ed. Oslo: Johan Gruntd Tanum, 36 pp.
    A review of teacher training in Norway.

Norsk Lektolag Gymnaskomitéen
   1967 *Videregáende allmenndannende skoler. 2-árige skoler med linjedeling. Uttalelse fra arbeidsutvalget. Norsk Lektorlags gymnaskomité.* Oslo: Cappelen. 44 pp., tables.
      A review of Norwegian regular and vocational education.
Radick, Carol
   1969 American and Norwegian education: a value comparison. Peabody Journal of Education 46:227–230.
Sirevag, Tonnes
   1966 Ten years of Norwegian school experimentation. International Review of Education 12:1–15.
Wiley, George M.
   1955 The organization and administration of the educational system of Norway. Foreword by Einar Boyeson. Oslo: Royal Norwegian Ministry of Foreign Affairs and Royal Norwegian Ministry of Church and Education. 276 pp.
      A study of formal structure.

POLAND

Apanasewicz, Nellie and William Medlin
   1959 Educational systems in Poland. Washington, D.C.: U.S. Department of Health, Education and Welfare, Office of Education. 32 pp., biblio.
Nowak, Stefan
   1962 Social attitudes of Warsaw students. Polish Sociologica Bulletin 1–2: 91–103.
Panstwowe Wydawntictwo Naukowse
   1962 Selected bibliography of Polish educational materials. Warsaw: Panstwowe Wydawnictwo Naukowe.
Pecherski, Mieczystaw
   1967 *Die Verwirklichung der Schulreform in Polen. Bildung und Erziehung* 20:31–43.
      A description of the complications of school reform in Poland.
Polny, Roman
   1968 *Über die Reform der allgemeinbildenden Mittelschule in der Volksrepublik Polen. Vergleichende Pädagogik* 4:25–42.
      A discussion of the reform of the universal middle schools in Poland.
Rosen, Seymour M. and Nellie Apanasewicz
   1964 Higher education in Poland. Washington, D.C.: U.S. Department of Health, Education and Welfare, Office of Education. 2 v., biblio., illus., map.
Singer, Gusta
   1965 Teacher education in a Communist state: Poland 1956–1961. New York: Bookman Associates. 282 pp., biblio.

RUMANIA

Braham, Randolph
   1963 Education in the Rumanian People's Republic. Washington, D.C.:

U.S. Department of Health, Education and Welfare, Office of Education. lx + 229 pp., biblio., diagrs., map, tables.

Grant, Nigel
1966 The changing school in Rumania. Comparative Education 2:167–179.

SCANDINAVIA

Dixon, Willis
1965 Society, schools and progress in Scandinavia. Elmsford, New York: Pergamon Press, Inc. 186 pp., biblio., index.

Sjostrand, Wilhelm
1967 Recent trends and developments in primary and secondary education in Scandinavia. International Review of Education 13:180–194.

SPAIN

Doherty, Ellen and George Male
1966 Education in Spain, Washington, D.C.: U.S. Department of Health, Education and Welfare, Office of Education. 36 pp., biblio.

Estarellas, Juan
1962 The education of Don Quixote. Comparative Education Review 6, no. 1:25–33.
The author describes the traditionalist, antiscientific, humanist education model in Spain. Neglect of primary schools is especially stressed.

SWEDEN

Bjerstedt, Ake
1968 Educational research in Sweden: some areas of current and potential development. International Review of Education 14:259–276.

Carle, Torbjorn, ed.
1966 Secondary education in Sweden. Trans. by Albert Read. Stockholm: National Board of Education. 104 pp.

Carlsson, Gosta and Bengt Gesser
1965 Universities as selecting and socializing agents: some recent Swedish data. *Acta Sociologica* 9:25–37.

Erickson, Herman
1966 Adult education and Swedish political leadership. International Review of Education 12:129–143.

Husén, Torsten
1962 Problems of differentiation in Swedish compulsory schooling. Stockholm: Svenska Bokförlaget. 63 pp., biblio., illus.

Marklund, Sixten and Pär Söderberg
1968 The Swedish comprehensive school. New York: Humanities Press. xxiii + 119 pp.

Orring, Jonas
1962 Comprehensive school and continuation schools in Sweden, a sum-

mary of the principal recommendations of the 1957 school commission. Trans. by Albert Read. Stockholm: Kungl. Ecklesiastik departementet. 154 pp., tables.

Paulston, Rolland
1966 The Swedish comprehensive school reform: a selected annotated bibliography. Comparative Education Review 10, no. 1:87–94.
1966 Swedish comprehensive school reform, 1918–1950: the period of formulation and adoption. New York: Columbia University. Ed.D. dissertation, 308 pp.

Education reform is represented as a reflection, particularly of post–World War II Swedish zeal for social change.

1968 Educational change in Sweden. Planning and accepting the comprehensive school reforms. Foreword by Torsten Husén. New York: Teachers College Press, Columbia University. x + 193 pp., apps., biblio., annotated biblio., apps., index.

Excellent study of reforms. 1918–1950. Annotated bibliography is especially useful.

TURKEY[2]

American Board Publications Department
1961 The report of the Turkish national commission on education. Istanbul: American Board Publications Department. (Study financed by the Ford Foundation.)

Athöv Türkkaya
1960 The faculty of political sciences of Ankara. Middle East Journal 14: 243–245.

Basgöz, I. and H. Wilson
1968 Educational problems in Turkey (1920–1940). Bloomington: Indiana University Uralic & Altaic Series No. 86.

Berkes, Fay K.
1960 The village institute movement of Turkey; an educational mobilization of society change. Ph.D. thesis. New York: Teachers College, Columbia University.

Davison, R. H.
1961 Westernized education in Ottoman Turkey. Middle East Journal 15: 289–301.

Eastmond, J. N.
1964a A comparison of education in Turkey and the U.S. Ankara: Ministry of Education (mimeo.)
1964b Educational attainment in Turkey. Ankara: Ministry of Education (mimeo.)
1964c School finance in Turkey. Ankara: Ministry of Education (mimeo.)

Erim, N.
1964 Problems of education, *in* Turkey, today and tomorrow. New York: Frederick A. Praeger, Inc. pp. 184–210.

[2] I am grateful to Peter Suzuki for most of the references on Turkey.

Fotos, E.
    1955 An appreciation of Turkish university life. Middle East Affairs 6:248–258.
Frey, F. W.
    1964 Education in Turkey. *In* Political Modernization in Japan and Turkey. R. E. Ward and D. A. Ruston, eds. Princeton: Princeton University Press. pp. 205–235.
Gündüzalp, Fuat
    1955 *Ogretmen meslek kitaplari kilavuzu* Istanbul: Maarif Basimevi.
Hekimgil, E.
    1959 Education in Turkey. Paper presented at the 22nd International Conference on Public Education. Geneva.
Karpat, K. H.
    1963 The people's houses in Turkey, establishment and growth. Middle East Journal 17:55–67.
Kasamias, A. M.
    1965 Social functions of the Turkish lise. USDHEW, Office of Education: Cooperative Research Project No. S-047. Washington: USGPO.
    1966 Education and the quest for modernity in Turkey. Chicago: University of Chicago Press. (Based on Ph.D. thesis on comparative education for the University of Wisconsin.)
          The most useful and up-to-date work on education in Turkey.
    1967 Potential elites in Turkey: exploring the values and attitudes of lise youth. Comparative Education Review, 11, no. 1:22–37.
Lilken, H. I.
    ·956 *L'enseignement et la recherche sociologique en Turquie*. Transactions of the Third World Congress of Sociology, VII. London: International Sociological Association, pp. 42–45.
Makal, M.
    1954 A village in Anatolia. London: Vallentine Press.
          Written by a schoolteacher.
Maynard, R. E.
    1961 The lise and its curriculum in the Turkish education system. Ph.D. dissertation, School of Education, University of Chicago.
Ministry of Education, Turkey
    1963 Report on developments in education during the 1962–1963 school year at the XXVIth Educational Conference, Geneva. Ankara: Ministry of Education.
Oguzkan, T.
    1955 Adult education in Turkey, Studies and Documents XIV. Paris: UNESCO.
Organization for Economic Cooperation and Development
    1965 Education and development. Country reports. The Mediterranean regional project: Turkey. Paris: OECD.
Ötuken, A.
    1950 General education and learning in Turkey. *Cultura Turcica* (Ankara) 2:5–27.
Ozdil, I.
    1950 Education in Turkey. Middle Eastern Affairs 10:285–290.

Pierce, J. E.
 1964 The Mosque school. *In* Life in a Turkish village. New York: Holt, Rinehart and Winston, Inc.
  See Chapter 9.
Reed, H. H.
 1955 Turkey's new Imam-Hatip schools. *Welt des Islams* 4:150–163. Discusses religious schools.
 1956– The faculty of divinity at Ankara. *Moslem World.* Pt I: 46:295–312;
 1957 Pt II: 47:22–35.
Robinson, R. D.
 1967 High-level manpower in economic development, the Turkish case. Harvard Middle Eastern Monograph Series. Cambridge: Harvard University Press. xiii + 134 pp.
Roos, Leslie L., Jr., and George Angell, Jr.
 1968 New teachers for Turkish villages: a military-sponsored educational program. The Journal of Developing Areas 2:519–531.
Roos, Leslie L., Jr., Noralou P. Roos, and Gary R. Field
 1968 Students and Politics in Turkey, Daedalus, 97:1:184–203.
Sassami, A. H. K.
 1952 Education in Turkey. Federal Security Administration. Washington, D.C.: U.S. Government Printing Office, Office of Education.
 1956 Recent trends in Turkish educational policies. School and Society 84:51–53.
Shor, F.
 1957 Robert College, Turkish gateway to the future. National Geographic Magazine 112:399–418.
Tuak, E. J. and A. R. Lanza
 1956 Business education in Turkey. Journal of Business Education 31:271–273; 355–357.
United States Department of Commerce
 1964 Bibliography of social science periodicals, monograph series: Turkey 1950–1962. U.S. Bureau of the Census. Foreign Demographic Analysis Division. National Science Foundation. Washington, D.C.: U.S. Government Printing Office. iv + 88 pp.
Verschoyle, T.
 1950 Education in Turkey. International Affairs 26:59–70.
Weiker, W.
 1962 Academic freedom and problems of higher education in Turkey. Middle East Journal 16:279–294.

USSR

Ablin, Fred, ed.
 1968 Contemporary Soviet education. Readings from Soviet sources selected from Soviet Education. Intro. by George S. Counts. White Plains, N.Y.: International Arts and Sciences Press. 305 pp.
  Discussion of formal education in the USSR. Emphasis on elementary and secondary education.

Anweiler, Oskar
    1968 *Die Sowjetpädagogik in der Welt von heute.* Heidelberg: Quelle &
        Meyer. 203 pp.
            A discussion of contemporary Soviet education.
Apanasewicz, Nellie and Seymour Rosen
    1964 Soviet education, a bibliography of English-language materials. Wash-
        ington, D.C.: U.S. Department of Health, Education and Welfare,
        Office of Education. vi + 42 pp.
Benton, William
    1966 The teachers and the taught in the USSR. Preface by J. W. Fulbright.
        New York: Atheneum Publishers, Inc. xiii + 174 pp., index.
            A review of lower school and higher education, educational television,
        the uses of film, propaganda in art, and other general topics.
Bereday, George Z., William Brickman, and Gerald Read, eds.
    1960 The changing Soviet school. Foreword by Herold Hunt. Cambridge:
        The Riverside Press. xvii + 514 pp., biblio., notes, index.
            A broad review of all aspects of Soviet education based on a tour
        of the USSR by a group of educators in 1958.
Bereday, George Z. and Jean Pennar, eds.
    1960 The politics of Soviet education. New York: Frederick A. Praeger, Inc.
        vi + 217 pp., notes, tables.
            Examines Soviet education since 1945 in a series of essays.
Brown, Donald, ed.
    1968 The role and status of women in the Soviet Union. New York: Teach-
        ers College Press, Columbia University. xii + 139 pp.
Chauncey, Henry, ed.
    1968 Soviet preschool education. I: program of instruction. II: theory and
        practice. New York: Holt, Rinehart and Winston, Inc. 182, 250 pp.
Cheselka, Andrew
    1968 The secondary school graduate explosion in the USSR, June 1966.
        Comparative Education Review 12, no. 1:76–79.
Grant, Nigel
    1964 Soviet education. Baltimore: Penguin Books. 188 pp., biblio., map.
Hechinger, Fred
    1959 The big red schoolhouse. Intro. by Paul Woodring. New York: Double-
        day & Company, Inc. 240 pp.
Johnson, William H. E.
    1969 Russia's educational heritage. Intro. by George S. Counts. New York:
    (1950) Octagon Books. xvi + 351 pp., apps., biblio., index, notes, tables.
            A detailed review of Russian education from 1700–1917 and its
        influence on contemporary Soviet education.
Katterle, Zeno B.
    1965 Schools in the Soviet. Foreword by Martin Essex. Washington, D.C.:
        American Association of School Administrators. 72 pp., tables.
            A review of the structure of Soviet education.
King, Edmund, ed.
    1963 Communist education. London: Methuen. xii + 309 pp., biblio.,
        biblio. foot., diagrs.

Lipset, Harry
  1968 Education of Moslems in Tsarist and Soviet Russia. Comparative Education Review 12, no. 3:310–322.
    Author examines the advances of Moslem populations under the Soviet regime in contrast to situation of other minorities such as the Jews.
Mickiewicz, Ellen
  1967 Soviet political schools: the Communist Party adult instruction system. New Haven: Yale University Press. ix + 190 pp.
Noah, Harold
  1966 Financing Soviet schools. New York: Teachers College Press, Columbia University. xxi + 294 pp.
Rosen, Seymour
  1963 Higher education in the USSR, curriculum, schools, and statistics. Washington, D.C.: U.S. Department of Health, Education and Welfare, Office of Education. ix + 195 pp., biblio. foot., illus., map, tables.
  1965a Part-time education in the USSR; evening and correspondence study. Washington, D.C.: U.S. Department of Health, Education and Welfare, Office of Education. x + 141 pp., biblio., illus.
  1965b Significant aspects of Soviet education. Washington, D.C.: U.S. Department of Health, Education and Welfare, Office of Education. v + 22 pp.
Rudman, Herbert
  1967 The school and the state in the USSR. New York: Crowell Collier and Macmillan, Inc. xviii + 286 pp.
Shapovalenko, S. G., ed.
  1963 Polytechnical education in the USSR. Paris: UNESCO. 443 pp., biblio., illus.
Shimoniak, Wasyl
  1963 A study of Soviet policies in Uzbekistan and their implications for educational and social change. Ann Arbor: University of Michigan. Ph.D dissertation. 415 pp.
    Basic and far-reaching social changes through education are discussed.
Yanowitch, Murray and Norton Dodge
  1968 Social class and education: Soviet findings and reactions. Comparative Education Review 12, no. 3:248–267.
    A discussion of recent Soviet research showing substantial influence of status and occupation of parents on children's chances for higher education.

UNITED KINGDOM

Anonymous
  1967 Primary education in Wales (The Gittins Report). London: HMSO.
Armytage, Walter
  1964 Four hundred years of English education. Cambridge: Cambridge University Press. xiii + 353 pp., biblio. notes.
  1967 The American influence on English education. London: Routledge and Kegan Paul, Ltd. x + 118 pp., biblio

1968 The French influence on English education. London: Routledge and Kegan Paul, Ltd. xiii + 114 pp.

1969 The German influence on English education. London: Routledge and Kegan Paul, Ltd. xi + 131 pp.

Bamford, T. W.

1967 The rise of the public schools: a study of boys' boarding schools in England and Wales from 1837 to the present day. London: Thomas Nelson. xv + 349 pp., biblio. foot., diagrs., tables.

Baron, George

1965a A bibliographical guide to the English educational system. London: The Athlone Press, University of London. 124 pp.

1965b Society, schools and progress in England. Elmsford, N.Y.: Pergamon Press, Inc. xviii + 228 pp., biblio.

Beasley, Kenneth

1966 London eliminates the 11+: the transfer document becomes the basis for secondary selection. Comparative Education Review 10, no. 1: 80–86.

A discussion of an important structural change in English school reform.

Berg, Leila

1968 Risinghill: death of a comprehensive school. Harmondsworth, England: Penguin Books Ltd. 287 pp., apps.

A moving account of resistance to change.

Campbell, Flann

1968 Latin and elite tradition in education. British Journal of Sociology 19: 308–325.

Cane, Brian

1967 Educational research in England and Wales. International Review of Education 13:152–161.

Carter, Michael

1962 Home, school and work; a study of the education and employment of young people in Britain. Elmsford, N.Y.: Pergamon Press, Inc. xi + 340 pp., tables.

1963 Education, employment, and leisure; a study of "ordinary" young people. New York: Crowell Collier and Macmillan, Inc. (abridgement of Carter, Michael 1962).

1966 Into work. Baltimore: Penguin Books, Inc. 239 pp., biblio. foot.

Carter's books deal with problems and plans of British young people who are seeking to use their education to gain employment.

Central Advisory Council for Education

1947 School and life, a first inquiry into the transition from school to independent life; report. London: HMSO. 115 pp., illus.

1954 Early leaving; report. London: HMSO. xii + 99 pp., forms, tables.

1959–

1960 15 to 18, a report. London: HMSO, 2 vols.

1963 Half our future. (The Newsom Report). London: HMSO.

1967 Children and their primary schools: a report of the Central Advisory Council for Education. London: HMSO. 2 vols.

These reports are the core of criticism and reform of the English education system with an emphasis on a shift from elitism and more attention to problems of school leavers and young people who go to work rather than on to more education.

Eggleston, S. John
1967 Some environmental correlates of extended secondary education in England. Comparative Education 3:85–99.

Floud, Jean, A. H. Halsey, and F. M. Martin
1956 Social class and educational opportunity. London: William Heinemann, Ltd. xix + 152 pp., biblio. foot., diagrs., tables.

Halmos, Paul, ed.
1963 Sociological studies in British university education. Keele: University of Keele. 204 pp., biblio. notes.

Hargreaves, David
1967 Social relations in a secondary school. London: Routledge & Kegan Paul, Ltd. New York: Humanities Press. xii + 226 pp., biblio., diagrs., tables.

Hunter, S. Leslie
1968 The Scottish educational system. Elmsford, N.Y.: Pergamon Press, Inc. xiii + 269 pp., illus.

Jackson, Brian
1964 Streaming: an educational system in miniature. London: Routledge and Kegan Paul, Ltd. New York: Humanities Press. ix + 156 pp., biblio.

Jones, R. Brinley
1968 Language and society in Wales. Comparative Education 4, no. 3: 205–211.

Jones, W. R.
1966 Bilingualism in Welsh education. Cardiff: University of Wales Press. Examination of a critical issue in Welsh education and national identification.

Kalton, Graham
1966 The public schools: a factual survey of headmasters' conference schools in England and Wales. London: Longmans, Green & Co., Ltd. xxxii + 179 pp.

Kasper, Hildegard
1967 *Die englische Grundschule: Neue Aspekte im Plowden Report. Zeitschrift für Pädagogik* 13:474–490.
An analysis of a basic reform report on British education.

Kazamias, Andreas
1966 Politics, society and secondary education in England. Philadelphia: University of Pennsylvania Press. 381 pp., biblio. ref. in notes.

Koerner, James
1968 Reform in education; England and the United States. New York: Delacorte Press. xix + 332 pp., biblio. ref. in notes.

Miller, Trevor
1961 Values in the comprehensive school: an experimental study. Edinburgh: Oliver and Boyd for the University of Birmingham, Institute of Education. 118 pp., biblio., illus.

Osborne, G. S.
1967 Scottish and English schools: a comparative study of the past fifty

years. Pittsburgh: University of Pittsburgh Press. 351 pp.

Passow, A. Harry

   1962 After Crowther—what? Comparative Education Review 5, no. 3:
         175–181.
         A description of the British Government's action and inaction on
         the recommendation (increase in age of compulsory school attendance,
         establishment of county colleges, and compulsory educational oppor-
         tunities for school-leavers) of the Crowther Report (Ministry of Edu-
         cation, Central Advisory Council for Education (England), 15 to 18.
         2 vols. London: HMSO: 1959, 1960).

Roberts, K.

   1968 The organization of education and the ambitions of school-leavers: a
         comparative review. Comparative Education 4, no. 2:87–96.

Sugarman, B. N.

   1966 Social class and values as related to achievement and conduct in school.
         Sociological Review 14:287–301.
         Focus on London.

Tajfel, Henri and John Dawson, eds.

   1965 Disappointed guests; essays by African, Asian, and West Indian stu-
         dents. New York: Oxford University Press. 158 pp., biblio.
         Highly critical comments on English society and education by
         Commonwealth students.

Vaizey, John E.

   1966 Education for tomorrow. Baltimore: Penguin Books, Inc. 121 pp.
         A review of the state of British education in the 1960s.

ᵀeness, Thelma

   1962 School-leavers; their aspirations and expectations. Foreword by C. A.
         Mace. London: William Heinemann, Ltd. 252 pp.

Wales University College

   1960 (Llyfryddiaeth) Dwyietheg. bilingualism; a bibliography with special
         reference to Wales. Aberystwyth: Jac I. Williams. 55 pp.

Weinberg, Ian

   1967 The English public schools: the sociology of elite education. New
         York: Atherton Press, Inc. xix + 225 pp.

Willey, Frederick T.

   1964 Education today and tomorrow. London: Michael Joseph, Ltd. 189 pp.
         A review of the current issues in British educational reform.

Wilson, John

   1962 Public schools and private practice. London: George Allen & Unwin,
         Ltd. 142 pp.
         The author examines the public and private aspects of British private
         schools. The elements in their "community," and their future role.

YUGOSLAVIA

David, Marcel

   1962 Adult education in Yugoslavia. Paris: UNESCO. 185 pp., biblio. foot.,
         tables

NORTH AMERICA

CANADA

Cheal, John E.
1962 Factors related to educational output differences among the Canadian provinces. Comparative Education Review 6, no. 2:120–126.
Review of considerable differences in educational situations in Canadian provinces.
Hobart, C. W. and C. S. Brant
1966 Eskimo education, Danish and Canadian: a comparison. Canadian Review of Sociology and Anthropology 3:47–66.
King, A. Richard
1967 The school at Mopass: a problem of identity. New York: Holt, Rinehart and Winston, Inc. xii + 96 pp.
A critical study of Indian education in one Canadian school.
King, A. J. C.
1968 Ethnicity and school adjustment. Canadian Review of Sociology and Anthropology 5:84–91.
Krukowski, T.
1968 Canadian private ethnic schools. Comparative Education 4, no. 3: 199–204.
Lawson, Robert
1967 A critical survey of education in western Canada. Comparative Education 4, no. 1:9–22.
Lupul, M. R.
1967 Education in western Canada. Comparative Education Review XI, no. 2:144–159.
Nash, Paul
1961 Quality and equality in Canadian education. Comparative Education Review 5, no. 2:118–129.
Conflicts in models (European, British, American), French-English problems, and elitist-egalitarian differences in educational goals are reviewed.
Rohner, Ronald P.
1965 Factors influencing the academic performance of Kwakiutl children in Canada. Comparative Education Review 9:331–340.
Sindell, Peter S.
1968 Some discontinuities in the enculturation of Mistassini Cree children. *In* Problems of developmental change among the Cree, Norman A. Chance, ed. Ottawa: Canadian Research Centre for Anthropology: 83–92.
Wintrob, Ronald M. and Peter S. Sindell
1968 Education and identity conflict among Cree Indian youth. A preliminary report, annex 3 of the final report, McGill Cree project. Ottawa: Rural Development Branch, Department of Regional Economic Expansion.

GREENLAND

Hobart, Charles
  1968 The influence of the school on acculturation with special reference to
       Greenland. The Journal of Educational Thought 2:97–116.

UNITED STATES

Barker, Roger G. and Paul Gump et al.
  1964 Big school, small school: high school size and student behavior. Stan-
       ford, Cal.: Stanford University Press. vii + 250 pp., biblio., diagrs.,
       tables.
Beals, Ralph and Norman D. Humphrey
  1957 No frontiers to learning: the Mexican student in the United States.
       Asst. by Ralph Arellano, Agnes Babcock, and Louis Stone. Foreword
       by Ralph Beals. Preface by Ralph Beals. Minneapolis: The University
       of Minnesota Press. xi + 148 pp., app., index.
       A study of Mexican college students in the U.S. with attention
       to their home lives, adaptations to the U.S. and American colleges,
       students' reactions and opinions, and a final chapter analyzing the
       current and future situations.
Bennett, John W., Herbert Passin, and Robert K. McKnight
  1958 In search of identity the Japanese overseas scholar in America and
       Japan. Foreword by Ralph L. Beals. Minneapolis: The University of
       Minnesota Press. x + 369 pp., apps., biblio., biblio. in notes, figs.,
       illus., index.
       An examination of the roles and adjustment problems of Japanese
       scholars in the U.S. and the returned student-scholar in Japan.
Benson, Charles
  1965 The cheerful prospect: a statement on the future of American educa-
       tion. Boston: Houghton Mifflin Co., Inc. 134 pp., index.
       A critical analysis of financing of American education, federal and
       state. Author suggests ways to utilize existing resources more effectively.
Bereiter, Carl and Siegfried Englemann
  1966 Teaching disadvantaged children in the preschool. Englewood Cliffs,
       N.J.: Prentice-Hall, Inc. 312 pp., biblio. foot., illus.
Boles, Donald E.
  1961 The Bible, religion, and the public schools. Ames, Iowa: Iowa State
       University Press. ix + 308 pp., biblio., index.
       An analysis of religious instruction in public schools with an empha-
       sis on issues surrounding Bible reading.
Brown, B. Frank
  1963 The nongraded high school. Englewood Cliffs, N.J.: Prentice-Hall,
       Inc. 223 pp.
       A case study of the Melbourne High School in Melbourne, Florida.
  1968 Education by appointment new approaches to independent study
       West Nyack, N.Y.: Parker Publishing Company. 175 pp., index.
       A discussion of the background of independent study concepts and
       their applicability to high schools in the United States.

Burnett, Jacquetta Hill
1969 Ceremony, rites and economy in the student system of an American high school. Human Organization 28:1–10.
Forthcoming
Pattern and process in student life: a study of custom and social relationship among the students in an American high school. New York: Teachers College Press, Columbia University.
Callahan, R. E.
1962 Education and the cult of efficiency: a study of the social forces that have shaped the administration of the public schools. Chicago: The University of Chicago Press. x + 273 pp., biblio. foot.
Clifford, Virginia
1964 Urban education; an introduction to the literature of research and experimentation. New York: Urban Education Collection, Auburn University Library, Union Theological Seminary. v + 277 pp. + 32 pp. (biblio.)
Cohen, Sol
1964 Progressives and urban school reforms: the Public Education Association of New York City 1895–1954. New York: Bureau of Publications, Teachers College, Columbia University. xi + 273 pp., biblio. in notes, index.
A historical study of a leading association in school reform in New York City.
Coleman, James S.
1965 Adolescents and the schools. New York: Basic Books, Inc. xi + 121 pp., index.
A comment on American precollege education with special attention to style and substance of education, financing, athletic programs, and congruence between society and education.
1966 Equality of educational opportunity. summary report. Washington, D.C.: U.S. Department of Health, Education and Welfare, Office of Education. v + 33 pp., illus.
A summary of the influential report about failure of the United States to provide Black citizens with equality of educational opportunity.
Conant, James
1961 Slums and suburbs: a commentary on schools in metropolitan areas. New York: McGraw-Hill, Inc. viii + 147 pp., tables.
The contrasts between suburban pushing of children beyond their capacities and slum absence of facilities are painted in this influential book.
1964 Shaping educational policy. New York: McGraw-Hill Inc. 139 pp., index.
Emphasis: the United States with case studies of California and New York.
1967 The comprehensive high school: a second report to interested citizens. New York: McGraw-Hill, Inc. vi + 95 pp., app., tables.
A discussion, based on the author's expertise and data collected on

the basis of questionnaires, on the present status and useful role of comprehensive high schools.

Covello, Leonhard
1967 The social background of the Italo-American school child: a study of the Southern Italian family mores and their effect on the school situation in Italy and America. Leiden: E. J. Brill N. V. 488 pp.

Cramer, M. Richard, E. Q. Campbell, and C. E. Bowerman
1966 Social factors in educational achievement and aspirations among Negro adolescents. Vol. I: demographic study. Vol. II: survey study. Chapel Hill: University of North Carolina Press. charts, tables.
A publication of part of a series of the Institute for Research in social science, University of North Carolina.

Cremin, Lawrence
1964 The transformation of the school; progressivism in American education, 1876–1957. New York: Random House, Inc. (Vintage Books). 387 pp.

Dennison, George
1969 The lives of children. the story of the First Street School. New York: Random House, Inc. 320 pp.
An account of an experimental New York City school for "problem" children. Discusses role of very small school (in terms of staff, space, and students) in urban education.

Dentler, Robert, Bernard Meckler, and Mary Ellen Warshauer, eds.
1967 The urban R's; race relations as the problem in urban education. New York: Frederick A. Praeger, Inc., for the Center for Urban Education. xii + 304 pp., biblio.

Deutsch, Martin et al.
1964 Communication of information in the elementary school classroom. New York: Institute for Developmental Studies, Department of Psychiatry, New York Medical College. ix + 228, 112, biblio.
1967 The disadvantaged child; selected papers of Martin Deutsch and associates. New York: Basic Books, Inc. xii + 400 pp., biblio.

Eddy, Elizabeth M.
1967 Walk the white line: a profile of urban education. New York: Frederick A. Praeger, Inc. xii + 187 pp., app., biblio.
An examination of relationships between formal educational networks and efforts to educate children of the urban poor in the United States. The author examines in depth nine schools in one city.

Eells, Walter Crosby
1959 American dissertations on foreign education; doctor's dissertations and master's theses written at American universities and colleges concerning education or educators in foreign countries and education of groups of foreign birth or ancestry in the United States, 1884–1958. Washington, D.C.: National Education Association of the United States. xxxix + 300 pp.

Endres, Raymond
1967 Elementary school functions in the United States: an historical analysis. *Paedagogica Historica* 7:378–416.

Fantini, Mario and Gerald Weinstein
 1962 The disadvantaged: challenge to education. New York: Harper & Row, Publishers, Inc. xvi + 455 pp., biblio. foot., illus.
Friedenberg, Edgar Z.
 1965 The dignity of youth and other atavisms. Boston: The Beacon Press. 254 pp.
   Critical essays and book reviews by an author who seriously attacks most education in the United States.
Froese, Leonhard, ed.
 1968 *Aktuelle Bildunskritik und Bildunsreform in den U.S.A.* Heidelberg: Quelle & Meyer. 256 pp.
Frost, Joe L. and Glenn R. Hawkes, eds.
 1966 The disadvantaged child: issues and innovations. Foreword by Samuel A. Kirk. Boston: Houghton Mifflin Company.
   A selection of articles concerning the identity of the disadvantaged; their characteristics; issues surrounding questions of intelligence and its measurements; the education of young and older children; and possible resolution of problems through teaching skills, training teachers, and assistance of and from individuals, families, and communities.
Freund, Paul and Robert Ulich
 1965 Religion and the public schools. the legal issue. Paul A. Freund. the educational issue. Robert Ulich. Cambridge: Harvard University Press. 54 pp.
   The Burton lecture and the Inglis lecture. General discussions of the problems inherent in attempting to present intellectual heritages in a secular setting. Focus: the United States.
Fuchs, Estelle
 1966 Pickets at the gates. New York: Free Press. x + 205 pp., biblio.
   A study of a crisis in a ghetto school and the reactions of the administration, staff, and parents, as well as the pupils. The author examines the school shutdown in New York City as a specific example of widespread trends in American urban education.
 1969 Teachers talk; views from inside city schools. New York: Doubleday and Company (Anchor Books). xiv + 224 pp., biblio. foot.
   An anthropological presentation of young teachers' culture shock in ghetto schools.
Gittell, Marilyn, ed.
 1967 Educating an urban population. Beverly Hills, Cal.: Sage Publications. 320 pp.
   Selections on the present urban problems in education, case studies on educational decision making, and possible approaches to change.
Goodman, Paul
 1960 Growing up absurd; problems of youth in organized systems. New York: Random House, Inc. 296 pp.
   A generally critical work on American adolescents.
 1967 Discussion: the education industries. Harvard Educational Review 37, no. 1:107–110.
   Comments on subordination of educational institutions to commercial purposes.

Goold, G. Howard
    1967 Discussion: the education industries. Harvard Educational Review 37,
        no. 1:116–119.
        Part of a discussion of the relationships between education-oriented
        industries and their influence on American education.

Gordon, Edmund and Doxey Wilkerson
    1966 Compensatory education for the disadvantaged; programs and prac-
        tices, preschool through college. New York: College Entrance Ex-
        amination Board. 299 pp., biblio.

Greene, Mary and Orletta Ryan
    1965 The school children; growing up in the slums. New York: Pantheon
        Books, Inc. 227 pp.

Greene, Maxine
    1965 The public school and the private vision. search for America in educa-
        tion and literature. New York: Random House, Inc. 183 pp., biblio.,
        index.
        An analysis of the nineteenth-century arguments for free, public
        education in literature in the United States. Authors such as Haw-
        thorne and Thoreau are discussed in this context.

Havighurst, Robert J.
    1964 The public schools of Chicago; a survey for the Board of Education of
        the City of Chicago. Chicago: Board of Education. x + 499 pp., illus.,
        maps.
——————, Maria Dubois, M. Csikszentmihalyi, and R. Doll
    1965 A cross-national study of Buenos Aires and Chicago adolescents. New
        York: S. Karger. *Bibliotheca Vita Humana.* 80 pp., tables.
        Data obtained from several different instruments about adolescent
        attitudes and aspirations are compared.

Herndon, James
    1968 The way it spozed to be. New York: Simon and Schuster, Inc. 188 pp.
        Author's teaching experiences in George Washington Junior High
        School in Oakland, Cal., primarily among Black students.

Holt, John
    1964 How children fail. New York: Dell Publishing Co., Inc. xv + 181 pp.
    1967 How children learn. New York: Pitman Publishing Corp. x + 189 pp.
    1969 The underachieving school. New York: Pitman Publishing Corp. ix +
        209 pp., biblio.
        A former schoolteacher's indictment of largely Black urban schools.

Keach, Everett T., Robert Fulton, and William E. Gardner, eds.
    1967 Education and social crisis perspectives on teaching disadvantaged
        youth. New York: John Wiley & Sons, Inc. xiii + 413 pp.
        A collection of essays on general topics of the disadvantaged youth's
        cultural values and family life, sources of the disadvantaged youth's
        problems in schools, and suggested remedies for these situations. Em-
        phasis is on the United States.

Keppel, Francis
    1965 The necessary revolution in American education. New York: Harper &
        Row, Publishers, Inc. xiv + 201 pp., app., index, tables.

A historical analysis of significant changes in American educational expectations and practice, the present situation, and requisite changes to make expectations and practice congruent. Emphasis is on pre-college education.

Kimball, Solon and James McClellan, Jr.
1962 Education and the new America. New York: Random House, Inc. xiv + 402 pp., biblio., index.
"Notes and references" section is useful. A historical, anthropological, and sociological analysis of the functions of American education.

King, Edmund
1965 Society, schools and progress in the U.S.A. Elmsford, N.Y.: Pergamon Press, Inc. 236 pp.

Kohl, Herbert
1967a 36 children. illus. by Robert G. Jackson, III. New York: New American Library, Inc. 227 pp.
Concentrates on Black children in a ghetto school in Harlem.
1967b Teaching the unteachable, the story of an experiment in children's writing. intro. by John Holt. New York: New York Review of Books. 63 pp., illus.

Krug, Edward A.
1964 The shaping of the American high school. Intro. by John Guy Fowles. New York: Harper & Row, Publishers, Inc. xvii + 486 pp., biblio., index.
Concentrates on the development of the American high school in the period 1880–1920.

Landes, Ruth
1965 Culture in American education: anthropological approaches to minority and dominant groups in the schools. New York: John Wiley & Sons, Inc. vi + 330 pp., app., biblio., index.
A description of a teacher-training project at Claremont. Landes argues that California is a microcosm of American social and educational development.

Leacock, Eleanor B.
1970 Teaching and learning in city schools: a comparative study. New York: Basic Books, Inc.
Students and teachers in classrooms in two middle-class and two low-income schools compared through observation.

McEvoy, James and Abraham Miller, eds.
1969 Black power and student rebellion. Belmont, Cal.: Wadsworth Publishing Co. xiii + 440 pp.
A collection of articles and analyses of Black-power efforts on various American universities.

Meranto, Philip
1967 The politics of federal aid to education in 1965: a study in political innovation. Foreword by Alan K. Campbell. Syracuse: Syracuse University Press. xiii + 144 pp., app., figs., index, tables.
A study of the shift in attitudes toward Federal aid to education, political and pressure groups, and changes within the political system, esp. in the House of Representatives

Minuchin, Patricia, Barbara Biber, Edna Shapiro, and Herbert Zimiles
1969 The psychological impact of school experience. New York: Basic Books, Inc.
   Comparative study of four urban schools with "modern" or "traditionalist" orientations.

Mitsuhashi, Setsuko
1962 Conceptions and images of the physical world: a comparison of Japanese and American pupils. Comparative Education Review 6, no. 2: 142–147.
   Author describes a cross-cultural test in which Japanese children scored much higher than American students. Some reasons for the differences are suggested.

Modill, Mary, Arthur Stinchcome, and Dollie Walker
1968 Segregation and educational disadvantage: estimates of the influence of different segregating factors. Sociology of Education 41, no. 3: 239–246.
   Focus: Baltimore, Md. school system. Authors conclude that private-public, city-suburban distinctions are primary factors in segregation which in turn affects academic performance of Black youth.

Morris, Richard T.
1960 The two-way mirror: national status in foreign students' adjustment. Assted. Oluf M. Davidsen. Foreword by Ralph L. Beals. Minneapolis: The University of Minnesota Press. xii + 215 pp., apps., index, tables.
   An attempt to relate adjustment of foreign students in the United States to a number of factors involved in students' self-conceptions, conceptions of other people's feelings about countries of origin, and so on.

Moskow, Michael H.
1966 Teachers and unions: the applicability of collective bargaining to public education. Foreword by Herbert R. Northrup. Philadelphia: University of Pennsylvania Press. xiii + 288 pp., biblio., index, tables.
   Focus is on teachers at the elementary and secondary levels. The author concentrates on the appropriateness and uses of collective bargaining for teachers in public schools.

Neuwien, Reginald A., ed.
1966 Catholic schools in action: a report. The Notre Dame study of Catholic elementary and secondary schools in the United States. Preface by Theodore M. Hesburgh. Notre Dame, Ind.: University of Notre Dame Press. xv + 328 pp., app., tables.
   A thorough look at enrollment, staff, goals, religious teaching, religious understanding, and student-attitude indexes, student opinions, and Catholic parents' attitudes and evaluations of Catholic schools.

Newmann, Fred and Donald Oliver
1967 Education and community. Harvard Educational Review 37, no. 1: 61–106.

Nichols, Robert
1968 U.S. Commission on Civil Rights, racial isolation in the public schools. Book review. American Educational Research Journal 5, no. 4: 700–707.

Park, Joseph, ed.

1965 The rise of American education: an annotated bibliography. Evanston: Northwestern University Press. xi + 216 pp.

Eleven sections including: textbooks; European backgrounds; studies in the development of American education; histories in higher education; elementary and secondary education; higher education; biographies, fiction, and journals; contemporary issues and movements in American education; American Antiquarian Society microprints; doctoral dissertations available on microfilm; guide to sources in history and education.

Passow, A. Harry, ed.

1963 Education in depressed areas; papers. New York: Bureau of Publications, Teachers College, Columbia University. xii + 359 pp., biblios., tables.

Powledge, Fred

1967 To change a child: a report on the Institute for Development Studies. Preface by Martin Deutsch. Chicago: Quadrangle Books, published in cooperation with the Anti-Defamation League of B'nai B'rith. vii + 110 pp., illus.

A study of the enrichment programs in the Institute for Development Studies. New York City.

Reissman, Frank

1962 The culturally deprived child. Foreword by Goodwin Watson. New York: Harper & Row, Publishers, Inc. xv + 140 pp., biblio., index.

Focus is on deprived children in the United States.

Sanford, Nevitt, ed.

1962 The American college: a psychological and social interpretation of the higher learning. Foreword by Morton Deutsch. xvi + 1084 pp., indexes.

Literature references are especially useful. A series of articles on topics such as changes in students as a result of college experiences, the various social relationships in colleges, and so on.

Schrag, Peter

1967 Village school downtown; politics and education; a Boston report. Boston: The Beacon Press. 191 pp.

Selltiz, Claire, June Christ, Joan Havel, and Stuart Cook

1963 Attitudes and social relations of foreign students in the United States. Foreword by Ralph Beals. Minneapolis: University of Minnesota Press. xiv + 434 pp., app., biblio., index, tables.

A study of foreign students' characteristics, social relations, adjustments, and attitudinal transformations in the United States while studying at the university level.

Sizer, Theodore

1964 Secondary schools at the turn of the century. New Haven: Yale University Press. xiv + 304 pp., apps., biblio., index.

A study of the causes and effects of the 1894 Report of the Committee on Secondary School Studies.

Trent, James W. and Jenette Golds

1967 Catholics in college: religious commitmenc and the intellectual life.

Foreword by John Tracy Ellis. Chicago: The University of Chicago Press. xiv + 366 pp., apps., biblio. in ref., index.

A discussion of Catholics' present and potential roles in colleges during a period of rapid change within the church, colleges, and society.

Useem, John and Ruth Hill Useem

1968 American-educated Indians and Americans in India: a comparison of two modernizing roles. Journal of Social Issues 24, no. 4:143–158.

Examination of implications of changes in this increasing exchange: shifts from missionaries to business and government employees among Americans and gradual shift to more senior Indians going to the U.S. Functions of both groups in modernizing processes are described.

U.S. Commission on Civil Rights

1967 Racial isolation in the public schools. Washington, D.C.: U.S. Government Printing Office.

Vol. 1, 276 + xi pp.

Vol. 2 (appendices), 293 + iii pp.

U.S. Senate Special Subcommittee in Indian Education

1967–

1969 Hearings before the Special Subcommittee on Indian Education of the Committee on Labor and Public Welfare, United States Senate, Ninetieth Congress, Ninety-First Congress.

Hearings, December 14, 1967–October 1, 1968 five parts, 2371 pp. Hearings in 1969 + appendix, 1706 pp. (entitled Indian education, 1969)

The education of American Indians; a survey of the literature. (February, 1969.) Brewton Berry. Foreword by Senator Ralph Yarborough. vii + 121 pp.

These volumes provide reprints, bibliography, testimony, and data that are exhaustive on the subject to date.

Watts, William A. and David Whittaker

1968 Profile of a nonconformist youth culture: a study of the Berkeley nonstudents. Sociology of Education 41, no. 2:178–200.

Abilities of nonstudents, concepts of their roles and roles of educational institutions, and roles in political action examined.

Wax, Murray, Rosalie H. Wax, and Robert V. Dumont, Jr.

1964 Formal education in an American Indian community. with assistance of Roselyn Holyrock and Gerald Onefeather. Supplement to Social Problems 11, no. 4. 126 pp., app.

An excellent study among the Dakota (Oglala Sioux) on Pine Ridge Reservation, South Dakota.

Wax, Rosalie H.

1967 The warrior dropouts. Transaction IV:40–46.

Especially useful for examining term "dropout" with reference to education of minorities in U.S. schools.

Wise, Arthur E.

1968 Rich schools, poor schools: the promise of equal educational opportunity. Chicago: The University of Chicago Press. xiv + 228 pp., biblios., index, index of (court) cases, tables.

An examination of the implications of recent U.S. court decisions on equality of opportunity in schooling.

PACIFIC AREA

AUSTRALIA

Ancich, Mary, R. W. Connell, J. A. Fisher, and Maureen Kolff, comps.
　1969 A descriptive bibliography of published research and writing on social stratification in Australia, 1946–1967.
　　Pp. 69–73 (entries on education) are especially relevant.
Australian Council for Education Research
　　Review of education in Australia. Melbourne: Melbourne University Press. In association with Oxford University Press.
　　1939—annual. This review includes a bibliography of educational reports and studies in Australia.
Biddle, Ellen and Hazel Smith
　1968 Educational standard of people of aboriginal descent living in the Brisbane metropolitan area. The Australian Journal of Social Issues 3, no. 4:13–25.
Bowden, Lord
　1965 The place of universities in modern society. Comparative Education 1, no. 2:45–62.
Bridges, Barry
　1968 Educational policy for aborigines. The Australian Journal of Social Issues 3, no. 4:26–32.
Cole, Percival, ed.
　1935 The education of the adolescent in Australia. Melbourne: Melbourne University Press. xii + 352 pp., index.
French, E. L., ed.
　1967 Melbourne studies in education: 1965. New York: Cambridge University Press. xv + 286 pp.
　1967 Melbourne studies in education: 1966. New York: Cambridge University Press. xvii + 264 pp.
Maclaine, A. G.
　1966 Educating the outback child in Australia. Comparative Education 3, no. 1:33–39.
Partridge, P. H.
　1968 Society, schools and progress in Australia. Elmsford, N.Y.: Pergamon Press, Inc. xvii + 246 pp.

MICRONESIA—PONAPE

Hughes, Daniel
　1969 Democracy in a traditional society: two hypotheses on role. American Anthropologist 71, no. 1:36–45.
Smith, Donald F.
　1968 Education of the Micronesian with emphasis on the historical develop-

ment. Washington, D.C.: The American University, Ed.D. dissertation. 328 pp.

A review of the policies and practices of Spain, Germany, Japan, and the United States in Micronesian education.

NEW GUINEA

Gibson, G. W.
  1968 A revolution in education: some aspects of bureaucracies, development and education. Comparative Education 4, no. 2:97–108.
Prince, J. R.
  1968 The effect of Western education on science conceptualization in New Guinea. The British Journal of Educational Psychology 38, no. 1:64–74.
Van Der Veur, Karol, and Penelope Richardson
  1966 Education through the eyes of an indigenous urban elite. Canberra: New Guinea Research Unit, Australian National Unit, Australian National University. iii + 99 pp., biblio., illus. (New Guinea Research Unit Bull. No. 12)

Index

abstract thinking ability, 74–77

acculturation, and rural-urban split, 317

achievement motivation, 68; cultural attitudes toward, 84–85; and independence training, 67

adaptation: and human world view, 93–94; and reform, 97; and social systems, 94–96

adaptation to cultural imperatives, 19–20

administration: attitude toward researchers, 104–106, 107; attitude toward small communities, 234; of high schools, 199–201; and teachers, 11

Amatenango, and education and national integration, 220–222

anthropologists: definition of national integration, 212; and educational research, 10, 12–14; role of, 230–231; and schools, *see* anthropology and education; and study of American society, 153; as teachers, 102

anthropology: compared with sociology, 153; and role of culture, 19*ff*

anthropology and education bibliography: on Asia, 349–355; on Europe, 355–372; general, 319–325; guide to, 308–311; on North America, 373–383; on Pacific area, 383–384; selection methods, 310–311; themes of, 311–318

Anthropology and education research, 98–99; and "assumption of dysfunction," 101; and attitudes toward statuses within schools, 101–103; benefits of, 111–115; and ethnography of schools, 144–149; explicating method, 110–111; and fieldwork, 99–100; and gaining entree and maintaining rapport, 104–106; prestige and status of, 108–110; problems and goals of, 103–104, 300–306; prospects for, 293–298; reporting findings of, 106–108; and small communities, 230–231; and treatment of schools as monolithic structures, 100–101

Anthropology Curriculum Study Project, 115

Australian aboriginal societies, 38

authority, legitimation of, 40–41

behavior: cultural patterning of, 20; and family-socialization, 26; of ghetto females, 278; human-animal comparisons of, 33; of Indian children, 254

bilingualism, 57; premature, 256; and school performance, 77–81

Black children, *see* culturally deprived; Potter, Rachel; Smith, David

books, attitudes toward, 72–73

Brookview school system: and Brookview community, 181–182; and control of school board, 189–190; and educational expansion, 192; and educational-political system, 188–189; effects of educational world on, 185–186; and political struggle, 194; and professional power versus local autonomy, 192–194; and relations with local community, 186; and religious influences, 187–188; and role of government, 191–192; and role of professional associations, 190–191; and social class influences, 187; tendencies in development of, 183–185; transactional model used for study of, 182–183

Bureau of Indian Affairs, 5, 232

bureaucracy, in schools, 146–147, 162

"bush" schools, 37–39

Caddo children, 261

Canada: local loyalties versus national loyalty in, 316–317; problems of minority education in; 315

Cantel, Guatemala: education and national integration study of, 222–224

Catholics, and Brookview school system, 181, 188

change: and anthropological educational research, 115; attitudes toward, 35; and concept of culture, 21; and educational research, 169; and reliance on education, 46

Cherokee Indian Baptist Church, 235

Cherokee Indian children, 46; educational problems of, 243–247; relationship of schools to, 235–239; *see also* eastern Oklahoma; education of American Indian children

art of teaching, 121–125; of Brookview school system, 184; and changes in generations, 164–166; and community culture, 15–17; and Dewey, 130–131; of folk Anglo-Saxons, 242; and integration, 168; and Jefferson, 129–130, 131, 132; of kibbutz, 21; need for, 163–164; of New York high school principals, 197–198, 204–207; and tasks of education, 166–167

educational research: and anthropologists, 10; and community study, 8–10; and data-collection procedures, 172–173; findings in lower-income, all-Black classroom, 176–177; findings in middle-income white classroom, 175–176; guidelines for, 170–172; methodological problems of, 169–170; and methods of analysis, 174–175; in middle-income Black school, 177–178; pseudoempirical, 8–10; and self-fulfilling prophecy concept, 171–172; and use of traditional field methods, 170

educational systems, *see* school systems

educational techniques, *see* instructional process

education compared with socialization, *see* socialization compared with education

education in complex society: and abstract thought, 74–77; approaches to, 67–68; and expectations of parents, 84–85; and language learning before school age, 77–82; and literacy, 68–74; and sex identity, 82–83

education of American Indian children: and conflict of values, 263–266; and duality of Indian life, 252–253; goals of, 268–269; and learning by looking, 256–259; and learning through language, 259–263; and patterns of socialization, 266–267; and research goals, 300–306; and styles of learning and cultural values, 267–269; and tests of learning prior to school entrance, 253–256; and "withdrawal" characteristics of Indian children, 9; and workshops for American Indian college students, 4–5

education of Negro children, purpose of study of, 273–274

education in United States: applicability to other countries, 13–14; and attitudes toward leisure, 160; and attitudes toward war, 158; and crisis, 156–157; and culturally deprived children, 161–162; in eastern Oklahoma, 243–247; and gross national product, 157–158; and historic necessity for stupidity, 158–159; methodological approach to problems of,

230–231; and occupational systems, 159–160; and "out of it" communities, 247–250; and political economy, 157; results of, 16; and vulnerability of educators, 160–161

educators: attitudes toward small communities, 234; and vacuum ideology, 6–7

elite: in Amatenango, 221; nation-oriented, 219; and society, 145; training of, *ix*

emotion, and socialization, 33

employment, in school systems, 146–148

enculturation, *see* cultural transmission

English-learning, 78–80

environment: and abstract thought, 74–77; and reading, 69–74

extrahousehold kinsmen, 26–27

family, and industrialization, 130–131

family learning, compared with outside learning, 35

family-socialization, 25–26

feedback, in school research reports, 106–107

field work, in anthropology of school research, 99–100, 112–113

figure matching tests, racial comparisons of, 254

flag, oath of allegiance to, 41

folk Anglo-Saxons: educational problems of, 231–234, 243–247; historic background of, 239–241

free drawing tests, 258

Gesell Developmental Scales, 253

ghetto children, *see* "culturally deprived"; Potter, Rachel; Smith, David

ghettos, compared with "out of it" communities, 247–250

government: and national integration, 223–224, 227–228; and school systems, 191–192

government programs: focus on schools, 145; in Oklahoma, 249–250; in Ozark region, 232

Grace Arthur General Nonverbal Intelligence Scale, 258

Grace Arthur Point Performance Scale, 263

grammar, competency for, 55

gross national product: and education, 157–158; and use of leisure time, 160

group pressures for conformity, 30–31

group relations, and national integration, 214–215

Guatemala, *see* Cantel

guilt, and socialization, 30–32

Guru, as teacher, 119–120

Gusii of Kenya: and parental control of

advantaged children, 55–65; present state of, 52–54

listening behavior, cultural influences on, 262

literacy, in primitive and complex societies, 68–74

Mandan-Hidatsa, 35

Manus-speaking people, 79n

mass education: and adult social roles, 133–135; concerns of, 131–133; development of concept of, 129–131; effects of, 149; and formation of a public, 135–143; origins of, 303

master-apprentice method, 119

Menomini, 20; communicative competence of, 54

Mesquakie Fox children, 59

Mexico, national integration in, 214–215, 217, 218; *see also* Amatenango

Mexican Revolution, 215, 218

middle class: of eastern Oklahoma, 246; and educational changes, 248; *see also* middle-class values

middle-class values: and lower-class children, 176; in school research, 114

minority education problems, 144–145; bibliography on, 314–315; *see also* culturally deprived; education of American Indian children; education of Negro children

models: of language structure, 52–53; for predicting school performance, 285–286; of societies, 136–137

modernization: and formation of elite, 219–220; and national integration, 208–209, 211; urban-rural differences in, 209–210; *see also* industrialization

modes of address, 57

monkeys, *see* nonhuman primate behavior studies

moral theory, and education, 140–141

mother: as teacher, 119; and use of guilt for socialization, 31–32

mother-infant relationship, and animal studies, 94

"nation-building," *see* national integration

national character, and schools, 151

national ideology, development of, 40–41, 211

national integration: and asymmetrical development, 210; "broker" concept of, 14–215, 216, 218; and Cherokees, 237–239; of closed corporate community and "open" community, 215–220; definitions of, 211–213; and eastern Oklahoma, 245–246; and education, 208–209, 211; effects of, 219–220; and

government support, 227–228; and institutions, 226–227; role of, 210–211; and Steward's theory of sociocultural levels, 213–214, 224–225

nature, attitudes of Indian children toward, 264–265

Navajo children, 260–261; and interpretation of photographs, 257

Negro children, education of, *see* education of Negro children

Neighborhood Youth Corps, in Ozark region, 232

New England, *see* Orchard Town Study

New York High School principals: attitudes toward culturally disadvantaged, 198; attitudes toward school crisis, 202–203; attitudes toward UFT, 198–199; backgrounds of, 196–197; and bureaucratization of school system, 199–201; as defenders of status quo, 195–196; and ideological defense of school system, 204–207; and middle-class model of education, 197–198; political activities of, 203; role of, 201–202

Nigerian elite, 312–313

nonhuman primate study: and human world view, 92–94; purposes of, 91–92; and social system as adaptive mechanism, 94–96

nonliterate societies: and education, 305–306; imitation learning in, 258–259

nonverbal classification test, 254–256

nonverbal development of Indian children, 254–256

Nyakyusa, and parental control of peer group behavior, 27–28

Ocean-Hill Brownsville, 250

Office of Economic Opportunity, 249

Oglala Sioux study: and attitudes of teachers and administrators toward Sioux society, 6–7, 8–9; background and hypotheses for, 4–6; and "cultural deprivation" theory, 15–16; design of, 6; and individualistic achievement goal, 7; *see also* education of American Indian children

Ojibwa, effects of Euro-American culture on, 19–20

Oklahoma, *see* eastern Oklahoma; Cherokee Indian children; folk Anglo-Saxons

Oklahomans for Indian Opportunity, 232

open communities: Cantel, 222–224; national integration of, 217–220

Orchard Town study of peer selection, 29

Ozark area, *see* eastern Oklahoma

parents: and peer-group activities, 27–29;

parents (*cont'd*)
and school system, 186, 284; status of, 101–103
particularistic values: and curriculum, 43–44; and identification, 44–45; and identity of teacher, 34; and institutionalized inequalities, 46; of peer groups, 27; and standardized curriculum, 39
peasant communities, 217; corporal punishment in, 32–33
peer groups, and socialization, 27–30
People's Republic of China, 313
photograph interpretation tests, and American Indian children, 257
picture vocabulary test, 255
Pine Ridge Reservation, *see* Oglala Sioux study
political conflict, in Brookview school system, 192–194
political economy: and education, 156–157, 161; and use of leisure time, 160
political participation: and education, 46, 133–143; of school principals, 203–204
political parties, and school systems, 188–189, 190
political scientists, and definition of national integration, 212
Potter, Rachel: family background of, 275; observations in home of, 276–277; observations in kindergarten class of, 286–287; results from kindergarten and first-grade analysis of, 282–283; and school culture, 284–285
Primary Mental Abilities Test, 257
primitive people, and writing, 70–72
principals: black, 146; role of, 147–148; *see also* New York City high school principals
problem-solving abilities, and bilingualism, 261
professional associations, 185; influence on school systems, 190–191; and local autonomy, 191–194
progressive education, 120, 134
Project Head Start, *see* Head Start programs
Protestants: in Brookview, 181; and individual achievement concept, 14
psychological theory: and changes in generations, 164–167; and education, 148
puberty rites, *see* initiation ceremonies
public: Dewey on, 138–139; formation of, 135–143
Public Education Association, 204
public opinion, and socialization, 30–31
public schooling, *see* mass education; schools
Pueblo children, social withdrawal of, 266
Puerto Rico, 213, 216–217

punishment: and child-rearing, 68; and socialization, 30–31; *see also* corporal punishment
pupils: development of, 10–14; pseudoempirical view of, 8–9; status of, 101–103
Puritan influence on educational theory, 140–141

reading, teaching of, 118, *see also* literacy; reading ability
reading ability, compared with literacy, 69–70
religion, and educational ideology, 12–14, 187–188
"responsibility," concept of, 141
retention of learning, 119
ridicule: and learning, 259; and socialization, 30–32

school administration, *see* administration
school board members, 150; election of, 188–189
school budgets, 188; and educational expansion, 192–194; vote on, 189
school performance: model for predicting, 285–286; and reward and punishment, 68; and teacher expectations, 171–172
schools: attitude of New York high school principals toward, 204–207; compared with other institutions, 150–152; description of, 150–152; fit with community, 233; folk Anglo-Saxon, 241–242; historical emergence of, 37–38; institutional changes in, 148; interactions in, 146; as middle-class institutions, 149; monolithic structure of, 100–101; purposes of, 36–37; relationship to Cherokees, 235–239; relationship to society, 144–149; research questions pertaining to failure of, 297–298; as research settings for anthropologists, *see* anthropology and education; role of, *ix*; as a social system, 123; in state societies, 39–42; by type of sociocultural environment, 294–295; urban and rural compared, 208–209; *see also* mass education; school systems
school systems: of Cherokees, 237–239; and community culture, 15–17; critical questions on, *ix-x*; discriminatory, 46; of eastern Oklahoma, 244–246; economic model for, 16–17; and Indian children, *see* education of American Indian children, Oglala Sioux study; and individualistic achievement goal, 7; methods for assessment of, 48–49; reasons for analysis of, *ix*; research in, 147–148; resistance to research in, 104–106; and working class,